Microsoft® Business Intelligence

FOR DUMMIES®

7

Microsoft® Business Intelligence

FOR DUMMIES®

by Ken Withee

WILEY

John Wiley & Sons, Inc.

Microsoft® Business Intelligence For Dummies®

Published by
John Wiley & Sons, Inc.
111 River Street
Hoboken, NJ 07030-5774

www.wiley.com

WILEY

About the Author

Ken Withee is a consultant specializing in Microsoft technologies. He lives with his wife Rosemarie in Seattle, Washington. He is coauthor of *Professional Microsoft SQL Server 2008 Reporting Services* (John Wiley & Sons, Inc.) with Paul Turley, Thiago Silva, and Bryan C. Smith.

Ken earned a Master of Science degree in Computer Science studying under Dr. Edward Lank at San Francisco State University. Their work has been published in the LNCS journals and was the focus of a presentation at the IASTED conference in Phoenix. Their work has also been presented at various other Human Computer Interaction conferences throughout the world.

Ken has more than 10 years of professional computer and management experience working with a vast range of technologies. He is a Microsoft Certified Technology Specialist and is certified in SharePoint, SQL Server, and .NET.

Dedication

I dedicate this book to my wife and best friend, Rosemarie Withee, who encouraged me daily throughout this time-intensive process. I owe her nearly a year's worth of late nights and weekends and hope to make it up to her during our long future together. I love you!

Author's Acknowledgments

I would like to acknowledge my grandma, Tiny Withee, who turns 96 this year and is still going strong. I would also like to acknowledge my wife Rosemarie Withee, mother Maggie Blair, father Ken Withee, sister Kate Henneinke, and parents-in-law Alfonso and Lourdes Supetran and family.

I would like to acknowledge my colleagues at Hitachi Consulting. I would like to send a special thank you to Paul Turley, Reed Jacobson, Aaron Daisley-Harrison, and Todd Folsom for putting up with my endless questions about the experiences they have had over their very successful careers.

I would like to thank Denny Lee and Thierry D'Hers for their support on the Microsoft side and the discussions about the Microsoft Business Intelligence technologies.

Thanks to Katie Mohr, Tiffany Ma, Blair Pottenger, Barry Childs-Helton, and the rest of the For Dummies team for providing more support than I ever thought possible. It is truly amazing how much work goes into a single book. Thanks also to my technical reviewer Chris Leiter for his insights and guidance.

Publisher's Acknowledgments

We're proud of this book; please send us your comments at http://dummies.custhelp.com. For other comments, please contact our Customer Care Department within the U.S. at 877-762-2974, outside the U.S. at 317-572-3993, or fax 317-572-4002.

Some of the people who helped bring this book to market include the following:

Acquisitions and Editorial

Project Editor: Blair J. Pottenger

Acquisitions Editors: Katie Mohr, Tiffany Ma

Senior Copy Editor: Barry Childs-Helton

Technical Editor: Chris Leiter

Editorial Manager: Kevin Kirschner

Editorial Assistant: Amanda Graham

Sr. Editorial Assistant: Cherie Case

Cartoons: Rich Tennant
(www.the5thwave.com)

Composition Services

Project Coordinator: Sheree Montgomery

Layout and Graphics: Ashley Chamberlain

Proofreaders: Lindsay Littrell, Toni Settle

Indexer: Ty Koontz

Publishing and Editorial for Technology Dummies

 Richard Swadley, Vice President and Executive Group Publisher

 Andy Cummings, Vice President and Publisher

 Mary Bednarek, Executive Acquisitions Director

 Mary C. Corder, Editorial Director

Publishing for Consumer Dummies

 Kathleen Nebenhaus, Vice President and Executive Publisher

Composition Services

 Debbie Stailey, Director of Composition Services

Contents at a Glance

Introduction *1*

Part I: Embracing a Microsoft Business Intelligence Solution *7*
Chapter 1: Surveying Microsoft Business Intelligence from 50,000 Feet 9
Chapter 2: Blazing a Trail through the Data Jungle 23
Chapter 3: Adopting Microsoft Business Intelligence 39

Part II: Wrapping Your Head Around Business Intelligence Concepts *57*
Chapter 4: Using Data to Inform and Drive Business Activities 59
Chapter 5: Taking a Closer Look at Data Collection 77
Chapter 6: Turning Data into Information 99
Chapter 7: Data Mining for Information Gold 123

Part III: Introducing the Microsoft Business Intelligence Technologies *145*
Chapter 8: Meeting SQL Server 147
Chapter 9: Excel — Digital Data Power to the People 175
Chapter 10: SharePoint Shines 211
Chapter 11: Expressing Yourself with Development Tools 247

Part IV: Incorporating Microsoft Business Intelligence into Your Business Environment *273*
Chapter 12: Setting Your BI Goals and Implementation Plan 275
Chapter 13: Evaluating and Choosing Technologies 297
Chapter 14: Testing and Rolling Out 315
Chapter 15: Training, Using, and Evaluating Results 335

Part V: The Part of Tens 353

Chapter 16: Ten Microsoft BI Implementation Pitfalls...............................355
Chapter 17: Ten Keys to Successful Microsoft Business Intelligence.....................363
Chapter 18: Ten Ways to Boost Your Bottom
  Line with Microsoft Business Intelligence 375

Glossary.. 383

Index 387

Table of Contents

Introduction 1

  About This Book 2
  How to Use This Book 2
  How This Book Is Organized 3
    Part I: Embracing a Microsoft Business Intelligence Solution 3
    Part II: Wrapping Your Head Around Business Intelligence
      Concepts 3
    Part III: Introducing the Microsoft Business Intelligence
      Technologies 4
    Part IV: Incorporating Microsoft Business Intelligence
      into Your Business Environment 4
    Part V: The Part of Tens 4
  Icons Used In This Book 5
  Let's Get Started! 6

Part 1: Embracing a Microsoft Business Intelligence
Solution 7

  Chapter 1: Surveying Microsoft Business Intelligence
  from 50,000 Feet. 9

    Introducing Microsoft Business Intelligence 9
      Knowing the components of Microsoft BI 10
      Tracing the terminology 11
    Getting to the Core of Microsoft BI 12
      Date warehousing and data marts 13
      Reporting on data 13
      Integrating data from many sources 14
      Analyzing data 14
      Data mining 15
    Microsoft BI Data Presentation 15
      Microsoft Office Excel 16
      Microsoft Office Visio 16
      Microsoft SharePoint 16
    Microsoft BI Development Tools 18
      Visual Studio 19
      Report Builder 20
      Silverlight 20
      Microsoft .NET 21

Chapter 2: Blazing a Trail through the Data Jungle 23

Exploring the Data Lifecycle 24
    Data generation and collection 25
    Data transformation and organization 29
    Data visualization and reporting... 31
    Data analysis.. 32
    Data mining.. 33
Understanding How Microsoft BI Fits into the Data Lifecycle................. 34
Juggling Data 36
It's a Flood of Data! Headed This Way!.. 37

Chapter 3: Adopting Microsoft Business Intelligence 39

Understanding the Adoption Process... 40
    Determining what to ask the BI genie.. 42
    Investigating your current Microsoft product usage 43
    Taking stock of your Microsoft knowledge 47
    Saving your sanity with a prototype 48
    Iterating the prototype to success 49
Documenting Your Key Business Processes.. 50
Understanding Where to Find Microsoft BI Guidance 51
    Taking advantage of in-house expertise 51
    Calling in the experts.. 51
    Tracking down individual experts 53
    Who you gonna call? Microsoft Support!.. 54
    Other resources online and on paper 55

Part II: Wrapping Your Head Around
Business Intelligence Concepts 57

Chapter 4: Using Data to Inform and Drive Business Activities 59

The Importance of Data in Making Business Decisions............................ 60
    Tracking down the relevant data.. 62
    Getting the right data to the right person at the right time........... 63
    BI and the risk of high-tech tunnel vision...................................... 65
Why All the Fuss about OLAP? 66
    What is OLAP?... 66
    What makes OLAP so fast? 67
    Why OLAP? 69
    Databases and cubes... 70
    Measures and facts (of life) 74
    Hierarchies of detail 75

Chapter 5: Taking a Closer Look at Data Collection **77**

The King of BI Concepts — ETL... 78
    Extracting data.. 78
    Transforming data 79
    Loading data 81
SQL Server Integration Services (SSIS) — Microsoft's ETL Tool 83
    Tossing the packages into the projects 84
    Connecting to data sources.. 85
    SSIS Toolbox... 86
    Data transformations.. 88
    Anything is possible with custom code................................... 89
A Simple SSIS Walk-Through 89
Exploring Data Generation 95
    Computers speed everything up... 95
    Enterprise Resource Planning (ERP)...................................... 96
    Rise of the machines 97

Chapter 6: Turning Data into Information. **99**

Data Storage for BI... 100
    Data warehouse... 100
    Data mart 106
    Data-storage patterns.. 108
    Models, schemas, and patterns 110
Understanding SQL Server Reporting Services (SSRS)........................ 111
    Business Intelligence Developer Studio (BIDS).......................... 112
    Report Builder... 114
Getting Familiar with SharePoint... 115
    Excel Services... 116
    PerformancePoint Services for SharePoint 117
    KPI lists.. 119
    Dashboards... 119
    Scorecards 120

Chapter 7: Data Mining for Information Gold **123**

Going Deep with Data Mining.. 124
    An algorithm defined... 124
    Data mining's role in the BI process................................... 126
Digging In to Data Mining in the Microsoft World......................... 126
    The Microsoft data-mining process...................................... 127
    Data-mining structures... 131
    Data mining models 132
Knowing the Microsoft Data-Mining Tools.................................. 133
    Integrating with Microsoft Office...................................... 133
    Visual Studio.. 135
    SQL Server Management Studio... 139
Using Microsoft Data Mining Algorithms 140

Part III: Introducing the Microsoft Business Intelligence Technologies *145*

Chapter 8: Meeting SQL Server 147
First Contact with SQL Server 148
Primary Components of SQL Server 149
    The SQL Server Database Engine 151
    SQL Server Reporting Services 155
    SQL Server Integration Services 162
    SQL Server Analysis Services 162
Looking at the Different Versions of SQL Server 163
    Core editions 163
    Specialized editions 164
Installing SQL Server 166
Checking Out SQL Server Tools 169
    SQL Server Management Studio 170
    Transact-SQL 172
    MDX 173

Chapter 9: Excel — Digital Data Power to the People 175
Excel as a BI Application 176
Generating Data 178
Collecting Data 179
Getting Organized 181
Show Me the Data! — Data Visualization 183
    Conditional formatting 184
    Charts and graphs 189
Analyzing Data: Pivot on This and Pivot on That 191
    Using Excel PivotTables 191
    PivotChart 195
Data Mining with Excel 197
    Using Excel to boss SSAS 197
    Pulling cube data for PivotTables and PivotCharts 200
Keeping Score with the Excel Scorecard 205
Knowing the Limits of Excel 207
Looking at the Future of Excel 209

Chapter 10: SharePoint Shines 211
Getting to Know SharePoint 212
    What exactly is SharePoint? 212
    Understanding the versions and editions of SharePoint 216
Making BI Information Available in SharePoint 218
    SSRS integration 219
    Excel integration 220
    InfoPath Form Services 226
    Using Key Performance Indicators 227
    Business Connectivity Services 228

Unleashing Human Business Intelligence with SharePoint 229
    SharePoint Web sites 230
    Document libraries 231
    SharePoint Lists 232
    Wikis 234
    Blogs 235
    Discussion boards 235
    Office integration 236
Learning What Was Added with SharePoint Server 2010 239
    Cruising with the Navigation Ribbon 240
    Providing a more fluid user experience 240
    Developing applications with Silverlight 241
    Integrating visualizations with PowerPoint themes 241
    Visio Services 242
    Sorting and filtering lists dynamically 243
    Using Business Connectivity Services 243
    Increasing efficiency with Office integration 243
    Taking SharePoint offline with SharePoint Workspace 244

Chapter 11: Expressing Yourself with Development Tools .... .247

Taking a Look at Visual Studio 248
    The Visual Studio interface 248
    Flavors of Visual Studio 250
    Visual Studio in the BI world 255
Examining the .NET Framework 259
    A language only a computer chip can love 259
    Intermediate Language (IL) 260
    The Common Language Runtime (CLR) 260
Exploring Report Builder 261
Diving In to SQL Server Management Studio 263
Getting to Know SharePoint Designer 264
Seeing the (Silver)light and Tasting Expression Blend 268
Understanding PerformancePoint 269

Part IV: Incorporating Microsoft Business Intelligence into Your Business Environment 273

Chapter 12: Setting Your BI Goals and Implementation Plan .... .275

Setting Your Business Intelligence Goals 276
    Understanding the components of business goals 276
    Examining technology goals 279
Determining Your Implementation Plan 281
    Comparing waterfall and iterative methodologies 281
    Discovering how things really work 285
    Identifying the power users 289
    Solidifying the goals of the BI project 290

Identifying the data needed to attain your goals...........................290
Setting a solid foundation for a BI implementation.....................291
Scope creep can be your friend 292

Chapter 13: Evaluating and Choosing Technologies 297

Assessing Your BI Capabilities 298
Identifying your current BI-friendly tools 298
Knowing your current licensing..303
Determining your current skill sets..303
Choosing Technologies to Incorporate 306
Understanding your business foundation 306
Putting together the BI technology puzzle 307
Plugging in the pieces..308
Utilizing Free BI Tools: Try Before You Buy...309
Trying SQL Server 311
Checking out SharePoint...312
Reducing Risk..313

Chapter 14: Testing and Rolling Out 315

Continuously Adding Value...316
Testing Your BI Implementation...316
BI testing diversity...317
Unit testing 320
Rolling It Out — Again and Again 323
Surfacing information...324
Having a BI Management Plan...327
Managing Change..328
Gaining early adoption 329
Transparency is crucial 330
Delegating ownership...331
Changing business processes 332
Introducing new technology without mutiny................................333

Chapter 15: Training, Using, and Evaluating Results 335

Tackling Training Efforts 336
Continuous education 336
Enabling self-service training 336
SharePoint training resources..337
SQL Server training resources 340
Training users at the grassroots level..342
Evaluating Results 342
Getting feedback with SharePoint 343
Incorporating Feedback...349
Creating a BI Culture 349
Inclusion...350
Communication and collaboration...350
Ownership...350
Merit-based recognition...351
Trust 351

Part V: The Part of Tens 353

Chapter 16: Ten Microsoft BI Implementation Pitfalls 355
Drowning Under the Waterfall 356
Getting Stuck on the Shelf(-ware)...357
Letting Politics Kill the BI Project..358
Ignoring IT 358
Disregarding Power Users 359
Snubbing Business Processes..360
Overpromising Results 360
Getting Squashed by Top-Down Decree 361
Skimping on the Foundation 361
Misjudging How to Use Consultants 362

Chapter 17: Ten Keys to Successful
Microsoft Business Intelligence...............................363
Reiterating an Iterative Approach 364
Obtaining Executive-Level Sponsorship....................................365
Assessing Your Current Environment 366
Developing an Implementation Plan 367
Choosing the Right People for the Implementation Team 368
Your in-house team members 368
Calling in consultants..368
Creating an Inclusive Environment 369
Fostering a Culture of Communication and Collaboration 370
Starting with the Right Goals 371
Reducing Risk..371
Maintaining Perspective 372

Chapter 18: Ten Ways to Boost Your Bottom Line
with Microsoft Business Intelligence 375
Increasing Efficiency 376
Improving Agility 377
Increasing the Visibility of Business Processes 378
Forecasting..378
Taking Advantage of Existing Skill Sets 379
Collaborating and Communicating..380
Reusing Code in Various Functional Areas 380
Consolidating Content 381
Increasing Productivity..381
Making Deep Use of SQL Server and SharePoint......................382

Glossary 383

Index 387

Introduction

- -

Any fool can make things bigger and more complex. It takes a touch of genius — and a lot of courage — to move in the opposite direction.

It's an old, tired joke among people in the armed services that "military intelligence is a contradiction in terms." And yet, intelligence in the military sense — accurate, timely information that can help produce an effective strategy — is more important these days than ever before. As organizations continue to pursue their goals in an economy that seems more like a battlefield, it's no wonder that they, too, feel the need for reliable information based on real and readily usable data — *business* intelligence. Unfortunately, gathering intelligence (let alone using it) takes time — which is in short supply, and sometimes the technology that was introduced to help a business meet its goals just adds to the confusion. Acronyms, obscure phrases, and seemingly unrelated buzzwords proliferate.

Hey, even "buzzword" used to be a buzzword, but now it has a Merriam-Webster definition: "an important-sounding, usually technical word or phrase, often of little meaning, used chiefly to impress laymen." (Wow! I'm impressed.) That is not to say that Microsoft Business Intelligence (BI) is full of technologies that are of little meaning. On the contrary! Microsoft BI is chock-full of some of the most useful software components you will ever use. Microsoft BI, like any other software realm, has a dizzying array of acronyms and terms that are used by those who understand the technology. Don't worry, however. By understanding the needs that the components of Microsoft BI fill within your business environment, you will be well on your way to throwing out acronyms with the best of them.

I resisted the temptation to call this book "Business Intelligence, OLAP, Data Warehouses, Data Marts, SharePoint, SQL Server, SSAS, SSIS, SSRS, PeformancePoint, ERP, CRM, .NET, Windows Server, Silverlight, Visual Studio, IIS, ASP.NET… Oh No! Say It Ain't So, Joe!" And not just because all that won't fit on the cover. The simple truth is that Microsoft BI is so much more than just understanding the language of acronyms. Microsoft BI is about taking best-of-breed business practices and matching them up with the technologies that will unlock their potential.

If you remember that every high-tech tool (and every buzzword) used in business started life as a response to a real problem in the business environment, you're on the right track: Start with what you know is real, and then find the right tools to work with it. Case in point: Underneath all the buzz, the need that brought business intelligence into existence remains: How do you turn raw data into a usable, reliable, timely information resource?

Well, I believe you can make a solid move in that direction by getting to know and use Microsoft Business Intelligence — a set of tools offered by those famous folks in Redmond to help you create that information resource — and maybe just transform your organization (while you're at it) into a strategic powerhouse.

Don't worry — by the end of this book you'll have a solid understanding of what each of these terms mean and how they fit into the big picture of Microsoft Business Intelligence. (You may even be calling it by its nickname, "Microsoft BI — pronounced bee-eye, not bye.")

After reading this book you will have a solid grasp on not only the acronyms for Microsoft BI but how it can be a tremendously valuable tool that can turn the mountains of data flowing through your organization into real and action-able information that will allow you to run your business in a more *intelligent* fashion.

About This Book

This book is about turning down the buzz and peering into a way to run your business more intelligently — on the basis of fresh, relevant data, ready to use and efficiently delivered.

This book introduces Microsoft Business Intelligence as a viable tool for building this utopia business vision. Sure, without guidance the technolo-gies, strategies, and concepts can seem complex and confusing, but my goal here is to give you a clear picture of what Microsoft Business Intelligence is, what it can do, and how to master the knack of implementing a Microsoft BI system. My hope is that when you finish reading, you'll have a good handle on the topic — and a useful direction in which to yank. The potential benefits to your organization include a more competitive position in the modern busi-ness landscape — for openers.

How to Use This Book

Microsoft BI can be like a big puzzle. Yes, you can jump in and put together small pieces of the puzzle but until the whole thing is complete you will lack an overall view of the big picture. This book is much the same way. You don't have to read the book cover to cover if you already have a solid understand-ing of some of the concepts, but reading each chapter will fill in some piece of the puzzle. If you are already familiar with the big Microsoft BI picture, then feel free to jump around. If you not, progressing through the chapters in order would probably be the safest bet.

How This Book Is Organized

Back when I started grad school, some professors used to start their courses by slinging terminology around that few of us understood, as if expecting everybody to catch up by floundering around. I found that the best professors would start at the beginning, building up the terminology and ideas as they went along. Then the discussions were better; the whole experience was better. I always appreciated that approach, so that's how I've organized this book (and, as you'll see, it's highly compatible with business intelligence). I start off like those great profs of mine . . . from the beginning.

Keeping in mind that business tools were developed to solve real business problems, this book presents both the problems and the Microsoft BI solutions that address them. Armed with this knowledge, you can examine the current state of your business and determine what problems you really face — and what BI tools can help you create real solutions. The idea is to get familiar with the toolbox, and then pick the right tool for the job.

Part I: Embracing a Microsoft Business Intelligence Solution

Part I lays out the fundamental concepts behind business intelligence, and uses the Microsoft BI capabilities as consistent examples. Chapter 1 provides a bird's-eye view of the Microsoft BI and what it offers. Chapter 2 looks at data as the blood running through the veins of modern business — and how Microsoft BI gets it to where it's needed. Finally, Chapter 3 outlines the process involved in adopting a Microsoft BI solution.

Part II: Wrapping Your Head Around Business Intelligence Concepts

Part II of this book introduces you to the fundamental business intelligence concepts while providing insight into how the Microsoft technologies fit within the business intelligence puzzle. Chapter 4 talks about data and how it can be used to drive your business decisions. Chapter 5 discusses the generation and collection of data from the vast tentacles of an organization. Chapter 6 walks you through turning data into information using visualizations and analysis. Finally, Chapter 7 talks about the Microsoft Data Mining technology and how it can be used to help you gain a key edge in a competitive business landscape.

Part III: Introducing the Microsoft Business Intelligence Technologies

Part III of this book discusses the technologies — the products, features, and capabilities — that make up Microsoft Business Intelligence. Chapter 8 walks you through the expansive SQL Server product, which functions as one of the two main components of Microsoft BI. Chapter 9 explores how Microsoft Excel can be used as a BI tool (instead of as a source of ungainly mutant spreadsheets full of conflicting versions of the same data). Chapter 10 examines SharePoint — the other main component of Microsoft BI — and its potential to transform an organization's way of doing business. Finally, Chapter 11 takes you on a tour of the tools available for developing and customizing the capabilities of Microsoft Business Intelligence to fit your business needs.

Part IV: Incorporating Microsoft Business Intelligence into Your Business Environment

Part IV of this book is where the rubber meets the road — or at least where the driver gets out the roadmap and locates the path to a new place: putting Microsoft Business Intelligence to work. Chapter 12 guides you through setting your goals for business intelligence and coming up with an implementation plan. Chapter 13 provides an outline for evaluating and choosing the BI tools that are right for your organization. Chapter 14 covers the testing and rollout phases of a BI implementation (a lot less stressful than rolling out a new jet). Finally, Chapter 15 discusses how to train your people, get them on the side of your new system, and start using business intelligence as a new way of working.

Part V: The Part of Tens

Part V of this book offers neat ten-packs of insights in individually wrapped chapters — each a quick reference to an important topic that will help you get the most out of Microsoft Business Intelligence. Chapter 16 outlines the ten most common pitfalls to watch out for when you implement Microsoft Business Intelligence. Chapter 17 lists the ten keys to BI success that every implementation should follow. Most importantly, Chapter 18 discusses ten ways you can use a Microsoft Business Intelligence system to boost your bottom line.

Icons Used In This Book

The familiar *For Dummies* icons offer visual clues about the material contained within this book. Look for the following icons throughout the chapters:

Whenever you see a Tip icon, take note and pay particular attention. It's a nugget I've dug up from years of involvement with Microsoft Business Intelligence, offered up to help out with your BI decision-making.

Get out your notebook whenever you see a Remember icon (or get out the highlighter if that's what worked for you in school). I point out key concepts that you should remember as we walk through Microsoft Business Intelligence. And here's your first thing to remember: There is an online cheat sheet for this book that you can find at www.dummies.com/cheatsheet/microsoftbusinessintelligence.

Throughout my consulting career, I've stepped on the business equivalent of land mines that have blown projects all to bits. Luckily, I've always had a good team, and we were able to glue the pieces back together. Pay particular attention when you see a "bomb" Warning icon — you don't want to explode a piece of your budget.

Here's where you can jump feet-first into those "important-sounding, usually technical words or phrases, often of little meaning, used chiefly to impress laymen." Just so you can spot them when they're coming — and already know something about them. The technical parts are indicated with a Technical Stuff icon and are for the brave souls who decide to actually wield a computer. The folks who don't can safely review the technical components of Microsoft Business Intelligence without having to actually install or interact with anything. Understanding is the key here; there are people within your organization who are highly-paid to actually do the technical things, and if you pick up a little of their dialect, it's a friendly gesture.

Let's Get Started!

My goal with this book is to give you insights into running your organization in a more intelligent (business-intelligent?) fashion. If your organization is like most, you have a mountain of data (much of it resembling a mudslide) flowing through your modern business every day. Hip boots won't do you much good there, but a thorough understanding of Microsoft Business Intelligence gives you something highly useful to do with the flow. Okay, here's where I get back to a little grad-school nostalgia: For me, there's no better way to understand something — in this case, Microsoft Business Intelligence — than to start right at the beginning. So with that in mind — provided you haven't already peeked at later chapters (hey, go ahead, there's no exam) — flip to Chapter 1 and off we go.

Part I

Embracing a Microsoft Business Intelligence Solution

The 5th Wave   By Rich Tennant

"I understand you've found a system to reduce the number of complaints we receive by 50 percent."

In this part . . .

You've heard the buzz about Microsoft Business Intelligence and how it can conquer the mountains of data your business generates. Terms (or, more aptly, buzzwords) and acronyms are thrown around that sound very innovative and advanced, but what do they really mean? How can you "mine" your data for the nuggets of information that will keep your business ahead of other businesses in an ever-changing economic environment?

You need a fundamental understanding of Microsoft Business Intelligence, including its terminology, concepts, products, and capabilities. You need to pull back the curtains and discover how the concepts can deliver on the promise of business intelligence and how Microsoft makes those concepts work. The chapters in this part introduce the fundamentals of Microsoft Business Intelligence and help you forge the way to creating a successful BI system.

Chapter 1

Surveying Microsoft Business Intelligence from 50,000 Feet

In This Chapter

▶ Getting a handle on Microsoft Business Intelligence

▶ Looking at the components of the Microsoft BI core platform

▶ Identifying Microsoft BI tools and features

▶ Customizing and developing Microsoft BI capabilities

If you cannot explain it simply, you do not understand it well enough.

— Albert Einstein

*I*n the vast world of technology-inspired buzzwords and jargon, it's easy to get dazed and confused and give up hope. Business intelligence (which, throughout this book, I'll also refer to as simply "BI") is no exception; I recently heard a complaint that the alphabet soup of Microsoft BI terminology is downright overwhelming. Fear not! This chapter gives you a bird's-eye view of the products and capabilities that make up Microsoft Business Intelligence.

You also find out how to speak Microsoft BI and gain an understanding of these coded sounds and acronyms that make up the language. You can then decipher the hype and draw your own conclusions about the role Microsoft BI plays in your organization.

Introducing Microsoft Business Intelligence

I was once on a consulting team for a large telecommunications company's BI project, using advanced BI software tools from some of the top names in the field. Our client company had a massive data store with a ton of data. We tried to build some very simple reports — but couldn't transform the data into what we needed. Getting that job done would take more than a year of bureaucracy and requests. We were stuck and desperate.

We met with a manager who was already turning out the kinds of reports we needed. He had a computer under his desk running a trial version of SQL Server — and was using that product's BI features to pull data from the database, transform it, and report on it. It was an eye-opening experience for me: This guy, with a free trial version of one Microsoft product, put together an impressive result while our team of professionals — highly paid, highly trained, using some of the best software on the market — struggled. The world just didn't seem right! From that day on, I vowed to figure out what Microsoft BI was all about; in this book, I share with you what I found out.

Knowing the components of Microsoft BI

Microsoft BI combines BI concepts with the built-in features of SQL Server, SharePoint, and Office products and makes those concepts happen. As Microsoft technology advances, the company has taken a head-on approach improving business intelligence — working relentlessly to make its products understandable and easy to use. The three mainstays of Microsoft BI are these primary components (illustrated in Figure 1-1):

✔ A core set of data tools and reporting features that are part of Microsoft SQL Server.

✔ The Microsoft Office products and SharePoint technology.

✔ A set of development tools that developers can use to customize and enhance Microsoft BI capabilities.

Figure 1-1:
The three
primary
components
of Microsoft
BI
technology.

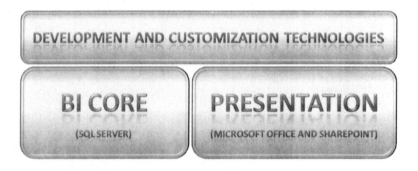

Many organizations have already paid for the licensing that enables them to use SQL Server, SharePoint, and many of the Microsoft Office products. Before you worry about a large cash outlay for licensing, check with your company's IT department to find out if you already have the technology you need for BI!

Tracing the terminology

Having worked in consulting for many years, I constantly walk into new situations and corporate cultures where I'm bombarded with acronyms and terms that make little sense to me (at first, anyway). I've noticed that when a group of people work closely together and have a common goal, they can easily create what sounds like an alien language. Okay, I'm just as guilty as the next person. Working with a new client, before long I find myself shortening the names of systems and processes to acronyms and then shortened again to, um, utterances (they're not exactly "words" most of us would use in a conversation). Rattling off these sounds can baffle an outsider: "You should use SSIS to ETL into a data warehouse so you can use SSRS and SSAS to surface data to MOSS." Say what?! *Hint:* "Surface" is a verb here. The rest is in Martian. (Kidding. But just barely.)

Here's a partial translation with some good news. Microsoft terminology often describes its products in terms of their specific features — until those features start to seem like separate products. So, for example, you may hear a lot about SQL Server Reporting Services (often shortened to SSRS, SRS, or even RS) and wonder whether you have to buy a separate license for it. Good news: You don't. SSRS is part of Microsoft SQL Server; if you own SQL Server, you already own this data-reporting capability. At the technical level, SSRS can send queries to gather data from other Microsoft products, as well as many different data sources that include such database products as Oracle, PostgreSQL, MySQL, TERADATA, SAP, and IBM DB2, just to name a few.

Microsoft has been sharpening its approach to business intelligence, consolidating products into an overall roadmap that simplifies the adoption and management of BI for its customers. For example, the company discontinued a former stand-alone product called PerformancePoint Server and added it to the latest release of Microsoft SharePoint. The term SharePoint is also often misunderstood. SharePoint will be covered in Chapter 10 but you should be aware that SharePoint includes many different features that often sound like their own products (and sometimes were their own products in a past life as is the case with PerformancePoint).

So, if you check with your IT gurus and find that your organization already owns Microsoft Business Intelligence technology, the next step is *implementation* — that is, getting it to do real work for you in your specific situation. All you need is an understanding of Microsoft BI concepts and functions — along with the technical skills to make them work for you — and the next section gets you started in that direction.

Getting to the Core of Microsoft BI

The core of Microsoft BI consists of the components that make up Microsoft SQL Server, as shown in Figure 1-2.

The Microsoft SQL Server Product

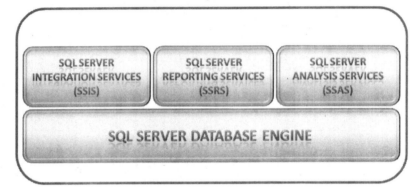

Figure 1-2:
The core components of the SQL Server product.

SQL Server started out as a database product but has grown to include additional capabilities that put core BI concepts into action. Table 1-1 outlines these core components and what they do.

Table 1-1	SQL Server Core BI Components
Product	*Description*
SQL Server Database Engine	The core program used to create standard relational databases, including data warehouses and data marts (detailed in the next section of this chapter).
SQL Server Reporting Services (SSRS)	Software for creating reports based on Microsoft (and nearly all other) data sources.
SQL Server Integration Services (SSIS)	Software for connecting to a multitude of data sources, transforming the data into a single useful format, and loading it into a Microsoft SQL Server database — all using the ETL (Extract, Transform, and Load) process detailed in Chapter 5.
SQL Server Analysis Services (SSAS)	A Microsoft version of OnLine Analytical Processing (OLAP, detailed in Chapter 8) that stores massive amounts of data in a special database called a Cube for very quick real-time analysis.

Date warehousing and data marts

Although computer systems help solve many problems in business, they use so many different kinds of programs that they can't always communicate easily with each other. A tremendous number of systems make up a modern organization — payroll, accounting, expenses, time, inventory, sales, customer relations, software licensing, and so on. Many of these systems have their own databases and ways of storing data. Combining data from the tangle of systems — let alone doing something useful with the combined data — becomes extremely difficult.

Business intelligence creates a "big picture" by storing and organizing data from many disparate systems in one usable format. The idea is to make the data readily accessible for reporting, analysis, and planning. A *data warehouse* is a central database created for just that purpose: making the data from all those sources useful and accessible for the organization. The idea is to give decision-makers the information they need for making critical business decisions.

A *data mart* is a more specialized tool with a similar purpose; it's a functional database that pulls particular information out of the overall Data Warehouse (or even directly from source systems depending on who you ask) to answer specific queries. For example, a manufacturing location may need to compile some specialized data unique to the process used to make a particular product. The overall data warehouse is too big and complex do that job (or to modify effectively to handle it), so a smaller version — in BI lingo, a data mart — can be created for this one manufacturing location.

The Microsoft SQL Server Database Engine manages not only data warehouses, but also data marts — and both types of data storage can become massive. Fortunately, SQL Server addresses this problem by storing one database across a cluster of many different servers. This approach accommodates the enterprise as it grows in scale.

Reporting on data

When you have a Data Warehouse, you likely don't want to look at rows and rows of data; instead, you want to visualize the data and give it meaning. Building reports that answer a particular question (or set of questions) means taking raw data and turning it into information that can be used to make intelligent business decisions. SQL Server Reporting Services (SSRS) — a component of SQL Server — builds reports by doing that bit of magic.

SSRS has features that can make your reports as fancy as you like — gauges, charts, graphs, aggregates, and many other snazzy ways to visualize the data. Check out more information on SSRS and reporting in Chapter 8.

Integrating data from many sources

The many different systems and processes that make up an organization create data in all shapes and forms. This data usually ends up stored in the individual systems that generated it — but without any standard format. Fortunately, SQL Server has a component — SQL Server Integration Services (SSIS) — that can connect to these many different data sources and pull the data back into the central data warehouse. As the data moves from the source systems to the Data Warehouse, SSIS can also transform it into a standard useful format. The whole process is known as *Extract, Transform, and Load (ETL),* and there's more about it in Chapter 6.

Analyzing data

As you can imagine, the amount of data contained in a modern business is enormous. If the data were very small, you could simply use Microsoft Excel and perform all of the ad-hoc analysis you need with a Pivot Table. However, when the rows of data reach into the billions, Excel is not capable of handling the analysis on its own. For these massive databases, a concept called OnLine Analytical Process (OLAP) is required. Microsoft's implementation of OLAP is called SQL Server Analysis Services (SSAS), which I cover in detail in Chapter 8.

If you've used Excel Pivot Tables before, think of OLAP as essentially a massive Pivot Table with hundreds of possible pivot points and billions of rows of data. A Pivot Table allows you to re-order and sum your data based on different criteria. For example, you may want to see your sales broken down by region, product, and sales rep one minute and then quickly re-order the groupings to include product category, state, and store.

In Excel 2010 there is a new featured called PowerPivot that brings OLAP to your desktop. PowerPivot allows you to pull in millions of rows of data and work with it just like you would a smaller set of data. After you get your Excel sheet how you want it, you can upload it to a SharePoint 2010 site and share it with the rest of your organization.

With PowerPivot you are building your own Cubes right on your desktop using Excel. If you use PowerPivot, you can brag to your friends and family that you are an OLAP developer. Just don't tell them you are simply using Excel and Microsoft did some magic under the covers.

When you need a predefined and structured Cube that is already built for you, then you turn to your IT department.

Data mining

Computers can be programmed to sort through enormous amounts of data looking for patterns. It's an exciting new frontier that goes by many different names — in business, the most common ones are *data mining, predictive analytics*, and *machine learning* — but this book sticks to "data mining". (Microsoft SSAS has a number of data-mining algorithms that I explain in detail in Chapter 7.)

The Microsoft data-mining algorithms are part of SQL Server Analysis Services, but you don't have to be a super computer ninja to access and use them. Microsoft offers a free Excel Data Mining Add-In that transforms Excel into a simple, intuitive client program for the SSAS data-mining algorithms (Chapter 9 has more about using Excel in data mining).

Microsoft BI Data Presentation

Microsoft provides BI data-presentation capabilities in its Office and Server products — mainly by consolidating stand-alone products into larger units that are easier to manage conceptually. For example, PerformancePoint Server (formerly a stand-alone product) became part of SharePoint as a feature called SharePoint PerformancePoint Services. Table 1-2 lists the Microsoft applications that do BI presentation.

Table 1-2	Microsoft Applications for BI Presentation
Product	**Description**
Microsoft Office Excel	Excel is an end-user desktop spreadsheet application that can contribute to BI throughout the journey data takes to becoming information, known as the data lifecycle. Excel has the ability to connect to the data warehouse, data Cubes, and other external sources of data and compile that data into charts, graphs, and other cool visualizations.
Microsoft Office Visio	Visio is an end-user desktop application for building flow charts and other diagrams. Visio has specialized templates for data mining.
SharePoint	SharePoint is a Web-based application that provides online collaboration and content management. Imagine SharePoint as an internal Web site, used for tasks such as storing documents, collaborating in real time, and viewing critical data about your company. SharePoint Web sites present the critical data housed on servers (those running Microsoft SQL Server as well as other backend systems such as SAP, Oracle, Dynamics, and custom developed solutions that have grown and been developed over the years) to users.

Microsoft Office Excel

As one of the most widely used Microsoft Office products, the Excel spread-sheet program is designed to organize, analyze, and visualize data. Excel is one of the most powerful desktop applications in the Microsoft BI arsenal.

An analysis tool for everyone

Excel is such a popular data tool that most of the client organizations I visit use it to run some critical portion of their business. One good reason is that Excel can be installed on a local computer with no need for administrators and servers.

The Data Mining Add-in

Microsoft creates Add-ins (new sets of capabilities) as a way to expand what its products can do; the Data Mining Add-in allows the Excel program running on your local computer to serve as a data-mining resource for SQL Server Analysis Services. You can run SSAS Data Mining algorithms using data that resides in Excel cells to yield important information about your business.

Microsoft Office Visio

The general idea behind Visio is to create flow charts — and to publish these documents to the Web as interactive diagrams with *drill-down* capabilities (users can click their way down to specific data). Microsoft offers a Data Mining Add-In for Visio that allows users to create interactive documents with real inlaid data. For example, a decision tree can be published to the Web with actual business data built in. When users go to the Web site containing that document, they can click a decision to view its results. (For more about Visio and its Data Mining Add-in, see Chapter 7.)

Microsoft SharePoint

One of the most talked-about Microsoft products as of late is definitely SharePoint. Modern businesspeople need to communicate constantly and maintain a tight connection to their products, markets, and business processes. SharePoint fulfills this need — so it's increasingly popular as a way to deliver Microsoft BI data. Some of the main features of SharePoint — Excel Services, PerformancePoint Services, and a tight integration with SQL Server Reporting Services — are well suited to the task. To see why, read on.

Excel Services

Excel Services addresses two primary problems that arise among organizations that use Excel extensively:

- ✔ When individual members of an organization become adept at using Excel, they often come up with custom spreadsheets that perform specific tasks very well but can be difficult for others to use. A customized spreadsheet can become so unwieldy that nobody (often even the original creator) understands how it works or how to update it.

- ✔ One original file can spawn hundreds of mutations as it's passed from person to person, e-mailed around, and modified slightly in between. Eventually no one can be sure which version of the Excel document is the "correct" one, and which versions have been changed, updated, or even tampered with.

SharePoint Excel Services addresses both problems by allowing an Excel document to be posted to a SharePoint Web site. Only one version of that Excel document can be viewed by users who have access to the SharePoint Web site. You can maintain security on the document by limiting how many users can update the original, and by limiting which users can view it. The actual Excel document appears as embedded in the SharePoint Web site. The entire, actual Excel document (or just a summary or graph from within the document), can form one piece of a larger BI picture that resides on the company's SharePoint Web site.

The concept of pulling many pieces of key data into a single view on a SharePoint Web site is called *dashboarding*. On a car dashboard, you have all the critical information about the car (speed, RPM, remaining gasoline, and oil pressure) right in front of you. Similarly, a BI dashboard provides all your critical business information in one easy-to-view location: a dashboard Web site.

PerformancePoint Services

PerformancePoint Services for SharePoint provides *scorecarding* (that is, a quick chart or scorecard that reports on progress toward goals) as well as dashboarding (that is, a report showing the status of a number of key metrics).

Reporting Services Integration

The Reporting Services component of SQL Server is a very powerful BI component: It not only creates reports, using many different data sources, but also stores those reports in its own application: Report Manager. Report Manager is a very powerful system for storing and managing reports but in the end it is yet another system for managing a particular type of content, a report.

One of the reasons SharePoint has moved to the center of the organization is that it can manage many different types of content including reports. SQL Server Reporting Services (SSRS) is tightly integrated with SharePoint. In fact, SSRS offers an Integrated Mode that puts the SharePoint server in control of managing all BI reports. As a result, reporting simply becomes another type of content contained within the SharePoint system and sits right along side other documents such as PDF, Word, and Excel as well as many others. The power of an Enterprise Content Management (ECM) system such as SharePoint provides the following benefits for storing reports:

✔ Users have to check the reports in and out.

✔ Document versions are controlled.

✔ Security is integrated into each document.

✔ Reports are embedded directly in SharePoint Web sites.

Microsoft BI Development Tools

Microsoft offers two general tools for developing and customizing its products' BI capabilities:

✔ **Visual Studio** gives the hard-core technical person or super-power–user a way to enhance BI processes and shape them to the needs of a specific business.

SQL Server includes a free version of Visual Studio that's designed especially for Microsoft BI: Business Intelligence Developer Studio (BIDS).

✔ **Report Builder** is designed for end users and business analysts; it provides the advantage of uniform reports that work well with Microsoft BI capabilities, regardless of organizational department.

In addition to Visual Studio and Report Builder, Microsoft has a couple of programming languages that are used in BI development. Silverlight is a technology that provides a rich experience through the Web browser, and Microsoft .NET ("dot-NET") is a framework and programming language designed to run on Microsoft operating systems.

Table 1-3 lists and describes these tools.

Table 1-3	Tools to Develop and Customize Microsoft BI
Product	**Description**
Visual Studio	A program for desktop computers, known as an Integrated Development Environment (IDE) and used primarily by developers and database administrators.
Report Builder	Report Builder is an end-user application that creates uniform reports. Like Office 2007 and later, Report Builder uses a Ribbon at the top of the user interface for navigation and access to commands.
Silverlight	This technology extends the functionality of a Web browser without requiring it to reload a Web page with every interaction. You have probably browsed to a page to search for a product or book travel. Whenever you click a button the page refreshes and flashes and loads again. Silverlight provides developers the ability to build Web sites that, once loaded in the browser, operate in a smooth fashion just like an application running on your local computer. The nice thing about Silverlight is that it is supported by multiple Web browsers.

Since Silverlight is a programming language its applications are almost limitless. Any scenario where you would need rich interaction through the Web browser is where you would use Silverlight. For example, if you were building an information system about your manufacturing equipment, you could use Silverlight in order to provide features such as the ability to click on a particular machine part and have the window magically transition into the detailed specifications without the need to flash, reload, and redisplay a new page. |
| Microsoft .NET | The Microsoft .NET technology is a programming framework used by developers to build applications on the Microsoft Windows platform. |

Visual Studio

Many Microsoft developers probably spend most of their working time in the Visual Studio program. Visual Studio has all the tools they need for creating Microsoft-friendly custom solutions in one place. Visual Studio provides project templates for developing nearly all aspects of a BI solution.

Microsoft has released a version of Visual Studio that includes only its BI components and which installs with the SQL Server product. This allows for BI development without needing the full featured Visual Studio product. When SQL Server installs it looks to see if Visual Studio is already installed on the computer. If it is installed, then it adds the BI functionality to this already installed program. If Visual Studio is not installed, then it installs the BI only version of Visual Studio called BIDS. BIDS stands for Business Intelligence Developer Studio, but in fact it is just Visual Studio with only the BI development components.

Report Builder

You can imagine, and may have already experienced, how unproductive it can be when business users have to go through the IT team in order to analyze data and build reports. Business users feel that IT doesn't understand what they are trying to say, and IT feels that business users just don't get technology. Both sides are probably correct, but that doesn't help get the right information in the reports and the reports to the right people at the right time. Microsoft has developed a desktop tool called Report Builder to avoid this unproductive process that is as easy to use as Microsoft Word or Outlook. (Check out Chapter 8 for more about Report Builder.)

Silverlight

You may spend much of your time in a Web browser working with various applications. In fact, if you work with SharePoint, then you probably access it through your Microsoft Internet Explorer Web browser. Whenever you open Internet Explorer and work with an application, you are actually using your desktop computer *and* Internet Explorer as a client to a program that runs on a server.

The server computer may be sitting in your company data center or out on the Internet somewhere, depending on the Web application. Each interaction, whether it's clicking a link or selecting a drop-down menu, sends a communication back to the server. Silverlight, a browser add-on, attempts to reduce much of that back-and-forth communication between client and server by allowing the local computer to run the program without constantly talking to the server computer. Silverlight gives your Web browser added functionality that makes browsing a Web site a much richer experience.

Microsoft .NET

When Web aficionados hear the term ".NET" (pronounced "dot net"), their first thought is almost always "domain name" extensions tacked on to the names of Web sites to identify Internet domains — .com, .net, or some other domain such as .org. The guess is understandable but wrong. Microsoft .NET is actually a software-development tool; it has nothing to do with the domain names you type into your Web browser.

In a nutshell, Microsoft .NET provides a framework within which software developers can create and customize programs to work well with Microsoft products — using various programming languages. It's handy for developing the BI capabilities of those products. Chapter 11 covers .NET in greater detail.

Chapter 2

Blazing a Trail through the Data Jungle

In This Chapter

▶ Checking out the lifecycle of data in an information world

▶ Understanding Microsoft Business Intelligence's role in the data lifecycle

▶ Discovering why the right data are more valuable than a lot of data

▶ Making use of the data glut generated by modern computer systems

The fewer data needed, the better the information. And an overload of information, that is, anything much beyond what is truly needed, leads to information blackout. It does not enrich, but impoverishes.

— Peter F. Drucker

*I*magine having the humanoid robot Data from *Star Trek: The Next Generation* as a consultant: A massive database that can sift through all the data ever known and turn it into information that the captain (okay, CEO) can use to make decisions . . . all in a human-friendly package. After he's spent a few days plugging in to all your computer systems and interviewing your people, you can ask him any question about your organization — and get a useful answer. The perfect business intelligence solution! Hopefully Microsoft is working on that. In the meantime, the present-day Microsoft BI capabilities can do almost as well.

These days, as never before, information is power. Hyper-competitive businesses live on the data that streams in from a complex tangle of people, systems, and processes. Before computers, armies of people needed weeks or months to compile business data — and more time to bash it into a usable format. In our modern world of computerized systems, you have mountains of data at your fingertips, with more data coming in all the time. The problem isn't so much collecting and compiling the data, but extracting just those nuggets of valuable information you need. Fast. Before your competition does the same thing with its own pile of data.

Microsoft Business Intelligence capabilities form a system designed to take on those mountains of data, get to the valuable information about your business, and help get that right information to the right person at the right time. When the decision-makers have this information, they know more of what they need to run the business better (even — dare we say it? — close to optimal).

Before launching you into that future, however, this chapter walks you through the data lifecycle — and gives you a working grasp of how Microsoft BI can help turn heaps of raw data into focused, useful information.

Journey with me now into the world of data — in the present!

Exploring the Data Lifecycle

Information and data are not the same thing: Data are a raw resource at the center of the business universe; information is born from data, but only after a lot of work. Understanding the data lifecycle — and how Microsoft BI can speed up the work of turning data into information when it's at the peak of its usefulness — gives your business the fuel it needs for warp-speed efficiency.

The operational processes and systems that make up a business stay busy in three ways: (a) getting things done, (b) generating data, and (c) storing the data they generate. And unless you have a way to get at those data tidbits systematically, there they sit — in the systems that generated them.

Microsoft BI capabilities treat all those disparate systems as sources, pulling data from them, transforming the data so it's easier to use and present, and storing the data in a central, networked location — a data warehouse. Specialized data-storage devices such as OLAP cubes and data marts also store data, but all these components have a common goal: not just to put the data somewhere, but to make it available to the organization.

OLAP stands for OnLine Analytical Processing. An *OLAP cube* is a special way to store data that allows end users to sort, group, and analyze massive amounts of data very quickly. Check out Chapter 4 for more about OLAP cubes.

When the data are ready for use, the business consumes it while it's still timely, fresh, and succulent — using reporting, analysis, and data mining. Figure 2-1 shows where those three capabilities fit into the data lifecycle and feed the Microsoft Business Intelligence system.

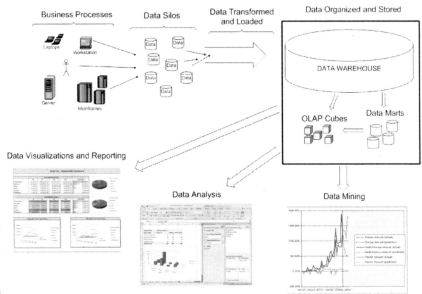

Figure 2-1:
The data
lifecycle.

Data generation and collection

Microsoft BI brings together potentially valuable pieces of data from the processes that run your business, but that's just the beginning. The next step is to organize the data into a format that offers insight into what's really happening in the overall business.

Business processes contain pieces of data about specific things, called *data points,* and often all you need is the means to extract them. Pulling these data points together into a picture, however, helps you evaluate the process. You might, for instance, spot a bottleneck that slows down the entire operation. (Say, final assembly of your electric automobiles has to wait till your balky supplier delivers the needed battery fluid — who knew?) Or a collection of data may tell you that the cost of one ingredient in your company's new fuel product is outrageous and driving up the total cost of producing it.

Businesses always need insights like those. Software companies have taken a step in that direction by creating products that bring individual business procedures into consistent formats and collect data about them. (Dynamics and SAP are examples; *Dynamics* is the Microsoft offering for computerized business process, and *SAP* is a German company and the leader in the field.)

Usually these software products also have a reporting mechanism to provide an organized picture of the data they store — but too often the systems
designed for particular business practices (say, manufacturing and human
resources) don't communicate with each other. All the data from these separate systems can create a bigger picture. Posing questions across systems
can then yield useful answers about the organization as a whole.

Business processes — the midwife for data

When I talk to executives about business intelligence, I'm often surprised to
see how many of them are nearly clueless about the processes that make up
their business. Top executives often get used to seeing only results. Ask them
how a particular part of their business actually gets done, and you may get
a funny look. Hey, it's understandable — a staggering number of processes
make up a typical mid-size or larger business — but even the chief should
have a basic understanding of those component processes. ("You mean we
actually *import* battery fluid for the electric cars? I had no idea.") They're
missing an opportunity to *improve* how the business runs.

Ongoing business processes (such as Point Of Sale (POS) and Purchasing)
are — potentially, anyway — constant sources of raw data (for example, the
product sale records for POS, or the price per item or pound records for
Purchasing). In this earliest stage of the data lifecycle, those raw bits of
fact have some maturing to do before they're any good to the business as
a whole — but first you have to generate them. And that means taking a
detailed, documented look at what makes your business tick.

The processes that make up a business are as critical to its health as they are
to business intelligence. Inefficient processes can quickly manifest into poorly
run businesses, and soon those businesses will be in trouble. Before you can
reap the full benefits of BI, you need a good working grasp of your business
processes and how you can make them more efficient. For example, is your
manufacturing showing constant delays at a particular step? When the process
is understood, efficient, and documented, you can go about capturing data.

The end result is that you first need to understand your business processes.
Once you understand the processes that make up your business, you need to
identify the critical points at which data can be generated. Finally, you need to
determine if the data are already being captured, and if not, how to capture it.

Small or large, the most successful businesses are vigilant about making their
processes more efficient. In smaller companies, employees are intimately
aware of what they have to do to make the company function. In larger companies, executive management tends to see business processes in broad terms;
it's the departments and groups that have a more intimate understanding of
what has to happen, and in what order. Everyone in the company understands
(or should) that business processes must be continually improved. Business
intelligence adds a new dimension to this understanding: Reliable, accessible,

usable process data are a step toward that improvement — for example, how much battery fluid do we have to stockpile to keep the electric automobile final assembly going smoothly, and how much warehouse space will it take up?

Collecting that data means intervening in the business process you want to get a handle on — in particular, capturing a *metric* (that is, a measurement, such as "how much battery fluid do we have on hand, month by month, for our super car final assembly?"). After all, any self-respecting business process has to be regular enough to be measurable. If all that potential quantitative data about a process isn't captured, it just drifts off into the ether, never to be heard from, used, or analyzed again. Here's where BI becomes a source of goals — in this case, to capture any data that's useful in making decisions for your company.

Ways to collect data

There are a number of ways to collect data. The simplest and oldest method is for a person to observe something and write it down on a piece of paper. Then another human can enter this data into a computer system or spreadsheet program such as Excel.

A higher-tech method is for the same human to observe an event in the business process (say, the whole final assembly of an electric car, up through adding the battery fluid) — poised over a computer. Instead of writing down the data on paper, the observer records it directly into the computer system in a digital format (as text, video, whatever).

An even more advanced method has the person interacting with a computer system from the get-go: The computer program *automatically* records the interactions and captures data it observes, and the person simply performs his task. For example, a person may be tasked with purchasing supplies for the company. The purchasing system may be computerized so that every purchase is made through the computer and is automatically recorded and cataloged in a database. The person simply performs his task, and the data are captured.

Beyond this point, we get to a method that doesn't require any human interaction at all: It's all done with computers, robots, scanners, conveyer belts, and so on. The task is performed by automation and is recorded in a database without any human interaction.

Data generation is, in essence, any point in a process that *can* be measured and recorded. When you think about all the diverse processes that make up your organization and how many data points would describe each one . . . well . . . let's just say the amount of data is enormous, and more is coming in all the time. It takes a computer system to turn all that data into information. *Business intelligence* is simply a system designed to do that job, and when it is done using Microsoft technologies it is called Microsoft Business Intelligence.

Data collection is all about having a mechanism in place to capture and store the data. Many self-contained computer systems already have such a feature. For example, suppose you purchase a system for tracking the licensing on a software product you've developed. The computer program that tracks this licensing stores information in a database as the users interact with the application. The data, now captured, just sits around in storage, waiting for somebody to use it. This data in disparate system is often referred to as *data silos*.

Data silos

While I was in graduate school in San Francisco, I attended a lecture by a researcher who was putting the data of his entire life in a digital format. He brought in all of his pictures, notes, and books and scanned them into a database. He inventoried all of his belongings and entered them into the database. He carefully recorded all of his activities on the Web and recorded them in the database. The goal of his project was to understand how people's lives can be digitized and to exploit how cheap digital storage had become. In the end, this one person had a massive database of his life.

Now imagine the same thing happening with a business. Even a small business generates massive amounts of data as its daily activities go on — enough to dwarf what's in a database of one human life. That would be enough of a challenge if all those activities stayed exactly the same over time, but business processes change.

You may start a small business by keeping track of your inventory on a pad of paper. As your business and inventory grow, you may install a small software program on the computer in your office to keep track of your inventory. As you grow even larger and have multiple locations, you may find a specialized software program that can be installed on a server that multiple people in your company can connect to and interact with. Imagine this sequence of events happening throughout the many pieces of your business as it grows. Before long, a hodgepodge of computer systems, processes, and data-storage mechanisms are all doing their various things within your business — and not talking to each other about what they're doing. Figure 2-2 shows how data from various business processes becomes isolated over time.

A *data silo* is a data-storage mechanism that's isolated and disconnected from other systems and data. Like an upended cylinder that stores grain on a farm, it's "standing out in its field" — usually all by itself. For example, your inventory software may store its data in a proprietary format that isn't connected to (or compatible with) the other computer systems that the business uses.

You may be using Microsoft programs to generate and collect data (during those first two phases of the data lifecycle), but if your business is like a lot of others, it's probably using a mix of different systems that have grown and changed over the years.

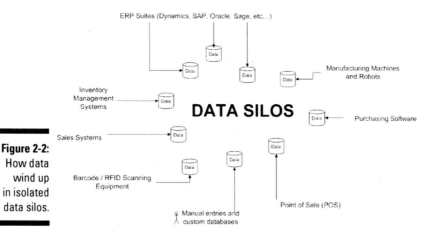

Figure 2-2:
How data
wind up
in isolated
data silos.

It's true that some of your systems may have been orphaned when the software companies that created them went out of business, merged with larger companies, or let some of their products die off. Does that mean the data in your legacy systems are unusable? Well, no. You're in luck for two reasons:

- You do *not* have to replace all your current systems with Microsoft products in order to implement Microsoft BI. Honest.

- Microsoft Business Intelligence is designed to turn all the data in those disparate locations — the contents of those data silos out in the boondocks of your business — into valuable information.

All of which brings up the next phases of the data lifecycle, namely . . .

Data transformation and organization

Data that is scattered around in different systems can answer some specific departmental questions. But isolated data aren't much use beyond their own little bailiwick. To answer questions that require data from operational systems across the business, you have to implement at least these three BI concepts:

- **Data warehouses and data marts:** These are places where you can bring the data together so it's easy to access.

  A *data mart* is simply a smaller, specialized data warehouse; it uses the same SQL Server database engine, as described in Chapter 1.

- **Cleaning:** Forget the soap; this means giving the data a single, non-proprietary, usable format, regardless of what system it comes from.

- **Organizing:** Giving the data a consistent structure so it's readily available for consumption within the business.

To make these concepts happen, your business needs an organizational structure for the purpose — a massive database built using the Microsoft SQL Server database engine.

Don't be surprised if you have to run the SQL Server database engine on a cluster of computers, even on many different servers, to create the sort of super-computer-style database that can handle this job.

The operational systems throughout the organization have collected data into silos, but it'll just sit there unless you can get it into the overall data warehouse. The program that handles this chore (and connects to all those disparate databases) is called SQL Server Integration Services (SSIS); it's included in the Microsoft SQL Server software product.

SSIS communicates with all the different systems, pulls the data out of those systems, transforms it into a standard format, and then loads it into the data warehouse. The transformed data in the warehouse is ready to pull out into specific departmental data stores (data marts) or structures such as OLAP cubes for data analysis, as shown in Figure 2-3.

At this point in the data lifecycle, the data have been gathered together and organized. It's ready for the next stage: to be turned into information through reports, analysis, and data mining.

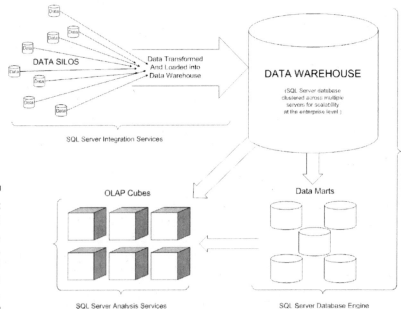

Figure 2-3:
Data extracted, transformed, and loaded into BI data structures.

Data visualization and reporting

Raw data by itself aren't very useful. Before it's usable in decision-making, it has to take on the form and relevance of information. That's what data visualization and reporting are for. The starting point is asking a question about your organization that cuts across departmental lines. Then you need a report based on the question that pulls the data from the data warehouse (or specific data marts) and puts it in a useful format that helps you answer the question.

For example, you may want to compare four salespeople in the region against their quarterly goals. You want to see their sales and expenses to date in a dashboard format, as shown in Figure 2-4.

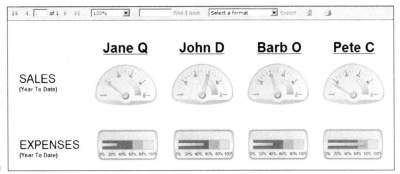

Figure 2-4:
Salesperson performance report.

The Microsoft BI feature that handles reporting is SQL Server Reporting Services (SSRS); it's included in Microsoft SQL Server. The reports that SSRS generates can come to you in a number of ways:

- ✔ You can view and route reports by using Report Manager, an out-of-the-box tool included with SSRS.
- ✔ You can integrate SSRS with Microsoft SharePoint.

  SSRS and SharePoint integration are covered in detail in Chapter 10.
- ✔ You can embed SSRS right into your intranet's Web sites.
- ✔ You can even build your own custom software program using .NET and SSRS to view, manage, and store your SSRS reports.

Think of reporting and data visualization as small projects: You come up with a set of business requirements for the report and then have an analyst build the report. Then, when the report is finished, it's constantly updated with new data (say, when salespeople make new sales or submit expense-account charges). Regardless of the new data coming in, the report itself doesn't change. It's a consistently useful place for the data to go.

The SSRS engine can generate complex reports that feel like you're drilling into a mountain of data. Those reports can bristle with parameters and groupings and can be interactive — but (again) the reports themselves don't change. They were built as static, logical structures on the server; there they stay, giving form to the data they pull from the data warehouse and from specific data marts (as shown in Figure 2-5).

Figure 2-5: Data are pulled from the data warehouse into visualizations and reports.

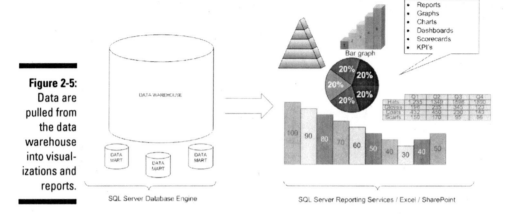

Reporting is still one of the most valuable mechanisms for understanding what's happening in (and to) a business. But sometimes you view a report and see something that doesn't look quite right but don't know why it bothers you. Then you have to decide how much effort it'll take to build another report — or find someone who can tell you what's wrong. Wouldn't it be nice if you could manipulate the data in real time, build a quick report on your own, and nail the cause of the anomaly? Well, one handy feature of BI systems is that they can build *ad-hoc reports* to answer such questions as they arise. The next phase of the data lifecycle — analysis — is built around just this scenario.

Data analysis

Data analysis is essentially ad-hoc reporting in real time; it's a tool for exploring questions while you're looking through your data. You may start off wanting to know your total sales, and then start slicing and dicing — say, dividing the sales data by region, organizing it by salesperson, by product, and by product group in a particular sales region. Then you may peer into time: What were those sales figures within the last week, during the same period last year, compared to the same week this year (or the current week), and so on. As you analyze the data, additional questions may crop up — and if they do, you can go down paths you didn't expect when you began.

Ad-hoc analysis manipulates the data in real time; exploring fresh questions as they arise is a big step up from static reporting. On-Line Analytical Processing (OLAP) makes it possible; the Microsoft OLAP program is SQL Server Analysis Services (SSAS).

Data mining

If SQL Server Analysis Services (SSAS) did nothing more than explore your data in real time, it would be the bee's knees. But its powerful data-mining algorithms make SSAS the *killer* bee's knees.

Data mining (also known as *predictive analytics* or *machine learning*) is the capability to dig through huge amounts of data, find the relevant stuff, and come up with predictions. The SSAS component of SQL Server includes a built-in data-mining engine with powerful algorithms designed to run on big, fast computers. (Chapter 7 digs farther into data mining.)

For example, an especially useful data-mining algorithm crunches historical data according to several criteria, looking for patterns and predicting future trends (as shown in Figure 2-6).

Figure 2-6:
A predictive
graph of
data-mining
results.

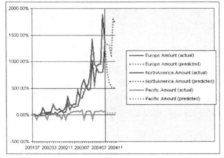

 You can take control of the data-mining algorithms built in to SSAS through an Excel interface on a client computer. The same everyday Excel program that you can install on your desktop machine can turn into a hot rod when it's connected to (and using the resources of) the big honkin' SSAS server. (For more about using Excel to run data-mining algorithms, see Chapter 9.)

Understanding How Microsoft BI Fits into the Data Lifecycle

The systems that make up a business are usually quite diverse. They include software programs from many different software companies, sometimes using a multitude of underlying databases, including their own proprietary systems. Often the mix includes suites of products known as Enterprise Resource Planning (ERP) systems that consolidate data from transactions. Your company may also have a SAP system, robots, scanning devices, and other business and automation programs. These systems generate and collect the data points that tell the story of what's going on inside your business. Microsoft BI isn't meant to replace these systems. Instead, it can add value — in a very cost-effective manner — by organizing all that disparate data and presenting it when it's needed.

Microsoft BI can enhance the data lifecycle at the following stages:

- ✔ Data transformation and organization
- ✔ Data visualization and reporting
- ✔ Data analysis
- ✔ Data mining

The program that actually connects to your many different systems and makes all their data play nice together is SQL Server Integration Services (SSIS), and it's included with the SQL Server product.

SSIS doesn't just plug in to those systems and shove their data into some SQL Server data warehouse willy-nilly; SSIS gives the data a single consistent format before storing it. The whole procedure — pulling the data from many different places, transforming it, and loading it into the data warehouse — is called Extract-Transform-Load (ETL); you can find the gory details of ETL in Chapter 6.

As you can imagine, a data warehouse quickly becomes a complex monster of a system that needs powerful computers to ensure responsiveness.

The SQL Server database engine is very powerful and can be scaled to accommodate larger needs. SQL Server scaling can be achieved by either scaling up to a bigger, more powerful server, or scaling out to include additional servers. Moving to a bigger server is referred to as a *scaleup* approach, and moving to additional servers is called a *scaleout* approach.

Having all your data hanging around in a data warehouse is convenient and a great way to feel organized, but turning that data into information is the last step (and the whole point). Microsoft BI capabilities can do that job; the good news is that you may already be using some of them. For example, SQL Server Reporting Services (a component of the SQL Server product) can connect to many different data sources and turn that data into various interactive reports. SSRS is ideal for connecting to the data in a SQL Server Data Warehouse, but it also can pull data from many other systems. Some systems SSRS can connect to include:

- ✔ Microsoft SQL Server
- ✔ OLE DB
- ✔ Microsoft SQL Server Analysis Services
- ✔ Oracle
- ✔ ODBC
- ✔ XML
- ✔ Microsoft SQL Server Reporting Services Data Models
- ✔ SAP NetWeaver BI
- ✔ Hyperion Essbase
- ✔ TERADATA

I discuss some details of SSRS connections to these products in Chapter 8.

Although creating reports at will with data from various products is handy and informative, those instant reports may leave you with more questions than answers. If, say, you generate a report on sales figures for all regions, you may notice that one particular region sells ten times more boxes of toothpaste than any other region in the world — and wonder why. Digging deeper into a report — quickly, of course — can be helpful; you can do this type of ad-hoc analysis with SQL Server Analysis Services (SSAS).

SSAS: A hidden gem

Although SSAS is part of the SQL Server product, many organizations that already own SQL Server scarcely realize they have SSIS, SSRS, and SSAS right at their fingertips! (Many IT departments just use the SQL Server database engine without ever taking advantage of the BI power available in the rest of the product.)

Many companies use the Excel spreadsheet that comes with Microsoft Office extensively — without exploiting the BI power of Excel. Microsoft has done a great job of connecting Excel to SSAS; to the end user, ad-hoc analysis almost seems like just another handy spreadsheet feature. Chapter 9 explores Excel in greater detail.

SSAS is handy for ad-hoc reporting *and* analysis. If its capabilities stopped there, you could still get lots of useful and timely information about your organization. But when you use the SSAS data-mining algorithms (detailed in Chapter 7) with Excel and with the Data Mining Add-In, you can go really deep into your enterprise for data to analyze.

The SharePoint product has become one of the most popular *Enterprise Content Management* (ECM) products available. SharePoint is an excellent ECM solution, but Microsoft has also continually added features and functionality, which now puts it at the center of many organizations. As a result, Microsoft has deeply integrated SSRS with SharePoint. SSRS reports can be stored in SharePoint libraries, which give the reports all of the content management, security, and other functionality that SharePoint has to offer. These SSRS reports can be integrated quickly into existing SharePoint sites through Web Parts with very little technical effort.

Enterprise Content Management (ECM) is simply a system for storing, managing, securing, and monitoring the massive amounts of digital content that flow through a modern organization. Before computers, an ECM solution would have been rooms full of file cabinets. Now that data are digital, an ECM solution is a software program, such as SharePoint, that tackles the task.

A *Web Part* is a developed component that can be plugged in to a Web site. For example, when you go to your favorite site, you may have a little section of that site that contains all of your stocks and current stock prices. Imagine if this portion of the page could be cut out and plugged in to another site. That's what a Web Part is designed to do. A software developer (for example) may tweak and customize the Web Part that lists stocks and stock prices and then plug that piece into a financial firm's Web site. Microsoft offers Web Parts that display SSRS reports; you can plug them right into your MOSS sites with only a few clicks of your mouse.

Recently, Microsoft has turned a stand-alone product called PerformancePoint Server into a feature of MOSS; its new name is PerformancePoint Services for SharePoint. As a MOSS feature, PerformancePoint Services for SharePoint offers capabilities for visualizing data — including scorecards, dashboards, and analytics — as detailed in Chapter 11.

Juggling Data

Executives who feel completely overwhelmed with the data coming in from different parts of their organizations often feel as if they're "juggling" data. Okay, I'm no juggler, but I can imagine some of the difficulties. Just about anybody can juggle one ball at a time by throwing it up and catching it; some folks may be able to handle two balls, one for each hand. But throw in a third, and I (for one) definitely drop all of them.

Managing data are much the same. Business decision-makers often have to juggle the equivalent of five or six balls at a time. At some point, however, the seventh or eighth ball comes in, the data juggler gets overloaded, and all the balls get dropped. Sometimes it's more efficient to leave that last ball out. That's why business intelligence seeks to form data into a limited number of manageable pieces that make sense right away and can be easily digested and understood. The idea is to provide decision-makers with only what is important and useful in making decisions.

It's a Flood of Data! Headed This Way!

If you had a really huge screen that could show a mind-bogglingly big spreadsheet, how long do you think your organization would take to generate a million rows of data? What would all that data look like, and how long would it take to sift through it and make sense of what it's telling you? Okay, trick question — I didn't even say how many *columns* of data each row has. What the heck, call it ten. If each row has only 10 columns of data, a million rows instantly becomes 10,000,000 data points!

What if your organization generated that much data every day?

Even small organizations generate massive amounts of data. For example, here's what's generated when one consumer makes one purchase at a typical retail store:

1. If the customer presents a store-issued "rewards card," the cashier scans it. The scan identifies the customer to the point-of-sale (POS) cash register and logs the purchase in two databases: the rewards-card database and the customer database.

2. The item that was purchased is logged in the inventory database as having left the building.

3. The payment is logged in to the accounting database.

4. If the supply of the item is running low, the purchasing database is notified that the item has to be re-ordered.

5. If the customer pays with a credit card, that information goes to the accounting and financial databases that handle authorization and payment.

6. When the receipt prints out, there are also coupons that print out for the next visit. The information on these coupons is stored in a coupons database.

(Wow. You really start something when you buy a pack of gum these days.)

As you can see in Figure 2-7, a single transaction interacts with a number of databases and systems.

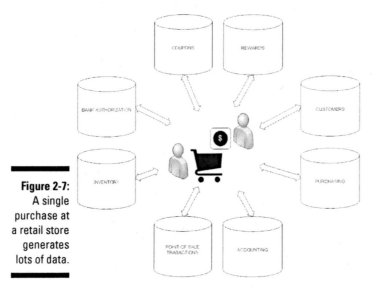

Figure 2-7:
A single
purchase at
a retail store
generates
lots of data.

What happens if the pack of gum is part of a 50-item grocery purchase? Suppose it's a crowded business day, right before a holiday weekend — say a thousand customers go through the store, and nearly *everybody* buys *at least* that many items. Here's the extra-credit question: How many data points make up that one business process? (Yikes.) Then think about how many processes make up your organization. Overwhelming? Understatement. That's why business intelligence exists: to turn these mountains of digital data into valuable information.

Chapter 3

Adopting Microsoft Business Intelligence

In This Chapter
- ▶ Adopting Microsoft BI for your business
- ▶ Discovering Microsoft goodies you may already have
- ▶ Identifying your most important business processes
- ▶ Getting guidance from Microsoft BI experts

Information technology and business are becoming inextricably interwoven. I don't think anybody can talk meaningfully about one without talking about the other.

— Bill Gates

*O*ne of the best things about my job as a consultant is going into businesses and describing all of the ways Microsoft BI can help them. The Microsoft BI tools are impressive, but the first questions are usually about licensing costs. That's why I like to have members of the IT department in the presentations with the executives — to keep things in perspective and to make sure all parties are included. Having IT in the room helps to determine in a few minutes whether the company is already licensed for many of the Microsoft BI and presentation capabilities. Often IT is already using SQL Server and Microsoft Office, and the company already owns the licensing. Sure, if our clients want to get BI going for the entire enterprise, they may have to pony up for additional licensing. But if they want to try Microsoft BI features at the prototype level on a small scale, they may see some real value generated pretty quickly. All they need to figure out is how to implement the features they already have.

In this chapter, you walk through the general ideas and steps necessary in adopting Microsoft BI. It's important to understand not only the licensing of Microsoft BI but the business processes with which Microsoft BI builds a long-term, and committed, relationship. Throughout the chapter, I also share some of my personal experiences and give some examples that you'll relate to as you go through the implementation process.

Understanding the Adoption Process

Undertaking any BI project is complicated and can seem overwhelming. But when you divide the plan into smaller, iterative steps, it becomes easier — and there's a much higher probability of success. (I can't drive home enough how important it is to iterate, iterate, iterate on a solution.) I like to see real results in the first few weeks of a project. It may be a very small result, but I want to have something out there that everyone can look at, critique, and discuss. Building a first prototype BI system also allows you to discover some of the major roadblocks before millions of dollars and vast resources go into developing and adopting the system. With a small prototype, you can chart your course as you go. The prototype is like a scout who's slashed a small trail through the jungle. You won't get any vehicles through the path yet, but you'll sure know the best route to take. The scout has probably gone up, down, and all around, but in the process she likely has discovered the best route.

The following are the general steps involved in a Microsoft BI implementation:

1. **Decide what you need to know about your organization in order to develop a BI system.**

   Determine the questions you need to answer as well as the target users who need those questions answered. Are the target users technical analysts, factory workers, executives, or all of the above?

2. **Investigate your organization's current Microsoft licensing and determine what BI capabilities you currently own.**

   It's also a good idea at this initial phase to bring in a Microsoft licensing expert in order to get a handle on just what additional licensing will cost should you choose to move forward with an implementation.

3. **Investigate your organization's current Microsoft technology aptitude.**

   Are your people already familiar with Microsoft products and operating systems? Do your IT people already use Windows Server, SQL Server, or SharePoint? Do your information workers already use Windows-based computers, Microsoft Office, or SharePoint?

4. **Determine whether you already have the needed skills on hand (including in-house project management and Microsoft-savvy IT skills), as well as "the vision thing."**

   Should you work with a partner? If you do, make sure that your partner is familiar with getting Microsoft BI to work in the real world. Don't be pressured into incurring a massive up-front cost. Build a relationship and work with your partner through the iterations (as in, "try, try again") to reduce risk.

5. **Start small and build a prototype to answer a few important questions.**

   Continue to iterate and expand the project as scalability and comfort level increase. Include representatives from all levels of the organization in order to increase employee ownership of and engagement in the implementation. The list should include executives, assistants, analysts, information workers, and IT, just to name a few.

BI in the building of a highway through wilderness

If your BI project encounters rough going, here's a project that offers inspiration: The highway running from the Pacific Northwest of the Continental United States up through Canada and into Alaska — one of the major accomplishments of the last century (circa 1942). The Alaska-Canadian (ALCAN) Highway runs through some of the harshest landscape on the continent and is a testament to the importance of having information about your route *before* you set out for your destination.

The designers of the ALCAN Highway faced multiple challenges — from dangers to pests — while building a road through the vast wilderness of the Northwestern region of the continent. In addition to the remote and isolated landscape, the workers had to deal with

- ✔ Solidly frozen soil (permafrost) that began to melt as soon as the road was cleared for construction.

- ✔ Muddy areas of quicksand known as Muskegs that threatened to swallow construction equipment and halt all activity.

- ✔ Unbearable cold that caused frostbite to any portion of skin exposed to the open air for mere minutes.

- ✔ Swarms of giant mosquitoes that attacked skin through layers of clothing.

If these hazards sound vaguely familiar to you, you're not alone in that impression. Software-based projects often face frozen habits, sticky details, a frigid reception, and swarms of irritating details; no wonder they risk failure more than almost any other type of project.

Here's what your IT crew can pick up right away from the designers of the ACLAN Highway: If they'd just plowed a straight path without first scouting the land and building an initial trail, they *would* have failed. Instead — and first — they used dog sleds, horses, and aerial surveillance to plot a plausible route. Then they built a prototype road, using hand saws, axes, and shovels. If they found a Muskeg or an especially difficult piece of terrain, they altered the trail. Only when the path was mapped and determined to be accessible would the heavy equipment come in to build a solid foundation for the actual road.

If you plan your BI implementation by first scouting out your route using a prototype, you can discover problems and clear a path toward success, all with minimal cost and resources. Then use the knowledge gained to scale up resources, time, and cost — with fewer unknowns and a higher likelihood of success.

Imagine an eerie riff on an electric guitar, and a baritone voice saying tersely, "In all types of software projects, there is a place known as the Twilight Zone . . ." The path to a successful project involves unknowns. Everyone always tries to guess at these unknowns, but until you've been through the process, all you can do is guess. That reminds me of a recent project that had a *really* overactive project manager — obsessed with forecasting every task down to the exact hour. Now, I can understand the need to have timelines and deadlines, but creating a custom solution doesn't exactly go like clockwork. Successful software projects demonstrate that an exact timeline is only possible after the fact; if you know exactly how long anything takes, then you've already forged (and traveled) the path to get there. So this is the most important point I can possibly make: *Start with a prototype of your BI project.* Then you give the people who have to do the large-scale implementation a vital advantage: Someone has scouted the landscape. They get a good working sense of the roadblocks, snags, and risk points, and can develop a map that shows how to proceed. I like to call this a "gut-check prototype" — it gives you a good idea of the path to take so you can then bring on additional resources with a greater probability of success — which calms everybody's guts *much* better than pink stuff in a bottle.

Determining what to ask the BI genie

Determining what you need to know about your company is one of the fundamental tasks of a BI implementation. Discovering BI is exciting; it's understandable to want to put it into action as soon as possible. But taking the initial steps of figuring out the questions you need answered will pay big dividends down the road.

I like to walk executives through an exercise called "Ask the BI genie." It goes like this: Try to wipe your mind of all you know about your organizational systems. Step back and look at your business as an outsider. Now imagine a BI genie appears and tells you to ask any business question you want and you'll receive the answer. Write these questions down. Only after you have a solid list of "what" and "when" questions should you move on to the "how" of building a solution.

For example, let's say you're in the business of manufacturing and selling cheese. Obviously you'll want to know about the manufacturing process, demand, marketing, product placement, promotions, and coupons. Imagine millions of data points reflecting everything you could want to know about the cheese business — from the time it takes milk trucks to unload to how many batteries are stored for the indoor forklifts. All these metrics are important to some portion of the organization — and in time you can incorporate them into a BI solution. For the time being, however, it's simpler to develop a prototype based on a few "key" (biz-speak for "most important") questions. If (for example) you step back and decide that the most important metrics are annual sales and profit margin (because a business that doesn't make money won't be a business much longer), have at it: Start by streaming these simple metrics to an executive dashboard application as part of the nightly data load. A more encompassing solution will emerge bit by bit as you examine each important question.

Investigating your current Microsoft product usage

Before you can start turning your mountains of data into valuable information, you need a clear picture of your current software situation in terms of three essentials: licensing, skills, and processes.

Checking your current licensing

Software licensing is one of the most difficult and frustrating parts of modern business — it's hard to do with a level head. Every time the industry introduces a must-have product or capability, whole herds of companies rush out and purchase licensing in hopes of not falling behind the competition. In the '90s, one such Next Big Thing was Enterprise Resource Planning (ERP). Oracle and SAP (big ERP players back then and now) sent sales reps to dazzle the brass with presentations of whiz-bang technology and must-have modules. Before long, organizations had purchased millions of dollars' worth of licensing. Nice new packages of duly licensed software came in the door — and simply sat on closet shelves collecting dust, with their "must-have" modules never implemented. A sarcastic new term was born — *shelf-ware*.

Microsoft licensing has always seemed to have a much higher adoption rate. For example, nearly every company I've ever worked with uses Microsoft Office for productivity — and runs Windows operating systems and server technology in at least some portion of the company. Microsoft takes advantage of this wide usage with *Volume and Site Licensing:* Under Site Licensing, one payment to Microsoft licenses the use of its software *throughout an organization.* This saves the IT team from having to nitpick the details of who has installed what software, in what version, on which computers. With Volume Licensing, only the actual licensing is purchased, with no need to ship all the extra media, installation guides, and packaging. The IT team simply installs software whenever it's needed and has the ability to "true-up" any additional growth licenses on an annual or semi-annual basis.

If your company already runs Microsoft products, then check to see whether you already have a Volume or Site License agreement with Microsoft. These agreements are usually custom tailored for the size and type of organization and the products that need to be licensed. Start your licensing discovery by working with your IT department and Microsoft representative to determine if you already have the proper licensing to run the Microsoft BI technologies. Even if your Volume or Site Licensing contract does not specifically mention

Microsoft Business Intelligence, you may still have the necessary licensing to begin obtaining real BI value from the products you're already using. Many of my clients are surprised to find that the products they use came with built-in BI tools (*Hint:* SQL Server and SharePoint). As a result, if their IT people already know those products inside out, they can put together a prototype BI solution in a matter of weeks. It's like looking for your glasses and realizing they were on top of your head the entire time!

Microsoft has a site dedicated to information about Volume Licensing. Check it out at www.microsoft.com/Licensing.

Mapping your IT environment

I like to document a company's most important IT processes and see what BI tools would enhance them. I then print out these diagrams on giant wall-size paper and stand back to get an overall view of what's going on. It's a great perspective, especially if you create it twice: When mapping your IT environment, do both a "before" map and an "after" map. The technique is the same, but the maps show where your IT environment currently is and where it's going. Make sure that the current map is completely accurate and up to date. No fibbing or fudging allowed. Otherwise . . .

A major mistake that I often see is that the map represents what leadership believes *should* happen instead of what *is* happening. Having the people performing their duties build the maps with the understanding that they should document *exactly* what they do to accomplish a task and not what their managers *think* they do. They should not feel threatened to produce what they think management wants to see. This exercise alone is often eye-opening; the discrepancy between what management thinks happens and what actually happens is often significant.

Figure 3-1 is a very simple version of such a *process map* — it shows *swim lanes* (visual divisions of responsibility) and where Microsoft BI technology fits into the overall picture. Figure 3-1 illustrates the projected processes "after Microsoft BI" — those that should be in place after implementation to achieve the best efficiencies. Here's an example of an "after Microsoft BI" process:

1. The company president requests a very specific inventory report.

   In the dark ages before BI, this specific report may have been impossible to obtain, or could have taken many months to accomplish.

2. An analyst receives the request (as shown in the "after" map).

3. The analyst looks in the Inventory section of the Report Library (a SharePoint site on the company intranet) to determine whether the report already exists (a *big* step up from "impossible" right there).

   If the report exists, problem solved.

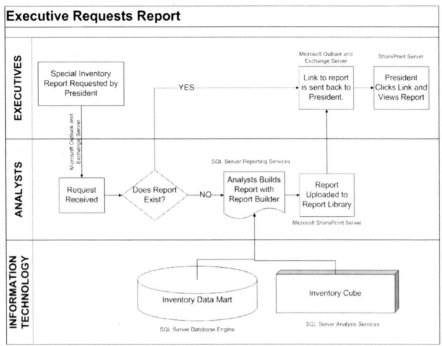

Executive Requests Report

Figure 3-1:
Simple
process
flow with
swim lanes.

4. If the report doesn't already exist, the analyst opens a Microsoft BI tool known as Report Builder by clicking a link on the SharePoint site.

5. Using Report Builder, the analyst pulls data quickly from the Inventory data dart and/or OLAP cube and organizes the information in the way the president has requested.

6. When the report is complete, the analyst saves the report to the Report Library and e-mails a link to the president — who can click the link to open and view the report.

Report Builder is a technology that allows the user to download the application to a local computer with only one click of the mouse. Report Builder is a report-creating tool that looks a lot like Microsoft Word 2007 or Excel 2007 with the Office ribbon at the top and that is easy to use throughout. SharePoint and SQL Server Reporting Services (SSRS) are tightly integrated so the reports have all the functionality SharePoint has to offer:

✔ Users with appropriate access privileges can check reports in and out.

  This is one of various SharePoint features that improve document security.

> ✔ Various report versions are possible but their use is restricted.
>
> This feature allows versatility while limiting possible confusion.
>
> ✔ Users with appropriate network privileges can have reports embedded in My Site.
>
> A My Site personal space on the SharePoint intranet site is available to everyone with access to the SharePoint system — assuming, that is, that the functionality has been enabled by the SharePoint administrators.

The president may love the new report and want it placed in his or her personal My Site page that is displayed whenever Internet Explorer is opened. Best of all, after the BI system is up and running, this whole process can happen without any IT involvement. It's an example of two major benefits that go along with a Microsoft BI solution: ease of use and self-powered information flow with no need to consult IT on the details. IT simply makes the data available in an organized and accessible data store; Microsoft end-user tools give non-IT employees the connectivity and functionality to turn data into information and share it easily.

In your initial prototype, you can focus on a few highly important questions and then create a map that connects the corresponding business processes with the needed Microsoft BI technology. My clients are often surprised to discover that the use of Microsoft products throughout their organizations means their people already possess skills that come in handy for implementing Microsoft BI. Of course, a long-term policy that fits Microsoft BI into the company vision and direction should come from leadership, but with minimal up-front investment, a prototype BI system can start providing better efficiency and BI advantages in very little time.

Determining which Microsoft software to purchase

Many technology vendors make you shell out for licensing software in massive bundles. Only after you've purchased all of this "proprietary" software can you attempt to actually customize it to your company's needs and gain real value from it. That value usually comes, if ever, many months (or even years) down the road after massive projects have wrestled it into place. The Microsoft software that makes up BI is often used in many organizations in some form or other. So your people have a useful skill set already, and you may already own the licensing. Even if you don't own licensing for Microsoft BI yet, you can download the tools for free in a trial version, kick the tires, determine where the product fits in your big picture, and *then* purchase licensing. Meanwhile, here's a leg up: Table 3-1 outlines the software you need to get started with Microsoft Business Intelligence.

Table 3-1	Microsoft Business Intelligence Software
Software	*Description*
Windows Operating System	The Windows Operating Systems are made up of clients and servers. The client OS includes versions such as XP, Vista, and the current Windows 7. The server OS is designed to run server products, and includes versions such as Server 2003 and Server 2008.
SQL Server	The SQL Server product includes most Microsoft BI core capabilities, including
	SQL Server Database Engine: The traditional database engine that is used to store data. Many companies use SQL Server for this purpose alone and don't realize the product also includes BI capabilities.
	SQL Server Reporting Services (SSRS): Used for reporting.
	SQL Server Integration Services (SSIS): Used to extract data from operational systems, transform it, and load it into a data warehouse.
	SQL Server Analysis Services (SSAS): Used for ad-hoc analysis of reports in real time, using very large datasets.
SharePoint Server	Software for collaboration, content management, and Web-portal creation. SharePoint is often used as intranet server software; it's a natural place to make BI data available to end users.
Office Excel	A popular data-crunching tool installed on many end-user desktops. Widespread familiarity with Excel makes it a good front end for SQL Server.

Microsoft BI continues to integrate these capabilities; a recent example is of the former stand-alone product PerformancePoint Server. Now called PerformancePoint Services for SharePoint, it's a built-in feature of SharePoint.

Taking stock of your Microsoft knowledge

Many organizations already have a rich skill set with Microsoft products. Microsoft has done an excellent job of integrating the BI tools into the products people use every day. For example, many people already use Microsoft Office for their day-to-day activities. Microsoft BI and collaboration servers have a tight integration with the Microsoft Office products to create a seamless transition into the BI world.

Like the Internet, only private

An in*tra*net is different from the Internet. Your intranet (a.k.a. *local area network*) is only available to your organization. A typical example contains human-resources information, internal company reports, project data, or other sensitive information that must remain internal to the company. Outsiders can't visit intranet Web sites or see their content; they're on a network that's only accessible by company employees. The Internet, on the other hand, is accessible by anyone. You may get *to* your intranet through Virtual Private Network (VPN) software that creates a secure channel through the wilds of the Internet, but your intranet itself is separate from the rest of the world.

Information workers may use products such as Windows for their PC, Outlook for their e-mail, Excel for number-crunching, Word for writing memos, and SharePoint for collaboration and intranet connection.

A further potential BI advantage comes with Microsoft products: They're commonly used by IT departments. Typical examples include

- ✔ Windows Server as the server operating system
- ✔ Active Directory to manage users and passwords
- ✔ Exchange Server to handle e-mail
- ✔ SQL Server for databases
- ✔ SharePoint Server to provide collaboration and intranet connection

If your organization runs Windows and Office nearly everywhere in-house, chances are good that it already has some basic BI tools waiting to be used.

 Before starting any BI implementation, find out which programs people are already comfortable with. Think about the possible downtime a complete change in platform (or even a different "look and feel") could produce. For example, people who already use Excel likely won't balk if a Data Mining tab appears on their Excel program, but they may struggle to adopt a new and unfamiliar user interface.

Saving your sanity with a prototype

I'm always surprised at the amount of money, time, and people it takes to put massive BI systems in place. Alas, these implementations often end in disappointment or (worse) complete failure — *after* millions of dollars and thousands of hours have gone into putting the system together. At that point, the company may have to make do with a BI system that's inadequate, frustrating, and avoided by users.

Thanks to a software development playbook known as Agile Development, I've found it's best to start by developing a quick prototype that accomplishes a goal, even if "it's ugly but it works." A group of three to five people can whip up a down-and-dirty prototype in three to five weeks that can

- ✔ Give you a handle on BI feasibility (you can gut-check that the data exists).
- ✔ Help you discover roadblocks early and with minimal cost.
- ✔ Show you the business value that key metrics can provide.
- ✔ Fine-tune your IT crew's grasp of Microsoft BI capabilities. The first attempt usually has some difficulties; later iterations of the BI system, bringing in additional processes, get easier.
- ✔ Provide a look into all aspects of the implementation process with minimal cost. Creating a prototype is like sending a scout into uncharted territory in order to map the terrain.

Iterating the prototype to success

I like to think of *iteration cycles* (one try after another, learning as you go) like walking: By itself, each step seems insignificant, but when you put these steps together you can cover huge distances. If you misstep, you can easily take a step back, adjust, and continue on course with little effort and cost. If, conversely, a project is planned and implemented all at once — and fails — the cost is tremendous and often involves going back to the beginning and starting over.

Microsoft BI, in contrast with other types of software projects, provides value early on — information derived from the data generated by operational systems — for minimal outlay. With each new iteration (improved and expanded version), the project picks up additional data points — which continue to deepen and refine the knowledge about the organization that's available in the data warehouse. Information workers and analysts can then produce more valuable information as the depth and breadth of data grows.

For instance, imagine a financials example. It's important to understand the sales numbers, cost numbers, profit numbers, marketing impacts, and all other numbers in between. A typical analysis may start out with just one big number — total sales. From there it may make sense to divide the sales into regions or states and then down into stores. This information is valuable and can be the first iteration. The next iteration may now include additional sales figures such as the cost numbers and then the profit numbers. Each iteration continues to build on the previous iteration. If at some point a big mistake is made in the way the data is collected, that iteration can simply track back on course without affecting the entire BI system.

Another analogy I like to use for the implementation process — admittedly scarier and more gruesome than my walking — is rock climbing: If the climber iterates — plants safety equipment and rope holds at intervals on the way up — then the farthest he or she ever falls is to the last secured point. If, however, the climber just goes straight for the top and falls at some point, the fall is all the way back to the bottom. Nobody wants the project to fail; make sure you iterate from the beginning.

Documenting Your Key Business Processes

Actual business processes — such as sending invoices, manufacturing a product, and ordering new supplies — have always been at the heart of business. These days that heart relies on computers and software. So the first step toward the benefits of business intelligence is to map out and fully understand the processes that make up your business.

Some of these processes are so vital that their health indicates the health of the company. They serve organizations as "canaries" — much like the caged canaries miners used to take down the mine with them to provide some warning if toxic gases were present. Business leadership uses "canary processes" to keep a handle on what's about to happen in a company. The corporate canaries themselves are often people in essential departments who speak up about problems they see — and base what they report on direct experience with the processes that make up their work. Be sure to identify your canary processes early on — and develop the first iterations of your BI prototype system around at least one of them.

There's a business buzzword for a similar concept — Key Performance Indicator (KPI) — that's similar to a canary process, but it doesn't necessarily tell you that danger is on the horizon. Here's an example: Suppose your business is in retail, and the company leadership has identified a particular sales region as the canary for sales overall: What starts selling well in stores in (say) Hollywood, California, indicates what will probably happen in other parts of the world as trends take hold. But sales overall — a typical Key Performance Indicator that's *always* important to your business — can only tell you what *has* happened, or is currently happening. It keeps mum about what's likely to occur in the future.

Understanding Where to Find Microsoft BI Guidance

Microsoft BI is arguably the most approachable and easily adopted set of BI tools available. But you also have other valuable resources available on your BI journey. And you may not have to hunt far to find some of them . . .

Taking advantage of in-house expertise

Don't be too surprised if a rich pocket of hands-on Microsoft expertise turns up at your company, even if a lot of your software doesn't come from Microsoft. Some companies that say they're SAP shops or Oracle shops are still running SQL Server for some portion of their IT departments — and developing custom applications using Microsoft .NET and Visual Studio. Most of the information workers in those shops are running Microsoft Office productivity applications and have been getting around the company intranet using SharePoint. The longer they've been doing that, the likelier it is that you'll find some "power users" among them. It's natural to extend such technology skills to Microsoft BI, which is based on SQL Server, Office, and SharePoint. So: Find out who's a whiz with Microsoft products.

Calling in the experts

The technical talent of full-time employees is often extensive; what's lacking is experience in Microsoft BI implementations. Bringing in a gang of consultants can give you access to experienced guides who have likely been through the process of getting BI up and running on a much larger scale. Every organization is different, so plan on dedicating at least some employee time to interacting with the consultants. The consultants can manage the overall project, bring in experience where needed, provide training and communication, and navigate the political landmines that the project encounters.

If your organization has engaged a large consulting company, resist the temptation (or, sometimes, pressure) to sign up for a multimillion-dollar project without trying a small prototype BI project in-house first. (If this theme seems familiar, then you *have* been paying attention!) If budgeting or internal project requirements demand that you sign on to the entire project up front, make sure a prototype phase is part of the agreement from the get-go. Consider putting a clause in the contract that allows you to cancel the agreement and explore other options if you're unsatisfied with the prototype phase.

Some of the largest and most well-known consulting companies that have specialized Microsoft BI practices include Slalom Consulting (disclosure: my current employer), Avanade, Accenture, and Infosys.

Large consulting companies are global and have vast resources, but they can also have expensive fees. Closer to home are local- or regional-level "boutique" consultancies that may have greater focus on a specific technology or industry, but also have smaller talent pools to draw upon. (That means fewer people available for *your* project.) Also look into local contractors and freelance consultants, but make sure they know their stuff. These individuals usually move from project to project and are usually pulled into projects as subcontractors.

Table 3-2 lists the pros and cons for each of these expert types:

Table 3-2	Experts — Pros and Cons	
Expert Type	*Pros*	*Cons*
Large global constancies	Deep experience, lots of resources for projects, access to Microsoft product teams, top-notch managing of people, time, cost, and other project resources.	Expensive, usually only reserved for very large projects, usually large travel expenses.
Boutique consultancies	Specialized knowledge of a specific technology or industry, locally available network and talent, generally less expensive than large consultancies.	Often lack the resources for certain vital aspects of consulting such as ERP integration, point-of-sale expertise, or software development. You may have to farm out parts of your project to multiple boutique consultancies. Often they have less end-to-end project-management experience with large projects.
Private contractors	Relatively inexpensive, often local talent, very focused on a specific BI tool or its components (such as Reporting Services).	Often lack project management experience, expect project to be run for them and to be given instructions, and aren't subject to oversight by professional managers.

Tracking down individual experts

I'm always amazed at how deeply pro-level experts delve in to their chosen fields of technology. Someone who's gained recognition for that passion from Microsoft — or has earned a reputation as a guru in the user community — can provide high-level insight when your project needs it. If you need to fill skill gaps in your technology teams, look in the following places for the experts:

- **Most Valuable Professional (MVP):** The Microsoft MVPs are divided into specific Microsoft products and capabilities. For example, there might be a Microsoft MVP for Reporting Services, for Excel, or for Visual Studio. These people are recognized by Microsoft as technology rock stars — known for sharing knowledge with the overall community. The Microsoft MVP directory (`https://mvp.support.microsoft.com/communities/mvp.aspx`) lists them by their specific fields of interest.

    The MVP list also lists those fields of interest (as shown in Figure 3-2). You can select a specific topic and then sort the list by name, technical expertise, technical discipline, country or region, state or province, and city or municipality.

- **User groups:** The Microsoft user groups are an active bunch. I've been involved with user groups for many years and I'm always impressed by the technical expertise, level of passion, and camaraderie in these groups. The user groups are generally organized by Microsoft product or function. One of the most highly organized user groups is the Professional Association for SQL Server (PASS), which can be found at `www.sqlpass.org`. PASS has an annual conference with many great Microsoft BI resources and seminars. You can find other local user groups focusing on topics such as SharePoint and Business Intelligence by using your favorite search engine. Generally, the Microsoft-focused groups are held monthly in a Microsoft or sponsor's location. These meetings usually involve presentations by subject-matter experts, networking, and job announcements.

- **Trainers:** Microsoft products are so popular that it isn't hard to find training programs. In fact, some companies specialize in training public and corporate audiences to use Microsoft software to their best advantage. These trainers are some of the best resources for guidance and expertise while you're developing a Microsoft BI system. They've seen just about every way a Microsoft product can be used, and they field questions from people who use those products every day. Hiring trainers as you go through your Microsoft BI implementation may make all kinds of sense for your company.

- **Blogs:** These days, given the power of search engines, nearly any technical problem you run across has already been experienced, solved, and blogged about. As the adoption of Microsoft BI gets even more widespread, you can be sure that your implementation team won't feel it's being dragged down a road untraveled.

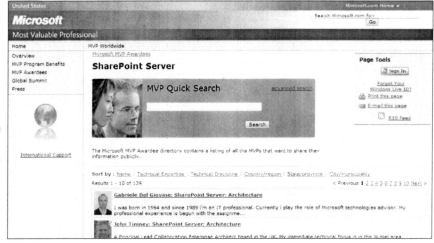

Figure 3-2:
MVPs for
SharePoint
listed on
Microsoft's
Web site.

There is no shortage of Microsoft technology experts, but when you pay good money for licensing, you also want to have the ability to call the company that creates the product. That is where Microsoft Support comes into play.

Who you gonna call? Microsoft Support!

The starting point for Microsoft Support is its Web site (http://support. microsoft.com). From there you can choose your products, look through online support, or start a support request (using e-mail, an online form, or phone), as shown in Figure 3-3.

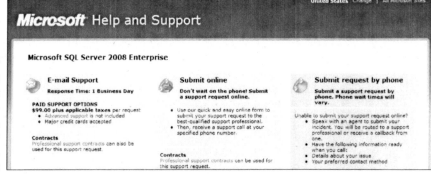

Figure 3-3:
Microsoft
support —
e-mail,
online, or
phone.

Your Volume or Site Licensing Agreement may already discuss Microsoft Support options, so make sure that you know what support you're already paying for *before* you purchase additional options.

Other resources online and on paper

As you may imagine, you can find a great deal of information about Microsoft products, systems, and solutions — whether in cyberspace or actually written down on paper (how retro). Here are some of those additional resources:

- **Microsoft Developer Network (MSDN):** This Web site is a treasure trove of information on the Microsoft technologies. Check the site out at `http://msdn.microsoft.com`. On the site the technologies are listed on the left-hand navigation pane. Select a technology, and all the information you could ever want pops up. The site contains videos, getting started material, downloads, and other articles.

- **TechNet:** The TechNet Web site is a technology resource for Information Technology workers. The site can be found at `http://technet.microsoft.com`. For example, clicking SharePoint Server in the left-hand navigation brings up product evaluation information, planning and architecture, design and building out sites, deployment, and operations. Figure 3-4 shows the SQL Server page of the TechNet site.

- **Whitepapers:** Many organizations perform tests, write down their methodology, and otherwise document Microsoft products and solutions. Microsoft itself, and its partner network, have created many whitepapers that can be found on the MSDN and TechNet sites. A quick search using your favorite search engine also yields whitepapers from all the top consultancies, research organizations, and MVPs.

- **Magazines, journals, and newsletters:** Many respected organizations send weekly, monthly, and quarterly newsletters. Two of the most popular are

  - *MSDN* magazine - `http://msdn.microsoft.com/en-us/magazine/default.aspx`

  - *The Architecture Journal* - `http://www.architecturejournal.net`: Note that the Architecture in the title refers to computer architecture

Figure 3-4:
The SQL
Server page
on TechNet.

Part II
Wrapping Your Head Around Business Intelligence Concepts

The 5th Wave   By Rich Tennant

"We've got a machine over there that monitors our quality control. If it's not working, just give it a couple of kicks."

In this part . . .

As with any new approach to doing business, business intelligence is full of new terminology and concepts. When I talk to someone working in a field I'm not familiar with, they seem to be speaking a different language. Concepts that seem so natural and simple to them mean absolutely nothing to me. They might think they're explaining something in very simple terms, but even the simple terms sound like Martian. It is like trying to teach someone a foreign language by only speaking to them in that foreign language. Sure, a person can pick up some of the language after a lot of time and misunderstanding — and hurts more than it has to.

If you're like me, you need a quick understanding of which concepts are important so you can get a perspective on implementing business intelligence. This part gives you an understanding of the most important BI concepts and how Microsoft delivers them in its products.

Chapter 4

Using Data to Inform and Drive Business Activities

In This Chapter

▶ Understanding the role of data in business decisions

▶ Converting data into information

▶ Exploring OLAP analysis concepts

▶ Familiarizing yourself with OLAP terminology

> *The only one who behaves sensibly is my tailor; he takes my measurements anew every time he sees me.*
>
> — George Bernard Shaw

There's an old management saying: "You can't manage what you can't measure." I know many creative types who would beg to disagree, but in business intelligence, the saying holds true. Imagine if you were told you have just become the CEO of a manufacturing company. Hooray! Now you're told the bad news: Nobody has any idea how many people work for the company, how many products are produced or sold, how many vehicles are owned for delivering the sold products, or how much money is in the bank. Yikes! One of your first tasks would be to start measuring these things — ASAP.

What you measure is, essentially, data generated by the processes that make up a business. If you can't measure business activities, then you can't know whether they're improving or getting worse . . . and if you don't know something is getting worse, you can't manage it in order to improve it! Small wonder that measuring and analyzing business processes are basic to business intelligence.

Measuring change means you care about it and want to try to affect its course. Sure, you can easily just "hippie out" and let the change flow in whatever direction the wind blows. That may be a groovy lifestyle for some, but it's no way to run a business. As the different gears and levers of business move, they change the course of the business. Measuring the change that each lever has on the business allows you to track the consequence of moving that particular lever. As the measurements come together and are plotted against the way the lever was moved and by how much, you begin to get a picture of how to fine-tune your use of the levers to optimize your business.

For example, if you're running a manufacturing company, you may be interested in measuring material costs, production times, and distribution costs. Using the data generated by measuring these processes, you can use the data mining algorithms contained within SQL Server Analysis Services (SSAS) to run a predictive analysis. Knowing what may happen to your overall business is a critical piece of information that you can use to make major business decisions.

In this chapter, we explore the role data plays in making decisions and running a business. In order to make a decision, you need information about the question at hand. Information is born from data, and thus data are critical components of business intelligence. We also explore some key technologies that were born from the challenges that massive amounts of data produce. In particular, OnLine Analytical Processing (OLAP) has a number of concepts that directly relate to turning raw data into information. Unfortunately, OLAP is filled with buzzwords and theories that sound like something out of a sci-fi movie. In this chapter, you discover the problem that the technology solves and then fill in the terminology that solves each problem. In the Microsoft BI world, the OLAP universe falls squarely in the SQL Server product, and in particular SQL Server Analysis Services (SSAS).

The Importance of Data in Making Business Decisions

You need to know what's happening in your business in order to make the decisions required for success (and, okay, a bonus). But hold on a minute; visiting this new territory means getting a handle on the lingo — and there are many terms in BI that refer to measuring. Knowing what they mean is crucial to making the correct decisions. Here's a quick list of the terms you'll hear most often:

- ✔ **Benchmark:** A standard used as a desirable starting point, or industry recognized value, for comparing one measurement against other measurements. For example, you may have a 10-percent benchmark profit margin for a particular retail store. You would then compare actual sales against the benchmark number.

- ✔ **Count:** Refers to the rows in a database. Excel also has a Count function for tallying numerous types of data.

- ✔ **Fact:** Numeric data that you want to analyze. In OLAP terminology, numeric data "lives" in a Fact Table, so it's common to use *fact* and *measure* interchangeably when referring to numeric data. The actual database table that these numeric data live in is called a *Fact Table.* A database is usually made up of numerous tables (think of a table as an Excel sheet with rows and columns). The table that stores the numeric data you want to analyze (fact / measure) is the Fact Table in OLAP terminology.

- ✔ **Indicator:** A piece of data that is consistently present when some part of your organization's business process is performing in a way you want to know more about.

- ✔ **Key Performance Indicator (KPI):** A factor known to be crucial to an organization's success — for example occupancy rate and revenue per available room, in the hotel industry. A KPI can be used to measure the performance of your organization, whether in part or as a whole.

- ✔ **Measure:** A term you will hear often in the business intelligence world that simply refers to a numeric value, or measurement, that you're interested in aggregating, grouping, and using in evaluative comparisons. An example of a measure is sales figures. You may divide sales figures by geography and then again by store.

- ✔ **Metric:** A measurement of something, usually given in the form of a numeric value. For example, you may have a metric that tracks the output of a particular manufacturing machine — say, the total output of finished Widgiematics in an eight-hour workday. (Truth to tell, "metric" is really just another word for *measurement.*)

I often hear about businesses run on the basis of a "gut feeling." I don't buy it. Even people who think they're running a business on pure instinct are getting input from *somewhere.* Often they're lucky enough to have a talent for keen observation of important facts, as if they were entire BI systems in themselves. That's enviable — as far as it goes. And this system may seem to work for smaller companies — but as businesses grow or the people attuned to the company (usually the founders) leave, the entire system can disappear in an instant. Having a real, hardware-and-software BI system in place — independent of a particular person — provides insurance against such sudden changes.

Jack Welch, the chairman and CEO of General Electric from 1981–2001, once said that he measures *everything.* From a BI perspective, this is a great practice; BI is, at its root, a measurement system. But *everything?* How do you go about such an enormous task? Figure 4-1 illustrates a realistic approach:

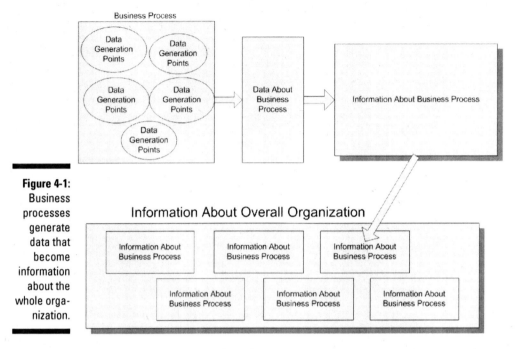

Figure 4-1:
Business
processes
generate
data that
become
information
about the
whole orga-
nization.

First, you have to divide your business into *processes* and then break down those processes into *data-generation points.* These points are where you find the crucial data to turn into the most useful information. Your BI system gathers the data that come in from the individual processes, and puts it in a usable format — in a data warehouse — where it's available (as information) to the overall business. Each individual business process makes up part of the big picture — backed up by solid, quantified information. That's the essence of Microsoft Business Intelligence.

Tracking down the relevant data

The primary purpose of BI is to get the right information to the right decision-maker at the right time. Having relevant data readily available helps fulfill this purpose — but what's relevant can vary, because every organization is different. When I first discuss BI with an organization, I like to find out what makes the organization tick and what its most relevant data are — the stuff that makes or breaks its effectiveness. The "right data"; they're the lifeblood of your BI system.

I like to follow these steps for determining the right data:

1. **Identify the data you need for making decisions about your organization.**

   For now, don't worry about whether the data are available — just come up with the list of questions you need the data to *answer.* This list of questions serves as the basis for the information that the BI system needs to provide.

2. **Determine which business processes produce the data that would answer your questions.**

   Map out the processes that make up your business (**Hint:** Assembling cars and delivering them to dealers are separate processes.) Figure out which data-generation points are available — and what data you need to assemble to get the correct information about the process. (For example, are all parts of the assembly process up to speed?)

3. **Ensure the data are being captured in a digital format.**

   For example, the data may already be stored in an operational system in a database or file. If the data are not currently available in a digital format, then you'd better adjust the process to capture it and store it in a digital format. This adjustment may be as simple as having someone enter the most important data items into an Excel spreadsheet. The Microsoft BI tools that extract data can connect to a vast number of different systems and formats — but the data have to be digital in the first place, and stored on a computer, for it to work!

4. **Microsoft BI kicks in and accesses the right data.**

   The software that connects the various systems and grabs the data is called SQL Server Integration Services (SSIS). The good news is that it's included with the Microsoft SQL Server product.

Getting the right data to the right person at the right time

Now that you've identified the data you need, determined which business process produces that data, and ensured that the data are being captured digitally, Microsoft BI can pull the data from the source systems and turn it into information for the decision-maker (also known as *the right person*).

Microsoft BI takes the relevant data, transforms it into a usable format, organizes it, and loads it into a data warehouse. When the data are stored and organized, they're ready to be turned into information and viewed by the right decision-maker at the right time. The Microsoft BI products used to display the data are SQL Server Reporting Services (SSRS), Excel, and SharePoint (PerformancePoint, Excel Services, PowerPivot, Dashboard pages, and KPI lists).

These steps walk you through the process of turning data into information and getting it to the right person at the right time:

1. **SQL Server Integration Services (SSIS) connects to the source systems and gains access to the digital data.**

2. **SSIS cleans up the data and transforms it into a format that's usable across the organization.**

   For example, the date format may differ between different systems. SSIS transforms these dates into a standard format before loading it into the data warehouse.

3. **SQL Server Analysis Services (SSAS) is used to build OLAP cubes that allow for ad-hoc analysis of the data.**

4. **SQL Server Reporting Services (SSRS) is used to build reports, using the data in the data warehouse as a source.**

   The result is that a number of questions (the ones you created in the previous section) are answered, which means the reports now contain valuable information.

   An *OLAP cube* is simply a specialized data structure designed to store data in a way optimized for summing and analyzing. SSAS OLAP cubes use the data warehouse data as a source.

5. **Excel connects to the SSAS OLAP cubes, analyzes the data, and builds reports from the data.**

   Excel can serve as a client for SSAS cube analysis, even though the actual data lives on a powerful server in the data center. Excel and Visio can also connect to SSAS and take advantage of the data-mining capabilities. Reports and charts can then be created and published.

6. **SharePoint surfaces the information in the form of SSRS reports, Excel Services documents, PerformancePoint, Scorecards, Dashboards, and KPI lists.**

BI and the risk of high-tech tunnel vision

So is BI a set-it-and-forget-it solution? Well, when a BI system is in place and the measurements are flowing into those nice dashboards, a company might get too comfortable and believe everything can run on autopilot. That's when I often tell a personal story about the dangers of depending too much on a tool that's meant to guide you but not make decisions for you.

I like to think I have a pretty good sense of direction. I've always been able to read a map and find my way by knowing the general direction I'm supposed to go. A while back, we started using a GPS for our car. One winter, I had a project down on the Oregon coast. I'd drive down from Seattle; the GPS said I'd be there in three hours.

A couple of hours into the drive, the GPS had me turn off of the main freeway (I-5) and onto a road that follows the Columbia River down into the Pacific Ocean. I was thinking about the project at hand — not paying much attention to where I was going — after all, the GPS had never failed me before. The next turn I made was onto a rather unassuming road (with no painted lines) that led up into the mountains. I started getting a little concerned when logging trucks started rolling by headed in the opposite direction and a light snow began to fall. I got really concerned when the snow turned into a downright blizzard and I could barely see the road.

I began to watch the GPS more closely, and it told me I should turn in only 2 miles. As I approached the turn, I stopped dead in my tracks — the road had not even been driven on! There were no tracks in the snow whatsoever, and the road looked very narrow and wound further up into a mountain.

At this point, I was relieved to find out that I had cell-phone reception. I called the client (who, thankfully, was familiar with Oregon back roads) and he told me that if I would have taken that road it would have been 20 miles of steep mountain switchbacks. He advised me to backtrack to the main road and follow it out to the ocean and down the coast. I followed his advice — and a little over an hour and a half later, I was there.

Yes, the GPS was *technically* correct — the route it wanted to take me was much shorter than the route I ended up taking, but without some common sense and good judgment I may have been in real trouble in the remote mountains of Oregon.

This experience was a real eye-opener — it made me realize how technological tools can make a person lazy. Nowadays, I always scout out my trips on a map Web site before I take a route I'm not familiar with. I consider the GPS a tool that can assist me in my journey but will not deliver me to where I want to go without me having to make decisions and use common sense.

And yes, there's a metaphor (and a moral) in there somewhere.

A BI system should be used much like a GPS — as a tool that provides you with the information you need in order to make the correct decisions. If you do as I did with the GPS, you get tunnel vision; the tool could end up causing more harm than good. I later found out that our GPS has a setting that will only route you on main highways. Likewise, though it pays you to keep creating improved iterations of your BI system to yield better information, the decision-maker still has to choose what to *do* with that information. That said, why is BI so tempting to set and forget? Well, there's another way to ask that question . . . .

Why All the Fuss about OLAP?

If a database boils down to a bunch of related data that's organized so it's easy to get at — and stashed where people can get at it (usually in a computer system), what else is new? Well, OLAP is (relatively) new. And to say it makes databases more efficient is like saying you can cut baloney fast with a Swiss Army knife: You can — but you can do *so much more*.

What is OLAP?

In 1993, E.F. Codd (known as the father of the modern database) proposed a new type of database design: OnLine Analytical Processing (OLAP). In essence, OLAP stores data in a way that is designed for fast data retrieval (read analysis).

The type of database that OLAP went beyond was called OnLine *Transactional* Processing (OLTP). The obvious difference between OLAP and OLTP is that third letter — *A* for *analysis* replaces *T* for *"transactional"* — the emphasis shifts from "Transaction X took place and we need to store the data very efficiently" to "Data Y exists in the database and we need to perform analysis on it without waiting for hours for reports to run." Table 4-1 highlights the differences between OLTP databases and OLAP databases — and what they mean.

Table 4-1	Comparison of OLAP and OLTP Databases
	Description
OLTP (Transactional)	These databases are set up to receive and store data very quickly. For example, imagine observing an hour's worth of transactions at your local grocery store. Every purchase requires storing many different pieces of data in a number of databases. If hundreds of customers make purchases at the same time, the database system has to be able to handle all these pieces of information. The goal of an OLTP database is to reduce, or eliminate, data redundancy.
OLAP (Analytical)	These databases are optimized for analyzing data rather than receiving and storing data. For example, if you already have a huge database (usually an OLTP database) full of grocery-store purchases, you can use OLAP to slice up the data and look at it from different angles. You can see (for example) total sales divided up by store, by time frame, and by cashier — and then jump to looking at profit margin divided up by product, product group, purchase, and time of day. Since the purpose of an OLAP database is to increase analytical performance, much of the data is stored redundantly. For example, you may have sales data per store, and then the same sales data aggregated and stored by region, by state, and by product group. The data are stored redundantly, but this makes analyzing the data and asking for aggregated data very fast.

Now you can impress your friends and colleagues by telling them that you're thinking about (ahem) "implementing some Microsoft BI to uncover inefficiencies in the production process by using OLAP to analyze the data coming in from the inventory OLTP databases." And they'll think, "Wow. I wonder what that means." With this book under your belt, you can tell them.

What makes OLAP so fast?

You may wonder what makes OLAP so special and fast. The secret is in the ways it helps people analyze data — most of which sound like somebody's going crazy with a drill:

- **Drilling in:** This analytic technique breaks a number (usually a sum) into the other numbers that make it up. For example, you may look at your total sales figures for the state of California and want to drill in to see how each individual store is performing. Using this method, you can view sales data by county or zip code, and then by neighborhood, and then by individual store.

- **Drilling out:** This method is (obviously) the opposite of drilling into the data: You move from specific details to more general data. An analyst can look at the sales data for a particular product in a particular store, drill out to see that product's sales for all stores in the city, and then drill out farther to see how sales of the product are doing in the entire state or country.

- **Drilling through:** To get to the information you want to see (say, the details of sales figures for a particular store), you click one link after another until you get to the actual source data (individual transactions contained in the OLTP system) originally aggregated to form the number you started with. For example, when analyzing the sales of a particular store, you notice that one particular product is a very hot seller. You, of course, want to know why — but the data have been summed up for that product for that particular store. So you drill through to view your transactional data at its most detailed level: actual entries in the system that made the sales. During this process, you may then notice some helpful correlations — say, that the hot seller is always included with another product or sells best a particular time of day.

- **Grouping:** If you've ever used a PivotTable in Excel, then you know about grouping data by pivoting columns and rows. When you pivot a row or column, the data are then grouped in a different way. For example, you may have sales figures with sales people down the left column and products and store location across the top. If you want to shift the groupings of sales figures and move products down to the left-hand column, then you would simply click the product field and drag it to the row. This may seem like a simple concept, but the number-crunching going on behind the scenes is amazing. Each field has to be summed up again with every change, using the criteria of the row or column that was pivoted.

The Excel PivotTable is a very powerful feature, and I often see it used to manage entire portions of a business. Microsoft has recognized the appeal and familiarity of Excel and has released a feature in Excel 2010 called PowerPivot. *PowerPivot* provides Excel with the ability to pull in tens of millions of rows in order to perform an ad-hoc analysis.

OLAP databases are optimized to store data in a way that speeds up these analytical tasks. For example, data are *pre-aggregated* (summed up and stored in the database when the database is processed instead of when the summed data are requested) so that when you drill in or drill out, the computer doesn't have to sum up the component numbers; the computer simply looks up the previously calculated value and presents it. The same is true with grouping: The database has already pre-calculated various values that you may need when you pivot the data. When you want to drill to find out what product groups are selling well within a certain geography, the data have already been calculated for you, and it's simply presented as a result of your request.

Why OLAP?

Well, why not? Seriously, though, the answer is simple: It's a fast way to handle complexity. Businesses have to make decisions quickly in a changing market-place, often by summing up and grouping huge amounts of data and analyzing them ASAP. Imagine (for example) that you have your sales figures (or any other numeric metric) handy, but you're evaluating your sales strategy so you want to see total sales sliced up and grouped in various ways — in real time. As you view one grouping of sales figures, other questions arise that can only be answered by changing the way the data are grouped (say, including more data or less data and then recalculating the results). If you have a very small business and a talent for arithmetic, you may be able do this by hand — or (if your business is more up to date) by using the PivotTable function in an Excel spreadsheet. But imagine what you'd face if you ran a huge company whose sales figures filled up *billions* of rows of data. A personal computer — and in particular Excel — would give up in despair at this huge mound of information (although PowerPivot, which is a feature of Excel 2010, increases the power of Excel dramatically). OLAP provides similar abilities of the Excel PowerPivot functionality but on a massive enterprise scale.

Transactional databases (OLTP) are great for vacuuming up and storing information, but they can't handle the many different lookup and sum opera-tions required for data analysis. With OLAP databases — designed with real-time analysis in mind — complex data-crunching takes seconds or minutes instead of hours, days, or weeks. The crowd goes wild. OLAP takes up perma-nent residence in the BI toolbox.

Many companies have developed products that implement OLAP in various ways. Microsoft's implementation of OLAP is included as a feature in SQL Server Analysis Services (SSAS) and is part of the SQL Server product. In the Microsoft world, people often use the terms OLAP and SSAS interchangeably (hey, call it brand loyalty), depending on the context of the conversation.

Microsoft's original name for its implementation of OLAP was OLAP Services. Later, when Microsoft included a Data Mining engine, the name changed to Analysis Services (OLAP by itself doesn't refer to data mining). This also left the door open for Microsoft to include other analysis capabilities in its Analysis Services in the future.

Analysis Services is a component of the SQL Server product. If you already own SQL Server, then you already own SSAS and Microsoft's OLAP implementation and Data Mining engine. (SQL Server contains a potent array of BI features, covered in greater detail in Chapter 8. See also Chapter 13 for more about checking the licensing of your existing Microsoft products — and making the most of the BI tools you may already have.)

Databases and cubes

An OLAP *cube* is nothing more than a specialized data structure designed for fast analysis. (OLAP database = A database divided into one or more OLAP cubes.)

An OLAP cube (by itself or one of many) is part of an OLAP database but isn't the entire database. Therefore *OLAP cube* and *OLTP database* are not the same thing. If you hear excited database geeks buzzing about "cubes," they mean OLAP cubes; if they're talking "databases," they usually mean OLTP databases. If you want to maintain that knowledgeable look, don't use *cube* and *database* interchangeably.

Because of their design, OLTP databases are often called *relational databases*. The data in the table are only stored once in the system; what makes it so doggone usable is the *relations* you can set up between it and the data in other tables in the same database. For example, imagine having a list of your customers in an Excel spreadsheet. If a customer changes his or her name, you have to go through the whole document and update all instances of that name. Imagine, however, that you just have a number in the table that represents the customer in the Name column — and that number refers to *another* worksheet that actually contains the customer's name. Then you need only change the name of the customer in that worksheet, in one spot. The two tables relate to each other and share information.

Storing a piece of data in just one place within a database is called *normalization*. There are many different levels of normalization that only the truly technically-obsessive care to discover. The main thing to keep in mind is that you can divide the databases you use in a BI system into two primary categories: normalized (OLTP) and de-normalized (OLAP).

In an OLTP (relational) database, you normalize the data in different tables when you store it in one place (that's the ideal, anyway) and relate it to data stored in other tables. OLAP databases, on the other hand, have to make stored data available for quick analysis — which means storing it where it's easy to access, even if that means duplicating it in various places — which makes the data *de-normalized* to that extent.

OLAP databases also have to be multidimensional — but if that sounds a bit too geometrical, don't worry: In database-speak, a *dimension* is a particular aspect of a data item, usually one you can use to head a column. If (for example) cars come in green, blue, and purple, then `Color` could be one of their dimensions — and if green is selling better, a decision-maker may want to know how many green cars are presently ready to ship. But suppose that the cars can have chrome trim and satellite radio as options; `trim` and `satellite radio` could be two more dimensions to deal with. (Typical questions may include, "How many green cars with chrome trim did we sell this year?" and "Did the green cars with satellite radio model do as well?") Every way you can possibly divide the data is a dimension — and an OLAP database has to group its data in whatever way the analysis demands. Table 4-2 summarizes the terminology differences between OLAP and OLTP databases. The accompanying sidebar ("Cubes, dimensions, geometry, and cheese") has a little fun with it.

Table 4-2	Database Terminology	
	Normalization Classification	*Structural Classification*
OLAP database (analytical)	Data are de-normalized, (optimized for analysis and fast retrieval of large amounts).	The database is multi-dimensional (includes many different ways to divide the data).
OLTP database (relational)	Normalized (optimized to gather, store, update, or delete large amounts of data quickly, in one place if possible).	Relational (the data in any tables are related to data in other tables). For example, all customer names can be stored in their own table instead of in an Orders table; the Orders table contains a small key that points (relates) to the Customers table.

Cubes, dimensions, geometry, and cheese

Okay, here comes the geometry: A good old-fashioned cube is a three-dimensional shape, and each side is of equal length, as shown in this figure. Now, class, how do you get from there to an OLAP cube? Truth to tell, my geometry teacher never asked that question. But the answer's pretty straightforward: By analogy.

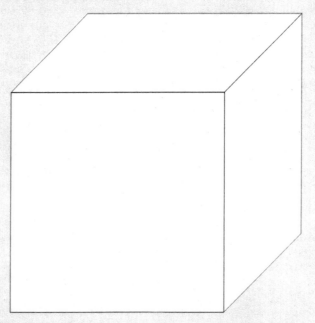

Various analogies can describe the concept of an OLAP cube and a data dimension. For example, imagine a data item as three sides of a cube. What the heck, make it a Rubik's Cube — a three-dimensional puzzle that has a different color on each of its faces (after it's been solved, anyway). Take away the top, bottom, and front faces of the cube. Call the remaining three faces of the cube "Sales Figures" and imagine the space they contain as a numeric value: the total sales figures for a company. Each of the remaining three sides is a way to divide total sales: One side represents sales in all states, the second side represents sales of all products, and the third side represents sales in all years. Now you can take any value from each side and draw a line through the middle, to a value on another face of the cube; at the intersection, you can get a value for that particular combination of sales "dimensions" (state, product, and year), as shown in this figure.

Where the dimensions intersect is the numeric value you're trying to find, as shown in this second figure.

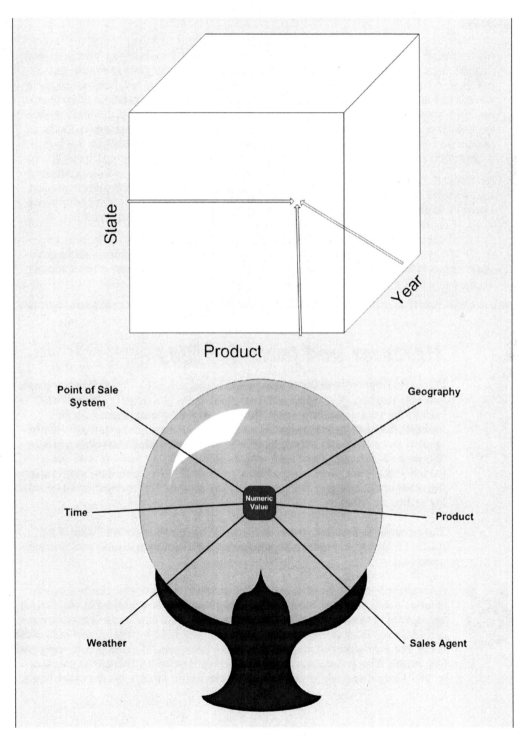

(continued)

(continued)

Now, an OLAP cube can have as many ways to divide data (dimensions) as you want. You can have more than three, of course, each represented as a line through the contained space. For the moment, three sales dimensions are enough to demonstrate how handy it is to pinpoint an item of data and get an immediate inkling of what it means to your business.

Another analogy I use is a cube of cheese: You start with one of those wire-mesh dicers you see on TV. Push it through the cheese, and the block of cheese becomes long, rectangular pieces of cheese. This would be the equivalent of slicing sales figures into Regions. Now pluck out one of the rectangles of cheese, say the rectangle that represents California. Take another dicer (representing Products) and push it down on the piece of cheese that represents California. You now have more, smaller rectangles of cheese, and each of these now represents a product sold in California. But you want to divide this product sold in California even further, say by salesperson. You pull out the Salesperson dicer and push it through the cheese. You can now pull out the one piece that represents the sales for a particular product, region, and salesperson. (Sorry, there's no cube of cheese to show you here. I ate it.)

You can still call this device a cube, of course — but just think of it as an incredibly useful capability of OLAP. Or a plate of yummy hors d'oeuvres. Your call.

Measures and facts (of life)

Discussing the facts of life is always a difficult subject — "you take the good, you take the bad, you take them both, and there you have . . . measures." Luckily for you, a *measure* and a *fact* are simply different names for the numeric data you're interested in analyzing. For example, you may want to analyze sales data and inventory levels, asking profound questions such as, "Do we have enough green cars with satellite radio on hand to ride the trend for the rest of this fiscal year without retooling?" The sales data may contain the sales in dollars, and the inventory may contain the current count of satellite radios on hand.

The numeric values are stored in a special table called a Fact Table. Just think of a fact or a measure as two names for the numeric data that you are analyzing.

A measure does not have to be a strict numeric value coming from a source system. A measure just needs to be something that is quantifiable and can be aggregated. A measure can be invented as well. You can create a measure out of thin-air by using an expression much like you would create a new column in Excel. For example, you may want to know how many dollars of cars were sold last month. The dollars starts out as a numeric value and simply aggregates up all of these numeric dollar values for the entire month. On the other hand, you may start with something like color, which is not a numeric value in the source system. When the colors are counted, however, the result is a numeric value that can be analyzed in the OLAP system.

SQL Server Analysis Services (SSAS) puts the measures in a structure called a Measure Group, which is simply a handy place to (well, yeah) put grouped measures. That way SSAS doesn't have to look all over the database looking for those pesky measures, and can manage related measures all together rather than separately.

Hierarchies of detail

Rejoice: A few BI terms actually sound like normal language and make sense — for example, *measure/fact* (synonyms discussed in the previous section). Here's another: *hierarchy* — a way to order and relate your data's dimensions at higher or lower levels depending on how detailed they are. *High-level* analysis is lofty, abstract, big-picture, and (okay) sometimes too vague if you're detail-oriented. *Low-level* analysis gets down to the nitty-gritty, the brass tacks, the fiddly bits, the individual grains of rice in the bag — which may be why *granular* is biz-speak for "very detailed."

For example, if you're considering a time dimension, you may start at a fairly high level representing years, come down the hierarchy a level or two to consider fiscal quarters, drop down another to represent months, and another to represent weeks. The collection of time dimensions forms a hierarchy, as shown in Figure 4-2.

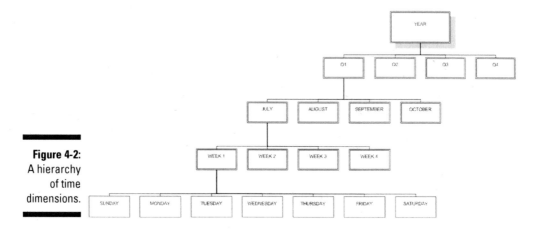

Figure 4-2:
A hierarchy
of time
dimensions.

But hierarchies aren't just for time — they can be used for any way you want to divide your data. Additional examples of hierarchies include your products, organizational charts, and geography. You can create a hierarchy of geography — starting way up there with a world dimension, coming down to Earth with a country dimension, swooping down to a state dimension, then a city dimension, a store dimension — and before you know it, you've landed in the front window of your company's store just down the block from here, and everything's all (eww) granular.

The lowest level of detail that the hierarchy goes down to is called . . . you guessed it . . . the granularity.

Although hierarchies of detail are common, you're not limited to any particular set. If you have the data available in your organization to create multiple hierarchies of dimensions, go for it. The most useful analysis connects your organization-specific data in ways that offer insight into the larger trends that decision-makers have to face.

Chapter 5

Taking a Closer Look at Data Collection

In This Chapter

▶ Exploring the Extract Transform Load (ETL) process

▶ Understanding how SQL Server Integration Services (SSIS) does ETL

▶ Checking out a simple example of SSIS in action

▶ Discovering the components of modern data generation

Leaders have to act more quickly today. The pressure comes much faster.

— Andy Grove

*B*efore data can be turned into information that an organization can use, it has to be collected and transformed into a standard format. The many different systems that generate data often speak only their own languages. Imagine that you're the leader of a group of people and everyone gets a clue to a puzzle. Putting the puzzle together unlocks the key to massive fortunes. The catch is that each person speaks a different language. Everyone knows only his or her piece but can't put the entire puzzle together. What you need is someone who can speak all the languages, collect all the clues, and then translate them in a way that makes sense to you, the decision-maker.

In business intelligence, the tool that speaks those multiple languages is called an *Extract Transform Load (ETL) tool.* In Microsoft BI, the ETL tool is called *SQL Server Integration Services (SSIS)* — and it's included with the SQL Server product.

In this chapter, you discover how ETL works and how SSIS is used to extract, transform, and load data into a data warehouse.

The King of BI Concepts — ETL

Extract, transform, and load — ETL — is the process of pulling data out of source systems and organizing it in a central data warehouse. Figure 5-1 shows an overview of how the ETL process works to extract data, transform it into a standard format, and load it into a data warehouse.

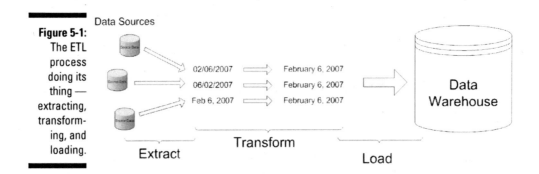

Figure 5-1: The ETL process doing its thing — extracting, transform-ing, and loading.

Here's a bracing, brisk walk through each phase of the ETL process.

Extracting data

Data extraction may sound fairly simple. If only that were true. As you take a closer look at your organization's source systems, you realize that the raw data are strung out all over the place. This is the moment when you scratch your head and wonder what the heck those systems are actually doing. Because your data hang out in multiple source systems, finding the specific data you're after can seem like finding a needle in a haystack. This is the moment when you remember that you have Microsoft BI capabilities (just daydream with me for a minute here) — and you call upon SQL Server Integration Services (SSIS).

SSIS is the tool for extracting data because you have to *connect* to the source systems before you can get at the data they contain. Source systems can take many shapes; the tool used to extract the data has to connect efficiently to the whole menagerie. For example, your data may be contained in Excel files, Access databases, simple text files, and some other form of database. SSIS can connect to the source systems that use these file types — and more — using no more than its built-in functionality. Once SSIS has connected to the data, it's ready to move to the next phase of the ETL process — transformation.

If (on the rare occasion) built-in SSIS functionality can't handle a particular connection, don't fret: Microsoft has provided a way to write custom code for SSIS, using the .NET framework (which makes just about anything possible). In addition, many third-parties have developed software that integrates with SSIS and extends its functionality. Before you call in a developer, make sure that someone hasn't already developed exactly what you're looking to accomplish.

Transforming data

I'm always amazed at the drastic data-storage differences among different computer systems. Wouldn't it be nice if all of the software companies and developers got together and agreed on how to store data? This would allow all systems to know how to speak to every other system. In this perfect scenario, you wouldn't even need a transformation process when you had to pull and aggregate data — you could just grab whatever data you needed, put it together to fit your need, and then store it all in a nice, tidy data warehouse for in-house consumption (yum, yum)! Unfortunately, in the messy real world, data storage varies wildly between databases — a hodgepodge of software programs, input sources (human or robot), scanners, and other gadgetry that generates data. Every system seems to have a different method, often the whim of the developer who originally created the program.

Well, that's why data transformation — essentially getting useful information out of the mess — is necessary. It isn't simple; often your data has to undergo cleansing, the mapping of its numeric values, calculation of new values, and aggregation. Here's a look at the down-and-dirty details of . . .

Data cleansing

Data cleansing involves taking data and code in various different forms and making them uniformly consistent with each other. An example is the process of taking different date formats and turning them into the same format. If the only date format you ever needed was 01/01/01, then you'd have no problems retrieving any date from anywhere in your organization's data. However, what if the date format for June 2, 2002 is stored as 06/02/02 in your U.S. office's system and as 02/06/2002 in your U.K. office's system. If you don't cleanse the data, making sense of what the data means is almost impossible.

Another great example of the need for data cleansing is in naming conventions. For example, if you have a list of professions in a reference tracking system, one system may use the word "lawyer," another system may use the word "attorney," and another system may abbreviate it to "Atty" or "Att." All these terms refer to a legal professional, but they're all represented in different ways. To make this information useful, first you have to determine the terminology you want to see — and then *map* all the different terms to one term (that is, specify one term to stand for all the equivalent terms used in the different systems). Your one chosen term will represent the whole profession in your cleansed data. Having standard naming conventions reduces confusion and allows analysts and decision-makers to perform their tasks more easily.

Mapping numeric values

Developers often store lists of data using numbers and expect the programs that use the data to decipher what the numbers mean. For example, you may be accessing data from a marketing database and need to correlate a marketing campaign against different targeted age groups across different regions. The age groups may be listed as 0, 1, 2, 3, 4, and 5. These numbers correspond to age groups 1–18, 19–25, 26–39, 40–55, 56–65, and 66 and older, respectively, but without the key, the data are not very helpful.

Another way to think about the key is to think of a legend on a map. If you're looking at a map, you need some sort of reference to give you context about what you're looking at — the cities you're driving between may look really close until you realize that 1 inch is equal to 1,000 miles! A key is just something to give the analyst context about what she's analyzing.

When you load the data into the data warehouse, you want to transform the numeric values into something more meaningful for a data consumer. An analyst may be drilling into the data in the data warehouse and notice that 60 percent of respondents were in Age Group 4. What does Age Group 4 mean? Now he has to go track down the key. By transforming the data, the analyst instantly sees that 60 percent of people were between 56 and 65 years of age.

Calculating new values

You'll often have stand-alone data, but in order to create information you'll need to perform a calculation using various data components. This new value is derived from existing data, but it represents a completely new data point. Here's an example of a newly derived value: You may have a list of products, their associated costs, and retail prices. You want a new column to represent gross margin, so you create that column (based on two of the original columns) by subtracting retail price from associated costs in order to derive the gross margin per product. This newly-derived data can now be stored in the data warehouse and used by analysts. The analyst's job is much easier because she doesn't have to go through the exercise of trying to figure out how to get the value she really needs for her analysis; she simply grabs the gross margin values from the data warehouse and uses them in her reports.

Aggregating values

The data in the source systems is usually more detailed than you need for your analysis, so you may want to sum up all of the sales per product for each day and then again for weeks and months.

Aggregating simply means to combine and sum up the independent values into groupings. Determining what the groupings should be is very important since these groupings are what analysts use to perform their analysis and build reports.

Storing these aggregates in the data warehouse provides the necessary data for the analyst — and nobody has to develop a complex query to get the data.

Each situation is different, and you may encounter other transformations that must take place between the source systems and the data warehouse. Taking the time to transform the data properly saves a great deal of time and headache later on. By properly transforming the data, you give the report developers and analysts a leg up: They can quickly and efficiently turn the data in the warehouse into information the decision-makers can use right away.

In reality, the analysts and report developers could connect to the source (transactional) systems directly, but the amount of time and frustration they'd have to plow through to build even simple reports wouldn't be worth the trouble. For example, imagine trying to connect to your inventory systems, accounting systems, and delivery systems in order to build a report. You know the systems are out there, but getting to them, getting the data out, transforming the data into a standard format, and then reporting on it would take a great deal of time and resources. If all of this data are already in a data warehouse, then most of the task has already been accomplished.

Loading data

The final phase of the ETL process involves loading the transformed data into the data warehouse. *Loading* simply refers to the task of filling up the data warehouse with actual data. Loading the data is a fairly straightforward process — *after* the data warehouse has been designed — but you have some practical decisions to make first. In particular, you need to decide how much history you want to store. For example, you may pull data every hour, every night, or every week — what interval makes sense for your business? You can choose to overwrite the data in the database or keep the history of the various values so you can run historical reports. Most likely, you'll use some combination of these two approaches — tracking some data at intervals to build up a useful history and overwriting other data at each new load.

Okay, why does data take so many forms?

Recorded data have been around since humans first started keeping track of things. Long ago, merchants recorded who owed them what by making marks on clay tablets. Each merchant likely had his or her own technique, but the general process was the same. Today the need is no different. You have to keep track of your business or organization, but you use computers and software — a lot faster, and no need to dry or bake the records when you're done.

Software has its own complexities. That's partly because almost anyone can develop a software program — including folks who've never programmed anything before but download the free version of Visual Studio Express and start coding away 20 minutes later. But as a program develops, questions proliferate that the programmer has to answer with decisions: How do you want to store data? What names do you give to the different logical containers for the data? How are people and other computer systems going to access your data?

Techniques for storing data can be as simple as storing everything in a file with a name and an equal sign (such as "FirstName=Joe") and then build some basic programming code for accessing that data. Suppose yours is about that straightforward. Then imagine that people really like your software — and hundreds of businesses begin to use it. Down the road,

these same businesses start implementing BI systems — and have this sudden need to combine data stored in your program with data yanked out of other software programs that store and name *their* data differently.

And then there's the question of compliance with standards. Although many large software makers have implemented their own versions of industry standards for interacting with data — say, different proprietary versions of SQL — not all of them agree on how strictly to apply that standard. Suppose your product implements SQL in a way that works fine for your purposes but conflicts with a different SQL implementation in somebody else's product — and both are chugging away in the same BI system. Such unique (and sometimes quirky) systems prevail in nearly every organization.

If you're a stalwart in one of those businesses with a new BI system, struggling to get all that diverse data into a report to the brass, you need one tool that can connect to many different data sources, pull the data out, put it into a standard format, and load it into a central data repository or data warehouse. Here you're talking ETL — extract, transform, and load. What you need (aside from a BIG bottle of aspirin) is the Microsoft BI tool for ETL: namely, SQL Server Integration Services (SSIS), a feature of Microsoft SQL Server. Oh, you have it? Take five.

It is important to start the BI process by determining what questions you want answered instead of trying to implement a solution that can answer any possible question.

When you start the BI process, focus on the "what" and not on the "how." Doing so helps you avoid falling into what I like to call "solution quicksand." I've worked with one or two project managers who were so obsessed with the details of "how" they were going to do this or that specific task that they completely forgot the whole point of "what" they were trying to accomplish.

As the data warehouse grows, you can continue to iterate and add additional information. Having a basic starting point allows you to determine what data you need to load — and in what fashion — to answer the questions you put to your database.

SQL Server Integration Services (SSIS) — Microsoft's ETL Tool

Terminology dies hard, and you'll often hear people refer to Data Transformation Services (DTS), a previous version of Microsoft's ETL tool. As Microsoft revamped the product and continued to add features, the ever-more-muscular ETL tool was renamed *Integration Services* in SQL Server 2005.

You can design an ETL process fairly easily in SSIS because it provides drag-and-drop development. It's a very straightforward process that happens in Visual Studio, as shown in Figure 5-2. On the left side of the screen is the Toolbox, containing components called *tasks* that you can drag over and drop on the design surface. (For more on the Toolbox, see the upcoming section titled "SSIS Toolbox.") As you drag additional components to the same place, you're not just collecting on-screen objects — you're building an ETL process.

Visual Studio is the primary application used for development tasks. Whether building ETL processes, OLAP cubes, or SSRS reports, your BI development needs will most likely be fulfilled with Visual Studio. When SQL Server is installed, there is an option to install Business Intelligence Developer Studio (BIDS). Although Microsoft has done a poor job in terminology, it's done a great job with the technology. BIDS is nothing more than Visual Studio with only the components specifically useful for BI development. If, for some reason, you already have a version of Visual Studio (maybe you're a software developer as well), then SQL Server will install the BI development functionality directly into your existing Visual Studio environment.

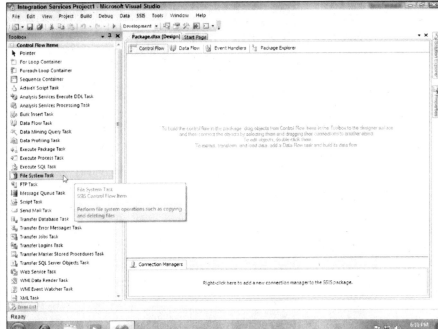

Figure 5-2:
Drag-
and-drop
develop-
ment of an
SSIS
project.

Tossing the packages into the projects

The term *project* is a generic term for any Visual Studio project. A Visual Studio project is a logical container that can contain multiple SSIS packages, as seen in Figure 5-3. What you create when you build an SSIS ETL process is called an SSIS *package.* I often hear people using *project* and *package* interchangeably, but if you're allergic to the careless use of terms, don't mix these two up. For more information on projects in Visual Studio, check out Chapter 11.

Figure 5-3:
A Visual
Studio
project can
contain
multiple
SSIS
packages.

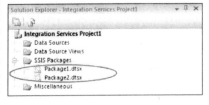

The filename extension for SSIS packages is `.dtsx`. It's the last vestige of an old name: Before the Microsoft ETL tool started going by the name SSIS, it was known as Data Transformation Services (or DTS). The x tacked onto the end means that the file is stored in a format known as eXtensible Markup Language, or XML — a standard markup language similar to HTML and used for storing text in a way that computers can read easily. (Isn't it nice how technophiles used a clever play on words to come up with the XML acronym? It'd be way too easy for everyday people to come up to speed if the abbreviation was simply EML, so it's XML to keep out the uninitiated — and, okay, to avoid confusion with the old Extended ML programming language. Maybe they were confused too.)

Connecting to data sources

SSIS can connect to many different data sources, including the following:

- **ERP systems:** Dynamics (NAV, SL, AX, GP, CRM), SAP, Epicor, Siebel, Oracle, Lawson, JD Edwards, Sage, and Hyperion, for example.

- **Database systems:** For instance, Microsoft SQL Server, Oracle, IBM DB2, Teradata, Microsoft Access, MySQL, PostgreSQL, and many others.

- **Files on a computer:** For example, Flat Text files, XML files, Excel files, Electronic Data Interchange (EDI) files, and Comma Separated Value (CSV) files.

- **Computer protocols:** Microsoft Message Queuing (MSMQ), HTTP and HTTPs, SMTP, and FTP, for instance.

You add a connection by right-clicking in the bottom of Visual Studio design pane within the Connection Manager section. Right-clicking in this section pulls up the dialog box displayed in Figure 5-4.

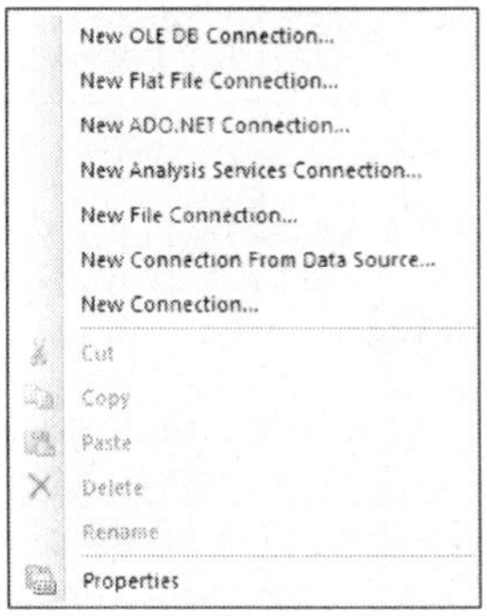

Figure 5-4:
The Connection Manager dialog box.

New OLE DB Connection...
New Flat File Connection...
New ADO.NET Connection...
New Analysis Services Connection...
New File Connection...
New Connection From Data Source...
New Connection...
Cut
Copy
Paste
Delete
Rename
Properties

You can choose any of the quick connection types, or you can select New Connection to create a connection with any of the out-of-the-box connection types, as seen in Figure 5-5.

Figure 5-5:
The SSIS
out-of-
the-box
connection
types.

Type	Description
ADO	Connection manager for ADO connections
ADO.NET	Connection manager for ADO.NET connections
CACHE	Connection manager for cache
EXCEL	Connection manager for Excel files
FILE	Connection manager for files
FLATFILE	Connection manager for flat files
FTP	Connection manager for FTP connections
HTTP	Connection manager for HTTP connections
MSMQ	Connection manager for the Message Queue task
MSOLAP100	Connection manager for Analysis Services connections
MULTIFILE	Connection manager for multiple files
MULTIFLATFILE	Connection manager for multiple flat files
ODBC	Connection manager for ODBC connections
OLEDB	Connection manager for OLE DB connections
SMOServer	Connection manager for SQL Server transfer tasks
SMTP	Connection manager for the Send Mail task
SQLMOBILE	Connection manager for SQL Server Compact connections
WMI	Connection manager for the WMI tasks

SSIS Toolbox

The components in the Toolbox are at the heart of SSIS development — a set of capabilities, already packaged as programming objects, that you can drag from the Toolbox and place on the design surface as you build your SSIS package. Being able to drag and drop complete functionality instead of coding it by hand greatly improves efficiency and ease of use. The Toolbox is dynamic and contains only the components for the design surface on which you're working. For example, there is a design surface tab for Control Flow, Data Flow, and Event Handlers, as shown in Figure 5-6. The Event Handlers tab is used to add functionality when an event (such as an error or warning) is discovered when the SSIS package runs. The Package Explorer tab is simply a tree view of the packages available in the SSIS project. Think of a *package* as a bundled-up piece of software functionality that's thought of as a single unit, or package.

The Control Flow Toolbox

When you're working with the Control Flow design surface, the components contained in the Toolbox are called *tasks*. You drag tasks from the Toolbox onto the design surface to build the SSIS package.

Once tasks are on the design surface, you can configure their properties by left-clicking them (to select a specific task) and then editing each property in the Properties pane that appears on the right-hand side of the screen, as seen in Figure 5-7.

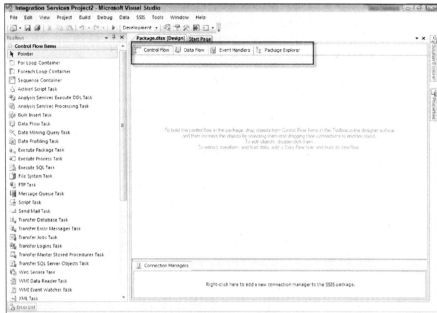

Figure 5-6:
The design surfaces tabs when working with SSIS in Visual Studio.

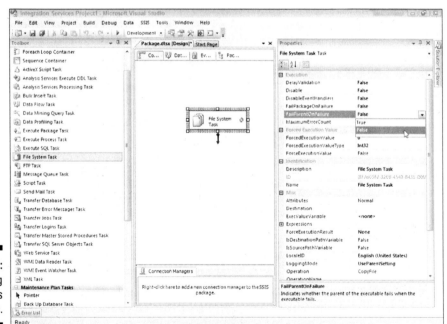

Figure 5-7:
Configuring a task's properties.

One of the most important tasks in the toolbox is the Data Flow Task, which moves data between systems and transforms it. Dragging the Data Flow Task to the Control Flow design surface provides access to the Data Flow design surface, which contains Toolbox components designed to work with data (see the next section).

As with many things in the Microsoft world, there are multiple ways to accomplish the same thing. For example, it may be confusing to think of dragging a Data Flow Task to the Control Flow design surface in order to start working with the Data Flow design surface. If you simply click on the Data Flow design surface, you'll see a message that says "No Data Flow tasks have been added to this package. Click here to add a new Data Flow task." Clicking the message does the same thing as manually dragging a Data Flow Task to the Control Flow design surface. Think of the Data Flow design surface as a way to build Data Flow Tasks that are on the Control Flow design surface. If you have multiple Control Flow Tasks on the Control Flow design surface, then you'll have to choose which one you want to work on when you're on the Data Flow design surface using a drop-down menu.

Data Flow Toolbox

The Data Flow Toolbox consists of three groupings of components: Data Flow Sources, Data Flow Transformations, and Data Flow Destinations. The Data Flow Sources grouping contains components designed to connect to data sources. The Data Flow Transformations grouping contains components that are designed to transform data, and the Data Flow Destinations grouping contains components designed to connect to data destinations. A general ETL process contains components from each of these categories, as demonstrated in the section "A Simple SSIS Walk-Through," later in this chapter.

Data transformations

Although SSIS has many components for transforming data, it's a good idea to get a grip on what you're trying to accomplish *before* you build an ETL process. So take a breath and a close look at the following checklist before building your ETL process . . .

1. Develop a complete understanding of the source data. You need to know what the system is storing and the relevance of the data to your questions at hand. What's coming in from where?

2. Understand the design of the destination system. The destination system is your data warehouse that has been developed to provide information to the big-kahuna decision-makers. How does it meet their needs?

3. Prepare mappings that will transform the data in preparation for loading into the source system.

   For a refresher on how mapping fits into data transformation, flip back a bit to the "Transforming data" section of this chapter.

Do not overlook these steps! Voice of experience here: It's too easy, especially when you're just starting out, to dive in to planning the BI "solution" without understanding the source data *first*. This approach leads to headaches later in the project — say, when you discover that the source data doesn't contain what you assumed it would. So be kind to yourself: Develop a complete understanding of the source data *before* you try to design and develop the overall solution. Ask some basic questions — like these, for openers: What business processes are serving as data sources? What, exactly, is being measured? How often? What data are kept to build up a history and what's overwritten? In what form — and format — is the data stored?

I'm a very visual person and I love documenting and printing large maps of the source systems. I often design these maps using Visio and print them on wall-size paper, then step back and take in the big picture. This allows me to avoid losing sight of the question(s) I'm trying to answer.

Anything is possible with custom code

Often, the standard components available in SSIS are all you need to get up and running before you can start merrily extracting, transforming, and loading the data from your source systems. However, Microsoft recognizes that sometimes situations arise that nobody could have anticipated. As a result, Microsoft has left the door open for you to augment your SSIS packages with custom code, using .NET programming capabilities. (For more on .NET, see Chapter 11.)

One benefit of custom coding is that anything's possible — you can hire a developer to write a piece of software that does just about anything you can dream. The (related) risk with custom coding projects is that they're often unpredictable. Unless you're working with a top-notch team, *scope creep* (a project's tendency to get bigger and more complex) can blow your budget before you can say "double-click."

A Simple SSIS Walk-Through

You may not want to transform yourself into a hard-core SSIS expert, but it's helpful to at least walk through a simple example. This one gives you an overview of how SSIS performs the ETL song and dance.

A simple set of data is used for this transformation. The source data are stored in an Excel spreadsheet and have dates in various formats, as shown in Figure 5-8. Keep in mind that this example is over-simplified with the data being sourced in Excel. In the real world, data would be spread out across different systems, files, and sources.

Figure 5-8: Sample data with dates in various formats.

The problem with the data is that the date February 6, 2010, appears in a number of different forms in different source systems. Imagine that your source systems store dates in their proprietary formats — and you want to gather and store the dates in your data warehouse, all in a format that's consistent with your company standard. Here's how to go about it:

1. **Open Visual Studio (also known as Business Intelligence Developer Studio (BIDS) if only the BI functionality is installed in the Visual Studio application) and create a new Integration Services Project by selecting File⇨New⇨Project, and then selecting Integration Services Project as shown in Figure 5-9.**

   The Integration Services Project is contained in the Business Intelligence Projects type.

2. **Ensure that the Control Flow tab is selected, and then drag a Data Flow Task from the Toolbox over to the Control Flow design canvas, as shown in Figure 5-10.**

3. **Click the Data Flow tab.**

   Now the Toolbox contains Data Flow Sources, Data Flow Transformations, and Data Flow Destinations. The source data are contained in an Excel file; this example loads the transformed data into a plain-text file. (In a real-world scenario, you'd load the data into a data warehouse, and the source data would probably be from many different non-Microsoft product sources.)

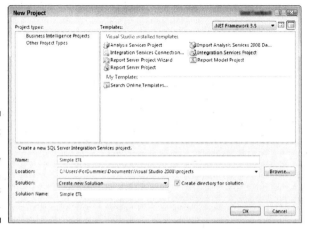

Figure 5-9:
Creating
a new
Integration
Services
Project.

4. **Drag over an Excel Source, Data Conversion, and Flat File Destination, as shown in Figure 5-11.**

5. **Configure the Excel Source component in order to complete a connection to an actual Excel document by right-clicking the Excel Source object and selecting Edit.**

   The Excel Source Editor dialog box appears.

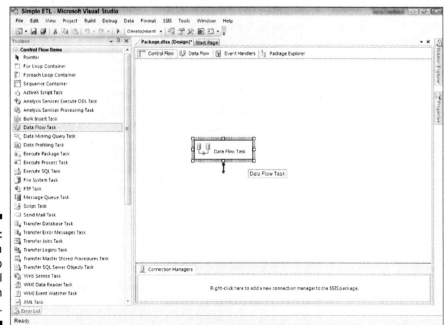

Figure 5-10:
Drag a Data
Flow Task to
the Control
Flow design
surface.

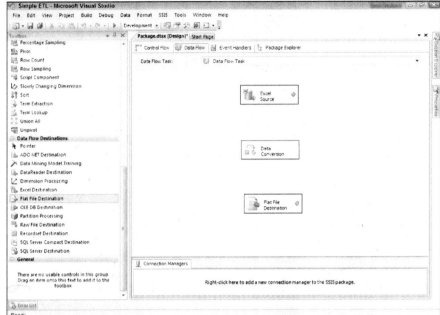

Figure 5-11:
Excel
Source,
Data
Conversion,
and Flat File
Destination
on the Data
Flow design
surface.

6. **Click the New button to create a new connection.**

7. **Browse to the Excel document and then click OK.**

8. **Specify the name of the Excel spreadsheet that contains the data.**

   The completed dialog box should look similar to Figure 5-12.

9. **Wire (connect) the components together.**

   In this scenario, the Excel document contains the source data to be extracted. The Data Conversion object performs the transformation, and the text file acts as the destination location for the load.

   a. *Right-click the Excel Source document and choose Add Path.*

      The From drop-down menu should already show the Excel Source.

   b. *Choose Data Conversion for the To drop-down menu and click OK.*

      In the Input Output Selection dialog box that appears, the Input drop-down menu should already have Data Conversion Input selected.

   c. *Set the Output drop-down menu to Excel Source Output and click OK.*

   d. *Now create the connection between the Data Conversion and the Flat File by performing almost identical steps; right-click the Data Conversion component and choose Add Path.*

e. Set the To drop-down menu to the Flat File Destination, click OK, and then set the Output drop-down menu to Data Conversion Output.

The components should all be wired together now — with an arrow displaying the direction of the data flowing through the process — as shown in Figure 5-13.

Figure 5-12:
Setting
up the
connection
to the Excel
source file.

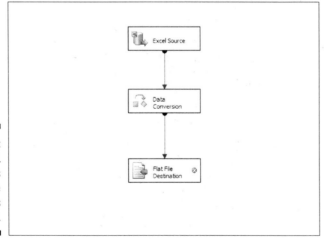

Figure 5-13:
The ETL
components
in a simple
ETL process
in SSIS.

10. **Connect the Flat File Destination object to the text file where you want the output to appear by right-clicking the Flat File Destination and selecting Edit in order to configure the component.**

11. **Click New to create a new connection, select Delimited, and then click OK.**

    The Flat File Connection Manager Editor appears.

12. **Browse to the directory where you want the output to appear and then enter a filename.**

    If the text file doesn't already exist, it'll be created. The completed dialog box is shown in Figure 5-14.

13. **The ETL process is now ready to be run: Press F5 or choose Debug⇨Start Debugging.**

14. **The process runs, and each component turns green, indicating that the process has successfully completed.**

15. **The dates are pulled in from the Excel source, flow through the Data Transform object, and are loaded into the text file.**

    The output is shown in Figure 5-15.

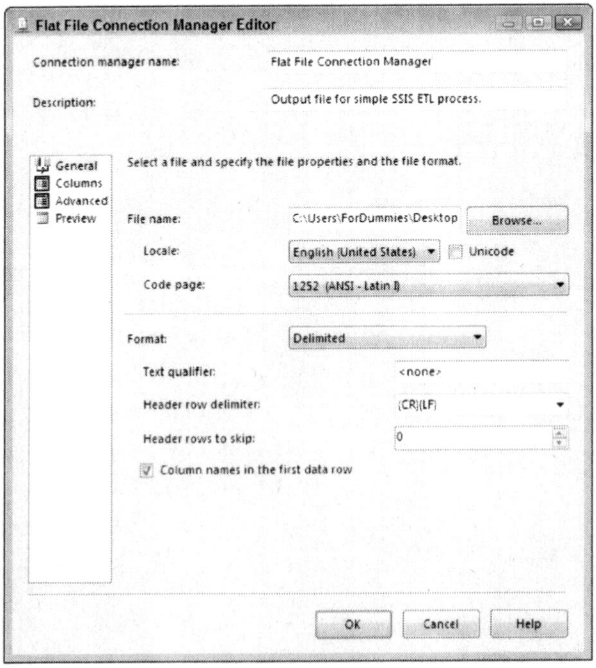

Figure 5-14: Configuring the text-file connection.

Figure 5-15:
Result of
SSIS ETL
process.

A real-world use of the ETL process would be much more complicated than this simple SSIS ETL example, but there you have a demonstration of the basic process. A real-world Microsoft BI system usually draws upon multiple source systems, performs more complex transformations, and loads the results into a SQL Server Data Warehouse.

Exploring Data Generation

Before computers were invented, data was collected and stored by people with writing implements and boxes. Somebody wrote information in a ledger or typed it into a form, and filed the resulting paper records in a filing cabinet (essentially a fancy box). At some point, the number-crunchers had to pull out their hand-cranked calculators ("adding machines") and sift through the accumulated papers to build reports. These reports would then be distributed to the company's head-knockers (uh, decision-makers) and the company would lumber along at a pace we'd see as glacial. But all companies did business this way; this slow method didn't create problems because the process was competitive. When computers burst onto the scene, the amount of data being produced — and the way business was done — changed forever.

Computers speed everything up

Computerizing business processes has drastically sped up the way companies do business. Take reports, for instance: Many business processes used to take armies of people days (if not weeks) to perform — and required massive amounts of filing and storage to document, so reports were a slow drag to create. We're talking months of labor, huge resources, and tremendous cost. No wonder report content was rarely updated, refreshed, or otherwise changed.

One fish, two fish, big fish . . . ERP

Originally, numerous software vendors provided ERP products; the most popular and widespread were produced by SAP, Oracle, Microsoft, Sage, Lawson, PeopleSoft, and JD Edwards. Then came the feeding frenzy: PeopleSoft purchased JD Edwards, and then Oracle purchased PeopleSoft. So Oracle is one of the big fish going ERP; the others are now SAP, Microsoft, Epicor, and Sage. Rumors continue to abound that Microsoft is positioning itself to purchase SAP, but as of this writing they're just rumors. With the explosion of Microsoft SharePoint as a communication and collaboration platform, I'm continually doing SharePoint/SAP interoperability work, so should Microsoft ever actual purchase SAP, well . . . Steve Ballmer, you give me a call!

Accounting was among the first business processes to embrace computers; the repetitive nature of all that number-crunching matched the nature of computers perfectly: They'd do huge amounts of it fast and never be bored. But as computers and software evolved, additional basic business activities began to adopt computers as valid business tools. At the same time, the cost of computers came down, and smaller companies could afford to jump on the bandwagon. By the 1990s, the computer had become part of the steering gear of the whole enterprise; companies were stumbling over each other to implement what began to be known as an Enterprise Resource Planning (ERP) solution.

Enterprise Resource Planning (ERP)

I like to think of ERP as (in effect) the computerization of a business. If you use computers to streamline the core processes that make up a business — in pursuit of that greater efficiency the computer has always promised — then what you're really doing is "implementing an ERP system."

The rise of ERP systems has paved the way for business intelligence — because corporate computer systems produce — in addition to all that speed and "enhanced productivity" — massive amounts of *data*. BI saves the data from just sitting there as a big pile of unused stuff, because its mission is to gather the data, transform it into consistent, usable information, and get it to the right decision-maker at the right time. As one company adopts a BI solution, other companies must follow suit (so to speak) to stay competitive. Thus a new revolution in the business world begins. As this chapter shows, the transformation of data is right at the heart of what makes BI the present must-have advantage.

Rise of the machines

It still amazes me how modern companies can use machines to streamline repetitive processes. Data are generated at a phenomenal pace without any human interaction. The need to handle this growing mountain of data leads to the use of Microsoft Business Intelligence.

At the center of the new machine workers are robots, scanners, and point-of-sale systems. Here's a closer look at how each of these fits into the BI picture.

Robots

Robots have evolved to perform complex and repetitive operations in all types of manufacturing. As robots perform their tasks, they produce a great deal of data that can be captured and analyzed by a Microsoft BI system. Some of the tasks modern robots are used for include welding, painting, assembling, cutting, casting, picking and placing, palletizing, inspecting, quality assurance, testing, and packaging.

Some of the most common types of modern robots include

- **Cartesian/Gantry robot:** A robot that moves from side to side and forward and backward as on a Cartesian plane. The movements of the robot are linear and at right angles. A small form of this type of robot may be used to pick up and place items in a box or move products from one conveyer belt to another. Larger robots may be integrated into the ceiling of a large manufacturing warehouse and can be used to cut or weld steel or move large items through an assembly process.

- **Selectively Compliant Articulated Robot Arm (SCARA) robot:** Robots that perform much like a Cartesian/Gantry robot however have movable joints instead of an X, Y grid movement. These robots take up a much smaller footprint than the Cartesian / Gantry robot.

- **Fully articulated robot:** A robot comprised of an articulated arm much like a human arm. The robot has joints and a gripping mechanism (fingers) that can be fine-tuned to perform very detailed tasks. The robot can move at nearly any angle and can perform complex operations.

Each of these robot-types performing their various tasks have data generation points that can be collected in a digital format and analyzed by Microsoft BI. The tremendous amount of data that robots produce is a wealth of information when incorporated into the overall Microsoft BI solution.

Scanners

Scanners are systems that can track items by scanning and recording locations. Each time an item is scanned, the information about that item and its location are stored in a database. This tracking provides a wealth of potential information, but it takes a BI system to access the data and provide context by combining it with data from other systems. Scanners are made up of two primary technologies.

✔ **Barcode scanner:** A barcode scanner uses a laser in order to read a barcode as an item passes through the laser. Barcode scanners are very popular and are used to track items such as products in the grocery store, luggage flowing through an airport, and packages moving around the country, to name just a few.

✔ **Radio Frequency Identification (RFID) scanner:** RFID allows a scanning mechanism to operate without actually "seeing" what it's scanning. The RFID scanner can detect the item whenever the item is within a given proximity.

Point of sale

The other day I was arriving home from running errands and realized I hadn't interacted with an actual human employee in any of the locations I had visited.

I started off going to the United States Post Office where I used a kiosk machine to weigh my package and pay for the shipping. I then just dropped the package in a drop bin next to the machine.

My next stop was the Home Depot where I picked up various items for around the house. I paid at a kiosk again on my way out. The kiosk directed me through the purchase without incident, and I was out the door quickly.

My final stop was the grocery store, where I picked up various items and again stopped at the kiosk on the way out in order to pay. The kiosk had me swipe my rewards and credit cards and then I was out the door without incident. On the way home I stopped for gas, swiped my card, and filled up our car.

Each of these transactions produced enormous amounts of data — but I didn't interact with a single human employee. As I was walking in the door, I realized that the machine revolution had long since arrived. Maybe they won.

Chapter 6

Turning Data into Information

In This Chapter

▶ Understanding centralized data storage in BI

▶ Finding out more about SQL Server Reporting Services (SSRS)

▶ Exploring SharePoint

> *There is at least one point in the history of any company when you have to change dramatically to rise to the next level of performance. Miss that moment — and you start to decline.*
>
> — Andy Grove

A modern organization generates a tremendous amount of data. If you were to peer into the source systems that hold the raw data you'd see rows and columns of data with little to no context into what it means to you and your organization. You may see numbers indicating how long a particular step in a manufacturing process took to complete or an inventory level for a particular ingredient at a particular point in time.

Taking this raw data and turning it into actionable information that directly relates to the decisions you need to make is what Microsoft Business Intelligence is all about.

In this chapter, you explore some of the technologies that take raw data and turn it into information. In particular, you explore a BI concept called a Data Warehouse and a Data Mart. You will gain an understanding of the Microsoft BI tools that are used to grab the raw data, organize it, and display it in a useful format — turning it into information.

Data Storage for BI

Even in the dark days before business intelligence arrived on the scene, people managed to slog through multiple data-generating source systems to find and pull out the data they needed for reports and such. But here's a sad truth: Doing that has always been a drag — and often the results would barely justify (if at all) the effort it took to get the information. Part of the problem was having to run around all over the enterprise just to hunt down isolated pieces of data in all those scattered systems. The folks who had to prepare reports must have wished they could find the data they needed in *one* place, ready to pull and use. That's why — no matter how you implement business intelligence — you'll always find a functional and efficient data-storage mechanism at the heart of a BI system. Microsoft BI offers two primary data-storage mechanisms to fill the bill — the data warehouse and the data mart — detailed in the next couple of sections. When all of the data are in one location and stored in a standard format you only have to look in one place instead of running around looking for the piece of data you need to complete your analysis.

Data warehouse

A *data warehouse* is a centralized storage location for (you guessed it) data generated by your business processes — where report developers, business analysts, and executives can go to gather information about the company when they need to make those big-time strategic decisions. A data warehouse serves not only as a central location that's easily accessible, but also as the go-to place for reliable, consistent data — about everything going on in the business. The name of the game here is not only having good data but also "Knowing where to find the goods," as illustrated in the accompanying sidebar.

Dual purposes of a data warehouse

A data warehouse is essentially a digital version of a real-world warehouse — it's a place to store stuff (in this case, data) until needed — but using this digital storage place brings challenges all its own, and they're a bit different: Though you don't have to wear a hard hat or use a forklift, you do have to contend with massive quantities of stuff (data) coming in at blinding speed, most of it in quirky packages (proprietary formats) that won't stack up well together with all the other packages that come in with their own (different) quirks. The data comes in from the source systems pretty quickly, but those source systems often have different formats for storing the data — and different mechanisms for connecting to the company network and receiving data.

Knowing where to find the goods

Here's a real-world analogy for how a data warehouse works and why it's needed. While I was growing up, one of my dad's best friends, Chris, owned an auto-parts business. On occasion, my dad and I would go down to the store to pick up a part. Because we knew Chris, we were allowed to go into the back and pick out the parts we needed. I remember being completely amazed at the storage system that lurked behind the scenes at the auto-parts store — row upon row of tall steel shelves in a massive warehouse. Each shelf had organized boxes that contained individual parts. There must have been thousands — tens of thousands — of parts, but the clerks could always find what the customer needed: They'd look up a specific part in a book, run back into the warehouse, and find it in only a couple of minutes.

The individual part manufacturers were the sources. The store would order from these various sources and then, when the parts came in, categorize, label, and otherwise organize them so they'd be easy to find in the warehouse's central storage system. Then, when a customer came in looking for a part, the clerk knew right where to look for what. If the store hadn't had a warehouse, Chris would have had to order the part from the supplier and wait for it to arrive in the mail. Customers who needed to replace a burned-out taillight, butterfly valve, or wiper blade *right now* — not when the part might straggle in through the mail — would have been annoyed, and would have marched right over to a competitor's store.

Now imagine a digital equivalent: Thousands of items of data, many of them in formats that may as well be multiple foreign languages, streaming into the same place from multiple source systems, all the time, every workday, at high speed. A digital equivalent of Chris organizes them, labels them in the same language, gives them the equivalent of catalog numbers, and stacks them neatly on nicely labeled digital shelves. A customer comes in, looking for the digital equivalent of enough parts to rebuild a car's front end. No problem.

Going back to the auto-parts warehouse, imagine that you have three different suppliers that produce the same part. Each supplier, however, gives the part its own unique identification number. The auto-parts warehouse needs to standardize these parts into a single standard identification number in order to keep their sanity. Imagine a customer coming in and needing a gas cap. The clerk tells the customer he's out of gas caps since the clerk only sees the gas caps made by Acme Motor Inc. The exact same gas cap made by AAA Motor Inc. would also do the job, but if the clerk can't find it and doesn't know it's the same part, then the customer is disappointed and dissatisfied.

If a data warehouse were *only* a place to put incoming data, you'd still have a hard time trying to get answers to a complex query: The process of finding and aggregating the needed data could take hours — okay, that's an improvement over weeks or months, but it's still a minor Ice Age if you're trying to get things done *fast.*

Fortunately, there's more to a data warehouse than just putting stuff on digital shelves. It's not only a central storage mechanism where consumers can find the data they're looking for in one central location, but also a place that gives the incoming data *a format that is consistent throughout all functional areas of the company,* as shown in Figure 6-1. This nicely formatted data are ready to consume — usually by turning it into information for decision-makers to use.

 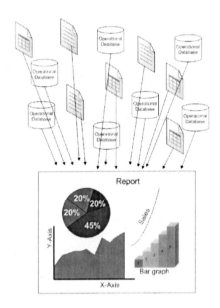

Figure 6-1: Getting report data from one central location versus multiple operational systems.

Having all the good stuff (ready-to-use data) in one central location greatly reduces the complexity of creating — or modifying — a report. The alternative is to keep flogging away at the old method until someone figures out why BI tools such as data warehouses are good to have.

For example, suppose one of the Widgiematic execs — in the bad old pre-BI days — has some diligent cube-dweller prepare a report that has to pull data from four different source systems — say, in sales, marketing, manufacturing, and product development — and then transform the mishmash of data into various diagrams, charts, graphs, and gauges that show how it all fits into the big picture so the execs can see how the business is doing. Well, at this point, Widgiematic has no BI system yet — so it takes the report developer months to get the report just right for the exec (who has remarked that it'd be *great* to have the information *yesterday*).

Suppose our hero finally finishes the report, decides it wasn't worth all that slogging because it's out of date already, and finds another job. He's long gone when the same exec — who's *still* trying to get an up-to-date perspective — gives some fresh-faced new hire the task of changing or updating the report — which is extremely complex. It'll take a long time for the new victim . . . uh, *person* . . . to retrace the original developer's steps through the various report elements, data sources, and report logic and come up to speed. Then the new hire finds an online article about BI, describing how a data warehouse would significantly reduce the amount of time and difficulty in preparing reports. A great light dawns. And next it reveals . . .

What runs a data warehouse: SQL Server database engine

Although the data warehouse is a fundamental concept in business intelligence, a fairly complex Microsoft BI technology makes it work: the SQL Server database engine. (In computer-speak, an *engine* is a program that does work for other programs; in this case, the work takes the form of manipulating a database.) SQL Server is often installed on multiple networked server computers; working together, these installations create a sort of super-database — the SQL Server federated database as shown in Figure 6-2 — that can handle vast amounts of data. (For more about the BI tools that come with Microsoft SQL Server, see Chapter 8.)

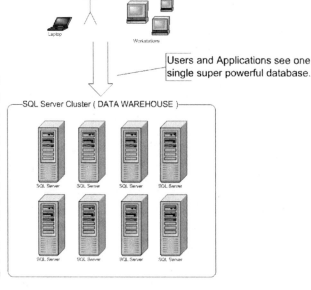

Users and Applications see one single super powerful database.

Figure 6-2: A SQL Server federated database is made up of multiple computers running the SQL Server database engine.

Making the case — reasons for a data warehouse

As Chapter 5 describes, the process of taking data from the source systems, transforming it into a standard format, aggregating it, and storing it in the data warehouse is known as Extract, Transform, and Load (ETL). Microsoft provides SQL Server Integration Services (SSIS) as your handy digital tool for ETL.

ETL is the BI capability that addresses the old problem of how to gather and use the data stored in source systems that often aren't connected to each other. The problem persists not only because companies limp along with a confusing tangle of storage formats (and no cohesive system in place to ensure data consistency), but also because — watch out — change happens. As a company evolves and grows, data sources, formats, and systems can become even more disparate — as is the case when these familiar business realities rear their heads:

- Acquisition of new companies
- Upgrading systems
- Change of ownership
- Change of system
- Relaxed standards for data entry
- Lazy data-entry processes and people
- User interfaces on programs used for data input omit proper validation

All these situations cause data to get truncated, ambiguous, convoluted, and otherwise messy. By getting requested data out of the source systems, cleaning it up, and storing it in a central location, the ETL process staves off chaos by bringing more order, usability, and coherence to your organization's data. When that happens, who knows what progress may follow? (The accompanying sidebar, "Master of the (data) world: MDM," offers a look at one authoritative possibility.)

Getting data out of a data warehouse

Whoa there. When you finally have your data all nicely tucked up in the data warehouse, it's ready to be turned into information. Then it's ready to be yanked suddenly out of storage and put to use. (The thought suddenly crops up: *Wait a minute. I thought data and information were the same thing.* Not so, seeker. Contemplate the sidebar sitting peacefully nearby for a bit more light on the subject.)

Master of the (data) world: MDM

Master Data Management (MDM) is a concept that's similar to the BI concept of a data warehouse, with an important difference: MDM tools and procedures don't just store and tidy up data; they address the problem of scattered data sources and multiple data versions by imposing aggressive, company-wide controls on the data to keep it consistent.

MDM solutions seek to establish one definitive ("master") version of the stored data and minimizing. Although MDM is not necessarily a part of BI, the result of deploying an MDM solution can help your business organize its data to a fare-thee-well, and provide one reliably accurate source for information. Here's a human-scale example of a problem that an MDM solution attempts to solve: Keeping an accurate mailing address when you're on the move.

My wife and I have had the most difficult time with a particular banking institution (I won't name it lest our account information mysteriously disappear). As we've moved around the country, we've kept the same bank for years — but as we've moved around the country, keeping our address correct has been nearly impossible.

We opened our account when we lived in San Francisco. For some reason our apartment number kept disappearing from our banking statement. We'd call and have the apartment number added back. Weeks later, the apartment number would disappear again. We continued this process until we moved to Boston and changed our address to our new Boston apartment.

Changing the address was a feat unto itself. We went to the bank's local branch, but the folks there couldn't change the address because our account *originated* in California. A banker had to call the original branch in California to change our address. At the same time, we ordered new checks; a couple of weeks later

they arrived . . . with our *old* address in San Francisco! We called the bank's 800 number and got the bank to change the address and reprint the checks. A couple weeks after that, our new statements arrived in the mail: Lo and behold, the address was our Boston address. Hooray! But a couple of statements later, our Boston apartment number disappeared from our address. We went back to the local Boston branch to get our apartment number put back on our address; the banker informed us that the only address the branch had on file for us was in San Francisco.

We now live in Seattle. Luckily, our address doesn't have an apartment number.

Why all the hassle? Well, I never blame the customer-service people; they're only working with the tools available to them. My guess (barring the intervention of aliens who like practical jokes) is that the bank has a number of different systems that don't talk to each other. I imagine that the people we've talked to over the years have had to deal with the quirks of those different systems, some of them in different branch offices in faraway states. Someone may change an address in one system while the same bit of data in another system goes unaltered. Our bank probably had (say) a system for addresses on checks, a system for addresses in the Boston area, and yet another system for addresses in California — each sitting in its little bailiwick, doing its isolated thing. Call it a hunch.

An MDM solution consolidates all these systems and creates only *one* address for each data item. Having only one address solves a lot of problems because the organization can create a simple tool for customer service agents or even a customer self-service portal on the Web site that allows people to change their own addresses without having to hunt up a customer-service agent.

Data are not (necessarily) information . . .

Data and information may sound like the same thing, but they're different because data tells you a specific detail and information gives you actionable answers to specific questions. In a nutshell information gives you — *context.*

What the report developers and executive brass are looking for is information in forms that speak efficiently to business issues — visualizations, reports (including scorecards, about which more in a minute), dashboards (ditto), graphs, charts, gauges, tables (familiar features at many a meeting), and SharePoint KPI lists (nothing gets the ol' neurons firing like a look at the Key Performance Indicators over your morning cup of corporate brew). The Microsoft tools that your company stalwarts use to produce these visualizations and reports include SQL Server Reporting Services (SSRS), SharePoint Excel Services, PerformancePoint Services for SharePoint, SharePoint KPI Lists, and some good-old, Microsoft Office end-user standbys: Excel, Word, and Visio. (For more about the SharePoint features that contribute to Microsoft BI, see Chapter 10; for more about SSRS, see Chapter 8.)

If you're looking for the brass tacks of how data turns into the information that dazzles the decision-makers, the first tool to examine is the younger cousin of the data warehouse — the data mart. Its story is next.

Data mart

A *data mart* is a data-storage mechanism similar to a data warehouse, only smaller and specialized. A data *warehouse* stores data for the entire organization; a data *mart* stores data for a particular functional unit, division, or department within the organization.

Purpose of a data mart

A data mart is useful when a particular portion of the company has special needs that aren't contained in the enterprise-wide data warehouse. For example, a manufacturing location may want to run a number of specialized tests based on different scenarios. The company doesn't need to integrate this specialized behavior into the overall data warehouse because the only group that cares about this information is a single manufacturing department. In this scenario, a data mart can be built that meets the needs of the department without putting the information in the overall data warehouse.

Origin of data in a data mart

It may be smaller than a data warehouse, but even the data mart has two theories for how best to use it to handle data flow. The first theory says that data should flow directly from the source operational systems into specialized storage, and that data marts should be that storage, as shown in Figure 6-3.

Figure 6-3:
Data
flowing
directly
from source
systems to a
data mart.

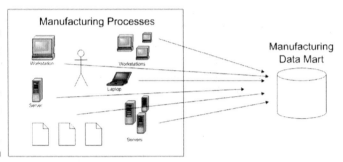

The idea behind this theory is that creating a data warehouse is a huge undertaking and is never really finished. By creating the data mart first, you can fulfill the specialized needs of a particular department without incorporating its needs into the overall data warehouse.

A second theory says that all data should flow from the operational systems into the data warehouse first, and then from the data warehouse into the data mart, as shown in Figure 6-4.

I subscribe to the second theory — data from throughout the organization should flow into a central data warehouse in order to achieve the same consistency and order throughout the entire organization. Building the data warehouse as one iteration after another gives you some advantages:

- Each iteration of the data warehouse is an improvement, with fresher — more organized — data, so the project progresses continually.

- You get quick functional wins — for example, sales data implemented for accounting are also useful for manufacturing and marketing and manufacturing data are also useful for accounting — along the way.

- Sourcing any needed data for a particular functional unit from the data warehouse helps ensure data consistency.

This arrangement also keeps the various functional areas from creating "secret" (okay, maybe just idiosyncratic) storage mechanisms that aren't shared throughout the organization.

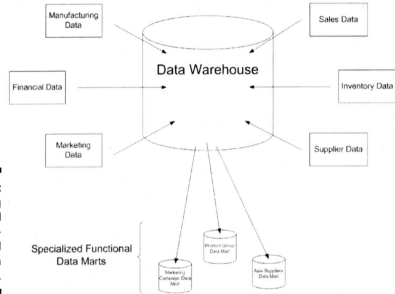

Figure 6-4:
Data flowing
to a central
data ware-
house and
then to data
marts.

Data-storage patterns

In BI lingo, you often hear people talk about dimensional, relational (or normalized), and hybrid storage patterns. A *data-storage pattern* (also called a *data model*) is the particular way a data-storage structure is designed to hold data. Any given data model generally occupies one of three main categories — dimensional, normalized (or relational), or hybrid — so the next several sections take you behind the buzzwords for a look at how these models work.

Dimensional models

When you design a data model, you create a visualization that represents the tables in the database. The actual data you analyze usually takes the form of numeric values — such as sales figures, inventory, marketing dollars, or anything else you can quantify. These numeric values, also known as *measures* or *facts,* are usually contained in a table in the center of the design, which goes by an unassuming name: the *fact table.* You also have tables representing the *dimensions* (that is, ways to divide up the data) hovering around the outside of the fact table. A *multidimensional* database hasn't been turned suddenly into a geometric solid — it just contains data that has a lot of different ways to be measured and examined, and these usually show up as column headings in its tables.

On paper, dimensional models look like a star or snowflake — and they're often referred to as star or snowflake patterns — depending on the design of the database. Figure 6-5 shows a visual representation of star and snowflake database designs.

Star

Snowflake

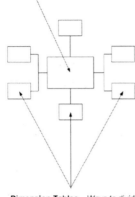

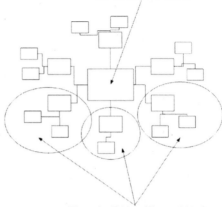

Fact Table – The numeric data you are interested in analyzing.

Fact Table – The numeric data you are interested in analyzing.

Dimension Tables – Ways to divide up or slice and dice the numeric data.

Dimension Tables – Ways to divide up or slice and dice the numeric data.

Figure 6-5:
Star and
snowflake
multi-
dimensional
design
models.

The star database design has one fact table in the middle, surrounded by tables representing the dimensions. A snowflake database design is very similar — but the dimension tables for a snowflake database have additional tables attached to them that reduce the amount of data stored in any single dimension table.

Relational models

Relational data models are often also called *normalized models. Normalized data* means that the data are stored only once — not duplicated in multiple systems — so it takes up less space. Imagine storing customer contact information such as names, addresses, phone numbers, e-mail addresses, and Web information in tens of thousands of places. If the data are normalized, the information is only stored in one location, and all other locations contain a number (known as a *key*) that points to the location of the actual data.

Hybrid models

Databases that follow the *hybrid* model store some data in a dimensional way and other data in a relational way. This approach can create complexities for the consumers of the data, but when properly constructed they can provide the best of both dimensional and relational worlds. An example of a hybrid model would be storing data that have been summed up, or *aggregated,* in a multi-dimensional model and the transaction level data that feeds the aggregations in a relational model. Mixing and matching models are theoretically providing the best of both worlds, however I've found that the added complexity makes it extremely difficult to implement a hybrid model in a way that's easy and straightforward for users.

If you're a decision-maker who's looking for the best approach to implementing BI, don't spend much time thinking about the type of data model to use for the data warehouse or the data marts. Instead, focus on *the result you want to accomplish* and *the questions you want answered* from your BI system. Your concern is the big picture; focus on *what* information you need to drive efficiency and make decisions, not on *how* to implement the details of the central storage model. You provide the business guidance and let the BI architects decide on the best data model to implement.

Models, schemas, and patterns

The term *model* is used often — and loosely — in talk about technology. In this book, however, it's a safe bet that I don't mean the kind of model you'd put in a wind tunnel. Here a model means a pattern that guides the design of a database or its components, the way the star or snowflake models (mentioned in the previous section) serve as the basis for building a data warehouse or data mart. In the next section, "Understanding SQL Server Reporting Services (SSRS)," I refer to a SQL Server Reporting Services (SSRS) Model — a type of data pattern specific to SSRS, and an example of how an appropriate data model is vital to a formidable BI tool.

In my consulting career, however, I find that people bandy terms about almost at random — model, schema, and pattern pinch-hit for each other. Many people argue for specific differences amongst the terms, and dictate when one term should be used over another. Eventually, it boils down to a kind of local preference: One organization describes the guiding principle behind its database as a schema, another calls the same thing a pattern, a third calls it a model ("tomahto, tomato, potahto, potato . . ." never mind).

As a consultant, I have to take a practical approach: I move between projects at different companies, and have to decipher what people are actually referring to when they talk about a model, schema, or pattern. I adopt my clients' terminology so I know that everyone involved is talking about the same thing — but the second I go to the next client, the terminology differences begin again. As your faithful author, at last I get to settle on one preferred term to use throughout the book. And I choose (drum roll, please) . . . model. (Okay, if you've been reading along in the chapter so far, you knew that. But if you just dropped in, there it is.) Here's a look at a model in action, as part of a Microsoft BI tool. . . .

Understanding SQL Server Reporting Services (SSRS)

SQL Server Reporting Services (SSRS) is the primary reporting component in Microsoft Business Intelligence. SSRS is a powerful reporting engine that can incorporate data from a number of different data sources into the reports it produces. The versatile connectivity that works this magic is shown in Figure 6-6.

Figure 6-6:
Connection types available in SSRS.

The strength of SSRS lies in its tight integration with Microsoft data-delivery mechanisms such as SharePoint. SSRS also comes with its own Web-based delivery mechanism known as *Report Manager.* Best of all, SSRS is easily integrated into any type of custom desktop or Web-based application, regardless of whether the application comes from Microsoft.

SharePoint has become a powerful *content-management system* that gives your organization control over some potentially troublesome aspects of the information constantly zipping through its network. Features like these do the job:

✔ **Document versioning:** No more naming a document `Important_Document_v124_edited_by_Ken_12-02-2009_re_edited_by_Rosemarie_02-06-09.docx`. With versioning you have one name for one document, and SharePoint takes care of the versions. You can review previous versions and roll back should the need arise.

✔ **Document check-in and check-out:** One of the constant battles of working on documents is keeping track of who has made what changes and when. I can't tell you the number of times I've spent hours editing a document only to find out the document I was working with was stale and not even being used anymore. With Check-In and Check-Out functionality, you check-out a document when you're working on it and check it back in when you're done. While you have the document checked out, nobody else can fiddle around with the document, and the result is only one true document.

✔ **Document security privileges:** Some things in life aren't meant to be shared with everyone. SharePoint security allows you to set specific permissions for people or groups within your organization. Maybe only accounting should be able to see financial numbers, and maybe only HR should be able to see company policies that are in the works.

✔ **Workflow monitoring:** Workflow has been around forever. You may already use e-mail as your workflow mechanism. Someone gives the task of creating a new document to the new guy on the block. Once he's done creating the document and taking a stab at the content, he e-mails it to his manager. The manager takes a look, makes some changes, and e-mails it to an executive. The executive takes a look, makes some changes, and wants legal to sign off on the document, so he e-mails it to the attorneys. This entire process is workflow. With SharePoint, however, workflow is baked into the product, and the workflow happens automatically without the need to manually attach a document to an e-mail message. SharePoint takes care of e-mailing the next recipient of the document with a nice link that he can simply click to view and approve the document.

In addition, SSRS can be tightly integrated with SharePoint so that the SSRS report files are stored and *surfaced* — made available to the users who have requested the information they contain — through SharePoint sites. Bringing together reports from different functional areas at the same SharePoint site enables SSRS to serve as a *dashboard* for business processes: One place, like your car's array of gauges, that you can give a quick once-over to see what's going on and identify any problem areas. (Chapter 10 provides a closer look at integrating SharePoint and SSRS.)

Business Intelligence Developer Studio (BIDS)

The *Business Intelligence Developer Studio (BIDS)* environment is really just a BI name for good-old Microsoft Visual Studio — except this version of Visual Studio includes a set of specialized projects and Toolbox components designed to build Microsoft BI functionality such as SSRS reports, SSIS packages, SSAS cubes, and data mining models. One of the nice things about Microsoft Business Intelligence is that you can develop almost all your BI capabilities in a single Integrated Development Environment (IDE) — namely, BIDS.

An *Integrated Development Environment (IDE)* is a software program designed for development tasks. When you think of writing a letter, you may use Microsoft Office Word, Notepad, or WordPad; each of these software applications can write text on a computer, so you can think of each one as a sort of document-development environment. An IDE is a software application designed for software developers and used to develop entire applications. In the Microsoft world, the IDE that you'll use most frequently is Visual Studio (called BIDS when it includes only BI functionality). (Chapter 11 covers Visual Studio in detail.)

When you're on familiar terms with Visual Studio, you can move from simple to sophisticated projects — from developing SSRS reports to SSIS packages to custom .NET code — without having to figure out a new development environment. An SSRS project in BIDS is shown in Figure 6-7.

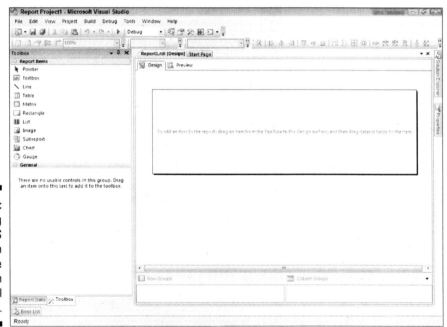

Figure 6-7:
Developing a SSRS report in BIDS (the BI version of Visual Studio).

Report Builder

Report Builder is a report-development tool designed to allow users with no previous development experience to create rich reports. Report Builder's look and feel may call to mind some standard Office 2007 and later products such as Word and Excel (as shown in Figure 6-8).

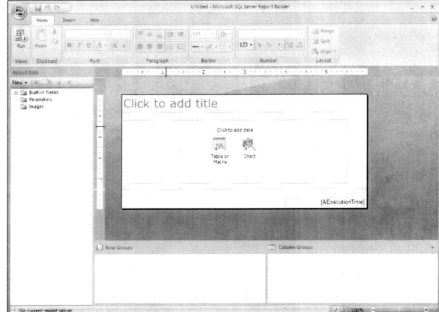

Figure 6-8: Report Builder is an Office-like application that allows end users to build reports.

Report Builder is geared to everyday business users and analysts; they can build reports the way they want to, using up-front controls, instead of struggling within a set of limited program options. No need to bounce the report back and forth between report creator and decision-maker until the two of them slowly bash it into shape. The report can be built efficiently and quickly to fulfill a specific need.

Report Builder supports the full range of SSRS capabilities, including these:

- ✔ Data visualizations such as charts, graphs, gauges, images, and drawings.
- ✔ Report layouts such as tables, matrices, and lists.
- ✔ Text boxes that allow for rich text such as different fonts and text sizes, bold, underline, italics, and colors much like when you want to spice up a Word document.
- ✔ Exportation capabilities from the database into Microsoft Word documents.

The Insert tab on Report Builder (see Figure 6-9) contains the components that can be used to create a rich report.

Figure 6-9:
Report
Builder
Insert
Ribbon
showing
components
that can be
inserted.

In addition to the SSRS core functionality, Report Builder also includes many user-friendly features such as wizards, shared data sources, and query designers. With Report Builder, users can directly open, edit, and save reports stored in SharePoint or the stand-alone product Report Manager (for more on Report Manager, see Chapter 8).

Getting Familiar with SharePoint

Much of the versatility in Microsoft BI comes from the sheer number of BI tools that can work more powerfully when you plug them into SharePoint. Microsoft SharePoint started as an application whose main mission was to make secure networked collaboration easier — but Microsoft has quickly added BI-friendly functionality to later versions. New features like these are especially timely:

✔ SharePoint 2007 pulled in the previous product known as Content Management Server, which provided SharePoint with a full-featured content management system.

✔ SQL Server 2005 SP2 introduced an Integrated mode that tightly coupled SSRS with the SharePoint environment.

✔ SharePoint 2010 pulled in the previous product known as PerformancePoint and enabled functionality such as dashboards and scorecards embedded directly in a SharePoint site.

✔ SharePoint 2010 introduced a powerful set of engines that provides users with the ability to view and interact with Excel documents that are embedded into a SharePoint site — all without leaving the Web browser. In addition, the powerful features of Excel 2010 (such as PowerPivot) are also viewable and intractable from the SharePoint site they are embedded in.

As if that weren't enough, SharePoint integrates tightly with the entire Microsoft Office product suite — and has become the dominant system of choice for building corporate portals and implementing content management.

These days Microsoft uses SharePoint as its primary delivery mechanism for business intelligence through features such as these:

- ✔ SSRS integration with SharePoint
- ✔ Excel Services
- ✔ PerformancePoint Services for SharePoint
- ✔ KPI lists
- ✔ Dashboards and scorecards

For a closer look at each of these, read on; for more on SharePoint, see Chapter 10.

Excel Services

Microsoft Office Excel has become one of the most popular spreadsheet programs of all time. I often walk into clients' offices and discover that they're running crucial portions of the business *using nothing but Excel.* (How '90s is that?) Some workgroups even have expensive ERP systems in place, but still choose to use Excel as a kind of "shadow" system instead of the main ERP system (which just sits there).

Okay, I can understand that often people want to keep using a familiar software program — and the skills they've developed while using it — along the lines of "if it ain't broke, don't fix it." Unfortunately, the results tend to suffer. Some Excel documents start to take on a monstrous life of their own — with complex functions, look-ups, and cross-references. Often the analysts who built those mutant Excel documents have moved on and are no longer with the company — and nobody wants to touch those things out of fear that they may break something and make the data disappear. So they continue to use the complex business logic captured in the Excel document.

SharePoint and Excel Services to the rescue. SharePoint allows you to put Excel documents online — and control how they're used or changed. Moving Excel into SharePoint provides some handy content-management features mentioned earlier in this chapter — such as security, check-in and check-out, versioning, and workflow.

Excel Services allows you to embed an Excel document in a SharePoint Web site. This feature ensures that users throughout the company can view the same Excel document without having to e-mail the document around, thus avoiding the possibility that the original document mutates into many different versions.

The security component of SharePoint can limit management capabilities for the Excel document to only a few key people. SharePoint security can also limit the number of users who can view the document — a document can be available for the entire company or restricted to selected people. Both of these configurations allow one person to upload a document and multiple people to view it, as shown in Figure 6-10.

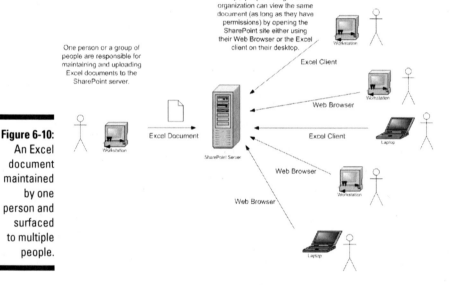

Figure 6-10: An Excel document maintained by one person and surfaced to multiple people.

PerformancePoint Services for SharePoint

As with many products, PerformancePoint has a history, continues to evolve, and just keeps getting bigger and more capable. PerformancePoint Server originally consisted of three components:

  ✔ **Business Scorecard Manager:** This component provided — and made powerful use of — *business scorecards* (a report card for business).

- ✔ **Analysis of OLAP cubes:** This component was obtained through the acquisition of a company named ProClarity, whose products can analyze the data cubes created by SQL Server Analysis Services (SSAS).

    For a closer look at OLAP cubes, see Chapter 4.

- ✔ **Planning Server:** This component started life as a financial planning piece that never really caught on.

Recently Microsoft announced that the financial-planning portion of PerformancePoint Server would be discontinued and the scorecarding and analysis portion would be rolled into SharePoint as a feature known as PerformancePoint Services for SharePoint. With this feature added, SharePoint moves closer to a central BI role for entire organizations, especially with these features:

- ✔ PerformancePoint

- ✔ SQL Server Reporting Services integration

- ✔ Excel Services

- ✔ PowerPivot for SharePoint

- ✔ Business Intelligence Web site templates

- ✔ Key Performance Indicator lists

Result: Two products are now the primary pieces of Microsoft Business Intelligence:

- ✔ **SQL Server:** This forms the core of Microsoft BI, and takes care of the behind-the-scenes server functionality.

- ✔ **SharePoint:** Behold — information generated for BI purposes now surfaces in a collaborative environment — anywhere you want it, throughout the organization. Some call it collaborative BI, I call it Human BI or HBI.

In addition, if you want to put a business dashboard in some of those far-flung corners of the organization, you can whip one up in PerformancePoint, using a tool called Dashboard Designer. With this tool, even users who aren't familiar with software development can create powerful visualizations — including dashboards, scorecards, and strategy maps — and upload them to the SharePoint environment, where anyone with sufficient permissions can view them. Dashboard Designer also allows you to export the same data and visual components used in your snazzy new dashboard to Excel spreadsheets or PowerPoint presentations.

As of April 1, 2009, PerformancePoint Server can no longer be purchased as a stand-alone product. Companies that have purchased Microsoft Office SharePoint Server 2007 Enterprise Edition will automatically be licensed to use Microsoft Office PerformancePoint Server 2007, and can expect to see the Monitoring and Analytics functionality included in SharePoint 2010. The Planning Server component, although discontinued, will be made available (with source code) to Enterprise Agreement customers as the Financial Planning Accelerator.

KPI lists

A *Key Performance Indicator (KPI)* is a measurement that gives you an especially clear indication of how a portion of your business (or your entire business) is performing. In SharePoint there is a special type of list specifically designed for KPIs — the *KPI list*.

The SharePoint KPI list can be added to a SharePoint site and configured to show green, yellow, and red icons to indicate KPI status. This color scheme is known as stop-lighting since the colors coordinate with those of a stoplight. The green (of course) means everything is on track, yellow indicates a warning, and red indicates something that needs immediate attention. Check out more information on KPI lists in Chapter 10.

Dashboards

In the SharePoint world, a *dashboard* is a specific type of page where you can insert reports, graphs, charts, and KPI lists in order to create a central location for functionally-relevant information. PerformancePoint Services for SharePoint even allows you to create custom dashboard elements.

A SharePoint dashboard is (in principle, anyway) just like the ones in a car or airplane — it's a central location where various different types of vital information show up as visual indicators. You can create dashboards in Excel, custom pages, or even on a PowerPoint slide. Generally, in the BI world, you want your dashboard to be updated automatically with real-time data; for this reason, the dashboards in SharePoint and PerformancePoint Services for SharePoint are likely to be most useful for you. (Think of a gauge that shows airspeed on an airplane dashboard while it's in flight — may as well use an optimistic metaphor, right?)

Scorecards

A scorecard is very similar to a dashboard. The main differentiator is that *scorecards* are generally designed to measure progress toward a goal. For example, you may have a scorecard that measures the current sales measured against a sales goal.

You can think of a dashboard as giving you information about a particular process and a scorecard as telling you how well you're meeting a specific target goal. Often, scorecards have colors associated with each metric in the form of green for good, yellow for warning, and red for all hands on deck!

Business balancing act — The Balanced Scorecard

In 1996, Robert Kaplan and David Norton wrote *The Balanced Scorecard* (Harvard Business School Press). No, they weren't describing how to keep a scorecard from falling off the tip of your nose. Their idea is to create a specialized scorecard that measures the individual processes and procedures that make up an organization — and to compare the results you get against the overall goals of the company. The theory behind the balanced scorecard has evolved over time, but this basic concept remains the same. Figure 6-11 shows what a balanced scorecard looks like.

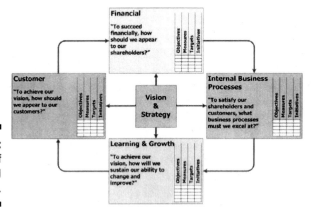

Figure 6-11: Diagram of a balanced scorecard.

The balanced scorecard is made up of the following four perspectives:

- ✔ **The business process perspective:** This perspective attempts to monitor the processes that make up the business. It allows individual managers who are responsible for individual processes to be well informed. The managers can see how a process aligns with the overall business and how it affects the business.

✔ **The financial perspective:** This perspective ensures that the budgeting for profit and cost centers is balanced throughout the organization in regard to the overall goals of the organization. For example, a primary goal of the organization may be to boost research and development during a slow economic period in order to strengthen product lines during a recovery. The financial perspective provides a scoring mechanism available to members of the organization to help them determine the current budgeting direction and potentially make adjustments to meet the organizational goals.

✔ **The customer perspective:** This perspective recognizes that the customer is king and that an organization needs to ensure the customer is happy in order to ensure the viability of the business. There are a number of ways to measure customer satisfaction, and whatever methods are chosen are integrated with the scorecard and monitored as the customer perspective.

✔ **The learning and growth perspective:** This perspective focuses on the employees learning new skills, their growth, and their attitudes, as well as the overall culture of the organization. As organizations become increasingly knowledge-based, it is important to recognize that the people who work for the companies are the main resource and most valuable assets. Scorecard elements such as mentors, buddies, cultural events, knowledge transfer, intellectual property, work-life balance, training, and learning make up this perspective on the scorecard.

There is also a Microsoft-centric approach to the balanced scorecard that goes by the term FOSH. The Microsoft approach divides the scorecard into the following for key areas:

✔ **Financial:** What is the overall financial outlook of the organization?

✔ **Operational:** How well is the company meeting its operational goals such as production and distribution?

✔ **Sales:** This is the customer-focused segment. How do our customers see us? How do we rank in our industry?

✔ **Human Resources:** What is our employee turnover? Employee satisfaction rate?

Microsoft and the balanced scorecard

The most difficult part about implementing a balanced scorecard is the fact that it's a systemic management system and requires a tremendous amount of effort throughout the organization. Now for the good news! After the system is in place, you can use the reporting capabilities of various Microsoft products to display the metrics that are most important and relevant to your organization. The products to use this way include these:

- ✔ SQL Server Reporting Services
- ✔ Excel (especially as a "front end" application hot-rodded with BI features)
- ✔ SharePoint Dashboards
- ✔ SharePoint Excel Services
- ✔ SharePoint KPI Lists
- ✔ PerformancePoint Services for SharePoint

If you implement the theories behind the balanced scorecard by using SharePoint as an intranet portal, the members of the entire organization can have access to the BI perspective in a way that benefits particular parts of the company directly — by showing exactly how their work is affecting overall performance.

Chapter 7

Data Mining for Information Gold

In This Chapter

▶ Knowing data mining and its role in the BI process

▶ Understanding data mining in the Microsoft world

▶ Discovering the Microsoft Data Mining tools

▶ Applying the Microsoft Data Mining algorithms

> *If I had asked people what they wanted, they would have said faster horses.*
>
> — Henry Ford

To obtain solid information about your business, you need data, and lots of it. Data are used in all sorts of ways in order to get usable business information — these include creating reports and conducting analyses. But often the data you need are not at all obvious; they're buried under other data or hidden in proprietary formats in scattered systems. If that data are going to do your organization any good, data have to be found, dug out, and unlocked.

How much data about your business do you have available? Often as much as you can gather — and computer systems can gather a whopping amount. Unlocking as much of that data as possible — and finding useful patterns in it, in real time — can give your organization a competitive advantage. That's why one of the handiest tools in the Microsoft BI arsenal is a capability that treats your data as a valuable raw resource just waiting to be refined into information. It's called data mining, and it's what this chapter is all about.

Going Deep with Data Mining

Data mining is the process of using complex mathematical algorithms to search for patterns in large amounts of data. Because computers are great at crunching numbers and mathematicians are great at creating formulas that use numbers, it makes sense that mathematicians have created formulas that do all sorts of cool things with computers. A computer can feed millions (or even billions) of numbers into these math formulas. The math formulas, in turn, perform what looks like magic — looking for patterns in the data and making predictions. The more numbers fed into those math formulas, the greater the accuracy of the predictions.

With the massive amounts of data that modern computerized businesses generate, data mining is a hot topic among industry leaders.

Data mining also goes by a few other names — *predictive analytics, machine learning,* and sometimes *artificial intelligence.* Keep in mind, however, that complex mathematical algorithms are at the heart of these predictive systems. You don't have to know how the math works in order to use the systems — you need only worry about feeding in clean (standard formats) and relevant data, and then using the results.

An algorithm defined

In computer-speak, *algorithm* simply means a math-driven process for accomplishing some task. If they seem scary and mysterious at first, well, that's a natural reaction. . . .

I remember the first algorithm given to me back in undergraduate school. One of my professors was giving a lecture on them, and I was excited to find out about algorithms; I had heard the term used in movies when hackers were trying to break a secret code, but I didn't understand what it meant. The professor pulled out a loaf of bread, a knife, a jar of jam, and a jar of peanut butter. An algorithm, he explained, is a way of describing a process in a series of small steps that should be easily followed by something as dumb as a computer. The entire class was baffled.

Our assignment was to write an algorithm for making a peanut-butter-and-jelly sandwich. In our next class, he took our algorithms and performed them *exactly* as we had written them. If an algorithm said to "put the jam on the bread," he would set the jar on the bread and call it complete. The point is that a computer will only do *exactly* what you tell it to do; it has no notion of context — and certainly no common sense.

Number systems explained

Computers are based on a number system known as *base two*. A counting system with base two means that you can only have two possible digits. When counting from zero to ten in the normal base-ten numbering system, you would count 0, 1, 2, 3, 4, 5, 6, 7, 8, 9, and then you would run out of symbols (you have only ten possible digits in this system). You would need to go to the next column and start over with zero in the first (rightmost) column. Moving to the next column (a power-of-ten column) would cause the first column to go back to 0 and the second column would become 1 to represent a count of ten things. The resulting symbol would be 10.

In a base-two numbering system, you start counting ten objects again by saying, "0, 1 . . . " but then you run out of symbols, so you have to move the 1 over to the next column (a power-of-two column), which represents two of something. There you would put one of your two available digits, and write 10 (one-zero) to represent two of something. Then you would go to three and add another 1, which you'd write as 11 (one-one). Again, you run out of symbols, so you move over to the next column, which represents four of something; the number becomes 100 (one-zero-zero).

So to count ten of something in a base-two system, you count 0, 1, 10, 11, 100, 101, 110, 111, 1000, 1001, 1010. Notice that each time you have to move to another column you have a power of two. Computers use base two; that's why you see numbers in the computer world as powers of two — such as 32-bit, 64-bit, or 8 bits to the byte, or 1,024 bytes equals a kilobyte, or 1,048,576 bytes equals a megabyte. A single gigabyte is a whopping 1,073,741,824 bytes!

Remember: Each byte is 8 bits, so a gigabyte is made up of 8,589,934,592 little pieces of silicon that are either on or off representing a 1 or a 0 digit.

Base 10	Base 2
0	0
1	1
2	10
3	11
4	100
5	101
6	110
7	111
8	1000
9	1001
10	1010

Computers use the base-two numbering system because they work with electricity and silicon. As a semiconductor, the silicon can either conduct or not-conduct electricity; when it conducts, it's on (represented by a 1); when it's not conducting, it's off (represented by a 0). If electricity in a circuit could have more than two possible states — and exist somewhere between on and off — then computers could work with a larger-base number system, but until quantum computers (and those in-between electrical states) are figured out, we're stuck with the base-two numbering system — also known as *binary*. The base-ten numbering system that most people are familiar with is called *decimal*.

This lesson continued to hit home with me as I learned to program and apply various aspects of computer science throughout the years. So: If you're satisfied to think of an algorithm as a (very carefully stated) set of steps for a computer to follow, you have the essence of it; if you're curious about algorithms as mathematical creatures, check out the accompanying sidebar, "Number systems explained."

Data mining's role in the BI process

Data mining needs clean and organized data in order to be effective. That's why a data warehouse is the best source for the data you use in your analysis — that's because the ETL process (more about ETL in Chapter 5) has already cleaned — transformed — and organized the data so it's ready to use. If you get your data from source operational systems, it comes to you in proprietary formats that make using it a major hassle. So a word to the wise . . .

Make it standard practice to mine your data from data warehouses or data marts, *after* it's been through ETL.

Now, all that nice clean data usually become information by going through the processes of reporting and analysis — but data mining takes that refinement a step farther. Reporting and analysis can give you great insights into what has happened and why, but they can't predict what will happen in the future or locate patterns that may not otherwise be visible. For these tasks — fortunately — you can rely on the data-mining capabilities of Microsoft BI.

Digging In to Data Mining in the Microsoft World

SQL Server Analysis Services (SSAS) has a set of data-mining algorithms built in, and SSAS is part of the Microsoft SQL Server product.

Users of SQL Server often figure that the SSAS component of SQL Server must be the same thing as the OLAP engine (for more about OLAP, see Chapter 4; the OLAP engine is profiled in Chapter 8) — but there's more to SSAS than that. True, the marketing department at Microsoft used to call the OLAP engine OLAP Services, but that was back when "Web services" was the hot buzz phrase. When Microsoft added the Data Mining component to SSAS, it also gave it a new name: The analysis component of SQL Server was reborn as Analysis Services — and now its secret weapon was the Data Mining engine. This rebranding left the door open for additional analysis features to be included under the same product name — and it's a good bet that'll happen as BI continues to expand its capabilities and range of users.

The Microsoft data-mining process

Okay, given that no pickaxes or hard hats are required, what do you actually *do* when you go off to the data mines? Well, first off, you don't have to go anywhere. You start by asking some pointed questions about your business — carefully — and then tell the Microsoft data-mining tools to go mine some data (heigh-ho, heigh-ho . . .). The whole Microsoft data-mining process consists of six major phases:

- ✔ Defining the problem so you know what you want to accomplish.
- ✔ Preparing the data so it's ready to work with.
- ✔ Exploring the data, keeping an eye out for patterns.
- ✔ Defining and using a data-mining model.
- ✔ Defining and using a data-mining structure to put the model into action.
- ✔ Deploying the results to your users through SharePoint.

The process is iterative; you keep trying out iterations at crucial points — and if you need to go back and redefine the questions you want your data-mining solution to solve, then that's what you do. After a few iterations, you get closer and closer to the data-mining approach that works best for your organization. The upcoming subsections take a closer look at each phase of the data-mining process.

Defining the problem

As with any part of a BI implementation, you begin by completely under-standing the problems you want solved and the questions you want answered. By focusing on *what* you need answered instead of *how* you'll answer it, you're free to get at the root of the information you need about your business. Don't worry about missing something at this point — because you'll come back to this step (at the next iteration) as you proceed. Additional questions will always pop up throughout the process, which makes iteration the most important aspect of a successful solution.

Preparing the data

When you've identified the problems and questions you want to (ahem) dig in to, you're ready to prepare the data that you'll use. The data-mining algorithms are very smart at solving very specific tasks, but they're incredibly dumb when it comes to using the data they receive if it comes in plastered with extraneous formats. The incoming data has to be clean and ready to use — and should conform to a company-wide standard.

As mentioned earlier in this chapter (and it bears repeating), the best place to get your data is your data warehouse. That's where the data has already gone through Extract, Transform, and Load (ETL) and is as squeaky-clean as business data can be.

If the data aren't already in a data warehouse, you have to decide whether it's worth the time investment to go through getting the required data *into* a data warehouse — or building a smaller data mart to hold the data you want to use. Your call.

The data for your analysis doesn't always *have* to come from a data warehouse, data mart, or OLAP cube; you just avoid some extra hassle if it does. Technically (which is often like saying "theoretically"), data sources can include any source that can be defined using the standard SQL Server data connection. In practice, that means you can create a connection to Oracle databases, SAP databases, IBM databases, text files, Excel files, and even open-source databases such as MySQL and PostgreSQL — but you may have to transform (clean) the data you get.

The Microsoft BI feature that you use to move and transform data is called SQL Server Integration Services (SSIS). It's part of the SQL Server product.

Exploring the data

To make sense of the output of the data-mining algorithms, you first need to poke around in the data and develop an understanding of it. Among the techniques you can use to explore the incoming data are these two classic approaches:

- ✔ **Averages and extremes:** Relatively quickly, you can take the averages of sets of numbers and determine the standard deviation from the average. You can also determine the minimum and maximum values — the extremes. This approach gives you an idea of the range and type of data you're working with.

- ✔ **Basic statistics:** You can take a sample of the data and perform some basic statistical analysis on that representative portion. For example, you can plot some of sales data from a particular region on a graph and determine the general distribution of values. Doing so gives you a feel for what to look for when you lay out the data in graphics.

Exploring the raw data as it comes in — even if you use no more than just these two techniques — gives you a handle on how the data you're working with fit into the context of what you know about the business process that generated the data. As you explore the data, additional questions that you want answered will almost certainly arise. After you've explored the data and listed those new questions, it's (you guessed it) iteration time: You revisit the first phase of the process by going back to the "defining the problem" phase, as shown in Figure 7-1.

After defining the problem again, in light of what you found while poking around in that first batch of data, you may need to prepare and explore additional data before you move on to the next phase.

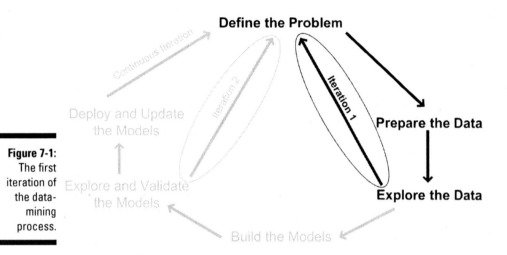

Define the Problem

Continuous Iteration

Iteration 2

Iteration 1

Deploy and Update the Models

Prepare the Data

Explore and Validate the Models

Explore the Data

Build the Models

Figure 7-1:
The first iteration of the data-mining process.

Building your models

After defining the problem, preparing and exploring the data, and iterating until you have a solid understanding (hopefully right before you get a solid headache), the next phase is to build a *data-mining model* — essentially a picture of the approach you expect to use in data mining. If you're already pretty handy at building queries, you could use the query language known as Data Mining Extensions (DMX) to build your data-mining model — after all, DMX already comes with SSAS —, but the most straightforward (and least painful) method is to use the Wizard through Visual Studio as described in the "Data Mining Wizard" section later in this chapter.

Exploring and validating your models

When you have your models built, you have to explore (view the trends and patterns that the models produce) and validate (ensure that the trends and patterns answer the questions that were proposed in the problem defining stage) them before you put them to work. The exploration process involves using the viewers that are part of the BI functionality of Visual Studio. The validation process involves determining if the data mining models actually answer the questions posed. After exploring and validating your models, you need to determine if the models are doing what you set out to accomplish. If they aren't answering the questions you have or the results seem inconsistent, then you need to loop back and continue to iterate.

You'll often hear Microsoft BI aficionados refer to Business Intelligence Developer Studio (BIDS for short) and the Data Mining Designer (though if they say anything about diamond drill bits, they're probably faking). I think of these two utilities as, essentially, Visual Studio in a BI costume. Visual Studio is an application for developing complete software programs, and sometimes different tasks need different functionality within the application. BIDS simply adds some handy BI functionality for specific tasks, one of which happens to be the design of data-mining models. If you're handy with Visual Studio, you'll be just as handy with BIDS, and vice versa — because (big trade secret) they're essentially the same tool.

When you get to exploring and validating your data-mining model, something hauntingly familiar will start to happen: You'll uncover additional questions that you could *really use* answers for. Before you know it, it's iteration time again! Gathering your patience, thinking about how you're improving your chances of getting *really good answers,* you go back and adjust the initial problem scenario. By using this process, faithfully doing one iteration at a time, you ensure that the project doesn't conclude with huge gaps where useful answers should be. It's normal, expected, and a "best practice" to keep redefining the problem whenever you need to, throughout the data-mining process. The resulting body of knowledge will be just as valuable as the resulting solution to your initial problem. Figure 7-2 illustrates what the iteration process looks like after exploring and validating the models.

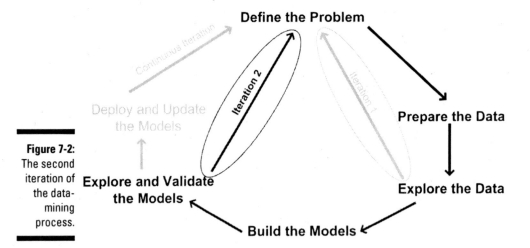

Figure 7-2: The second iteration of the data-mining process.

Deploying and updating your models

The final phase of the data-mining process is to deploy the models into a production environment as small-scale working prototypes and allow users to begin using them. As users begin to use the data-mining system, it's a good bet that fresh problems will arise and additional modifications will be required. Then the iteration and reiteration of the data-mining process continues on a larger scale, as long as there's data to process, as shown in Figure 7-3.

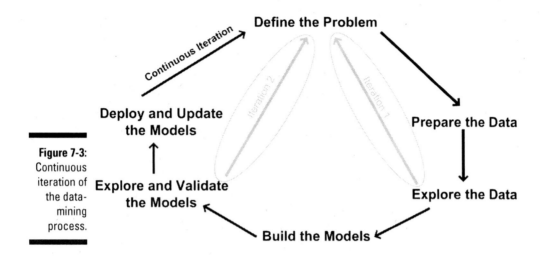

Figure 7-3:
Continuous
iteration of
the data-
mining
process.

As with any technical project, you should do multiple iterations for each phase in order to get the results and answers you want. For example, after defining the problem and preparing the data, you move on to exploring the data. During this second phase, you may uncover additional problems and have additional questions to answer. That's your cue to go back to defining the problem and preparing additional data before you sally forth with the next iteration — and that's how it goes for every phase of the project. The result of all those painstaking iterations is an inclusive project that has addressed and accommodated fresh questions as they arose throughout the project, instead of creating more questions than answers.

Data-mining structures

Think of a *data-mining structure* as a base upon which to build your data-mining models. This structure takes the form of a table that defines the data you intend to feed into the models — which measurements make it up, where it comes from, the nature of its connections to the data warehouse, data marts, or source systems — all arranged as headed columns similar to those in an Excel spreadsheet. For example, if you're in the business of selling groceries, you may want to use data mining to analyze your customers' buying habits. In this case, the data-mining structure could contain column headings such as Product, Product Group, Store, Time, Coupons Used, Customer Address, and any other relevant aspect of the data that tells you what you want to know.

In the interest of saving time and ensuring consistency, build a single data-mining structure that can be used by multiple models.

Data mining models

A *data-mining model* is where all the fun happens in data mining. Our favorite word, model, is thrown in again. In Microsoft Data Mining, a *model* is a collection of data mining "things." These things consist of a data-mining technique (mathematical algorithm) such as a decision tree or dependency network along with the connections to the source data, logs, configuration settings, and results. The whole ball of data-mining wax is called a *data-mining model.*

It's easy to confuse data-mining structures and data-mining models. An easy way to remember the difference is that a data-mining structure is like the frame of a house — it contains the raw data that will be analyzed. A data-mining model is like a fully-constructed home with all of its systems up and running — it's the end product of the process that begins with defining the structure: A consistent, planned use of Microsoft BI tools that

- ✔ Gathers data according to a well-formed pattern worked out through multiple iterations

- ✔ Can make predictions and try what-if scenarios

- ✔ Keeps your business running well because it can contribute timely, relevant data to the decision-making process

The results of processing (feeding data through the mathematical algorithm) are stored in the model itself — in effect, the model is a specialized database in its own right, built for the purpose of data mining. When you have those results, you have two ways to call them up from the model:

- ✔ You can use the built-in viewers in Visual Studio to see the results.

- ✔ You can create a query in the Data Mining Extensions (DMX) query language.

Learning DMX is beyond the scope of this book, however, it's simply a query language for data-mining models much like SQL is a query language for relational databases and MDX is a query language for OLAP databases.

Microsoft has released the Data Mining Add-In for Excel, which makes working with the data mining algorithms much easier. Using Excel as a client to interact with the algorithms is covered in Chapter 9.

Knowing the Microsoft Data-Mining Tools

The star development tool in the Microsoft arsenal — whether for BI purposes or any Microsoft-compatible software project — is Visual Studio. Microsoft has recognized that although many developers love Visual Studio, there are many more business users who want to use its powerful functionality on the server but don't want to end up doing more software development than business analysis. To give those business users easy access to the hefty powers of Visual Studio, Microsoft has added functionality to some of its other products so they can serve as familiar tools that pack a bigger BI punch; Excel, the outstanding example, flexes some of its new BI muscle in the upcoming section.

Integrating with Microsoft Office

Some of the good news for business users is that Microsoft has made the data-mining functionality of SQL Server Analysis Services (SSAS) available to the entire range of Office productivity software — primarily through the Data Mining Add-Ins for Excel. The result is a popular data-analysis tool that many people already have installed on their local desktop computers. The Data Mining Add-Ins allow you to use Excel — and the capabilities of Visio (a component of Microsoft Office used to build diagrams and flow charts) as a client to connect to and use data-mining algorithms on the SSAS server.

Best of all, you can access all those capabilities through a familiar Excel interface; they show up on-screen nicely arranged in a tidy Data Mining tab after you install the Data Mining Add-Ins. Figure 7-4 shows the Data Mining tab at home in the Excel ribbon.

Check out Chapter 9 for more information on using Excel to access the Data Mining algorithms.

The Data Mining Add-Ins consist of table analysis tools for Excel, a data-mining client for Excel, and data-mining templates for Visio.

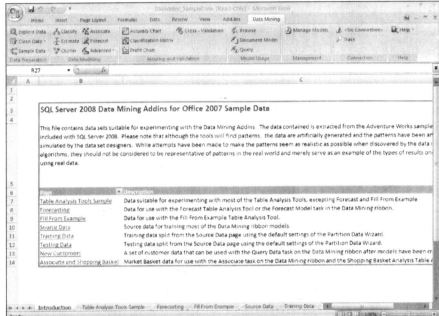

Figure 7-4:
The Data
Mining tab
in Excel.

Table Analysis Tools for Excel

The Table Analysis Tools for Excel add-in provides access to the SSAS data mining engine. You can use data in the spreadsheet and choose an algorithm from the Excel Ribbon. Without having to understand the innards of the algorithms or their complex data-mining concepts, you can get right down to business.

Data Mining Client for Excel

Using the Data Mining Client for Excel add-in, you can use Excel to create queries, explore data, perform testing, and manage data-mining models — all through access to the SSAS data mining engine. The data can be contained in an Excel file, or you can make the data available to external systems through the SSAS server connections.

Data Mining Templates for Visio

Using the Data Mining Templates for Visio add-in, you can build data mining diagrams that surface your data in Visio — a powerful program for creating process-flow diagrams (also known as flow charts). As you develop your diagram, you can include the actual data you dredge up with data mining as part of the overall process flow.

Visual Studio

The Visual Studio application is one of the most popular development environments in the Microsoft world. The actual Visual Studio application is a shell development environment that is extended with development functionality. For example, you may have project types in Visual Studio that allow you to write custom Visual Basic or C# .NET code. If you switch over to developing custom reports with SQL Server Reporting Services (SSRS), you could add functionality for writing reports to the Visual Studio application. The same environment is used for both development processes. Letting developers stay in their comfort zones by staying within a single environment as they move through various development tasks is important for productivity and efficiency. Find out more information about Visual Studio in Chapter 11.

Data Mining Wizard

The Data Mining Wizard lives within Visual Studio once the BI functionality has been installed.

You install the BI components to Visual Studio by selecting Business Intelligence Developer Studio (BIDS) from the SQL Server installation media. If you already have Visual Studio installed, the BI components will simply be added to your existing Visual Studio installation. If you don't have a version of Visual Studio installed, the SQL Server installation will install the Visual Studio shell with only the BI functionality. This version of Visual Studio with only the BI functionality is called BIDS.

You start the Data Mining Wizard by creating an SSAS project in Visual Studio, right-clicking Mining Structures in Solution Explorer, and then choosing Add Mining Structure (as shown in Figure 7-5).

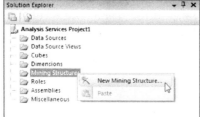

Figure 7-5:
Starting the
Data Mining
Wizard.

The Data Mining Wizard walks you through creating a data-mining structure and model, as shown in Figure 7-6.

Figure 7-6:
The Data
Mining
Wizard in
action.

The wizard allows you to choose a relational or cube data source (such as those found in your data warehouse). Next, choose the data-mining technique you want to use (as shown in Figure 7-7).

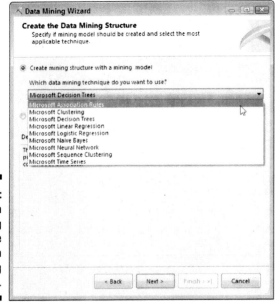

Figure 7-7:
Choosing a
data-mining
technique
in the Data
Mining
Wizard.

You choose the data to plug in to your data-mining structure from the available Data Source Views in the SSAS project you have underway. Depending on the data-mining technique you've chosen, the wizard walks you through building your data-mining structure and model.

Data Mining Designer

The Data Mining Designer — a BI tool that also comes with the BI functionality of Visual Studio — consists of design tabs that make the data-mining functionality easy to use as you develop the approach to data mining that best fits your organization. Figure 7-8 shows the Mining Structure design tab, the Mining Models design tab, the Mining Model Viewer tab, the Mining Accuracy Chart, and the Mining Model Prediction tab. These tabs appear on-screen after you've created a data-mining structure in your SSAS project (see the previous section).

Figure 7-8:
The Data Mining Designer is a set of tabs in Visual Studio.

Using the Data Mining Wizard creates design elements automatically in the designer tabs, but you can also create data-mining structures and models manually in Visual Studio if you need to.

The nice thing about developing Microsoft BI capabilities using these BIDS tools is that you can also use Visual Studio for almost every software-development project in your organization — and doing so practically guarantees that those projects will work well with Microsoft BI. Visual Studio has more BI uses than a pocket multi-tool has blades, including these:

- ✔ You can create projects that specify the ETL process with Integration Services.

- ✔ You can develop reports with Reporting Services.

- ✔ You can create OLAP cubes and develop your data-mining approach with Analysis Services.

- ✔ You can develop custom BI tools with .NET.

When you've become familiar with development for one type of project in Visual Studio, it's easy to move to a different development project with minimal training.

If you want to avoid Visual Studio (BIDS) altogether, you can also work with data-mining models using Excel and the Data Mining Add-Ins. Developers find Visual Studio to be a very comfortable environment, but many business analysts want to stay as far away as possible from any development environment — which is why Microsoft introduced the Data Mining Add-Ins for Excel. I have yet to meet a business analyst who doesn't use Excel. Excel is covered in detail in Chapter 9.

SQL Server Integration Services

The SSAS data-mining tools are really just the beginning. Another formidable BI component of SQL Server goes by the name SQL Server Integration Services (SSIS). SSIS provides tasks, data-flow transformations, and data-flow destinations designed to assist you in the data-mining process; the next section gives you a quick look at each of these features. (SSIS technology is covered in detail in Chapter 5.)

Tasks

Tasks are a key component of building an SSIS package. Visual Studio shows SSIS tasks on-screen at left, in a window called the Toolbox. You can drag and drop tasks onto the design surface of Visual Studio and then use the configuration window (shown at right on-screen) to fine-tune the tasks to your needs.

Some of the available SSIS tasks include these:

- ✔ **SSIS Analysis Services Execute DDL:** Execute this task when you want to run statements created in the Data Definition Language (also known as the DDL). DDL statements can be used to create, delete, or modify a data-mining structures and models.

- ✔ **SSIS Analysis Services Processing:** Use this task to automate the processing of a data-mining model. Processing a data-mining model consists of connecting to the data source, running the data through a chosen algorithm, and storing the results in the model.

- ✔ **SSIS Data Mining Query:** This task runs a query against a data-mining model or even against multiple models (which function as specialized data-mining databases, as you may recall from earlier in the chapter). The query itself is a statement created in Data Mining Extensions (DMX); it returns the results in a data set that you can store in a table. As database usage goes, that's so convenient it's almost decadent.

The Data Mining Extensions (DMX) language is actually an extension to the Structured Query Language (SQL) language. SQL is a computer language that's designed to run queries against a database. For example, a SQL query may look something like this:

```
SELECT column1, column2, column3, FROM MyDatabaseTable
```

> DMX is simply an extension to the standard SQL language that adds functionality for data mining. For example, instead of selecting columns from a database you would select columns from a data-mining structure such as a decision tree.

Data-flow transformations

Data-flow transformations are the components of SSIS responsible for (you guessed it) transforming data. These transformations can take the form of modifying, summing or merging, distributing, and cleaning up data.

The SSIS Data Mining Query transformation creates DMX queries that run against one or more data-mining models. The transformation contains a DMX query-building tool to simplify building the query. This transformation is similar to the Data Mining Query task, but instead of saving the output to a table, the transformation makes the output available to send to other destinations.

Data-flow destinations

Data flow destinations are the components of SSIS that output the results of a transformation to a specific location in your organization. For example, you may run a transformation and want to store the results to an Excel spreadsheet or a plain-text file.

The SSIS Data Mining Model Training destination can pass the data that's received into a data-mining model. You can use this destination to develop an SSIS package that compiles and cleans data from different sources and then sends it to a data-mining model that has been developed, for example.

SQL Server Management Studio

Given the various ways that "studio" crops up in the names of Microsoft BI tools, it shouldn't come as a surprise that there's one more: SQL Server Management Studio is a stand-alone application; it's separate from Visual Studio. Management Studio is designed to connect to and manage a SQL Server database. Although you can't use Management Studio to create or alter new data-mining models, you can use it in the following ways on *existing* models:

- ✔ Processing, browsing, and scripting models
- ✔ Creating prediction queries
- ✔ Deleting data-mining objects from the database

Using Microsoft Data Mining Algorithms

Multiple capabilities crop up in many Microsoft BI tools, and many of those tools come with SQL Server. In particular, the Data Mining Engine that comes with SQL Server provides algorithms that can manipulate your data in five different ways: classification, regression, segmentation, association, and sequence analysis.

Table 7-1 outlines the types of out-of-the-box algorithms that are available in the Microsoft Data Mining Engine, and gives you a brief summary of what they do.

Table 7-1	Microsoft Data Mining Algorithm Types
Algorithm Type	*Description*
Classification	You use these algorithms to predict one or more single numeric variables based on other variables in the data. The Decision Tree is an example of a classification algorithm.
Regression	You use these algorithms to predict what a continuous stream of numbers — based, for example, on past sales figures — will look like in the future. The algorithms look for patterns in the input data — for example, whether sales are lower in the summer months or peak during the holidays — and use the patterns they find to build a future prediction. The more data available to these algorithms, the greater the accuracy of the prediction.
Segmentation	You use these algorithms to divide data into units or groups that have similar attributes. The Clustering algorithm is an example of a segmentation algorithm.
Association	You use these algorithms to hunt for correlations between particular items of data — for example, you may find that beer and diapers are often purchased at the same time, in a single transaction, at a grocery store. The Market Basket Analysis is an example of an association algorithm.
Sequence Analysis	You use these algorithms to identify common sequences in a series of data. For example, if you analyze your Web site, you may discover that people often click its links in a certain order. Sequence Clustering is an example of a sequence analysis algorithm.

Understanding the algorithm types is important, but understanding how these algorithm types can be used to solve real-world business problems is more important.

The Microsoft Data Mining Engine also has a kind of open-ended versatility: It can use third-party algorithms. If some new BI vendor comes up with a fancy new algorithm, chances are excellent that you can plug it into the engine and have it work as easily as an out-of-the-box Microsoft algorithm.

The Microsoft algorithms can be used for functional business analysis. Some of the common business problems addressed by the algorithms include analyzing customer behavior, sales, inventory, and marketing effectiveness. Microsoft has identified some business cases for the data-mining algorithms (and I've included some comments you may hear in the corridors of Widgiematic, Inc. when the company's BI whizzes start using 'em):

- **Market Basket Analysis:** Use this algorithm to identify which items are generally purchased in the same check-out or shopping basket. This information can be used to compare how marketing promotions are performing or how product placement affects sales. ("Online sales of the Deluxe model jumped when our biggest retailer displayed it as 'A Must-Have Gadget for Summer Fun' — go figure.")

- **Churn Analysis:** Helps you identify the patterns behind customer *churn* (turnover). Understanding the reasons behind your churn rate can help you keep customers happy before they walk out the door. ("Our sales in the Midwest took a hit last year right after that fluff news piece on how a couple of 20-year-olds in North Dakota thought the flapdoodles on our Deluxe model were funny-looking.")

- **Market Analysis:** Assists you in grouping similar customers into different segments in order to better understand your customer demographics. This analysis can provide you with insights into your most profitable customer segments. ("So how do we get 20-year-olds in North Dakota to buy like 20-year-olds in California?")

- **Forecasting:** Allows you to input past data in order to predict future values such as inventory levels or sales information. The more data you feed into the algorithm, the better the prediction will be. For example, having an accurate forecast is important for making educated decisions about manufacturing capacity, as well as inventory levels and timelines for deliveries to locations and centers. ("At the rate the Deluxe Widgiematics are selling, we'll run out of flapdoodles for the final assemblies before the end of the quarter. Where can we get enough flapdoodles to keep California supplied?")

  Figure 7-9 shows an example of a Forecasting chart generated by using the data-mining functionality of SSAS in Excel.

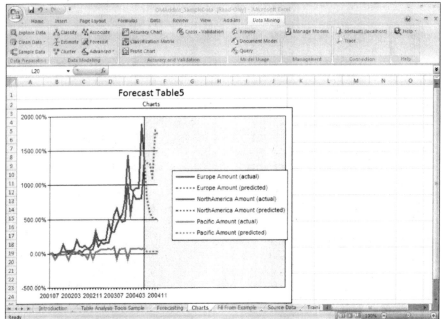

Figure 7-9:
Using Excel
with the
data-mining
Forecasting
functionality.

✔ **Data Exploration:** Permits you to explore the various components of your data. An example of a use for this algorithm may be analyzing the profit margin of a particular product across demographic segments. You could also use Data Exploration to determine how successfully a marketing campaign is performing. ("That new "Think Green" promo has started an uptick in regional sales over last year for Deluxe Widgiematics in Forest Green, even outside California.")

✔ **Unsupervised Learning:** Identifies relationships between components of your business that you may not have known existed. You may find out, for example, that implementing a new collaboration technology like SharePoint has boosted research-and-development productivity by allowing engineers from around the world to quickly interact with each other through discussion groups and wikis. ("Klaus in the Baden Baden design department says he's experimented with putting the flapdoodle on the other end — and you know, it actually works and looks kind of cool.")

✔ **Web Site Analysis:** You can use this algorithm to fully understand how customers and potential customers use your Web site. Once you understand usage patterns, you can develop and structure a Web site to create a better user experience. ("They're lingering on the Web page that shows the Deluxe model in Forest Green being used on the beach.")

- **Campaign Analysis:** Targets a marketing campaign and attempts to quantify the results. For example, you could analyze how a particular product or demographic responds to a particular promotional offer. ("So what *are* the 20-year-old Widgiematic owners saying about our offer to replace any bent flapdoodles on the Deluxe models free for a year?")

- **Information Quality:** Helps to clean and organize data coming into a system. Running an algorithm that assesses information quality may be useful when a large amount of manual data entry is required and not every data point can be checked. You may have mail-in forms from customers with information that has been entered into a system, for example. You could use the algorithm to determine the quality of the data that was entered. ("And right *there* is the day the server went down when all those promotion coupons came in at once.")

- **Text Analysis:** This algorithm can be performed to analyze feedback coming in from customers or clients. For example, you may want to determine whether there's a common theme showing up in feedback. Sorting through the mountains of forms manually wouldn't be practical (or much of a fate for a human being) why not use this tool to do it for you? ("It isn't just the green finish that they like on the Deluxe model — apparently they *really* like the way it looks with the chrome trim, the spinner, and the optional rubber duck.")

This list of business problems is by no means comprehensive. The use of the algorithms to solve business problems is only limited by your imagination and the data you have available for your organization. If you have really good BI tools *and* an active imagination, you're two steps ahead.

Part III
Introducing the Microsoft Business Intelligence Technologies

The 5th Wave   By Rich Tennant

"Look—what if we just increase the size of the charts?"

In this part . . .

This part introduces you to the products, features, and capabilities that make up Microsoft Business Intelligence. It's easy to get fuddled by acronyms and jargon, especially when they change and old features mutate and show up in different products— and Microsoft's offerings are no exception. Just trying to keep up with how applications interact with each other, which product does what, and how they develop superpowers when you hook them up to a server can be a headache. In fact, there are companies dedicated solely to following the Microsoft products, what they do, how that can change, and what direction each product is taking.

This part of the book offers a basic path through the maze of Microsoft Business Intelligence tools, including SQL Server, Office Excel, SharePoint Server, and the development tools.

Chapter 8

Meeting SQL Server

. . . .

In This Chapter

▶ Getting to know SQL Server

▶ Exploring the different versions of SQL Server

▶ Checking out the SQL Server components

▶ Going through the SQL Server installation

▶ Discovering the tools that work with the SQL Server components

. . . .

There seems to be some perverse human characteristic that likes to make easy things difficult.

— Warren Buffett

Consulting in a technological field often feels like traveling among different worlds inhabited by creatures who speak different alien languages. I've found that entering new "technology worlds" is often frustrating — because the people who live in those worlds know the ropes, rarely leave, and tend to expect a newcomer to know what they already know. Not that I blame anyone. Living in a technology world is like living in a cultural area. For example, we lived in Boston for a number of years — and many of our friends' families had never lived anywhere else. Some family member, generations before, had settled in the area, and the following generations never decided to leave. Many families had such deep roots that they never moved farther than a few blocks from the neighborhoods that they grew up in.

Being newcomers to Boston, we found it frustrating because often the neighborhood streets weren't marked with names — the general feeling was that you should "just know" how to get somewhere if you were going there. When we'd ask for directions (which was rather frequently), we'd be given landmarks with the usual remark that they didn't know the name of the streets but they knew how to get there. And the same is true in the technology world.

I recently did some work in the world of SAP technology. As I began working with SAP products, I felt like a bumbling idiot. (I won't say "sap" — after all, they pronounce it "S-A-P," letter by letter.) The people I worked with were very nice, and would try to explain things to me — but even the definition of an acronym was filled with other acronyms or buzzwords peculiar to SAP. What I needed was context! The SAP people had, in a sense, grown up with the SAP products. As new versions of SAP would come out or SAP would acquire and integrate specific technology, the SAP people were right there to fully process what was going on. In short, the SAP world in general made sense to them. They already knew that SAP was founded in Germany, that the letters stand for the German equivalent of "Systems Applications and Products," and that their products are designed for ERP (Enterprise Resource Planning — see Chapter 5). Not everybody who first encounters SAP knows that. But now you do. In case anybody asks.

Having all those new technology experiences (along the lines of SAP) has made me very empathetic toward people entering my Microsoft technology world. What they need is context! The SQL Server product makes perfect sense to me — and seems well organized and well documented — but I'm sure the SAP people felt the same way about their products. In this chapter, I provide context and direction for a core component of Microsoft Business Intelligence, SQL Server. Welcome to my "world."

First Contact with SQL Server

When I first heard the term "SQL Server," I found the name confusing. I knew that SQL was an acronym for Structured Query Language (SQL) and that it was used to query databases, but I wasn't sure why Microsoft would develop a special version of this language. After some research, I found out that SQL Server was the name that the Microsoft marketing folks had given to the database product. SQL Server does, indeed, do the job of managing a traditional relational database — but it has evolved to include additional features and functionality that can (for openers) extract, manipulate, store, analyze, and report on data. Today SQL Server is still the Microsoft database product, but it's like a jackknife that has evolved into a multi-blade tool, and from there into a box of power tools.

The best method I've come up with for understanding a product is to understand the problems that each of the product's features tries to solve. Looking at what a technology actually does — and how it solves business problems — is much easier than trying to wade through acronyms, jargon, and gosh-wow marketing material.

At the end of the day, technology should solve real-world problems; otherwise, it's may only be useful to the technological whiz-kids who created it. SQL Server solves many real-world problems, which provide some nice big rocks for breaking apart acronyms and slowing down the marketing spin. Throughout this chapter, I describe how each functional component works — and the business problem it's designed to solve.

Primary Components of SQL Server

Okay, here's the anatomy lesson: SQL Server has four primary components — database engine, reporting services, integration services, and analysis services. Figure 8-1 shows the way they go together.

Figure 8-1:
The compo-
nents of the
Microsoft
SQL Server.

Here's a quick look at what each component does:

✔ **Database Engine:** This type of component does the actual work of any traditional relational database. Naturally, most IT people think of the database engine first when they think of SQL Server.

✔ **Reporting Services:** Also known as SSRS, this is a BI component that creates reports from "clean" — that is, transformed — data (see Chapter 5) and manages access to those reports (see Chapter 10).

✔ **Integration Services:** Also known as SSIS, this component handles the ETL process (Extract, Transform, and Load — see Chapter 5) that gives the data coming in from source systems a standard format — and makes it usable by the entire organization.

✔ **Analysis Services:** Also known as SSAS, this component contains an OLAP engine for the online analysis of data (see Chapter 4) and a data-mining engine for finding the needed data for answering queries (see Chapter 7).

Engines and services, eh? Well, yes — but in BI, those words have nothing to do with your car's innards or with delivering pizza, as the accompanying sidebar ("What do you mean, *engine* and *service* . . . ?") explains. Upcoming is a closer look at each of these main SQL Server components.

What do you mean, *engine* and *service* . . . ?

In the software world, an *engine* is a software program designed to perform a specific task. For example, a *reporting engine* is a specific piece of software that developers have written that renders reports. This task-specific program is usually an integrated part of a larger software product, identified as the "engine" that the product uses to do that task.

The term *render* simply means that the reporting engine draws pictures, builds diagrams, and otherwise places the data in the report that has been developed. You can think of a report as being "built" once, but every time the report is "rendered," fresh data are inserted into the report based on what's in the database at the time of rendering.

Thus a *database engine* is task-specific software that stores and interacts with digital data. Many software companies have developed database engines. Some companies that sell popular database products include Microsoft (which makes SQL Server), Oracle, Sybase, Teradata, and IBM (which makes DB2). A number of open-source database engines, including MySQL and PostgreSQL, are available free of charge.

By the same token, *service* has a special meaning when you're talking about computer programs: It's a software program that provides results to other programs. In a database system, the services reside on the server, receive commands and queries from other locations on the network, and send results back to those locations.

The differences between a service and an engine are subtle and often interchanged. In the Microsoft world, you can see a list of all Services running on your computer by opening Task Manager and clicking the Services tab. The database engine, for example, has a number of different services running that are used for all types of things such as a notification service and an agent service that is used to execute administrative tasks, among others.

The SQL Server Database Engine

The database engine is probably the best-known component of SQL Server because it does the most basic and indispensable database task: It creates regular relational databases. That may be why many people think only of the database engine when they think of SQL Server. In fact, I often talk to IT people who weren't even aware that SQL Server contains functionality apart from the database engine — including some highly useful BI tools (more about those in a minute) just waiting to be used. For the moment, however, here's a closer look at using the SQL Server database engine to create (what else?) a database.

Creating a database

SQL Server gives you two ways to create a relational database:

- ✔ You can use the graphical user interface (GUI), which provides a program that walks you through the whole process of bringing a new database into the world.

- ✔ You can build your database from scratch, using a text-based component of the T-SQL language called Data Definition Language (DDL) to create a database object. The DDL has multiple functions, but at its core is a set of standard commands for creating, altering, and deleting a database object.

Everything that can be done in the GUI can be done using T-SQL, however everything that can be done using T-SQL cannot be done using the GUI, which is why many hard-core database administrators and developers prefer using straight T-SQL and avoid the GUI's all together.

Creating a database using the GUI

The GUI consists of a SQL Server management application called SQL Server Management Studio. You can use the GUI to create a new database by right-clicking Databases (which you'll find on the upper-left side of the Management Studio application) and choosing New Database, as shown in Figure 8-2.

Creating a database using the DDL

If you're the do-it-yourself type, you can create a new database by entering text into a new query window; when you do so in Management Studio, you use the Data Definition Language automatically. If you want (for example) to create a new database called `MyForDummiesDatabase`, the following command does the job:

```
CREATE DATABASE MyForDummiesDatabase
```

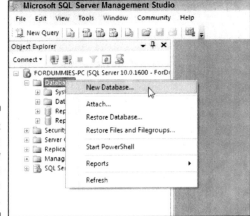

Figure 8-2:
Creating
a new
Database
using the
GUI.

After you click Execute to execute the command, the status of your new database-to-be shows up in the Messages window. Figure 8-3 shows the command that was executed, as well as the status as it appears in the Messages window.

If you want your new database to appear in the Object Explorer window (the window that shows the Databases at the upper-left corner of the Management Studio application), right-click the Databases folder and choose Refresh.

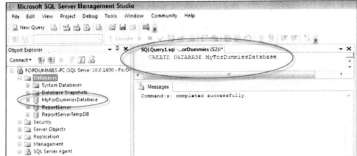

Figure 8-3:
Creating
a new
Database
using DDL.

In Figure 8-3, I created a new database in the Query window — which is part of Management Studio (the database-management tool included in SQL Server). If you're comfortable with a bare-bones command-line interface, you can use a tool called SQLCMD to write commands in the T-SQL language (or, for that matter, in the DDL, which is actually a specialized form of T-SQL) to tell SQL Server what you want done. When the SQLCMD utility is open (as in Figure 8-4), it looks like a DOS window. To launch SQLCMD, you simply type SQLCMD from a windows DOS command prompt.

Microsoft has been steadily moving toward providing a command-line mechanism for techies to administer Microsoft software. In essence, this new, super-powerful command line (think of DOS on steroids) is called *PowerShell*. Technical teams love working with applications using a command line because they can simply key in the commands and have them all run in one single batch or at a certain time without the need to manually click through a bunch of windows with the mouse.

Figure 8-4:
Creating a new database with the SQLCMD utility.

SQL Server clustering and high availability

As SQL Server evolves and sprouts more BI features, it plays an ever-increasing role in many organizations. As IT folks use SQL Server databases to develop *mission-critical* applications (business-speak for "failure is just too dreadful to think about"), they put even more of a premium on database reliability and availability. SQL Server helps ensure both of those qualities by reducing downtime and increasing reliability and availability using features such as failover clustering, database mirroring, log shipping, and replication.

Failover clustering

With failover clustering, the cherished data mart and data warehouse data are stored on two or more disks that are shared by multiple computers. Each of these computers is called a *node*. The business users connect to a virtual database name that simply points to the active node (computer). If one of the computers should fail, the virtual server name fails over (points) to a node that's healthy, and users don't see any interruption in data access.

Database mirroring

Database mirroring is a software solution that keeps an exact copy of the database in an additional database (the mirror database). Since there's always a second database that's an exact copy of the main database, you can simply switch over to the mirror database should something bad happen to the main database. The main difference between failover clustering and database mirroring is that failover clustering prevents against hardware failures and moves (points) an entire computer over to a completely different computer. Database mirroring works at the database level and, should something bad happen to the database itself, you can simply switch to the mirrored database.

In addition, database mirroring is a much simpler and cheaper (yet powerful) alternative to failover clustering. Another nice feature with database mirroring is that you don't have to let the copied (mirrored) database just sit there going to waste waiting for something bad to happen; you can provide read-only access to the mirror database which allows for reporting. Resource-intensive reports can use the mirror database when they're rendered, which alleviates some of the work the main database must perform.

Log shipping

Anytime something happens to a SQL Server database, a log entry is entered in a file. These log files can be used to recreate an entirely new database by simply performing the steps that were performed on the main database. These log files can also be used to maintain backup databases. The backup databases can be scheduled to automatically update based on the log files, which ensures you'll always have a quick backup should the main database fail.

Replication

Replication refers to replicating your data from your main data warehouse out to other computers. The main database is called the *publisher,* and the secondary computers are called the *subscribers.* For example, say your main data warehouse is in Seattle but you have offices all around the world. You may have your main Seattle database be the publisher and then have databases around the world that subscribe to the main database. Users around the world could then simply access the closest geographic database in order to improve performance when running their reports and performing their analysis.

SQL Server in the cloud

Sooner or later, at IT cocktail parties (or among friends at the water cooler who are trying to sound high-tech) you'll hear about software running "in the cloud." No, the software isn't being flown through a thunderhead (not usually, anyway). The expression comes from network diagrams that show some of the connections running into a cartoon cloud that represents the Internet (which is way too big and complex to cram into a diagram). In reality, software "running in the cloud" is running on servers that someone else manages and maintains, usually located *somewhere else* that's most easily accessed over the Internet.

Many of those servers-in-the-clouds are data resources set up by large corporations. Microsoft, for example, has invested billions of dollars in building powerful data centers that have massive computers running many of their software products as business resources designed to be accessed through the cloud. The overall strategy is called the Azure Services Platform — which you can explore in greater detail at

`www.microsoft.com/azure/default.mspx`

It may sound scary to have your critical data "out there" in the Internet. In all reality, the data are stored and guaranteed by none other than Microsoft. There are all types of service level agreements and data security guarantees. Microsoft can be confident in the security of the data flowing across the Internet due to high powered encryption. Even though the data are flowing across the Internet, it's heavily encrypted while in route and is only useful once it has been decrypted within your own secured corporate network. In order to ensure the security of the Azure platform, Microsoft partnered with the most trusted name in Internet security — VeriSign. If you've ever made a purchase online, chances are good that you've used VeriSign to secure the transaction.

The SQL Server offering of Azure is called *SQL Data Services* (SDS). SDS allows you to create a database out there in the clouds, on the hulking Microsoft servers, in a matter of minutes. The idea is to give organizations instant access to a world-class data center without making them worry about such details as plunking down a few million dollars to set one up.

If your organization has been growing like a movie monster and you need to scale up your database, you can simply change a configuration setting and have immediate access to more data-handling power. The traditional approach to scaling up servers involves accessing a larger data center, making expensive arrangements for additional electrical power, bigger air conditioners, more network bandwidth, and more powerful servers. SDS promises to greatly simplify the process by making SQL Server available with very little up-front cost — and nearly endless scalability with a minimal outlay of resources. (What does Microsoft get out of the deal? Well, just imagine the boost in brand loyalty.)

You can find details of the SQL Data Services (SDS) component of Azure at

```
www.microsoft.com/azure/data.mspx
```

SQL Server Reporting Services

SQL Server Reporting Services (SSRS) started life as a relatively modest add-on to SQL Server in 2004. Prior to the introduction of SSRS, many people used the Microsoft Access database product with reporting software from other companies. They had to pull data out of SQL Server if they were going to build reports; SSRS simply gave them a handy Microsoft tool for doing that. Since its introduction, however, SSRS has grown considerably, gained a reputation as a popular BI tool on its own merit, and is now a full-fledged part of SQL Server. If you're interested in using SSRS, you can install it simply by checking the box for it during the SQL Server installation process. SSRS can pull data and build reports from a number of data sources, not just SQL Server.

Given the history of SSRS and its popularity, a natural (and common) mistake is to assume that it's a stand-alone product. Nope. SSRS is a component of SQL Server, which you install as a feature. Even so, you can use SSRS on its own (provided you've installed SQL Server *and* specified the installation of SSRS), even if your data are stored in a non-Microsoft database.

Report Definition Language

A Reporting Services report consists of a text file in a format called *Report Definition Language* (RDL). The RDL itself is formatted as a document in Extensible Markup Language (XML), a more advanced cousin of HTML (commonly used in Web pages), and as such a standard designed to store and transport data using only text.

For example, a standard XML document consists of *tags* that define the data contained within the document. If you created your own XML standard, you may call it My Own Language (MOL). Say your MOL describes your life. You may have tags such as <job> </job> or <age> </age>. **Remember:** One of the rules of XML is that every opening tag has to have a closing tag; in XML, a closing tag is simply the opening tag name with the / symbol in front of the tag name. If you have an empty tag, XML allows you to take a shortcut and open and close it with the same tag by simply putting a forward slash after the tag name like so <job />. A sample of your MOL language may look something like this:

```
<MyLife>
    <FirstName>John</FirstName>
    <LastName>Doe</LastName>
    <Age>46</Age>
    <Job>Almost CEO</Job>
    <Birthdate>February 6</Birthdate>
</MyLife>
```

In the sample MOL, the <MyLife> tag is the opening and closing tag (</MyLife>), and it contains five tags, namely FirstName, LastName, Age, Job, and Birthdate. (I can already see that your MOL works a lot like RDL. Mind if I borrow it to use as an example? Never mind — I already did.)

RDL is more complicated than MOL, but it too is formatted as XML. The RDL that makes up a simple empty report looks like this:

```
<?xml version="1.0" encoding="utf-8"?>
<Report xmlns:rd="http://schemas.microsoft.com/SQLServer/reporting/
            reportdesigner" xmlns="http://schemas.microsoft.com/sqlserver/
            reporting/2008/01/reportdefinition">
  <Body>
    <Height>2in</Height>
    <Style />
  </Body>
  <Width>6.5in</Width>
```

```
<Page>
  <LeftMargin>1in</LeftMargin>
  <RightMargin>1in</RightMargin>
  <TopMargin>1in</TopMargin>
  <BottomMargin>1in</BottomMargin>
  <Style />
</Page>
<rd:ReportID>2b324b9f-2fec-4c44-b0f0-be36e755a664</rd:ReportID>
<rd:ReportUnitType>Inch</rd:ReportUnitType>
</Report>
```

The tags in the first line specify that the document follows the XML standard, version 1. The next line is the opening tag for the report, which is called <Report>. (Notice there is also a closing tag at the bottom called </Report>.) The opening Report tag also has an attribute that points to the location of the XML rules that the RDL document follows.

Other tags that describe the report follow next. In even a simple report, the RDL quickly becomes massive; for this reason, there are tools (see the next section) that can create RDL documents — which means you can use them to create reports.

I've known a few people who love writing the RDL document by hand. They say that after some time, you start to see RDL as blocks of functionality instead of line upon line of text. (Personally, I prefer a tool that allows me to drag and drop items to build the report. When I like having control of the details, I switch over to the raw RDL.)

You can open an XML document (or, for that matter, an RDL document) because it follows the XML standard) using nothing more than a simple text editor like Notepad.

XML doesn't "do" anything in particular (nor does RDL for that matter) — it's only a way to define and store data. You can think of XML as a standard for writing the text document and the RDL as the specific implementation of that standard. The Reporting Services engine takes these RDL documents and renders them as reports.

Report-building tools

Building a Reporting Services report using Notepad is acceptable, but if you want to do it faster (and make the report a bit fancier), Microsoft offers some tools to help you build the RDL. Traditionally, the primary tool for building reports has been Visual Studio. More recently, however, Microsoft has come up with a report-development environment geared to the needs and skill-sets of business users and analysts — with the familiar look and feel of Microsoft Office (in particular, the interface elements introduced in Office 2007 and expanded in Office 2010). This new report-building tool is called — wait for it — Report Builder. (Hey, there's comfort in obvious things.)

Report Builder

The *Report Builder* application is designed to give the end user easy-to-use power over the report-building process. The application isn't part of SQL Server, but it's designed to work directly with the SSRS engine, which is part of SQL Server. Report Builder can be accessed either by downloading it (free of charge) from Microsoft or, if your IT department has configured it, by simply clicking on Report Builder from within the environment you use to manage SSRS reports, namely, Report Manager (discussed below) or SharePoint.

If your IT department has set up Report Builder to download directly from the place where you manage your reports, you simply click a link, and a technology known as ClickOnce downloads the application to your local computer, and you're all set. Any time a new version of Report Builder is released, you'll automatically get it through ClickOnce after your IT department has made it available. You don't need to install or update anything — through the magic of ClickOnce, all updates to your local version of Report Builder happen automatically.

The alternative to ClickOnce is to download the application from the Web and then install it on your local computer much like Microsoft Word or Excel (except Report Builder is free). The application looks very similar to Word or Excel with the Office Ribbon at the top, as shown in Figure 8-5.

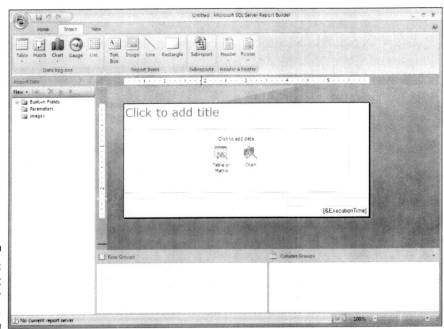

Figure 8-5:
The Report Builder application.

Report Builder is not limited to building its reports only from SQL Server data. It's a versatile tool that works just as well with data from various data sources, including databases from such vendors as SAP, Oracle, Teradata, and many others.

Report Builder is an application designed for analysts and other business users, but when it comes to most development tasks in the Microsoft world Visual Studio is the application most techies are familiar with.

Visual Studio and Business Intelligence Developer Studio

Visual Studio is the standard application used for developing software in the Microsoft world. It's so prevalent that many other software makers have designed their development products to interact with Visual Studio. This situation is really handy for Microsoft-savvy developers; they can just keep working merrily away in the Visual Studio environment, plugging in those other products — as well as the BI capabilities already built in to Microsoft products — without having to figure out whole new environments.

Reporting Services is a classic example; it includes features that function as add-ins to Visual Studio. Result: You can use this well-established development environment to work up your reports (which is very nice if you are already familiar with Visual Studio and use it day in and day out). You add the features in one of two ways when you install Reporting Services:

- ✔ If you already have a version of Visual Studio installed, the features are simply added to the version of Visual Studio you have.

- ✔ If you don't already have a version of Visual Studio installed, then Reporting Services installs Visual Studio for you — with only the BI functionality added. This stripped-down, BI-specific version of Visual Studio goes by the name *Business Intelligence Developer Studio* (BIDS — which also includes functionality for the other components of SQL Server including SSIS and SSAS).

Either way, you end up with a version of Visual Studio that provides all the report-building features of Reporting Services. Figure 8-6 shows what these look like in BIDS (notice it isn't as pretty and user friendly for building reports as Report Builder? Unless, of course, you are already familiar with Visual Studio, in which case it is beautiful).

Report models

The best way to understand the concept of a report model is to understand the problem that it solves. A typical reporting situation involves a database (containing, you know, *data*) and a person who knows how to build a report (or has been assigned to do it regardless). The person building the report has a mission: Get the data from the database and bash it into a report, ASAP. The data in the database are often stored in a complex way, which makes a real chore out of standard database procedures such as finding the correct data to build the report or (for that matter) building a query to *get* the right data.

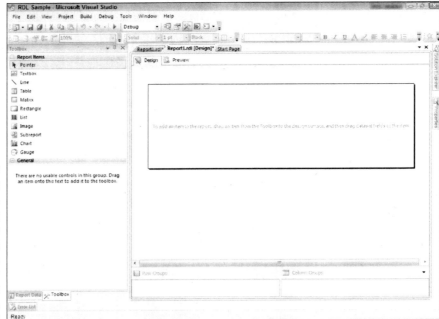

Figure 8-6:
Report-
building
features in
Business
Intelligence
Developer
Studio
(BIDS).

Traditionally, some kindly technical person would serve as an intermediary, taking the data requirements from the business user or analyst and then building the report to suit. This process may work, but it's time-consuming and can be frustrating.

An up-to-date alternative that saves on the aspirin is the *report model* — a structure that sits between the actual data and the person who builds the report, busily making the data accessible and understandable for the end users. (What a concept.) The end users then use tools such as Report Builder to put their reports together, saving time and headaches because the report model gives them a view into the data that's already ready to include in the report instead of the raw view that the database administrators see. Figure 8-7 illustrates this difference (progress — gotta love it).

This approach is often called *ad-hoc reporting* because the reports are often created quickly and are designed to answer specific questions. The report model presents the data in a way that makes sense to business users. Business users can then drag and drop fields and design quick-and-dirty reports to answer specific questions as they arise.

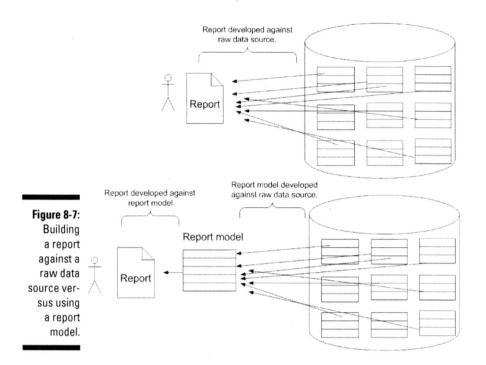

Figure 8-7:
Building
a report
against a
raw data
source ver-
sus using
a report
model.

Table 8-1 outlines the tools used to create and edit a report model when you're doing ad-hoc reporting.

Table 8-1	Tools for Creating and Editing Report Models
Tool	**Description**
Model Designer	The Model Designer lives inside Visual Studio and consists of specific functionality (in the Toolbox, Design Pane, Properties, and Project Explorer) used for building report models. You can start building a report model as a project, using the New Project Wizard that comes with Business Intelligence Developer Studio (BIDS).
Report Manager	Report Manager is a Web application, installed when Reporting Services is installed and used as a stand-alone application. Report Manager provides features for storing and organizing SSRS reports, specifying access to them, and delivering them to the appropriate end users.
SharePoint Server	SharePoint Server manages your SSRS reports — taking the place of Report Manager — when you use Reporting Services in a system that's integrated with SharePoint.

SQL Server Integration Services

SQL Server Integration Services (SSIS) is the component of SQL Server that extracts data from source operational systems, transforms it, cleans it, and then loads it into a data warehouse. SSIS used to go by the name Data Transformation Services (DTS), back when life was simpler; now it does the whole ETL (Extract, Transform, and Load) process (see Chapter 5).

When SSIS does ETL, the process consists of building *SSIS packages* in a Visual Studio file called a *project.* You can create a new SSIS project from within BIDS — which is, after all, a BI-specific version of Visual Studio — by launching the New Project Wizard and choosing the Integration Services Project.

Building an SSIS package involves three procedures:

1. You create a connection to a data source.

2. You use SSIS transformation *tasks* to clean and transform the data.

3. You send the transformed data as output to a destination.

You can find the tasks, data sources, and destinations in a Visual Studio Toolbox window. You simply drag and drop them onto a design surface, and then configure the components in a Properties window. (For a closer look at creating a simple SSIS package, flip to Chapter 5.)

SQL Server Analysis Services

SQL Server Analysis Services (SSAS) is the component of SQL Server that you use to analyze data, usually after it's been transformed. The SSAS component is made up of an OnLine Analytical Processing (OLAP) engine and a Data Mining engine.

If you happen to encounter an older version of SQL Server, you may find the analysis component hiding under its old name — OLAP Services. After the Data Mining engine was added, the component was renamed Analysis Services, a more flexible moniker that leaves the door open to include whatever future data-analysis technology Microsoft comes up with.

OLAP

OLAP is a standard that refers to optimizing a database for analytical activities such as aggregation, grouping, and slicing and dicing data in various ways. OLAP databases are known as *cubes,* the numerical data that is analyzed is known as a *fact* or *measure,* and the way of grouping the data is known as a *dimension.* (You can find more about the SSAS OLAP capabilities, along with details of what a "dimension" is in database-speak, in Chapter 4.)

Data Mining Engine

The Data Mining Engine is a component of Analysis Services that contains a number of mathematical algorithms that can be used on data. Data mining is also called *predictive analytics* or *machine learning,* and the components that do it are installed along with the Analysis Services feature (no extra tweaking required). Check out Chapter 7 for more information on data mining.

Looking at the Different Versions of SQL Server

SQL Server comes in various *editions* (versions), each encompassing features that accommodate businesses looking for levels of functionality (and price points) to fit their needs. You can see a comparison of all the SQL Server editions at

```
www.microsoft.com/sqlserver/2008/en/us/editions.aspx
```

Core editions

The two core editions of SQL Server are the Standard and Enterprise editions. These are the primary editions that most organizations license.

Standard

The Standard edition is a complete system and includes all the features required for data management and business intelligence, including basic reporting, ETL, and data analysis but allows only four processors maximum.

Enterprise

The Enterprise edition is the grand-daddy of all SQL Server versions. The Enterprise edition includes all available functionality and as many CPU's as the Operating System supports. The Enterprise edition also includes all of the advanced features that aren't included in the Standard edition such as enhanced functionality for SSRS (data driven report subscriptions, scale out report configuration, infinite click-through of ad-hoc reports), SSAS (sequence prediction, perspectives, custom rollups), and SSIS (data mining training destination, fuzzy grouping and lookup, and term extraction destination). If these advanced features sound, well, advanced, don't worry — your BI pros can guide you through the complete list of advanced functionality.

What I often see when working with clients is that they've licensed the Enterprise version of SQL Server (presumably because they figure, "Hey, we're an enterprise, right?") — but aren't taking advantage of all the features they're paying for. If SQL Server looks like the Next Big Thing in databases for you (or your organization), be sure to talk to a Microsoft professional or customer-service representative about all the features SQL Server. Figure out beforehand whether you require the Enterprise or Standard license. If you do require the Enterprise license — or your company has already installed SQL Server and is getting serious about BI — make sure you're taking full advantage of all of the features that SQL Server offers — in particular, its BI features.

In order to take full advantage of SQL Server, it helps to put together a team of people who can guide you through each of the features of the product in order to fully understand what you absolutely need and what you can live without until later iterations. The full list of features can be viewed at the following Web address.

www.microsoft.com/sqlserver/2008/en/us/editions-compare.aspx

Specialized editions

Microsoft recognizes that some market segments may not be ready for the full-up Standard and Enterprise editions of SQL Server. So it's created special editions — Express, Web, and Workgroup — to reach these market segments and encourage them to use, get to know, and (probably) get hooked on the capabilities of SQL Server.

Express

The Express editions of SQL Server consist of the following three editions:

- ✔ **SQL Server Express with Tools:** The core edition of SQL Server Express that includes SQL Server Management Studio (the tool used to manage databases).

- ✔ **SQL Server Express with Advanced Services:** This edition of Express expands on the core version to include support for Integrated Full-Text Search and Reporting Services.

- ✔ **SQL Server Express (Runtime Only):** The runtime-only edition of Express includes only the SQL Server database engine and is designed for integrated deployments and redistribution with other software products. For example, should you choose to develop a software application that requires an integrated database to store its data then you would use the runtime-only version of SQL Server and include it with your custom application (see the accompanying sidebar for an example). The runtime-only edition is also referred to as the *Compact* edition.

A database among the vegetation

I developed an application that embeds the Compact edition of SQL Server for field biologists while I was a graduate student at San Francisco State University. My thesis involved developing an application on a portable Windows mobile device that could be carried into the field in order to track vegetation types and densities. The biologist had been using pencil and paper in the field — and would then go through a torturous data-entry routine once back in the office. My application used a GPS-enabled device and a large, easy-to-navigate user interface to capture data in the field. The data was stored in a SQL Server Compact edition database. Once back in the office, it would automatically sync to a central server and upload its data using a Web service.

The Express editions of SQL Server are free and are designed for hobbyists, students, and anyone else who wants to become familiar with SQL Server (with the exception of the runtime only edition, which is designed for redistribution with custom software). The Express editions will give a new user a good grounding in how SQL Server works and (some of) what it can do. One of the main limitations of the Express edition, however, is that it only supports 1GB of RAM, a 4GB database, and one CPU.

Web

The Web edition of SQL Server is designed to provide low-cost database hosting. The database itself can be included in Web-hosting packages that include a database component; this edition also supports Web services, as you might expect. The Web edition of SQL Server has a streamlined set of features targeted at Web hosting — in particular, improved management and monitoring of web customers, increased scale-out needs, and maximum server utilization (no hardware restrictions).

Workgroup

The Workgroup edition is designed to be used by small groups within an organization (for example, a manufacturing team) — especially those that use Microsoft Access for their database needs. The Workgroup edition brings some of the power of SQL Server to these target groups at an affordable price — without the limitations of the free Express editions, in particular the database size is not limited, it supports 2 CPU's as opposed to the 1CPU in Express, and 4GB of RAM is supported instead of the 1GB limit imposed by Express. The idea is to familiarize users with these features and to facilitate later upgrades to the Standard or Enterprise editions.

Developer

The Developer edition of SQL Server contains all the features and functionality of the Enterprise edition and is designed for developers. The restrictions that come with the Developer edition mean that it can only be used for development, testing, and demos and can't be used in a production or real-world environment. The idea is that developers should be able to take advantage of all of the features possible under the Enterprise edition without having to bother with the actual licensing of the Enterprise edition.

Take the Developer version of SQL Server for a spin before plunking down the money required to obtain the Standard or Enterprise edition. This will give you a test run of the Enterprise edition without paying for the licensing upfront. The Developer edition has a nominal price of around $50.

Installing SQL Server

Many technical people are always on the watch for new technology; I sure am. When I hear about a new program, I like to download a copy of it, install it, and explore it — especially if a consulting client is using it — but sometimes the prey is elusive. In my recent foray into the SAP world, for example, I tried for days to find a trial version of the SAP software. It seemed I was constantly hitting a dead end. I felt that SAP software must be stashed in some remote cache, guarded by dragons (or at least imperial guards), where nobody was allowed to have a look at it. Even the documentation that I read online was password-protected on the SAP Developer Network. Hey, all I really wanted was a trial version so I could get a feel for how the pieces of software worked and how they fit together.

I'm sure that much of my frustration was due to the fact that the SAP world was new to me. I had never been to the SAP Developer Network before and had never registered for a free account. It turned out to be not that different from the Microsoft world, where you still have to register for a free account. Frankly, though, I'm hoping this chapter — especially this section — will make your experience finding the software much easier.

Microsoft makes a 180-day trial of SQL Server available, as well as free Express editions. The software can be downloaded or ordered on DVD at

```
www.microsoft.com/sqlserver/2008/en/us/default.aspx
```

The installation file comes in two forms that are available online:

- **ISO image:** This is a packaged file that can be burned directly to a DVD using a DVD burner.

- **Self-extracting file:** This is a file that you download and then double-click to extract and install the SQL Server files automatically.

Whichever form of installation you choose, you're presented with a number of options when you begin the installation. The first dialog box that opens is the SQL Server Installation Center (shown in Figure 8-8). Its options can help you with many aspects of SQL Server — such as planning for an installation, performing an installation, performing maintenance, using tools, viewing documentation, viewing pre-requisites, and running diagnostics.

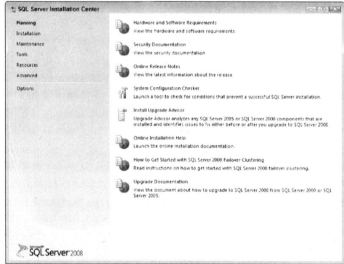

Figure 8-8:
The SQL
Server
Installation
Center main
screen.

From the SQL Server Installation Center, follow these steps to install a stand-alone instance of SQL Server:

1. **Click the Installation tab on the left side of the screen.**

   The right side of the screen provides options for SQL Server installation, as shown in Figure 8-9.

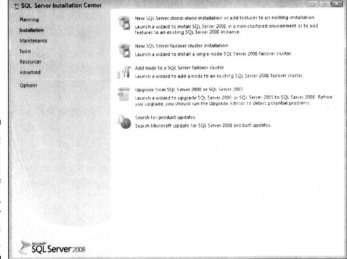

Figure 8-9:
The
Installation
screen of
the SQL
Server
Installation
Center.

2. **Click the New SQL Server Stand-Alone Installation or Add Features to an Existing Installation option (this is the first option in the list).**

   This option allows you to install a stand-alone instance SQL Server or add functionality to an instance of SQL Server that's already installed.

3. **As the wizard works through the installation, you're given the opportunity to install the core SQL Server components of Microsoft Business Intelligence.**

   Figure 8-10 shows the options for installing the Database Engine Services, Analysis Services, Reporting Services, Business Intelligence Development Studio (BIDS), Integration Services, and the Management Studio tool, along with many others.

   If a feature has already been installed on the server computer on which you're attempting to install SQL Server, that feature is checked and grayed out.

Although the wizard is helpful and walks you through the installation with documentation, some hardy souls prefer to install software using the command line. SQL Server can indeed be installed using command-line parameters; you can find out more about this method at

`http://msdn.microsoft.com/en-us/library/ms144259.aspx`

Analysis Services

Reporting Services | Database Engine

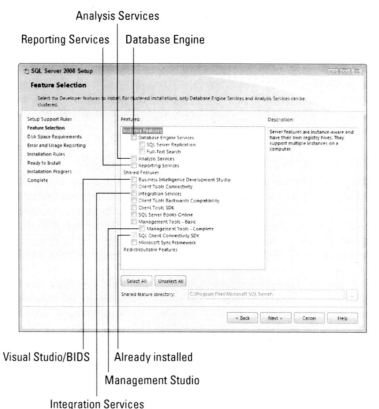

Figure 8-10:
The Feature
Selection
screen of a
SQL Server
installation.

Visual Studio/BIDS | Already installed

Management Studio

Integration Services

Checking Out SQL Server Tools

SQL Server comes with a number of tools you can use when you want to get the most out of this centerpiece of Microsoft BI while you're becoming more adept at it. Those tools help you manage SQL Server instances (installation), as well as develop and build projects that use SQL Server capabilities.

A SQL Server instance refers to a self-contained SQL Server installation on your server. You can install SQL Server multiple times on the same computer as long as you give each instance its own name. In the world of technical jargon, these instances of SQL Server are called, aptly enough, *named instances*. In a test environment you may have a named instance for every member of your team running on the same server. This allows every person to have their own private SQL Server instance without interfering with others and without you having to purchase a computer for each person. When you start a SQL Server tool, you specify the named instance you wish to connect to. If you're the only one running SQL Server on the computer, then most likely you'll use what is called the *default instance* of SQL Server.

SQL Server Management Studio

The primary tool that database administrators use to manage SQL Server databases says so in its name: SQL Server Management Studio (often referred to as simply Management Studio). Management Studio handles all aspects of SQL Server tasks (such as configuration, general database management, administration, security, and data retrieval). In addition, you can use it for writing development scripts.

Terminology confusion with Management Studio

Before SQL Server 2005 came out, the primary management tool was called SQL Server Enterprise Manager. You may often hear people mixing up the names. ***Remember:*** With SQL Server 2005 and beyond, the management tool is called Management Studio. Also, prior to SQL Server 2005 the primary application used to build SQL queries was called Query Analyzer. The Query Analyzer functionality was rolled into Management Studio as well.

In essence, Management Studio is a software program that serves as a place to develop other programs — called an *environment* by tech people — that acts as a user interface for SQL Server. The Management Studio application is shown in Figure 8-11.

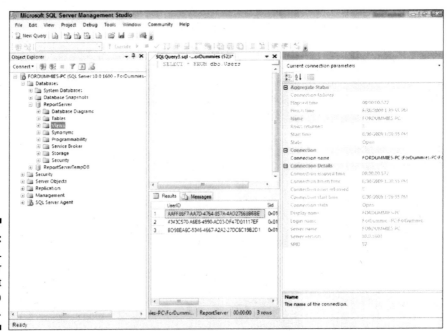

Figure 8-11:
The SQL Server Management Studio application.

The Object Explorer window on the left side of the screen lists the available programming objects — such as databases, tables, and views, in addition to security and management objects. In Figure 8-11, the center window is being used as a SQL development window: Note that the written SQL shows up in the text editor (the top half of the center window); the results are displayed in the bottom half of the same window. The Properties window on the right side of the screen displays the properties assigned to the particular object you've selected.

Although Management Studio is a completely separate application from Visual Studio, its environment is very similar. That's intentional. The idea is to help anyone who's familiar with one Microsoft environment (whether for development or management) make an easy transition to working with other environments.

Development in Management Studio

The development component of Management Studio provides a number of feature-rich script editors with such handy bells and whistles as color-coded key words and IntelliSense. Even someone who's new to writing code will find it friendly.

IntelliSense gives the program the capability to help the user with typing correct SQL syntax. IntelliSense takes the first letter (or letters) in a word and provides a list of possible syntactically correct options. For example, if you want to type the name of a database for your query, you can type the first letter and a drop-down list of every object that you may want to choose appears. You can then just scroll down to the word you want, click it, and keep working. If you don't see your keyword in the drop-down list, you can continue to type additional letters of the word; the drop-down list will continue to narrow until only the word you want is selected.

IntelliSense is an especially convenient feature because the names that database administrators typically give to objects are often difficult to remember (and not exactly user-friendly). As with any computer programming language, certain words are special to the language. These special words are called *keywords*. For example, SELECT is a keyword in the SQL language because you type it when you want to select columns from a database. As a result, you couldn't name one of your database columns SELECT. These keywords show up with different colors so you know instantly what words are keywords as you're developing. Color-coded key words and IntelliSense are shown in action in Figure 8-12.

Keywords

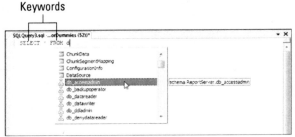

Figure 8-12:
IntelliSense
in SQL
Server
Management
Studio.

Transact-SQL

Whether you think of SQL as a shorthand form of the word "sequel" or as initials that stand for Structured Query Language (opinions differ in the database community), one thing's for sure about SQL: It's a standard for defining a query language that can retrieve data from just about any relational database.

The SQL standard for retrieving data seeks to be independent of existing database technology — the idea is to avoid incompatibility headaches. For example, if your SQL query retrieves data from a database that runs SQL Server, the query should *also* be able to retrieve the same data from an Oracle or IBM database (assuming that the tables in those databases have the same names).

Having a common query language that can work with various makers' database products is great, but it doesn't take full advantage of the strengths built in to each system. As a result, the software companies that develop database products have extended and tweaked SQL into versions of the language that are specific to their particular systems. For example, Transact-SQL (T-SQL) is one such *superset* of the SQL language — it's sprouted extensions designed to work with the Microsoft database system. Oracle also has a superset of the SQL standard; its specific functionality, geared to the Oracle database, is known as Procedural Language/SQL (PL/SQL).

If you use T-SQL commands, you have to enter them into a software application that understands the query and executes it against the specified database. The most user-friendly methods for writing a T-SQL query include using the text editor that's part of SQL Server Management Studio (or, for that matter, the one in Visual Studio). There's also a command-line utility called SQLCMD that's installed automatically with SQL Server as well as SQL extensions for the DOS on steroids command-line utility called PowerShell. (For more about T-SQL, see Chapter 11.)

MDX

Multi-Dimensional Expressions (MDX) is a query language designed to query multidimensional OLAP cubes (see Chapter 4 for a refresher on multiple dimensions and OLAP). What the T-SQL extension of SQL does for traditional relational databases, MDX does for OLAP cubes with equal aplomb.

Whether you're using T-SQL to query a relational database or MDX to query an OLAP cube, the result is usually a *dataset* — a file containing data presented in the form of columns and rows. (It looks similar to an Excel table.) After a dataset is returned, its data are ready to use and present — usually in the form of a report.

Chapter 9

Excel — Digital Data Power to the People

In This Chapter

▶ Understanding Excel's popularity

▶ Creating data

▶ Gathering data

▶ Organizing data

▶ Visualizing data with charts and graphs

▶ Using pivot tables and pivot charts to analyze data

▶ Data mining with Excel

▶ Tallying the score with the scorecard

▶ Understanding the limits of Excel

▶ Peering in to the future of Excel

You are neither right nor wrong because the crowd disagrees with you. You are right because your data and reasoning are right.

— Warren Buffett

*I*n case you've been hiding under a rock and haven't encountered Microsoft Excel, it's not only a spreadsheet, but one of the most versatile and widely used software applications of all time. Excel is used by a broad spectrum of people — from Grandma keeping track of her sewing materials to multi-billion dollar international corporations forecasting profits and losses. For a vast number of companies small and large, across many industries, Excel is at the heart of the organization.

Excel is unique because its uses span the entire data lifecycle — data generation, data collection, data organization, data visualization, data analysis, and data mining (for more about these stages, see the mini-table in the next section and check out Chapter 2). This versatility makes Excel a one-stop shop for business intelligence (BI), and widely popular as a tool for extracting not only data but *metadata* (information about data).

The six stages of the data lifecycle — and (for that matter) business intelligence itself — are all about turning raw data into ready-to-use information for making intelligent business decisions.

When Excel became part of the Microsoft Office suite and wound up on nearly everyone's desktop computer, everyday businesspeople had a powerful tool for handling data digitally — much *more* data, and much quicker. End users started to drop the shackles of printed reports delivered in binders. Suddenly a wider range of people could come up with their own calculations — and the spreadsheet began a reign that continues today.

In this chapter, we take an intimate look at Excel's role in the data lifecycle and business intelligence. We explore how Excel can be used to create, store, organize, analyze, and manipulate digital data. We look at how Excel can be used as a desktop tool that connects to the powerful SQL Server Analysis Services (SSAS) server and also how Excel can be used to build scorecards, dashboards, and other reports using a plethora of graphs, graphics, and charts.

Excel as a BI Application

Used in the context of Microsoft BI, Excel gives everyone — at all organizational levels — the power to turn data into information. Excel is a dominant business tool for three main reasons, each of which makes it a natural for BI use:

✔ It's easy for everyday (non-technical) people to use and understand.

✔ It provides everyone with familiar, user-friendly access to BI functionality.

✔ It has uses that span the entire data lifecycle (as illustrated in Table 9-1).

One reason Excel works well as a *front end* (that is, a user-friendly set of controls for BI processes) is that its user interface is deliberately intuitive. Microsoft sought to make all Office user interfaces consistently intuitive by introducing the Ribbon — a large bar across the top of the program window that contains the icons, zones, and tabs needed for using the programs. The idea is to help the user get to the needed functionality with a quick scan of the Ribbon.

Table 9-1	Using Excel Throughout the Data Lifecycle
Stage of Data Lifecycle	*Typical Use for Excel*
Data generation	Excel is deceptively easy and common as a data entry mechanism. When data is entered into Excel, it begins its life as digital data and can then be used throughout the rest of the data lifecycle just as data coming from other sources such as ERP, custom solutions, robots, machines, and scanners.
Data collection	Often data are stored in backend systems, but business users are comfortable with manipulating and analyzing the data in Excel. Excel has a number of ways that data can be imported for analysis as will be explored the Collecting Data section below.
Data organization	Excel organizes data in a number of ways including Excel files, Worksheet tabs within files, and rows and columns.
Data visualization	The power, and addictiveness, of Excel lies in its ability to quickly build charts and graphs for data visualizations. A business user can quickly put together a visualization that can be used to make critical decisions all without leaving her desktop or interacting with a report developer. These quick-and-dirty analyses are what drive many ad-hoc decisions in the business world.
Data analysis	Using features such as the PivotTable, PivotChart, PowerPivot, and SSAS connectivity Excel can be used to quickly analyze massive amounts of data in a comfortable format.
Data mining	When the Data Mining Add-In is added to Excel, it becomes a client for the powerful data mining algorithms that reside in the SSAS server. Data mining is explored in depth in Chapter 7.

When the Excel program window is expanded (maximized as opposed to sized down), the Ribbon expands dynamically to display more visual information on-screen about the available features. Figure 9-1 shows the Excel Ribbon in a sized-down window; Figure 9-2 shows the same Excel application maximized. No Excel configurations were necessary (what a concept!) to make this increased view of features available. Even so, many people hardly notice this improvement, other than recognizing that it's easier to find the functionality they're looking for and get on with the job.

Figure 9-1:
Excel
Ribbon
with a
sized-down
window.

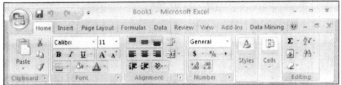

Figure 9-2:
Excel
Ribbon with
a maximized
window.

Microsoft is fully aware of Excel's familiarity to a wide range of users — and its versatility as a tool that spans the data lifecycle. No wonder the company has gone to great lengths to continue the product's dominance — and BI is an integral part of that strategy. Excel puts all that familiarity and versatility to work as a fresh advantage when it's used as a front end that bosses around the powerful BI features of SQL Server. SQL Server Analysis Services (SSAS) is typical of those features — *back-end* capabilities that aren't built in to Excel per se, but will do as it says when they're properly connected to Excel. Imagine starting up a powerful data mining algorithm — or browsing and analyzing an SSAS OLAP cube — by doing no more than clicking an icon in Excel. It could go right to your head.

Generating Data

It's amazing how many processes are involved in the simplest aspects of business; generating data is a typical example. Fortunately, taking an idea for a data-generation point from concept to reality is deceptively simple using Excel:

1. A business user creates a simple form in Excel (say, an inventory of flap-doodles on hand for Deluxe Widgiematic final assembly, and a record of how many units come in each quarter from the flapdoodle supplier) and sends it to the person who has the needed information.

2. Whoever is involved in the business process (say, the Foreman in Charge of Flapdoodles) fills out the form and e-mails it back.

3. Voilá — someone has generated data where there was none before. Now all the company has to do is turn it into ready-to-use information (more about that in a minute).

So far, this process of generating data is easy and straightforward — and requires very little opportunity cost. Even the largest companies are still run by people, and as people in business become aware of a need for data they don't have, they often choose Excel as a handy tool for generating that data. Some smaller companies still rely entirely on Excel for data generation — but there's also a larger BI perspective that looms — at least potentially — in the background. Stay tuned.

BI is about knowing what's going on in your business — and that means know-ing its processes. A *data-generation point* is any point in a process at which data can be created (entered into a digital format). It can be as simple as a date/time stamp or as complex as a general ledger accounting adjustment. Every process has data-generation points. The amount of data that can be generated by a process is limited only by imagination (to perceive a need for data) and resources (to go get it.)

Collecting Data

You can use Excel to collect data from a number of different sources. The first — and most obvious — place is from actual real-life humans. (Come on. Surely your organization still has some of those around?)

A purchase-order form, shown in Figure 9-3, is easy to create in Microsoft Excel. This form can be used for something as simple as a home-based craft business or as complex as a large corporation. After the data are entered into the form, it can then easily be imported into a back-end database, using Microsoft tools such as .NET Web Services or SQL Server Integration Services (SSIS — see Chapter 5). At that point, a simple Excel form has become a data source for business intelligence.

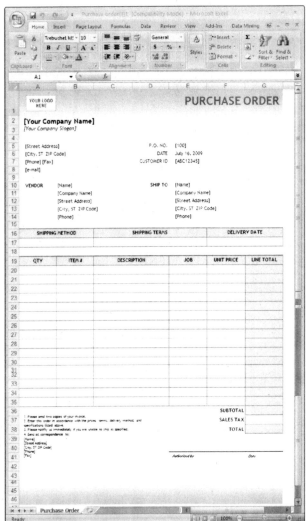

Figure 9-3:
A purchase order form in Microsoft Excel.

As powerful as Excel is at collecting data from people, it's equally powerful at collecting data from other computer systems. Excel has a Get External Data feature on its Data tab (see Figure 9-4) on the Ribbon. It's designed to connect easily to other computer systems and import data.

By using the Get External Data section, a user can collect data from Access databases, directly from Web sites, text documents, databases, cubes, XML data, and pretty much any other source that allows a standard database connection known as *ODBC* or *OLEDB* (for more information, see the "ODBC and OLEDB" sidebar in this section). Not shabby for an application that used to be sold as a tool for organizing recipes.

The Get External Data feature

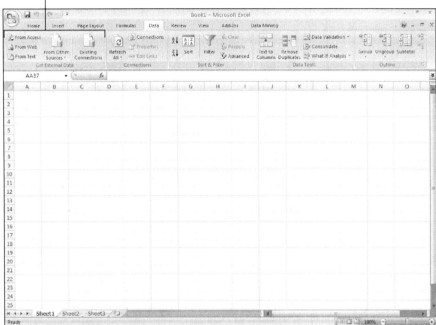

Figure 9-4:
The Get
External
Data section
of the Data
tab in Excel.

Microsoft Business Intelligence is, in essence, a range of features included in various Microsoft products — and each has its place in the data lifecycle. For a detailed look at which features of which programs fit the functional needs of your business at each stage of the data lifecycle, take a spin through Parts I and II of this book.

Getting Organized

Excel lives to organize data. An Excel document is subdivided into Sheets with tabs across the bottom. Each tab is its own spreadsheet; you can rename tabs and cross-reference other tabs. As you can see in Figure 9-5, this organization is simple and straightforward; it takes minimal time to organize data into groups, rename the tabs, and paste data into the spreadsheets. A Summary tab that links to other sheets and summarizes the data also helps with the organization and is easy to create. For small amounts of data, Excel is a great data organizational tool, but Excel documents tend to grow out of control as datasets become larger. At the enterprise level, they're like shambling mutants.

ODBC and OLEDB

Open DataBase Connectivity (ODBC) and Object Linking and Embedding, DataBase (OLEDB) are standards that define interfaces for accessing data. They emphasize connecting various Microsoft applications to a database (ODBC) and sharing the same programming objects among applications (OLEDB).

For example, imagine you write a software program that stores a bunch of data (that is, a database) in a computer. To do its job, your database program has to give people a way to access that data. Wouldn't it be great if someone could send a command such as `GetMyDataPlease(row 1)` and have your database program return the first row of the data, just because that person put "row 1" in the parentheses? Okay, suppose you build that capability into your database application. So far, so good. . . .

Then somebody else writes another database program that does the same data-storage job that yours does (uh-oh — competition!) — and uses pushy language for the same command: `GetMyDataNOW()`. Employees who've been using your database know the commands you specified, and use them to interact with the database; some may have used those commands in their own software programs (called *clients*) to access the data in the database.

Now suppose the boss decides he really *likes* the pushy new program, and he tells everyone

that the company is switching to the second database. That means all employees have to throw out their knowledge of the commands you wrote into your database program — and learn a brand new set of commands in order to interact with the new database. There is mass gnashing of teeth and a quiet epidemic of splitting headaches. How do you avoid this? With ODBC and OLEDB.

ODBC and OLEDB are sets of standards that define an *API*, or *Application Programming Interface*. These standards are the equivalent of the commands in the example above. Instead of the first database using the command `GetMyDataPlease()` and the second database using the command `GetMyDataNOW()` in order to return data, both database programs would use one command *defined by the standard*.

If both database programs in this example followed one of these standards, then the users would only have to know the commands specified in the standard. They wouldn't have to worry about how the software actually put the standards into practice. Fortunately, nearly every modern database program follows either the ODBC or the OLEDB standard — which means Excel can pull data from any of them.

Charts are a handy and powerful way to summarize and visualize data. Excel has a smorgasbord of charts and graphs available; Figure 9-5 shows a pie chart, a column chart on the Summary tab, and raw data on the Region 1 Data and Region 2 Data tabs. (For instructions on how to build charts and graphs, flip to the section "Charts and graphs," later in this chapter.

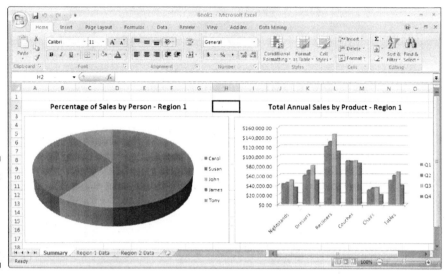

Figure 9-5:
Sales data organized and summarized in Excel.

As a consultant, I get to peer into many types of businesses throughout various industries; I'm always amazed at the amount of data people can keep organized with Excel. These rough-and-ready "databases" made of overstuffed Excel spreadsheets grow over the years — and begin to take on lives of their own. The massive amount of data spread across many sheets makes perfect sense to the users who've created and maintained them, but to a newcomer (or consultant) they seem downright overwhelming. This is a well-intentioned misuse of Excel — and it's detailed in the "Knowing the Limits of Excel" section, later in this chapter.

Show Me the Data! — Data Visualization

One of the most powerful features of Excel is that you can use it to create visualizations of your data — which is incredibly handy at the stage of the data lifecycle known as (wait for it) data visualization. As visual creatures, humans rely on what they see when they're making sense of the world. Hit 'em with charts, graphs, colors, and effects, and suddenly data starts to make all kinds of sense. Excel, well, *excels* at turning your data into visual components; this section details the features that do the job.

Conditional formatting

Excel provides a Conditional Formatting tool that bases its visualization of data on the contents a cell: If, for example, you have one cell showing the number of a product in inventory and you want the cell to turn red if inventory falls below 5 units, then you can use the Color Scales component of Conditional Formatting. It's a helpful capability when you're analyzing sales figures, profits and losses, daily totals, and so on. The Conditional Formatting tool hangs out on the Home tab of the Excel Ribbon.

When you're dealing with a large list of related numbers, you can apply conditional formatting to create a quick, at-a-glance view of the data — for example, using green or red to make your sales figures easier to see, and arrows pointing up, down, or across to show whether your product sales are trending up or down or staying flat. You can see a relative position of a number in a column because the whole column fills up with a color based on that position.

Conditional formatting has several main categories of uses:

- ✔ **Visualizing relationships using Data Bars:** In a set of numbers, it's often helpful to see how a particular number compares with other numbers in a large series of data points. The Data Bars feature fills a cell with a colored bar, the length of which shows the relation of the number in that cell to the other numbers in the dataset. Although you could use a pie chart or bar chart for this purpose, a simple set of bars that fill up the actual cells gives you not only the number but its position in the list of numbers — at a glance — which gets your point across quickly.

  Figure 9-6 shows the default colors for Data Bars (Navy, Green, Red, Yellow, Blue, and Purple). (Okay, they're shown here in black and white, but they're prettier on-screen. Just trust me.) You can customize Data Bars to reflect various aspects of your data by using the Managed Rules feature on the Conditional Formatting tab. Figure 9-7 shows an example of Data Bars in action.

  Managed Rules allows you to define your own custom rules using custom formulas. For example, if your gross revenue is in column A and your profit is in column B, you can create a formula to turn the row green if the profit is greater than a specified percentage of revenue or red if it is less.

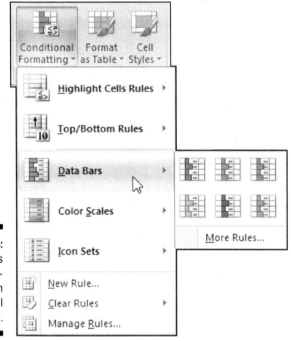

Figure 9-6:
Data Bars available with Conditional Formatting.

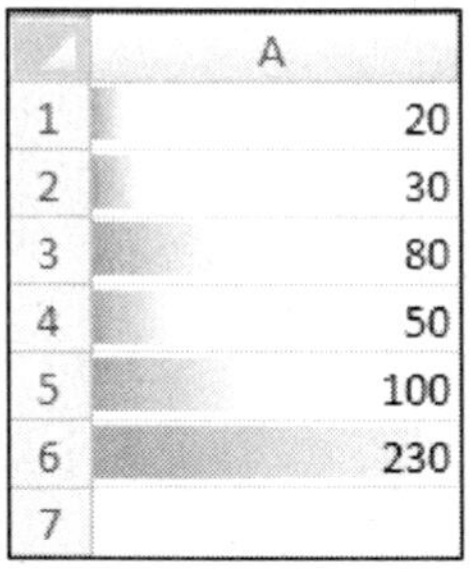

Figure 9-7:
Sample view of Data Bars in Conditional Formatting.

	A
1	20
2	30
3	80
4	50
5	100
6	230
7	

✔ **Visualizing problems using Color Scales:** You can use Color Scales (shown in Figure 9-8), to change the color of a cell in response to a particular condition that applies to the data it holds. The condition can be simple (say, if a number is greater than 50) or complex (if the cell holds a custom formula based on cells from other sheets and external files).

For example, if you're given a massive list of profit-and-loss calculations, the printout may look like a giant blob of numbers at first. If you turn all the cells green that contain positive (profit) numbers and turn the cells that contain negative (loss) numbers red, someone looking at the spreadsheet can see instantly if the green cells outnumber the red (or vice versa). Right away, even before the people at the meeting start slinging numbers, they can get a quick sense of whether sales results are generally positive or negative. Figure 9-9 shows an example of Color Scales in action.

✔ **Visualizing trends using Icon Sets:** Excel offers a number of icons that you can use to depict data trends. Some of the most commonly used icons are arrows and stoplights, but other icons take other forms — flags, circles with different phases darkened, check marks, and data bars that look like the network-signal bars on a cell phone. You can use the Conditional Formatting feature to display icons that point out various conditions — up to five — based on the data (as shown in Figure 9-10). Figure 9-11 shows Icon Sets in action.

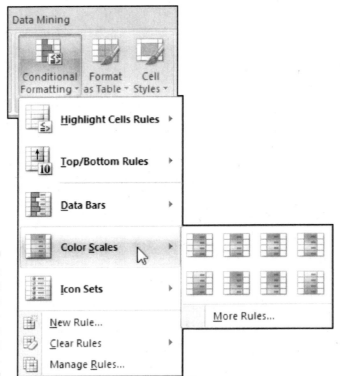

Figure 9-8:
Default
Color Scales
avail-
able with
Conditional
Formatting.

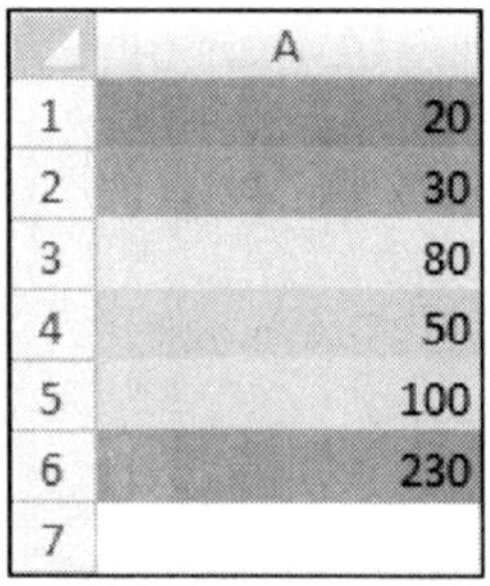

Figure 9-9:
Sample
view of
Color
Scales in
Conditional
Formatting.

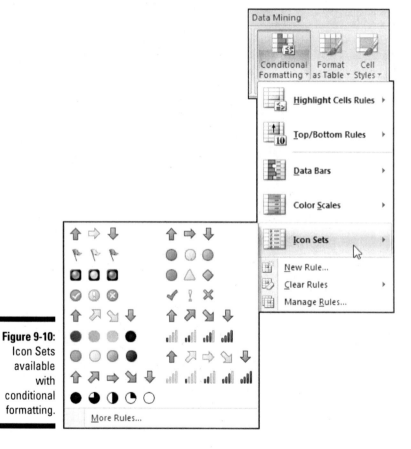

Figure 9-10:
Icon Sets
available
with
conditional
formatting.

Figure 9-11:
Sample
view of Icon
Sets used
for spotting
trends.

	A	B	C	D	E	F	G	H	I
1		Total Sales by Person By Quarter							
2		Q1	Q2		Q3		Q4		
3	Jane	$15,000	$21,000 ⬈		$27,000 ⬈		$37,000 ⬆		
4	John	$30,000	$28,000 ⬂		$30,000 ➡		$24,000 ⬇		
5	Tom	$25,000	$35,000 ⬆		$42,000 ⬈		$45,000 ➡		
6	Suzan	$45,000	$48,000 ➡		$44,000 ⬊		$40,000 ⬊		
7									

Here's a simple example of conditional formatting: It determines whether a number is greater than or less than 50 (hey, gotta start somewhere). The dataset contains three numbers: 40, 55, and 60. The exercise looks like this:

1. **Open Excel and enter the three numbers.**

   Type 40 in cell A1, 55 in cell A2, and 60 in cell A3.

2. **Highlight the dataset by clicking the left mouse button and dragging until all three cells containing the numbers in your Excel sheet are highlighted.**

3. **Make sure the Home tab is selected in the Ribbon at the top of the window and then select Conditional Formatting⇨Highlight Cells Rules⇨Greater Than (as shown in Figure 9-12).**

   The Greater Than dialog box appears.

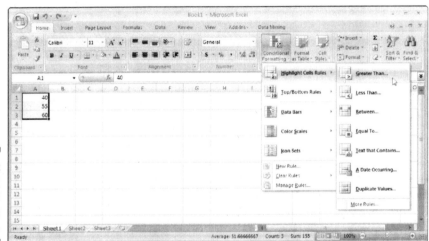

Figure 9-12:
Selecting
Conditional
Formatting
in Excel.

4. **You can type in a value or reference a different cell that is in the same spreadsheet, a different spreadsheet, or even a different Excel file.**

   For this example, type 50, choose Green Fill with Dark Green Text, and then click OK.

5. **Repeat Steps 3 and 4, but this time select Conditional Formatting⇨Highlight Cells Rules⇨ Less Than.**

   The Less Than dialog box appears.

6. **Type 50, choose Light Red Fill with Dark Red Text, and then click OK.**

   The result should look similar to Figure 9-13.

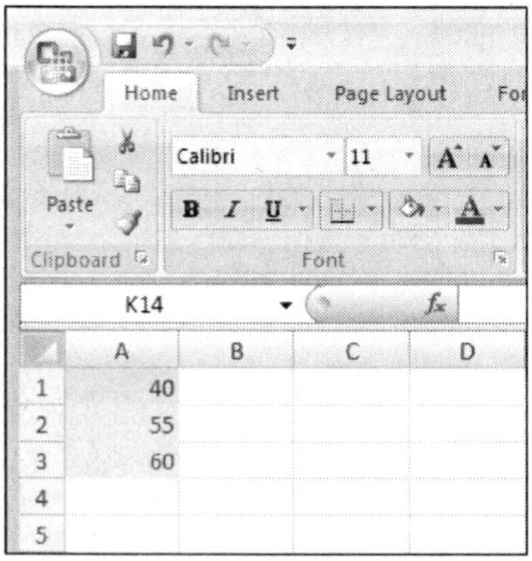

Figure 9-13:
Conditional
Formatting
with Greater
Than and
Less Than.

Charts and graphs

The charts and graphs that Excel offers for visualizing data are among my favorite aspects of Excel because (no surprise here) they look good — and the credit for a snazzy-looking chart rubs off on the presenter. These graphs and charts are simple to create, modify, manipulate, and transfer into other Microsoft applications (I simply use Excel to create a chart or graph and then insert it into a Word document or PowerPoint presentation). Charts and graphs are a traditional and easy-to understand method of visualizing data relating to sales, costs, production levels, inventory, forecasts, and other aspects of business.

The Charts section is on the Insert tab of the Excel Ribbon, as shown in Figure 9-14. If you're in a hurry and want to insert a chart quickly into your Excel document, no problem: Make sure you have a cell somewhere within your data selected (Excel will take a guess at your data — the alternative is to highlight all of your data set by clicking and dragging until your data are selected), choose a chart group from within this section, select the type of chart that works best for the presentation of your data, and then simply click the chart type. Excel inserts the Chart into your document.

The Insert tab

Figure 9-14:
The Chart
groups
available in
Excel.

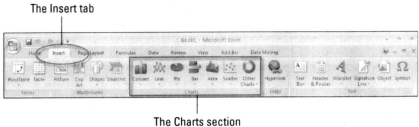

The Charts section

Use the drop-down feature for the chart type (Column, Line, Pie, Bar, Area, Scatter, and Other) on the Ribbon to quickly add a chart to your document. You can also view all of the available charts by clicking the small arrow in the bottom-right corner of the Charts group in the Ribbon. The arrow is pointing down and to the right, and when clicked it expands the full Insert Chart dialog that lists all of the possible charts available, as shown in Figure 9-15.

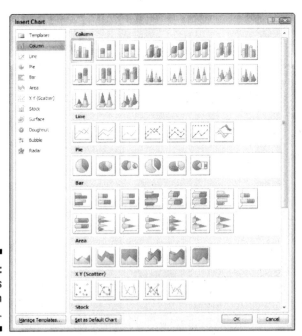

Figure 9-15:
The charts
available in
Excel.

Analyzing Data: Pivot on This and Pivot on That

One of the most widely-used and popular features for analyzing data in Excel is the PivotTable. A *PivotTable* allows users to aggregate data that has been collected in Excel into various groupings. These groupings can be rearranged instantly in order to view the data in different ways. Another popular feature in Excel is the *PivotChart,* which is a chart that's created from a PivotTable and used to see the data in a chart format.

Using Excel PivotTables

As an Excel feature, the PivotTable is an especially handy tool for aggregating data into groups — and for changing those groups and aggregations in real time: All you have to do is drag criteria around the screen, from row to column; there's no need to re-sort and re-sum your criteria; the PivotTable takes care of these calculations and adjustments automatically. Check out this simple example in order to get a handle on how a PivotTable works.

Suppose you have a small company with two stores and four products. Your products consist of regular honey, creamed honey, honey sticks, and honey gift baskets. Of course, this example is simplified, but it gives you a dataset that demonstrates exactly how a PivotTable works in Excel. The raw data are organized with a store location, product, and sales price, as shown in Figure 9-16.

Using a PivotTable, you can quickly analyze raw data in Excel (whether entered by hand or imported from a source database). To insert a PivotTable in Excel, follow these steps:

1. **Select a cell somewhere within the data.**

2. **When you've selected the cell you want, click the Insert tab in the Ribbon and choose PivotTable, as shown in Figure 9-17.**

   The Create PivotTable dialog box opens, offering a number of different options, including where to find the data you want analyzed and where to put your brand new PivotTable. Excel is smart enough to figure out where the data are because you've already selected a cell in the data region (back in Step 1) before inserting the PivotTable.

   You can also add data to Excel from an outside source by selecting Use An External Data Source.

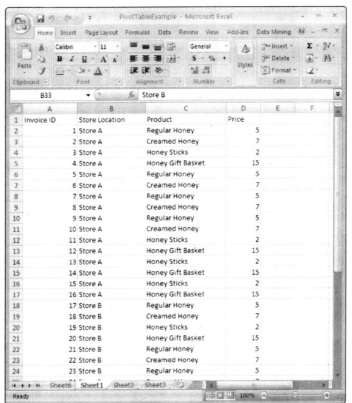

Figure 9-16:
Raw data in Excel.

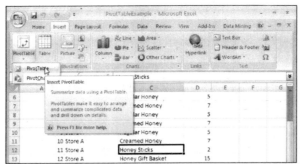

Figure 9-17:
Adding a PivotTable in Excel.

3. Indicate where you want the new PivotTable placed, as shown in Figure 9-18.

In this case, I prefer to put the PivotTable in a New Worksheet tab.

4. **Click OK.**

   Behold the new PivotTable — all nicely created and ready for analysis, as shown in Figure 9-19.

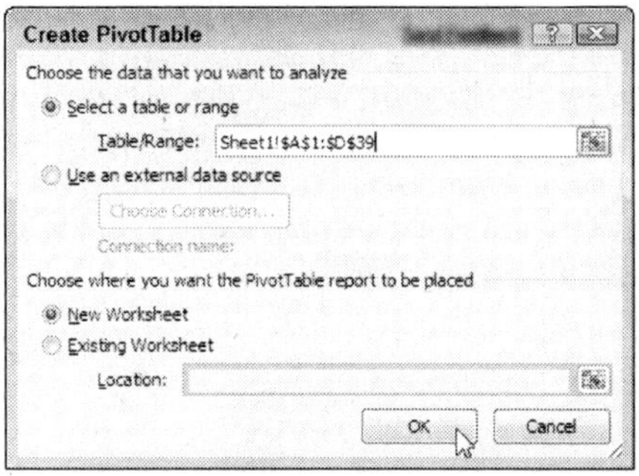

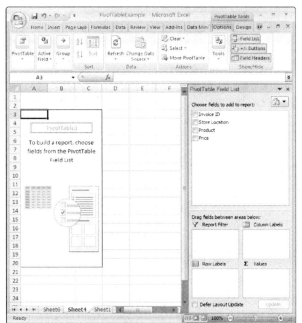

Figure 9-18: The Create PivotTable dialog.

Figure 9-19: A newly created PivotTable.

The PivotTable starts with a placeholder image in the main screen on the left side of the window and the PivotTable Field List on the right side. The Field List shows the available fields at the top and four boxes on the bottom. If you drag the fields down into the boxes, the PivotTable is updated automatically to reflect the new organization of the data.

If you want to check the results, just drag various fields into different boxes. Working with the example of the honey company in Figure 9-20, I've placed the Price field in the Values box to sum up prices (the field you place in the Values box should be numeric data so the values can be summed); I've also put the Store Location field in the Columns box, and the Product field in the Row Labels box. Note that the default behavior of dragging a numeric value to the Values box is to sum the values. You can also perform other calculations by clicking the down arrow on the field within the Values box and choosing Value Field Settings. The possible summaries include Sum, Count, Average, Max, Min, Product, Count Numbers, Standard Deviation (against a sample size or against the entire data population), and Variance (also against a sample size or against the entire population).

Figure 9-20:
A PivotTable
in Excel.

You can do a quick slice-and-dice of a dataset by dragging the fields to different columns and rows and changing the data you want summarized. If there are multiple fields in the row column, the data will be grouped according to its position in the Row Labels box. For example, starting from Figure 9-20, you may want to alter the groupings and add a new pivot point called SalesPerson. First, you would need to import or enter the SalesPerson column and then you could continue and expand your analysis. After you have a SalesPerson field, you can drag it to the Row Labels box. Having multiple columns in the same Row Labels box simply adds another grouping.

A PivotTable's power over data is easy to see, even in this simple example.

PivotChart

A PivotChart is (as you may expect) an Excel chart created from a PivotTable. Okay, but why do that? Well, first you use the PivotTable to massage and analyze your data, and then you create a PivotChart to show all that well-analyzed data in a chart format.

After you've inserted a PivotChart into your Excel spreadsheet, you get a little extra magic as a bonus: When you update the PivotTable, you also update the chart that's based on it — automatically. You can also change the chart type on the fly, try various charting visualizations, and find the one that works best. Follow these steps to create a PivotChart (using the honey-company example from the previous section):

1. **Select a cell within the PivotTable, and then click the PivotTable Tools tab in the Excel Ribbon.**

2. **With the PivotTable Ribbon displayed, click the PivotChart button, as shown in Figure 9-21.**

   The PivotChart button displays a list of the chart types you can use.

The PivotTable Tools

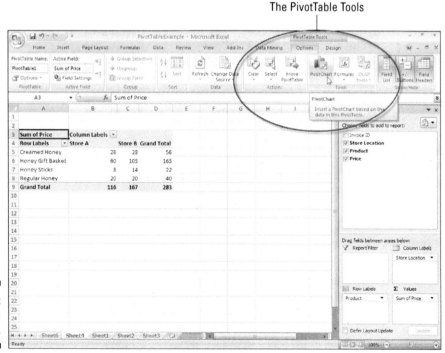

Figure 9-21: Selecting a PivotChart.

3. **For this example, select a simple 3D Column chart.**

   The chart is inserted in the middle of the spreadsheet, but you can move it around to fit nicely on the screen.

4. **With the PivotTable and PivotChart on-screen, play with the data a bit, using the filter menu — or manipulate the data by dragging and dropping fields in the Row Labels and Column Labels boxes.**

   Figure 9-22 shows a typical result. Notice that Store B sells noticeably more Honey Gift Baskets than Store A. Armed with knowledge like this, you can track down the source of the difference.

   The PivotTable chart type can be changed with a few simple clicks. Click PivotChart Tools tab in the Excel Ribbon and then click the Change Chart Type button. Keep trying different chart types until you find the one you want.

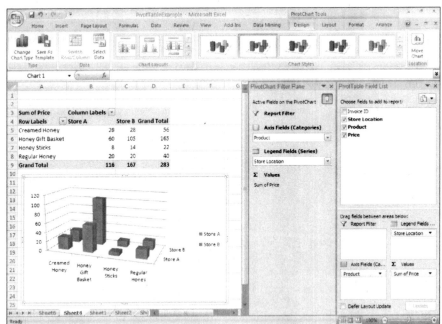

Figure 9-22:
A PivotTable and PivotChart in Excel.

The PivotTable and PivotChart are especially powerful and easy-to-use tools for that purpose.

Excel brought on even more powers of analysis: It helps you connect to and analyze OLAP data cubes (those standard BI fixtures I describe in Chapter 4).

A data cube works much like a PivotTable, but it's stored in SQL Server Analysis Services (SSAS). Cubes generally focus on some form of numeric data that can be grouped by different criteria (called *dimensions* in database-speak). For example, the numeric data could be sales figures, and four possible dimensions could be

- Time (year, month, week, day)
- Salesperson
- Location of sale
- Item sold

A cube built on these criteria could take the total sales figures and slice and dice them using any combination of these dimensions — say, how many Honey Gift Baskets did Carl sell, or how many were sold in the Tucson store last summer (when the killer bees were out)? Dimensions can include any criteria for which data are available.

Of course, to make data available in the cube, you have to have some BI apparatus in place — in particular, the tools to generate data from a business process, and then collect and organize the data. If data are generated in response to a specific criterion (say, a specific item sold), then you can apply that criterion at every stage of the data lifecycle — and it can become a dimension of the cube.

Data Mining with Excel

Excel's capabilities make it a powerful data tool in its own right, but its popularity provides an additional advantage: Because Excel is already widely used throughout the business world, it's already familiar to a legion of users — so Microsoft has given them some handy data-mining buttons that call on the power of SQL Server Analysis Services (SSAS). *Data mining* (as described in Chapter 7) uses algorithms to dig in to and sift through data in bulk amounts, looking for the nuggets of information that give businesses insight and advantages over their competition.

Using Excel to boss SSAS

(Hey, it's a lot more useful than sassing the boss.) The engine that runs the core Microsoft Data Mining algorithms is built in to SQL Server Analysis

Services (SSAS). Microsoft has released a Data Mining Add-In for Excel that grants the humble spreadsheet formidable data-mining powers (Chapter 7 describes those, including the various available algorithms and what they accomplish).

No need to break out the chalk and blackboard; you can make ready use of these algorithms from within Excel. The process works like this: Excel runs on your desktop, and the Data Mining Engine (part of SQL Server Analysis Services) runs on a server somewhere in a data center. Your computer and the server in the data center communicate with each other using the network. Excel can connect to that server as a client and use the power of the SSAS algorithms that hang out on the server.

Of course, before you can use Excel to unleash SSAS data-mining capabilities, you have to install the Microsoft SQL Server 2008 Data Mining Add-In for Microsoft Office. (Details, details.)

Instructions for downloading and installing the Microsoft SQL Server 2008 Data Mining Add-In for Microsoft Office can be found at

```
www.microsoft.com/downloads/details.
          aspx?FamilyId=896A493A-2502-4795-94AE-
          E00632BA6DE7&displaylang=en.
```

It's worth the hassle: The Add-In is what gives Excel the superpowers to perform data mining, as described in Table 9-2. Note that the Add-In is also used for Office Visio as described in the table.

Table 9-2	Data Mining Add-In Functionality
Feature	**Description**
Table Analysis Tools for Excel	Provides tasks that use the data-mining features of SQL Server 2008 on spreadsheet data.
Data Mining Client for Excel	Provides a client application that you run from within Excel to create, test, explore, and manage data-mining models (for more about those, see Chapter 7).
Data Mining Templates for Visio	Gives you a way to use Microsoft Visio from within Excel to create and share data-mining models.

When the Data Mining Add-In is installed, a new tab (see Figure 9-23) appears and makes the new capabilities available on the Excel Ribbon.

The new Data Mining tab

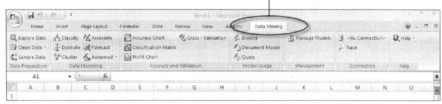

Figure 9-23:
Here's what data-mining functionality looks like in Excel.

To do its magic, the Data Mining Add-In requires an active connection to the SSAS server. You can ask your database administrator for the proper configuration information or you can download and install a trial version on your local desktop (but let your IT folks know if you do that — trust me, they'd want to know). When you open Excel with the Data Mining Add-In already installed, the add-in immediately demands SSAS access; you're prompted to take one of these actions:

- ✔ Install a trial version of SSAS. (Just remember, you'll have to either buy the thing or uninstall it later.)

- ✔ Connect to an SSAS instance that you administer (which is fine if you're the Big Kahuna of the company database).

- ✔ Connect to an SSAS instance that your kindly database administrator has configured for you.

Microsoft also provides a sample Excel document, complete with sample data, to use while you're trying the Data Mining Add-In. You can access this Excel spreadsheet at the following location:

```
Start > All Programs > Microsoft SQL Server 2008 Add-ins > Sample Excel Data
```

Figure 9-24 illustrates the Forecasting feature of the Data Mining Add-In, using the Sample Excel Data.

If you're trying to use the Data Mining Add-In for its namesake purpose and an error message pops up to tell you that a default database doesn't exist, then *somebody* forgot to run through the Configuration Wizard to set up the Data Mining Add-In. You can remedy this woeful situation by accessing the Wizard: Click the Data Mining tab in the Excel Ribbon and then select Help⇨Getting Started.

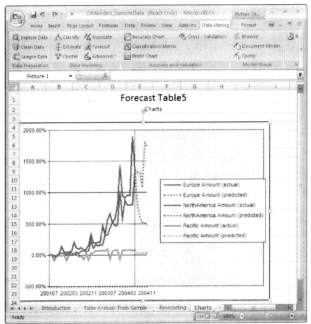

Figure 9-24:
Microsoft
Data Mining
in Excel —
forecasting
functionality.

Microsoft has compiled an online resource page dedicated to data mining — complete with content such as videos, whitepapers, articles, overviews, and links (no hard hats or pickaxes, though). You can find it at

    www.microsoft.com/sqlserver/2008/en/us/data-mining.aspx.

I've found the videos on data mining especially helpful. Check out the videos at

    www.microsoft.com/sqlserver/2008/en/us/data-mining-addins.aspx.

Pulling cube data for PivotTables and PivotCharts

Excel has grown to be a true OnLine Analytical Processing (OLAP) analysis tool and has the ability to connect to OLAP cubes and pull data back for analysis. (The Microsoft OLAP engine — SQL Server Analysis Services — is covered in greater depth in Chapter 8.) Excel has an advantage over other OLAP tools because many people have experience with Excel. Excel users can easily expand into the OLAP analysis functionality.

SQL Server Analysis Services (SSAS), a component of SQL Server, is the tool Microsoft offers for working with OLAP cubes. Using the Data Mining Add-In, Excel can connect to these data cubes and either browse them (by acting as a client) or pull in data for analysis within Excel.

After you've pulled some data into Excel (or connected to an OLAP cube located on the SSAS server), you can enter the newly acquired data into PivotTables and PivotCharts for analysis and visualization. The whole process isn't as difficult as it sounds.

Microsoft provides a practice OLAP cube that administrators can install on a test server as a resource for samples, tutorials, and trying SSAS capabilities in Excel. The cube contains data about a fictitious company called Adventure Works.

For the example in this section, I've installed the sample Adventure Works databases and Analysis Services cubes on a handy SSAS server to demonstrate how you can work with those cubes in Excel. More about that in a minute.

If you're feeling brave and are already familiar with administering SQL Server, you can install the samples yourself. You can find all the information you need for the samples at

```
http://msftdbprodsamples.codeplex.com/
```

Another option is to send this link to your administrator and cajole that kindly person into getting you up and running with the samples on a test server that's already in place.

Your database administrator may already have a practice Analysis Services cube in place (it can't hurt to ask). You can connect directly to the cube provided by your administrator or just follow along with our example to test-drive the combination of Excel and SSAS.

In this example, I'm naming my server MSBIFD, an abbreviation for *Microsoft Business Intelligence For Dummies* (Wiley Publishing, Inc.). The first thing to do to start exploring the data in the cube, of course, is to set up the connection the Analysis Services cube. With Excel open, follow these steps (you may want to read them first and check with your database administrator before jumping in):

1. **Select the Data tab from the Excel Ribbon.**

2. **In the Get External Data section, click the From Other Sources button in the Get External Data section.**

3. Select the From Analysis Services option from the drop-down list, as shown in Figure 9-25.

The Data Connection Wizard opens.

The Data tab

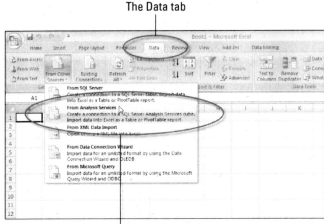

Figure 9-25:
Selecting the Analysis Services option for external connection.

The From Analysis Services option

4. Enter the connection information in the Connect to Database Server dialog box that appears and click Next.

The connection information can be provided to you by your database administrator. In this example, my server name is `ForDummies-PC` — but you can simply use a "." (period) if you have SSAS running on your local machine — and I'm using a credential that has permissions to connect to the local sample database I installed, as shown in Figure 9-26.

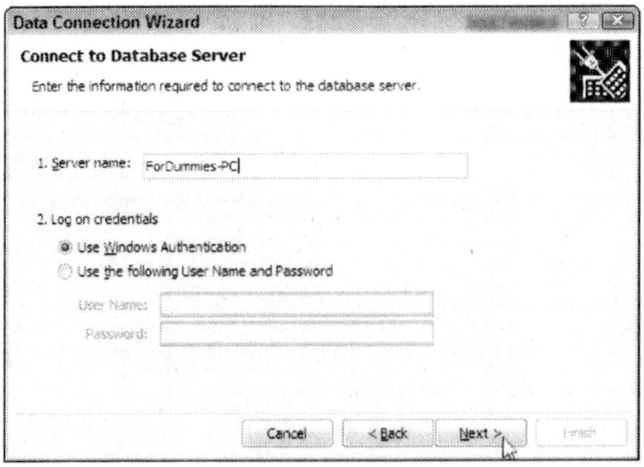

Figure 9-26:
The Connect to Database Server screen.

The Select Database and Table dialog box opens and asks you to choose a cube.

5. **Enter the name of your chosen cube if you know it; if you don't know the name, check with your database administrator. Click Next after selecting the cube you want to use.**

    In this example, I chose the sample cube that Microsoft provides that contains information about the Adventure Works company, as shown in Figure 9-27.

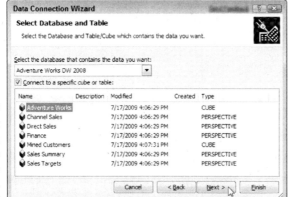

Figure 9-27:
Selecting
the
Adventure
Works cube.

6. **In the Save Data Connection File and Finish dialog box, enter the location to save the Data Connection file and then make some configuration settings, as shown in Figure 9-28.**

    The Data Connection file is a file with the extension .odc, which stands for Office Data Connection. Think of an ODC file as a file that stores all of the connection information to a data source or server. The advantage of the ODC file is that should you go to test additional functionality against the data source you are setting up, you simply have to point to the ODC file instead of walking through the wizard and inputting all of the connection fields. The other advantage is that if the connection information changes, you only have to update the connection information in the ODC file instead of all the other Excel files that use it for their connection information.

7. **Complete the configuration by clicking Finish.**

    The connection to the SSAS cube is now complete; a dialog box asks what you want done with the connection. You can choose to create a PivotTable, create a PivotTable and a PivotChart, or to do nothing with the connection.

Figure 9-28:
Here's
the Data
Connection
file and the
final con-
figuration.

8. **Choose to create a PivotTable and PivotChart and click OK.**

   All the data in the cube is now available for analysis.

9. **Drag Measures and Dimensions down into the PivotTable boxes.**

   Doing so starts a real-time aggregate analysis on the cube data. Figure 9-29 shows an example of this analysis on the sample cube.

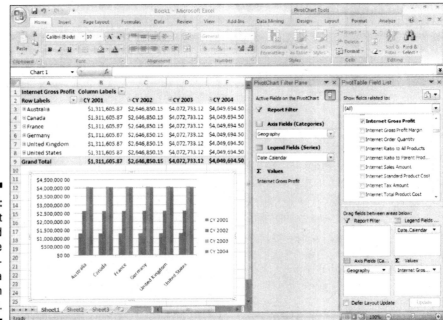

Figure 9-29:
A PivotChart
and
PivotTable
using real-
time data
from an
SSAS cube.

As demonstrated here, Excel combines the capability to collect data with the power to analyze data — especially when working in tandem with SSAS. No wonder it dominates the spreadsheet software market.

Keeping Score with the Excel Scorecard

To be sure, charts and graphs can be an attractive way to visualize data (as in the "Show Me the Data! — Data Visualization" section earlier in this chapter) — and you can apply conditional formatting (including Data Bars, Color Scales, and Icon Sets) to your heart's content, but why stop there? Often the company brass wants a hard-hitting summary of the data — or at least a cogent report — to go along with the pretty pictures. Fortunately, you can use these Excel visualization features to build summary reports based on Key Performance Indicators (KPI) — the business metrics that show how well a business is performing (Chapter 6 tells you more about KPIs). But you can go a step farther by using Excel to record and group those KPIs into a *scorecard* (like a report card when you were in school, but for business).

Although this section explores building Excel Scorecards, you should know that this task is often resource-intensive and time-consuming. The key to an Excel Scorecard is the data, and collecting and organizing that data are a lot of work. Fortunately, when you've created Scorecards that tell you what you need to know, you can use additional Microsoft tools to automate much of the work involved in keeping your Scorecards up to date. Chief among these tools are SQL Server, PerformancePoint Services, and SharePoint.

PerformancePoint Services is the tool you use to build Scorecards in SharePoint. It used to be a separate product; now it's become a feature of SharePoint — where it goes by the name PerformancePoint Services for SharePoint.

Using Excel to create a Scorecard is relatively straightforward. The key to the whole process is to fully understand how the data fits into your business and how it should be visualized. When you have that under your belt, Excel makes it easy to add visualizations and summaries that provide quick snapshots of the data for the harried decision-makers (you know — the ones who always joke about "my copious free time"). The catch: I've found it's often difficult to choose the best visualization for a particular problem. Excel helps by offering a range of graph and chart types; you can pick one and then simply change the chart type, option by option, trying visualizations until you find one that makes sense. I usually move quickly through types and styles of charts until one I like jumps out at me.

I created a simple sample Scorecard (shown in Figure 9-30) that uses many of the different visualizations available in Excel:

 ✔ The Gross Sales by Country section uses Icon Sets to show trending between quarters.

✔ Data Bars show the relative strength of each region.

✔ The Net Profit by Country section uses Color Scales to show the relative profit margin compared with other regions.

✔ Each region has a Pie Chart that shows Gross Sales and Net Profit.

✔ At the bottom of the Scorecard, a three-dimensional chart shows Gross Sales and Net Profit over the last decade, which is useful for quickly visualizing long-term trends.

As you can see in Figure 9-30, these elements can be combined in many different ways. The key to making Scorecards is (first) to determine the most important metrics to track (your KPIs will help you there) and then to pull the data together into visualizations.

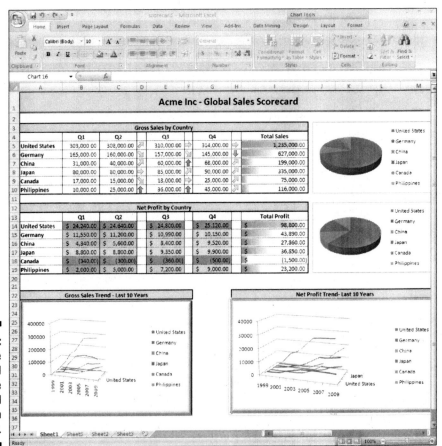

Figure 9-30: A sample Scorecard making use of Excel visualization functionality.

Knowing the Limits of Excel

People used Excel to manage their businesses long before business intelligence exploded into corporate practice and vocabulary. As BI tools go, Excel was early on the scene, started out handy, and got downright indispensable. As people (and their businesses) became more comfortable with digital data, however, they started using Excel as if it were the only tool in the BI toolbox — and it isn't. Some of the uses those folks came up with were clever and appropriate. Some were . . . problematic.

It turns out that although you can use Excel at every stage in the data lifecycle (see the Data Lifecycle table earlier in this chapter), it's still a spreadsheet at heart. If you use it on a scale much larger than one-user-on-one-desktop, problems emerge. Giant spreadsheets, crammed with row upon row of data and quirky, user-created functions, start wandering around the business and mutating. Their creators, all too often, move on; maintaining and updating the beasts can too easily become nightmarish.

To keep the strengths of Excel but to fit it into the BI arsenal as a more efficient tool, Microsoft developed a way to use Excel with SharePoint. It's a SharePoint feature called Excel Services. You can use it to post Excel documents to SharePoint sites, which makes them accessible through a Web browser. That takes care of the scalability. With SharePoint 2010 Microsoft has continued to advance Excel Services, which provides a richer experience (and more like interacting with Excel on your local desktop) through the Web. In addition PowerPivot, a feature of Excel 2010 and SharePoint 2010, allows power users to develop Excel spreadsheets that contain millions upon millions of rows of data. This massive amount of data is stored within the Excel document, which makes analysis of super large amounts of data as straightforward as it is to analyze smaller amounts of data in previous versions of Excel.

For now, Excel's scalability continues to improve as Microsoft teams it up with other BI tools:

- You can use Excel as a client with SQL Server Analysis Services (SSAS), which is built for enormous amounts of data.
- Although Excel's native capabilities may not provide the larger-scale analyses your business may need, you can connect Excel to server-based systems and continue to use all the Excel features that you're comfortable with, and tap in to the power of the server systems in the data center when you need the extra horsepower.

As with many things in life, Excel's greatest strengths can also be its greatest weaknesses. Its ease of use is one surprising example, as recounted in the accompanying sidebar, "Dodging the bus."

Dodging the bus

Excel is easy to get started with, but spreadsheets can quickly take on a life of their own — especially if someone comes up with a *really useful* one. The more it's used, the higher its *bus factor* — that is, how difficult it would be to re-create (or how difficult it would be to explain to a new user) if its creator were hit by a bus. What the business needs is a low bus factor — if someone new comes into a position, the new hire should be able to take over with relative ease. A monster spreadsheet — almost inevitably — carries a high bus factor; if its creator is nearly impossible to replace, the monster will cause fits of agony for a replacement. The complexity of a monster spreadsheet becomes overwhelming; often the person(s) who built the creature didn't document how it was developed, and may not recall (or even know) how it works.

And then there's the problem of the monster's mutant offspring. Because Microsoft Excel is already installed on many PCs in business

organizations — and a spreadsheet is a self-contained file that can easily be e-mailed around with a couple of mouse clicks — a monster spreadsheet zips around an organization like a rumor through a high school. People fiddle with different aspects of the formulas and functions in the document and e-mail it on. Many different versions, all working differently from each other, start to crop up and zip around. This chain spirals out of control. Pretty soon the original data that was pulled from the database loses its context (if you can even be sure it's the same data). It works like the game of "Telephone" — kids sit in a circle, someone whispers a secret to the next kid, who follows suit, as does the next kid, until the secret has passed around the entire circle — and comes back to the starting point changed in bizarre ways. That sort of thing is fun at a party; in a business, it's trouble in the making. Even if the spreadsheet's original creator manages to dodge the bus.

To limit the number of monsters roaming around the business, Microsoft provides an Information Rights Management feature in Excel: Document creators can restrict access to the documents they create and limit what other users can do to the poor creatures. Excel users can (for example) limit who can read the document, restrict the document from being copied or printed, and also set an expiration date for the document. The catch: This feature only works if it's fully adopted and used. That means setting up corporate policy and training that uses this feature and makes sure everyone knows how to use it.

Traditionally Excel could handle a mere 65,000 rows of data. Excel put that number up to just more than 1,000,000 rows of data in Excel 2007 and has now increased it to as many as a hundred million with Excel 2010 and PowerPivot. These numbers may sound huge, but they're dwarfed by the number of records that a typical corporation may generate. As a result, Excel has become more like a SWAT weapon for data: A business user may pull out a specific piece of information from the massive (billions upon billions of records) data store and run an analysis in Excel.

Excel documents are easy to manipulate and update by nature. If data from a server-based system are modified and e-mailed, the data loses its context; suddenly nobody's quite sure what the "real" (and reliable) version of the data is. By using Excel as the client to the OLAP server (SQL Server Analysis Services), you help to ensure that there's one source for correct data — the monsters can go away, the villagers can put away the torches, and everyone can get on with the business.

Looking at the Future of Excel

Microsoft has introduced new capabilities that help connect the modern information worker to advanced BI systems: Excel Services, part of SharePoint Server, allows companies to put Excel sheets on the Web. The actual Excel documents are stored in SharePoint Document Libraries and have all the features of SharePoint — security, versioning, check-in and check-out, and central backups, you name it — and when properly configured, they meet the strict new regulatory data-retention standards.

I discuss SharePoint in greater detail in Chapter 10, but for now, know that a Document Library is a SharePoint feature that serves as a sort of digital filing cabinet; it's a place to which you can upload your documents and control certain aspects of it, such as who gets to view and edit them. No monsters here.

In addition to publishing documents on the Web, Excel Services also has a Web service (part of the SharePoint Web services) that programmers can use to interact with Excel documents uploaded to SharePoint sites. If the data that a developer needs is contained in such an Excel document, access is entirely possible (given the system administrator's OK).

A *Web service* provides an interface for programmers to interact with in their programs. For example, the Excel Services Web service has procedures that programmers call from within their own programs when they want those programs to interact with Excel documents stored in SharePoint. The programs can run from any computer and just need to be able to contact the computer that contains the Web service; it's much like browsing the Internet. When you go to www.microsoft.com, for example, your computer contacts the computers that contain the content you're looking for — and your local Web browser displays the result.

Chapter 10

SharePoint Shines

In This Chapter

▶ Understanding SharePoint

▶ Knowing how SharePoint delivers business intelligence

▶ Setting free human BI with SharePoint

▶ Discovering what's new in SharePoint 2010

I'm a great believer that any tool that enhances communication has profound effects in terms of how people can learn from each other, and how they can achieve the kind of freedoms that they're interested in.

— Bill Gates

Microsoft has positioned SharePoint as the premier software product for business communication and collaboration; it's designed for the networked enterprise and for the Web. Business intelligence (BI) is about using that connectivity to run your business in the most efficient and effective manner possible. Information and data come from all aspects of a business, and collaboration and communication are key components to helping a business use the information and data it gathers. The core BI system that SQL Server provides is accessible through SharePoint — which allows everyone in an entire organization to communicate and collaborate, regardless of where team members are in the world.

As BI and collaboration continue to grow as hot topics, SharePoint has become one of the most successful products Microsoft has ever produced. But it's also a complex product with many valuable features and functions; those end up combined in so many ways that people think of SharePoint as just the feature set they're most familiar with using — and there's a lot more to it, as this chapter shows.

Getting to Know SharePoint

A recent Microsoft marketing campaign touts its business software products as People-Ready — emphasizing two core products: SQL Server and SharePoint. Whether gathering facts, digging for answers with data mining, or making communication, collaboration, and content management more efficient, Microsoft BI capabilities seek to be as usable as they are powerful. Increasingly, a modern company relies on a global workforce to stay competitive, and that means empowering its people — in this case, with SQL Server and SharePoint.

Business can no longer maintain a top-down control structure that assumes people are isolated and sitting around waiting for their next order. With the emergence of social networking sites such as Facebook, Twitter, and Linked-In, people are connected as never before — why not do the same in the workplace? That's where SharePoint comes in: It eases communication, collaboration, and document management by giving companies the means to ensure that their employees are connected — to each other, to the content that lives within the organization, and to each other's ideas, in a secured and control corporate environment.

Sharing knowledge has always been critical to a successful business — especially if a global organization is to take full advantage of its far-flung offices. Communication has to happen seamlessly among geographic locations that can span continents; an engineer in Seattle may have to connect easily with a developer in the Philippines.

Microsoft isn't the only company to recognize the importance of communication, collaboration, and content management in running an intelligent business. (Recently, Oracle purchased Stellent, IBM has FileNet, and EMC^2 has Documentum.) As other software companies rush to bring products that increase connectivity throughout an organization, however, the clear winner is still SharePoint.

What exactly is SharePoint?

Microsoft highlights these defining characteristics of SharePoint:

- SharePoint Server is a suite of integrated server capabilities. In essence, if you install SharePoint on your server, you give it a new range of information-wrangling powers that work together.

- SharePoint manages content (your business information) and provides enterprise-wide search capabilities. Wherever the needed information is in your organization, SharePoint can find it, make it usable, and keep it secure.

- SharePoint, when used to full advantage, accelerates business processes that require collaboration by making communication easier (and information easier to share) across departmental boundaries.

✔ SharePoint can help improve the administration of your company server, extend existing software applications with server-based capabilities, and help a wide range of software and hardware play well (and work well) together.

To get a handle on SharePoint, start from the bottom and work up through its components (which you can see in Figure 10-1).

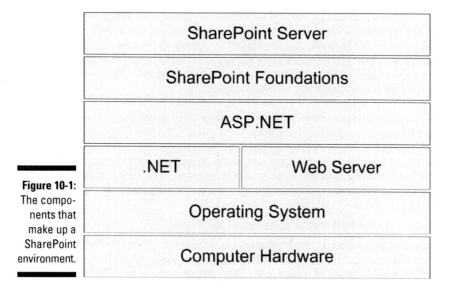

| SharePoint Server |
| SharePoint Foundations |
| ASP.NET |
| .NET | Web Server |
| Operating System |
| Computer Hardware |

Figure 10-1:
The components that make up a SharePoint environment.

Starting with the roots — computer hardware

Every computer system starts with physical components — central processing unit (CPU), memory, a hard drive, power supply, and motherboard. A computer can either be assembled in one of two ways: You can buy all of the individual pieces and put them together yourself or you can purchase an already-assembled computer from a vendor that specializes in building them, such as HP, Dell, and IBM. What this means to a BI system is that a range of components from various makers and vendors have to work together without compatibility hassles.

A new trend that you may have heard about involves virtual computers. A *virtual computer* is a self-contained computer operating system running within a host computer. The host computer is responsible for interacting with the actual hardware. The virtual computer, also called the *guest computer*, runs just like a normal computer but instead of interacting directly with the hardware it interacts with the host computer. There's always only one host computer that interacts with the hardware; however, you can have multiple guest computers all performing different server functions. In essence, what virtualization does is provide the ability for an entire operating system (such as Windows 7 or Windows Server) to run as an application within the host operating system.

Software that talks to the hardware — the operating system

The software that's makes all the hardware components actually do something — the *operating system* (OS) — usually comes in two major versions — one for end users (client) and one for the organization's network (server). In the Microsoft world, both OSs are called *Windows*. Windows 7 is the latest client OS and Windows Server 2008 R2 is the latest server OS. Note that the R2 means Release 2. The previous version of the Windows Server OS was called Windows Server 2008, without the R2.

If you're going to run server software such as SQL Server and SharePoint, you need to have the appropriate version of Windows Server OS installed on your server computer(s). Normally end users throughout the organization have the client OS running on desktop or laptop computers. All those personal computers have to connect to the server computers (running somewhere in a data center) in order to interact with the server software.

Software frameworks and servers — .NET and IIS

The .NET software framework runs on the Windows OS (both client and server versions) and keeps the various hardware components on speaking terms with each other. (I discuss the .NET framework — and its role in maintaining compatibility — in more detail in Chapter 11.)

Also running on the Windows Server OS is the Microsoft Web server called *Internet Information Services* (IIS).

In nearly any discussion of corporate networking, you'll hear the term *server* used to describe both hardware (the server computer) and software (the server operating system that tells the hardware what to do). True, a computer running a server operating system *is* a server, but so is the operating system itself (a computer can't function as a server without a server OS)— and (are you ready for this?) so is the software designed to work with a server OS. They're all called "server." (It's like saying, "This is my brother Darrell, this is my *other* brother Darrell, and this is *his* brother Darrell." Only worse.) But all sanity is not lost; get a grip and hang on for this example:

 ✔ Windows Server 2008 R2 is an operating system designed to run specialized software optimally — on a server computer.

> ✔ The networked computer on which you install the Windows Server OS is your server computer. Usually server computers are high-capacity and high-performance machines designed and built for that job.
>
> ✔ Server software applications act like short-order cooks and waiters: They serve up information to client computers in the form of Web pages, ftp sites, or e-mail communications. SQL Server and SharePoint Server are such applications.

Put those three aspects together, and you have a functioning server; just be careful which aspect of it you're talking about. And here's where the function of a server can help dispel the confusion of the term: What a server *does* is provide a consistent place where the network's users can access data. Because data can play many roles, servers can specialize accordingly — as (say) a database server, file server, or content-management server.

A computer language for the Web — ASP.NET

ASP.NET is an extension of the .NET software framework and is specialized to build Web applications (including custom Web pages) to run on (be served up by) the IIS Web server (Microsoft's Web server). ASP.NET is used to build custom Web pages, often using programming languages such as C#.NET or VB.NET. For more information about .NET and programming languages check out Chapter 11.

The first step into the SharePoint world — SharePoint Foundation

ASP.NET commands are what run SharePoint Foundation, previously known as Windows SharePoint Services (WSS), a basic set of software features that demonstrate some vital SharePoint capabilities. SharePoint Foundation is essentially a "lite", or base, version of SharePoint: It provides some collaboration and communications features (such as lists and document libraries) that developers can build into custom applications and Web sites. Because the SharePoint Foundation is built on the ASP.NET framework (an extension of .NET), it provides endless opportunities for customizing applications. SharePoint Foundation, however, doesn't offer powerful enough functionality to pinch-hit for industrial-strength SharePoint if an organization is large and complex. (But then, that's what the Enterprise edition of SharePoint is for, as detailed in the next section.)

A finished product — SharePoint Server

Microsoft used SharePoint Foundation as a solid foundation and then built SharePoint Server. The goal was to create a software product that could solve business problems with its built-in features, cutting down on time-intensive (and expensive) customizing of software.

As a full-featured version of SharePoint, SharePoint Server is designed as a large-scale, enterprise-level BI tool: Your organization can use it for content management, communication, collaboration, setting up portals, doing enterprise-wide searches for specific information, and the documentation of business processes (even including the design of forms).

Understanding the versions and editions of SharePoint

SharePoint can be broken down into versions and editions. A version is a release of the product that usually coincides with a date. For example, the previous version of SharePoint was released in 2007, and the latest version of SharePoint is being released in 2010. Each version is also segmented into two primary editions. The first is a "free" edition of SharePoint that comes along with the Windows Server operating system. The second edition is a deluxe edition that is purchased separately.

The previous version of SharePoint consisted of Windows SharePoint Services (WSS) 3.0 — free edition — and Microsoft Office SharePoint Server (MOSS) 2007 — deluxe edition. The next version of SharePoint consists of SharePoint Foundation 2010 (the successor to WSS) and SharePoint Server 2010 (the successor to MOSS 2007). One great aspect of the marketing terminology shift is that Microsoft actually simplified the product terminology! Now instead of the two major editions of SharePoint being called WSS and MOSS — do you remember what they mean? — the two SharePoint editions are simply called SharePoint Foundation and SharePoint Server. Easy enough to remember.

You may wonder why there isn't just *one* SharePoint edition. Here's the short answer: Because no two businesses are exactly the same in size, complexity, or mission — and Microsoft wants to offer editions of SharePoint that all will find appealing. Thus the "free" version of SharePoint and the deluxe version. It should be noted that "free" is relative. SharePoint only runs on the Windows operating system, and in order to get the "free" version you have to purchase the operating system. The "free" version can also be thought of as SharePoint "lite" because it contains features and functionality that are critical to organizations of all sizes, but it does not contain the enterprise features such as Business Intelligence including Excel Services, InfoPath Services, KPI's, Dashboard pages, and the Business Intelligence Center.

If everyone would simply adopt the latest version of SharePoint right away, then life would be simple. Unfortunately, you will likely encounter the previous version of SharePoint for some time to come until everyone finally pulls the plug on the old and moves on to the latest and greatest. Until that time arrives, let's explore the previous version of the product and then the latest version of the product.

WSS 2.0 and MOSS 2007 (previous version of SharePoint)

So the previous version of SharePoint has two primary editions — Windows SharePoint Services (WSS) and Microsoft Office SharePoint Server (MOSS). The licensed edition of MOSS is broken down again into two components: Standard edition and Enterprise edition.

Table 10-1 clarifies how these three editions — WSS, MOSS Standard, and MOSS Enterprise — differ in what they can do.

Table 10-1	SharePoint Features in Three Editions		
Capability	*WSS*	*MOSS Standard*	*MOSS Enterprise*
Communication	X	X	X
Collaboration	X	X	X
Enterprise-level content management		X	X
Portal setup		X	X
Enterprise-wide searches		X	X
Business-process documentation and forms			X
Business Intelligence features including Excel Services, KPI's, Dashboard pages, and Business Intelligence Center			X

SharePoint Foundation 2010 and SharePoint Server 2010 (latest and greatest version of SharePoint)

The latest version of SharePoint is still broken down into two primary editions just like the previous version of SharePoint. The "free" or "lite" edition that is included with the Windows Server operating system is called SharePoint Foundation. The deluxe version is called SharePoint Server. Microsoft has added a great deal of functionality to the deluxe version (SharePoint Server) and as a result break the licensing of the product into two primary categories. The first is geared toward Internet facing sites, and the second is geared toward intranet (internal) facing sites. Each of these categories, internal facing and external facing sites, is then broken down into a Standard and an Enterprise edition.

For more on these versions, check out

```
http://sharepoint2010.microsoft.com/product/editions/Pages/
                          default.aspx
```

The SharePoint development ladder

The easiest way to think about ASP.NET, SharePoint Foundation, and SharePoint Server is to picture them as rungs on a ladder of software sophistication: Each adds capabilities and value as you move up in complexity and scale.

Starting (relatively) simple, if you need a specific solution that provides features such as communication, collaboration, and document management, then you can pay developers to build all those capabilities from scratch. Just be prepared to make a time investment. Trust me on this one: Back in grad school, a team of us did just that, using the Java programming language. Our Web application was a content-management system that tracked electronic content and allowed people to check content in and out, as well as purchase content from an online store. This took us more than six months and involved team members from Germany, China, Columbia, and San Francisco.

So suppose you've given your Microsoft-savvy developers a similar task: "Build nearly everything from scratch for a solution that provides communication, collaboration, and document management." They may assume they'll have to work the whole thing up in ASP.NET. But if they start with the SharePoint Foundation framework, they can use the ready-made document-management and collaboration components of SharePoint — and then just build and customize the rest of the solution to your specifications. Definitely faster. But suppose your

company has finally graduated from "up-and-coming medium-size enterprise" to "newest monster on the scene." You need heavy-duty bang for your buck.

That's why Microsoft used ASP.NET and SharePoint Foundation to build nearly all the features you'd want in that custom-made solution into SharePoint Server. SharePoint Server is customizable, of course, but Microsoft has already done most of the heavy lifting by building the product. All you have to do is pay for it, install it, and put it into action. With that said, I have yet to meet a client who uses straight out of the box SharePoint Server. There are always customizations and tweaks to make it do exactly what you want. Think of SharePoint Foundation as a basic house that provides shelter and a warm and comfy place to sleep. If you are fine with the basics, then SharePoint Foundation may be all you need. If, however, you need a garage and kitchen and laundry facilities, then you need to move up to something Microsoft has already built for you. Unless of course you want to use ASP.NET (wood and nails) to build it yourself. When you think of SharePoint and Microsoft Business Intelligence, you should think of SharePoint Server because almost all of the BI functionality (Excel Services, PowerPivot for SharePoint, KPI's, Dashboard pages, and Business Intelligence Center) come with SharePoint Server.

Making BI Information Available in SharePoint

As SharePoint becomes a prominent part of more organizations, it's only natural that it takes center stage as a place to access and share BI information. SharePoint has quickly adapted to include business intelligence in its range of tasks — by including tight integration with SQL Server Reporting

Services (SSRS), Excel as a front end for business users, InfoPath Forms, Key Performance Indicators, and Business Connectivity Services (BCS) for integration with Line Of Business (LOB) systems. The following subsections take a closer look at these fixtures of the Microsoft BI landscape.

SSRS integration

SQL Server Reporting Services offers two primary methods for integrating its reports into a SharePoint environment, but you have to pick one when you install it: You can install SSRS in Native Mode or in Integrated Mode.

SSRS in Native mode

When SSRS stands on its own, it provides a Web application called Report Manager that you use to manage, secure, view, and organize reports.

SSRS has a couple of Web parts — Report Explorer and Report Viewer — that you can install into a SharePoint environment:

- ✔ Report Explorer is for browsing reports residing on the SSRS server from the SharePoint site.

- ✔ Report Viewer is a tool for embedding a finished report into a SharePoint page. The report still lives in Report Manager (a built-in feature of SQL Server), but it appears embedded in the SharePoint page itself.

You can also connect Report Explorer and Report Viewer to each other, which gives you another handy capability: You can browse for reports on the SSRS server using Report Explorer, click them to select them, and then display them in the Report Viewer — all on the same SharePoint page.

SSRS in Integrated mode

SQL Server Reporting Services is a powerful tool in its own right — but when you integrate SSRS tightly into SharePoint, you make it even more capable.

SharePoint Integrated mode made its debut as a feature of SSRS with SQL Server 2005 SP2. Coupling the SSRS engine with the SharePoint environment lets SharePoint take over the work of Report Manager completely — which means you have one less program to worry about in terms of security, content, subscriptions, versions, and so on. When SSRS is in Integrated mode, SharePoint manages SSRS reports — and connections to data — the same way it manages other content (such as Word and Excel documents). Result: Your SSRS reports gain SharePoint functions that make them all the more useful to business intelligence — such as check-in and check-out, versioning, workflow, and security. Reports can also be seamlessly integrated into SharePoint sites so end users can just go to a portal page to view reports.

Excel integration

Excel ranks as one of the most popular business applications of all time — which is a two-edged sword: Excel is familiar to a vast number of users but can also spawn confusing hordes of duplicate documents. End users often store Excel documents on shared drives with versions included in their names such as `My Excel Doc v293.xlsx`. When people need to collaborate on an Excel document, they often e-mail it back and forth and include their initials and a date in the document name of the updated version.

SharePoint treats Excel documents as it would any other type of content: It manages them — requiring users to check them in and out, controlling the proliferation of versions, providing tools for maintaining efficient workflow and ensuring appropriate document security.

Such content management is an essential feature of business intelligence. The component of SharePoint that makes it possible for Excel documents is called Excel Services. This component allows an Excel document to be embedded in a SharePoint site, managed *in one location* by one or more people, and then made available to anyone in the organization who has the appropriate access privileges to view the document (all without leaving the SharePoint site).

The need for such control comes from a bad habit that Excel documents have when they are created and passed around: They can become massive and take on a life of their own. I've been in organizations where people aren't even sure who originally created a much-used Excel document — all they knew was that (a) it performed the function they needed it to perform, and (b) they were deathly afraid to tinker with it for fear that something might break.

Figure 10-2 shows a happier result — an Excel document (in this case, the scorecard I develop in Chapter 9) embedded in a SharePoint site. Here a small screen resolution limits how much of the entire scorecard is visible without scrolling. But there would be only one version of the scorecard — and only one place to find it for access and easy maintenance: that same SharePoint site.

The following step-by-step instructions walk through adding an Excel document to a SharePoint Server 2010 library; and then embedding that same document within a SharePoint page.

 1. **The first step is to open the document library where you want to store the Excel document.**

    In this example I will store it in a library called Shared Documents. To open the document library, simply click on the link to the document library in the left-hand navigation as shown in Figure 10-3.

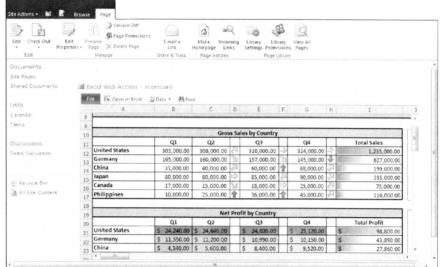

Figure 10-2:
An Excel
scorecard
displayed in
a SharePoint
site.

Figure 10-3:
Opening
the Shared
Documents
library in
SharePoint
Server 2010.

2. **Next click on Add New Document, which is highlighted by the green plus sign as shown in Figure 10-4.**

Figure 10-4:
Adding a
document to
the Shared
Documents
library in
SharePoint
Server 2010.

3. **In the Upload Document dialog box, click the Browse button to select the document you wish to add to the document library and then click OK.**

4. **Give the document an optional Title and then click OK as shown in Figure 10-5.**

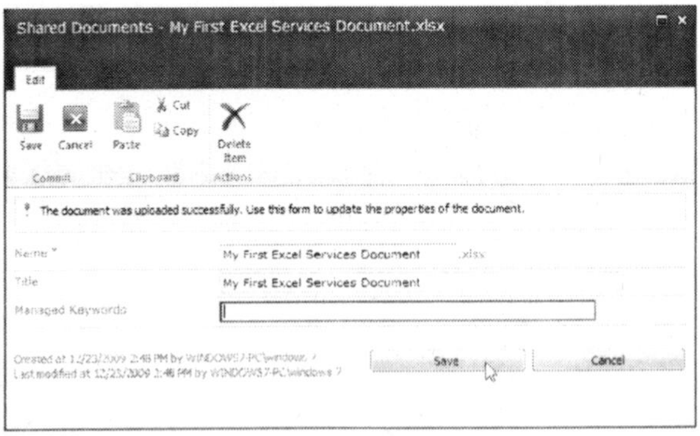

Figure 10-5:
Giving the
new Excel
document
a title while
adding it to
the Shared
Documents
library in
SharePoint
Server 2010.

5. **The document is now stored and managed by SharePoint. Hovering over the document and then clicking the context menu shows some of the content management functionality, such as versioning, available out of the box with SharePoint as shown in Figure 10-6.**

   Note that versioning can be turned on and off by your administrator, so if you don't see the Versioning button, then it has not been enabled.

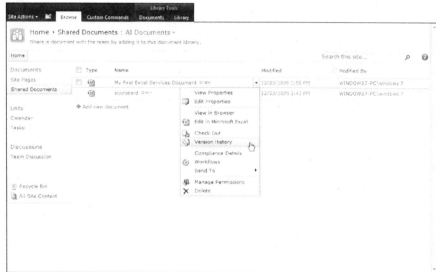

Figure 10-6:
Some of
the content
management
functional-
ity, such
as version-
ing, in
SharePoint
Server 2010.

6. **Now that the Excel document lives within SharePoint, you can easily add it to a Web site by navigating to the page where you want to embed the Excel document and then selecting the Page tab in the ribbon at the top of the page, as shown in Figure 10-7.**

   Note that if you don't have the ribbon at the top of the page, then you are probably not an administrator for this particular page. When you are viewing the page, the Browse tab is selected; when you want to administer the page, you select the Page tab.

Figure 10-7:
The Page
tab allows
for the
administra-
tion of a
page in
SharePoint
Server 2010.

7. **With the Page tab selected, click the Edit button on the left side of the ribbon. Clicking the Edit button puts the page in edit mode and allows you to add Web parts and content to the page. Under the Editing Tools tab select the Insert tab as shown in Figure 10-8.**

Figure 10-8: The Insert tab under the Editing Tools tab allows you to insert Web parts and other items into the SharePoint Server 2010 page.

8. **Click the Web Part button located within the Insert ribbon at the top of the page and then select Office Client Applications As from the Categories list and Excel Web Access from the Web Part list and then click Add as shown in Figure 10-9.**

Figure 10-9: Inserting an Excel Web Access Web part into a SharePoint Server 2010 page.

9. **The Excel Web Access Web part is now added to the page, but it needs to be pointed to the correct Excel document. Click the link titled Click Here to Open the Tool Pane to open up the configuration dialog box.**

10. **With the configuration dialog box open, click the blue button next to the Workbook field and then browse to the Shared Documents folder where you added the Excel document. Click the Excel document to select it and then click OK as shown in Figure 10-10.**

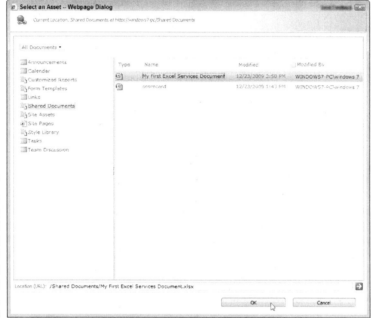

Figure 10-10:
Selecting
the Excel
document
from the
Shared
Documents
folder.

11. **Finally, scroll down to the bottom of the configuration dialog and click OK to close the dialog and view your Excel document within your SharePoint page as shown in Figure 10-11.**

    Note that to view the page as others would see it without the editing ribbon, click the Browse tab.

As you can see from the walk-through, Excel Services provides a rich set of features that allow you to integrate and embed Excel documents. Excel 2010 includes a feature known as *PowerPivot* that allows you to import and analyze tens of millions of rows. In order to analyze that many rows, PowerPivot also includes slicers and dicers that make working with massive amounts of data attainable. When your Excel 2010 document with PowerPivot is ready for prime-time, you can simply upload it to your document library and share it with the rest of the organization by embedding it within a SharePoint page. The rest of the users don't need to go and download the document since they can interact with the analysis all through their Web browsers.

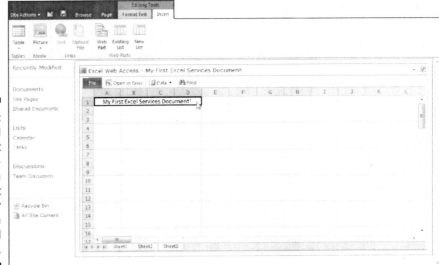

Figure 10-11:
An Excel
document
embed-
ded in a
SharePoint
Server
2010 page
using Excel
Services.

InfoPath Form Services

Like Word or Excel, InfoPath is part of Microsoft Office — and (also like them) it's used to create forms. InfoPath, however, gives developers the option of building *rich* forms that can validate data as it is entered as well as send and receive data rather than just contain it — and end users can open those forms just as easily as they'd open Word documents. InfoPath forms have cool features that can connect directly to data sources — and either pull data into the form or submit data to the data source. Useful for BI? You bet.

Using InfoPath, non-developers can also connect to Web services by using a wizard — and interact with systems built to comply with the Service Oriented Architecture (SOA) standard. This means the IT department can simply give access to a Web service and then allow power users to build forms for their individual groups without the need to involve the IT department. The IT department maintains control by defining the exact Web service and how the data should be handled.

InfoPath also contains many components that allow developers to add data validation and other form wizardry.

SharePoint has its own InfoPath Form Services feature for integrating InfoPath forms into a SharePoint site. The real power of InfoPath — and the reason for its popularity as a tool to use with SharePoint — is that the rich forms created in InfoPath can also be embedded into a SharePoint Web page: Data can fly fast and furious in two directions, all without leaving your trusted SharePoint-based intranet portal.

With InfoPath forms embedded in a SharePoint Web page, there's no need to install the entire InfoPath program on every user's computer. Users can take advantage of most InfoPath features by using a Web-enabled InfoPath form that they access through their Web browsers.

Most users never know (or care) that they're using InfoPath when they work with InfoPath Form Services. That's intentional. The user experience *should* seem like just another interaction with a form on a SharePoint Web site. Because that's what it is — only with a lot of sophisticated BI magic going on behind the scenes.

With InfoPath forms, you can collect and present data in real time as users interact with the company intranet or Internet sites. For example, you may have customers fill in a form that responds to your inventory shipments automatically: Instead of hiring software developers to build a custom program to track those shipments, you can put an InfoPath form on the SharePoint site that connects to a Web service, pulls information from your SAP system on (say) how many of a particular product you have in stock, and displays that number to the customer who's looking for the product. If the product's availability changes, the form is updated automatically through the live Web service.

Fortunately, you have help in working this kind of magic: You can use wizards to build a form in InfoPath and connect it to a Web service — without having to type a single line of code. Using this no-code approach greatly reduces the cost and complexity of developing forms for new situations.

Using Key Performance Indicators

A *Key Performance Indicator* (KPI) is a piece of information that is especially important for understanding how well your business is doing — and running it accordingly. (For example, sales figures — such as sales per store and sales per product — are typical KPIs.) No surprise that SharePoint has a component called a KPI — a specialized way to store specified data that also provides visualizations of the data, embedded in a SharePoint site. Figure 10-12 shows a SharePoint KPI — representing the morale of an organization — embedded in a SharePoint Web page.

Although a SharePoint KPI stores KPI information, end users are more likely to understand it when they think of the KPI as the data itself and not the delivery mechanism (which is embedded in a SharePoint portal environment and calls no attention to itself). SharePoint presents the KPI data and then just gets out of the way, making it easier to talk about the information and not the technology used to deliver it.

Figure 10-12:
A
SharePoint
Key Perfor-
mance
Indicator
displayed
in the
Business
Intelligence
Center of
SharePoint
Server 2010.

Business Connectivity Services

Business Data Connectivity (BCS) is a component of SharePoint that allows *Line of Business* (LOB; the systems that run your business) data to be interacted with (read/write) from within the SharePoint environment. For example, BCS could access customer records stored in a whole other part of your BI system that does customer relationship management (CRM) — and allow you to display and edit them in SharePoint.

To get SharePoint to work with LOB systems, you have to develop a document in eXtensible Markup Language (XML) that configures BCS to work with your SharePoint BI system.

Creating a configuration file from scratch may sound daunting, but XML files are essentially text; you can use any of various tools (even a simple text editor like Notepad) for the purpose. Some available applications make the task much easier; one of the most popular is MetaMan.

When you've worked up a BCS configuration file in XML, you can import it into SharePoint — which makes the data in the LOB systems accessible for analysis (another vital part of business intelligence).

Using the read-and-write capabilities of BCS, you can navigate to your company intranet, view LOB data, and update it as needed (provided you have the appropriate access privileges). Here's an example of why that's a BI advantage: Imagine you have a site on your company portal that lists all contacts for a particular product in a particular region. (The actual data are stored in a database that operates behind the scenes.) If you notice that a contact has to be changed, normally you'd open the application in which the data was created (if one exists) and make the change there — or (even more time-intensive) e-mail the person who's responsible for the data and ask that person to make the change. The SharePoint 2010 environment stream-lines this process: You can simply click the information you want to update, choose Edit Item (which brings up an editable form), change the information yourself, and let SharePoint instantly update the appropriate database — automatically.

BCS also makes it easier to take data that resides in SharePoint 2010 offline, using Office applications. If you suspect that a piece of information needs updat-ing, you can simply take the data offline for review, make the update, and let BCS sync your updated data with the source database — automatically — when you're back online.

Unleashing Human Business Intelligence with SharePoint

Any organization is home to a huge amount of knowledge and information — and SharePoint collects that knowledge and helps to distribute it. Those functions are critical to implementing business intelligence and staying competitive. Of particular importance to BI is the knowledge that an organization's people have and use — but may not have shared effectively yet.

Business is increasingly knowledge-based. Tapping in to what employees know about your industry, your products, and your business processes — and turning that knowledge into a collective advantage for the whole orga-nization — can help you stay competitive. SharePoint is designed to aid and abet this next wave of "human" business intelligence. Microsoft calls it being "People-Ready."

In addition to tapping in to the knowledge of the individuals that make up the organization, SharePoint is also a superb environment for surfacing, or dis-playing to users, BI information. When BI information is surfaced into a col-laborative environment such as SharePoint, the result is that discussions and knowledge finely tune and shape the meaning of the root information. For example, imagine surfacing BI information that calls out a particular product as a hot seller in a particular city. The crowd can begin discussing what this super city is doing right and how other stores in other cities might emulate its success to drive sales across the entire organization.

The following features and functionality are what make SharePoint a key com-ponent to your Microsoft BI system.

SharePoint Web sites

Using SharePoint to create and host a Web site is the foundation of the most powerful SharePoint capabilities. In essence, a SharePoint site is a collection of Web pages that are not only interconnected, but also set up to make communication, collaboration, and the sharing of information easier and more efficient.

Imagine going to your company intranet and creating sites dedicated to BI on such divisions as (say) human resources metrics, manufacturing metrics, or even particular product metrics. A site may be made up of KPI data, scorecards, dashboards, formulas, graphs, and charts. You could create these sites from scratch, using programs and development tools that have been around since the World Wide Web was first created — after all, people do that all the time — but SharePoint makes the whole task easier to undertake and its results more BI-friendly.

As a development tool, SharePoint makes creating, securing, modifying, and managing Web sites easy — and consistent from one site to the next.

Figure 10-13 shows an out-out-of-the-box SharePoint site. It's based on the Business Intelligence Center site template that comes with SharePoint Server 2010.

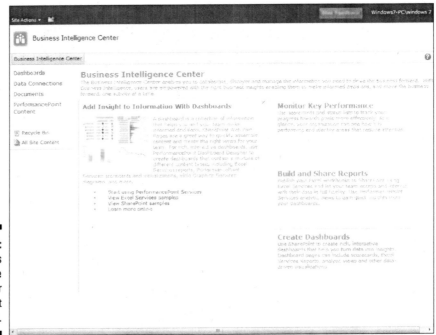

Figure 10-13:
Business
Intelligence
Center
SharePoint
Site.

A SharePoint site can be created by clicking the All Site Content link on the left-hand pane, clicking the Create button on the top of the screen, and then choosing Site in the Filter By type as shown in Figure 10-14.

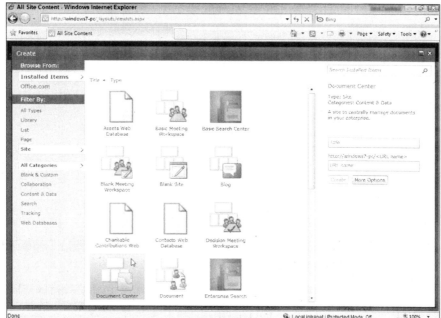

Figure 10-14:
Creating a
new site in
SharePoint
Server 2010.

Document libraries

A *document library* is a SharePoint tool for content management, used to store documents and regulate how they're used. Document libraries are where you can keep track of versions and control where a document goes, who gets to use it or change it, how safe it is from unauthorized access, who can subscribe to it, who's alerted if it changes, and how it fits into the overall workflow of your business and how.

Just as real-world libraries can contain all kinds of books and media, document libraries can contain different types of documents — Word documents, Excel spreadsheets, InfoPath forms, Web pages, text documents, reports, connection files, custom content types — you name it. Figure 10-15 shows a document library containing Word documents. Note especially how the drop-down menu for each document provides options for content management — in particular, Edit properties and document, Check-In/Check-Out, Publishing, Version History, Compliance Details, Workflows, Conversions, and Permissions.

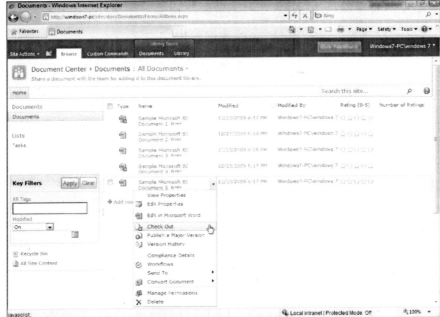

Figure 10-15:
Word docu-
ments in a
SharePoint
Server 2010
document
library.

A SharePoint document library can be created by clicking the All Site Content link on the left-hand pane, clicking the Create button on the top of the screen, and then choosing Library in the Filter By type as shown in Figure 10-16.

SharePoint Lists

A SharePoint List is a component that stores data as a list that resembles an Excel spreadsheet. SharePoint comes with a number of specialized lists designed to be useful for business — such as announcements, contacts, links, tasks, issue-tracking, surveys, and KPIs.

If those lists don't quite cover all the aspects of your business you want listed, you can create custom SharePoint Lists from scratch. A simple graphical user interface makes it easy. You can even add columns to your list without having to do any custom coding, as shown in Figure 10-17.

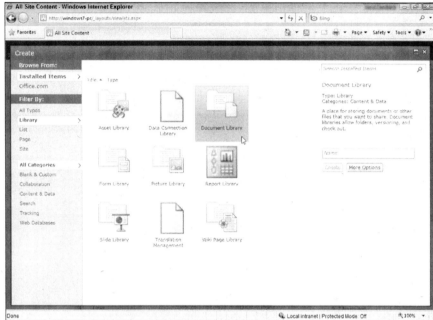

Figure 10-16:
Creating
a new
document
library in
SharePoint
Server 2010.

Figure 10-17:
Creating
a custom
column in a
SharePoint
List.

TIP

A SharePoint list can be created by clicking the All Site Content link on the left-hand pane, clicking the Create button on the top of the screen, and then choosing List in the Filter By type as shown in Figure 10-18.

Figure 10-18:
Creating a
new list in
SharePoint
Server 2010.

Wikis

The World Wide Web keeps coming up with new ways to handle information that have business uses. A *wiki* is an example — it's an interactive Web site that can be edited by a number of people. One of the most popular wiki Web sites is Wikipedia (www.wikipedia.org). SharePoint turns the wiki to business use as a tool for collaboration, documentation, and communication.

If you're developing a piece of software or a new product, you can use SharePoint wikis to create documentation. Since wiki's are interactive everyone can be involved in the documentation process, even users. (Now, there's a concept — I can already hear a collective "Hallelujah!" from future developers who've had to struggle with bad — or absent — documentation.) Different community members have access to the wiki page — and any time a new bug is introduced or fixed, community members update the wiki page. As a result, the Web site is always up to date and doesn't need a full-time administrative staff (or one poor overworked IT stalwart) to maintain it.

Blogs

Unless you've been living under a rock for the last few years, you probably know that a *blog* is a Web log or journal. Blogs showed up on the Internet as personal journals, became increasingly popular, cropped up in the business world as a way to get company messages out into the world, and are now important components of communication. SharePoint provides blogging features that are easy to integrate into the company intranet or Web portal.

Many organizations have started blogs for executives or different departments. The blogs act as a conduit for communication, allowing readers to comment, collaborate, and generate ideas about the content of the blog entry. CEO or executive blogs help keep the company informed and up to date on the company's direction — and on its progress toward organization-wide goals.

Discussion boards

A *discussion board* allows users to post topics on a Web site and get responses from other users. SharePoint includes discussion boards that are easily integrated into a site; Figure 10-19 shows an example.

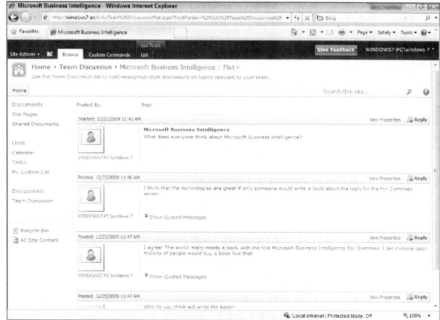

Figure 10-19:
A
SharePoint
discussion
board.

I have found that discussion boards are among the most valuable collaboration tools that an organization can employ. An engineer in San Francisco (for example) can post a topic for people around the world to read. Allowing employees throughout the company to discuss a topic ensures that they all have an opportunity to be involved in the conversation, contribute ideas and perspectives, and share their knowledge so it isn't hidden by geographic remoteness.

A SharePoint discussion board can be created by clicking the All Site Content link on the left-hand pane, clicking the Create button on the top of the screen, and then choosing List in the Filter By type as shown in Figure 10-20.

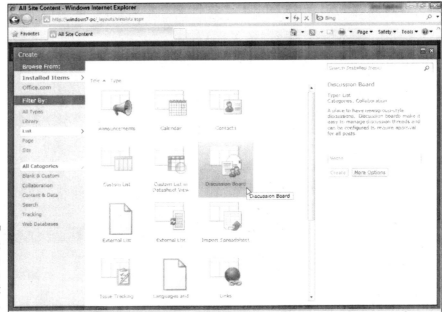

Figure 10-20: Creating a new site in SharePoint Server 2010.

Office integration

As SharePoint has become increasingly popular, Microsoft has integrated other popular applications into the SharePoint environment. Chief among these is its mega-popular productivity suite — Microsoft Office, which includes Word, Excel, Outlook, and PowerPoint. Integrating these familiar applications with SharePoint will hot-rod them along collaborative BI lines.

Word

Individual Microsoft Word documents have the same problem as individual Excel spreadsheets: They tend to spread out in an organization and get saved as stray versions in various forms, under different names. When you integrate SharePoint with Word, however, you get SharePoint document management: People can manage their documents within Word — but SharePoint controls the creation of versions and access to the documents.

Figures 10-21 and 10-22 show the check-in/check-out of SharePoint functions you can access from within Word. You can access the versioning feature by clicking the Office button (in Word 2007, Figure 10-21) or the File tab (in Word 2010, Figure 10-22) and then navigating to the Server tab in 2007 or the File tab in 2010.

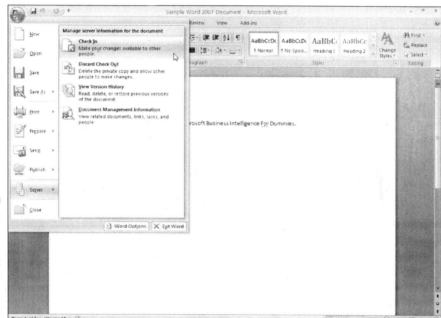

Figure 10-21:
Interacting with the SharePoint server from within Word 2007.

Outlook

Outlook is one of the software programs that information workers use most throughout the day. People are constantly checking e-mail, viewing and updating calendars, and looking up contacts. Recognizing this heavy usage, Microsoft provides SharePoint features that accommodate Outlook tasks performed throughout the day.

Of these features, one of the most popular is the discussion board. Although discussion boards per se aren't new — they've been around since the prehistoric era (in computer time) — SharePoint expands the usefulness of discussion boards by integrating them into the application where many people spend a great deal of their time, Outlook e-mail. For example, the discussion boards discussed previously in the chapter are very powerful, but over time it can be an annoyance to constantly have to go to the SharePoint site and click the discussion board to see what's going on. When you attach a discussion board to Outlook, any new posts to the discussion board will show up in Outlook just like when you receive a new e-mail.

To attach a SharePoint discussion board into Outlook, open a SharePoint discussion board in your Web browser by navigating to the SharePoint site and clicking on the discussion board link. Next click the List tab, and then choose Connect to Outlook (as shown in Figure 10-23).

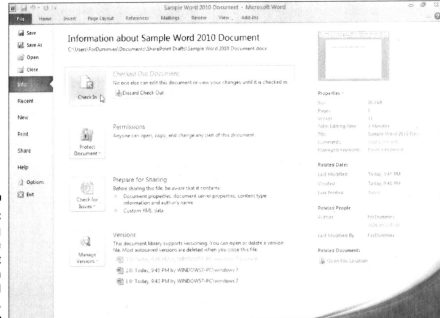

Figure 10-22:
Interacting with the SharePoint server from within Word 2010.

After you've connected a discussion board to Outlook, each new entry or topic thread in the discussion board shows up in the Outlook client as a blue number that indicates the number of new messages. Then the user can access the messages and read them right from the Outlook client; the procedure looks and feels just like using e-mail. The difference is that instead of receiving an e-mail to your Inbox you are being notified, and can read, a new posting to the discussion board that lives on the SharePoint site.

Figure 10-23:
Connecting
a SharePoint
discussion
board to
Outlook.

Learning What Was Added with SharePoint Server 2010

Although this chapter has used SharePoint Server 2010 for the examples, it is important to understand what was added, and what you gain, by moving from the 2007 product to the 2010 product.

Microsoft SharePoint Server 2010 — the newest version — includes many features and capabilities that organizations have been craving (each one detailed in the sections that follow):

- ✓ Navigation Ribbon
- ✓ Asynchronous user experience
- ✓ Silverlight add-in
- ✓ Integration of PowerPoint themes
- ✓ Visio Web rendering
- ✓ Dynamic list sorting and filtering

- ✔ Business Connectivity Services
- ✔ Increased integration with Office applications
- ✔ Offline workspaces

Cruising with the Navigation Ribbon

Beginning with Office 2007, Microsoft introduced the Ribbon, a band of visual controls across the top of all Office applications that allows users to find the functions they use without having to click and hunt through drop-down menus. SharePoint 2010 sites include a Ribbon as well — similar to the Ribbon in Office products but accessed through the browser the SharePoint Ribbon provides the same kind of convenient control over SharePoint functionality. Users of client machines view the Navigation Ribbon in their Web browsers, and can use it to interact with and manage a SharePoint site. For example, if you are an administrator you will find all of your administrative functionality in tabs in the ribbon.

When you are working with a document library you will find the functionality you need such as versioning history and check-in and check-out in the Ribbon. The Ribbon is context sensitive, meaning that you only see the functionality on the Ribbon that is relevant to the current page in SharePoint.

Providing a more fluid user experience

SharePoint 2010 moves toward what is known as an asynchronous user experience. "Asynchronous" may sound like something's out of sync, but sometimes that's a good thing: In this case, Microsoft is providing a more people-friendly experience for users of SharePoint Web sites. Here's why. . . .

As convenient and familiar as the Web is, it was never intended to provide the user experience that people expect from a software application running on an individual personal computer. The actual processes of Web applications, however, happen on the server — and users of client machines view the application through their Web browsers. As a result, continuous communication must take place between server and client to keep them in sync — and all that back-and-forth can bring an annoying interruption in the client machine's performance.

You may have noticed (for example) that clicking a drop-down button on a Web site causes the entire page to flicker and reload. This response is called a *post-back,* since the client is posting (reporting) your selection from the drop-down menu back to the server. Over time, post-backs become disruptive and frustrating. SharePoint 2010 allows the client application to post information back to the server asynchronously — that is, timing the post-back so it doesn't interrupt the user experience — resulting in a more fluid Web browsing experience.

Developing applications with Silverlight

Silverlight is a Microsoft plug-in program for Web browsers that developers can use to create custom applications and new features for Web pages. Silverlight allows Web browsers to run a special set of .NET commands, which means that when business users interact with a Web page a lot of the processing power driving the Web experience can be powered by their local machines instead of sending a bazillion messages back and forth to the server. SharePoint 2010 uses Silverlight all over the place, which gives the user the feeling that she's interacting with a programming running on her local machine instead of a SharePoint site running out on a server being accessed through her Web browser. SharePoint 2010 is also very friendly to developers creating functionality for SharePoint 2010 and provides mechanisms for hosting Silverlight right out of the box.

The end result is that when business users are interacting with a SharePoint BI feature such as a dashboard page, the Business Intelligence Center, KPI's, scorecards, and even Excel documents embedded in a SharePoint page, they have a fluid experience and can focus on the information and pay little attention to the technology driving the information. In essence, the technology becomes transparent and focuses the attention of the user on the information instead of a flickering and annoying Web page.

Integrating visualizations with PowerPoint themes

Given that data visualization is an essential part of the data lifecycle (see Chapter 6), why not use a familiar Microsoft application to give it a uniform look? Many organizations already use PowerPoint for presentations, and have spent time building specific PowerPoint themes for the organization; you may as well use them. In SharePoint 2010, those PowerPoint color themes can be uploaded and used throughout the SharePoint environment.

For example, many organizations that I visit have spent a considerable amount of time building PowerPoint themes, which represent the colors and fonts of the organization. When I look at their SharePoint sites, however, it is a rainbow of color with the colors being based on the whim of the person who created the site. It may seem like a small thing to be able to upload a PowerPoint color theme into SharePoint, but the result creates uniformity and also keeps the marketing people happy.

Themes can be used across the Office suite of products. After a theme is developed, it can be used in other Office products such as PowerPoint, Word, Excel, and even when creating e-mails in Outlook. Now with SharePoint 2010, these same themes can be imported into the SharePoint environment and used in Web sites as well. A handy tool used to create themes is called Theme Builder, and it can be found at the following location:

```
http://connect.microsoft.com/ThemeBuilder
```

Assuming you are an administrator of your site, you can upload a theme by clicking on Site Actions in the upper-left corner of the site and then choosing Site Settings. Under the Galleries section, select Themes and then choose the Add new item link at the bottom of the list of themes, select your theme, and then choose OK to upload your theme into the SharePoint Theme Gallery.

After your theme is uploaded, you can enable it for a site by again going to Site Actions and then choosing Site Settings. In the Look and Feel section choose Site Theme. Browse for your theme in the list of available themes and then click Apply. Viola! Your SharePoint site is now branded with your Office theme.

Visio Services

Visio is a well-established and powerful tool for data visualization. It's great at building everything from process flows to organizational charts. In the past, Visio diagrams could be developed and saved in a format such as PDF and then distributed throughout the organization. In SharePoint 2010, Visio diagrams can be rendered (displayed) directly in the Web browser — which moves end users closer to a seamless experience. All they have to do is navigate to the company intranet and view Visio content without having to fire up any other applications.

Visio Services works much like Excel Services (see walkthrough example earlier in the chapter). Visio Services allows Visio documents to not only be embedded directly into a SharePoint page, but the documents can be interacted with by zooming in and out in a seamless manner. In addition, Visio documents can contain diagrams that are driven by data that is contained in the Data Warehouse. The embedded Visio diagrams can obtain live updates without the user ever having to leave his browser. In essence, Visio Services brings Visio into the BI mix without requiring the user to understand or even be aware of what is happening behind the scenes.

Sorting and filtering lists dynamically

If you've ever worked with lists of data — especially in spreadsheet form — then you know how important it is to be able to sort and filter the data to examine its different aspects. In SharePoint 2010, users can sort and filter SharePoint List data simply by clicking the arrows and filters displayed at the top of each SharePoint List. This capability is especially useful for business intelligence because you can instantly perform a quick analysis on SharePoint list data without having to export it to an application such as Excel. For example, say you have a list containing more than a thousand customer comments. One of the tabs may be a rating system that allows feedback based on 1 to 5 stars. You can simply select the drop-down at the top of this column and sort the list from highest to lowest or lowest to highest. You may then want to sort the list by the date that the comment was received in order to understand if newer ratings have improved or become lower.

The ability to quickly filter a list may seem simple enough when you are thinking about interacting with data in an application such as Excel but when the same functionality is included out of the box in SharePoint 2010 and can all be accomplished without ever leaving the Web browser the benefit quickly becomes apparent. Again, the technology dissolves into the background, and to the business user they may assume every list on the Web should have the same functionality. Trust me, this ease of use and integrated transparency is not widespread.

Using Business Connectivity Services

Business Connectivity Services (BCS) is the predecessor to the Business Data Catalog (BDC) which was part of SharePoint 2007. The BDC was useful for pulling information from Line Of Business (LOB) systems into the SharePoint environment, but it was primarily a read only, or one-way, trip. The BCS technology expands upon the BDC functionality by providing read and write access to the LOB systems. See the section earlier in the chapter for more information about BCS.

Increasing efficiency with Office integration

Integrating Office, SharePoint, and LOB systems improves the efficiency of your larger BI system by saving effort and time: Certain business tasks can use data from multiple data sources without requiring users to open several applications. For example, consider the everyday action of filling out a purchase order in a Word document with this integration in place:

1. The Word document is already connected to a content type in SharePoint, which in turn is connected to the LOB system or database.

2. Integration between the applications allows the employee to select a customer from the LOB system's list without having to open any other application; Word works with SharePoint to get the job done.

3. The Word document is automatically populated with the most up-to-date information from the LOB system. The employee doesn't have to switch to another application to obtain the needed customer information.

Taking SharePoint offline with SharePoint Workspace

In 2005, Microsoft acquired a company called Groove Networks. The Groove software allows users to create workspaces that are shared among the members of a group. The workspace is synchronized to all group members' computers when they're online without having to be stored on a central server. The result is that a user can work on her own documents when she's offline and as soon as she's online again her changes are synchronized to everyone else in the workgroup. In this manner, everyone always has the latest copy of everyone else's work (assuming everyone goes online once in awhile).

Having a group of people and computers helps to ensure that data will always be backed up — in this case, in each group member's computer, while the work is going on. If one person's computer crashes, it's easy to sync with the other users after the sick computer is repaired.

SharePoint Workspace uses this Groove technology: Users have the ability to work with their SharePoint sites offline and then have the changes synced with everyone else, and the server, when they are connected again.

SharePoint Workspace 2010 is a member of the Office 2010 family and installs on your local computer just like you would install Word 2010 or Excel 2010. Figure 10-24 shows a screenshot of the SharePoint Workspace 2010 application after start-up.

Notice that there are options to create a new SharePoint Workspace, Groove Workspace, or Shared Folder. A SharePoint Workspace is a SharePoint site that you can take offline. A Groove Workspace provides a virtual workspace as described at the beginning of the section in which users sync their work with all other members when they come back online, and a Shared Folder creates a folder on your local file system that you can then share with others.

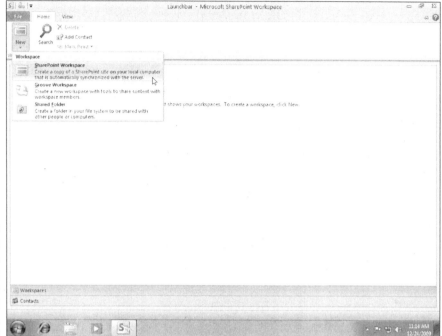

Figure 10-24:
The
SharePoint
Workspace
2010
application.

Chapter 11

Expressing Yourself with Development Tools

In This Chapter

▶ Diving in to Visual Studio

▶ Exploring the .NET Framework

▶ Taking a look at Report Builder and SQL Server Management Studio

▶ Examining SharePoint Designer

▶ Understanding the transition of PerformancePoint into SharePoint

▶ Exploring the PerformancePoint development platform

> *Complexity kills. It sucks the life out of developers, it makes products difficult to plan, build, and test, it introduces security challenges, and it causes end-user and administrator frustration. Moving forward, within all parts of the organization, each of us should ask "What's different?," and explore and embrace techniques to reduce complexity.*
>
> — Ray Ozzie

*G*etting a good working handle on the Microsoft development tools is pretty straightforward. You don't need to study up on the intricacies of every tool, but if you understand each tool's basic use and how it differs from the other tools, you're equipped for a tour of the overall BI landscape. This chapter aims to bring those tools into your comfort zone.

One of the primary Microsoft development tools is Visual Studio. After you familiarize yourself with Visual Studio, it's easy to move between development projects without having to claw your way up a huge learning curve. Some of the other tools that belong in your basic BI kit include Report Builder, SQL Server Management Studio, SharePoint Designer, PerformancePoint Dashboard Designer, and the Expression Suite — as well as the common thread that ties nearly all components of Microsoft development together: the .NET Framework.

Taking a Look at Visual Studio

Visual Studio is a software-development application of a type referred to as an Integrated Development Environment (IDE) — that is, a text editor designed specifically for writing code. IDEs such as Visual Studio have specialized features such as auto-formatting, color-coding of key words, and the capability to run and test newly written code within the IDE application. Of course, software code is really nothing more than text — so you can write it in text editor as simple as Notepad — but the features an IDE make that whole undertaking easier.

Microsoft designed Visual Studio as a basic IDE with generic features — but you can add some pretty fancy functionality (such as BI functionality to work with Analysis Services, Reporting Services, and Integration Services) that installs directly into the Visual Studio application. The advantage is that you can develop many different types of Microsoft-compatible programs with minimal hassle and an efficient time investment.

The Visual Studio interface

If you don't currently have Visual Studio 2010 installed on your computer, you can download a trial version from the following location:

```
http://www.microsoft.com/visualstudio
```

After Visual Studio is installed on your computer, you can open it by clicking Start⇨All Programs⇨Microsoft Visual Studio 2010, as shown in Figure 11-1.

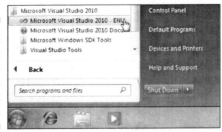

Figure 11-1:
Launching
Visual
Studio from
the Start
menu.

When Visual Studio first opens, you're presented with a start page that provides quick access to the most common Visual Studio tasks (such as creating or opening a new project or program), as shown in Figure 11-2.

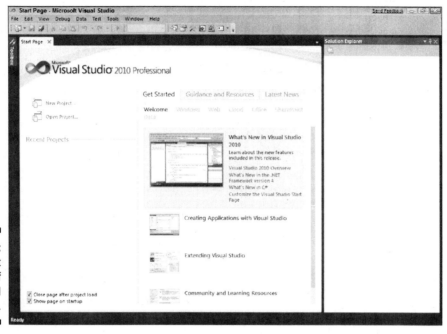

Figure 11-2:
The Start
Page of
Visual
Studio.

You can create a new project either from the start page or by clicking
File⇨New⇨Project. The New Project dialog box that appears (see Figure 11-3),
offers a range of project types — which ones you get depend on what plug-
ins you've installed with Visual Studio.

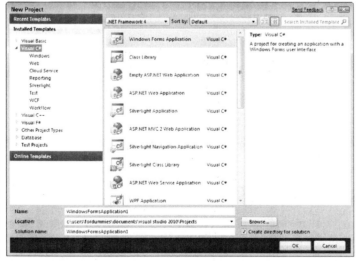

Figure 11-3:
The New
Project
dialog box
in Visual
Studio.

When a project is open in Visual Studio (as in Figure 11-4), it shows some common on-screen elements that are the same regardless of what type of development you're doing:

✔ The Toolbox pane on the left provides controls that are specific to the type of project being developed.

✔ The center pane is divided in to two parts: The upper portion is used for design (what type depends on the type of project you're developing); the lower portion is an information or code window that contains debugging information.

✔ The right side of the window is where you find panes for the Solution Explorer (upper-right) and Properties (lower-right). The Solution Explorer provides a window you can use to view the files contained in the program you're developing; the Properties window displays the properties for the currently selected object.

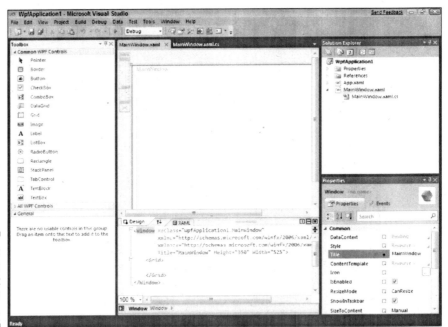

Figure 11-4:
A typical project in Visual Studio.

Flavors of Visual Studio

I often hear the voices of my clients raised in confusion over the difference between Visual Studio and Business Intelligence Development Studio (BIDS). No problem: Think of Visual Studio as a container for all types of Microsoft development functionality (for example BI development). The different groups at Microsoft create development tools that are used within the Visual Studio container. Visual Studio also comes in some stand-alone editions designed for writing code, such as these:

- ✔ Express Editions is for students, hobbyists, and those individuals wanting to gain familiarity with programming in the Microsoft environment.

- ✔ Professional Edition is for teams that are focused on delivering custom applications such as stand-alone Windows and Web applications.

- ✔ Premium Edition is for teams that have specialized needs such as Database development, more advanced testing, modeling, debugging, and modeling needs.

- ✔ Ultimate Edition is for teams that need the most advanced features such as Web performance and load testing, historical debugging information, and advanced diagramming. In addition, the Ultimate edition includes features for lab management.

An excellent chart showing the differences between Professional, Premium, and Ultimate can be located at the following URL and is shown in Table 11-1.

`www.microsoft.com/visualstudio/en-us/products/2010/default.mspx#compare`

Table 11-1	Comparison of Visual Studio 2010 Editions		
Product Features	*VS 2010 Professional*	*VS 2010 Premium*	*VS 2010 Ultimate*
Team Foundation Server	****	****	****
Version Control	x	x	x
Work Item Tracking	x	x	x
Build Automation	x	x	x
Team Portal	x	x	x
Reporting and Business Intelligence	x	x	x
Agile Planning Workbook	x	x	x
Test Case Management	x	x	x
Visual Studio Team Explorer 2010	x	x	x

(continued)

Table 11-1 *(continued)*

Product Features	VS 2010 Professional	VS 2010 Premium	VS 2010 Ultimate
Development Platform Support	****	****	****
Windows Development	x	x	x
Web Development	x	x	x
Office and SharePoint Development	x	x	x
Cloud Development	x	x	x
Customizable Development Experience	x	x	x
Testing	*	***	****
Unit Testing	x	x	x
Code Coverage		x	x
Test Impact Analysis		x	x
Coded UI Test		x	x
Web Performance Testing			x
Load Testing			x
Database Development		****	****
Database Deployment		x	x
Database Change Management		x	x
Database Unit Testing		x	x
Database Test Data Generation		x	x
Debugging and Diagnostics	**	***	****
"Pinnable" Data Tips for easier data inspection	x	x	x

Product Features	VS 2010 Professional	VS 2010 Premium	VS 2010 Ultimate
Post-mortem debugging support for .NET (dump debugging)	x	x	x
Breakpoint improvements (search in Breakpoints window, label, import/export)	x	x	x
New WPF visualize	x	x	x
Enhancements for debugging multi-threaded applications (Parallel Stack and Tasks)	x	x	x
64-bit support for mixed-mode debugging	x	x	x
Static Code Analysis		x	x
Code Metrics		x	x
Profiling		x	x
IntelliTrace (Historical Debugger)			x
Architecture and Modeling		*	****
UML® Layer diagram viewer		x	x
Architecture Explorer			x
UML 2.0 Compliant Diagrams (Activity, Use Case, Sequence, Class, Component)			x
Layer Diagram and Dependency Validation			x

(continued)

Table 11-1 (continued)

Product Features	VS 2010 Professional	VS 2010 Premium	VS 2010 Ultimate
Lab Management			***
Test and Lab Manager			X
Virtual environment setup and tear down			X
Test Case Management			X
Manual Test Execution			X
Manual Test Record and Playback			X
Lab Management Configuration			X

When you install one of these editions of Visual Studio, you're really installing the Visual Studio container — with its general development capabilities — as well as the features specific to each edition (such as the database development functionality in the Premium edition).

When you install SQL Server and select the box to install the Business Intelligence Development Studio, what you're installing is the Visual Studio container application plus some features designed to help you create BI capabilities — these, for example:

✔ Tools, templates, and wizards for developing SQL Server Analysis Services (SSAS) projects.

✔ Tools, templates, and wizards for developing SQL Server Integration Services (SSIS) projects.

✔ Tools, templates, and wizards for developing SQL Server Reporting Services (SSRS) projects.

If you already have Visual Studio installed and you click the same box to install BIDS, the installation process simply adds BI functionality to the edition of Visual Studio you're running.

The editions of Visual Studio are outlined in Table 11-2.

Table 11-2	Editions of Visual Studio
Version	**Description**
Express editions	This edition is free to download and use; its capabilities are limited accordingly. The Express Editions include Visual Basic, Visual C#, Visual C++, and Visual Web Developer. It's designed to introduce the individual developer to Visual Studio.
Professional edition	This edition includes the bulk of the tools required for using the .NET framework to develop applications.
Premium edition	This edition includes all of the features of the Professional edition as well as advanced features including more sophisticated tools for database development and testing capabilities.
Ultimate edition	This edition includes all of the features of the Premium edition as well as features for Web performance and load testing, advanced modeling capabilities, and lab management functionality.

Visual Studio in the BI world

As a part of Microsoft BI, Visual Studio works somewhat like a build-it-yourself toy: You can build BI functionality by using Visual Studio with the BI functionality installed.

If, during installation of SQL Server, you install only the container version of Visual Studio and the plug-in BI features included in SQL Server, then the program you end up with is called Business Intelligence Development Studio (BIDS). It is, however, simply Visual Studio with only BI functionality, but you will hear people refer to it as both Visual Studio and BIDS. Figure 11-5 shows the check box you choose to make that happen.

Among the BI features that turn Visual Studio into BIDS, you'll find a number of new BI-related project types that show up on-screen when you click on File and select New Project. Using these project types, you can develop custom applications that use SQL Server Reporting (SSRS), SQL Server Integration Services (SSIS), and SQL Server Analysis Services (SSAS) to best advantage, as shown in Figure 11-6. The upcoming subsections offer a look at the BI project types available in BIDS.

Select this option

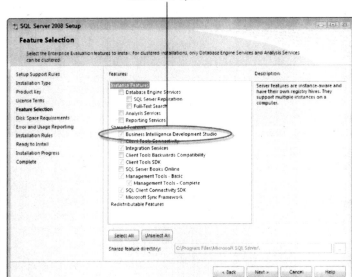

Figure 11-5:
Installing
BIDS from
the SQL
Server
installation
media.

Figure 11-6:
BI project
types in
Visual
Studio.

Analysis Services Project

The Analysis Services Project is the BIDS project type used to develop applications for OLAP and data mining (for more about those, see Chapters 4 and 7 respectively). An Analysis Services Project contains folders such as Data Sources, Data Source Views, Cubes, Dimensions, Mining Structures, Roles, Assemblies, and Miscellaneous, as shown in Figure 11-7.

The folders store development files in a logical fashion. For example, if you're building a data-mining solution, you right-click the Mining Structures folder and select New Mining Structure to launch the Data Mining Wizard.

Import Analysis Services Database

The Import Analysis Services Database project launches the wizard that walks you through importing the contents of an existing Analysis Services database into a project for further development. (For more about Analysis Services, see Chapters 4, 7, and 8.)

Figure 11-7:
Using
Solution
Explorer
to view an
Analysis
Services
Project
in Visual
Studio.

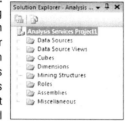

Figure 11-7:
Using
Solution
Explorer
to view an
Analysis
Services
Project
in Visual
Studio.

Integration Services Connections Project Wizard

The Integration Services Connections Project Wizard launches a wizard that guides you through creating an SSIS package (for more about those, see Chapter 5). The wizard walks you through the data connections and destinations required to build the package. Figure 11-8 illustrates using the wizard to select a data-source provider. The wizard offers connections to a number of data providers — including SQL Server, Excel, Flat File, DB2, Oracle, SAP BI, Sybase, and Teradata.

Integration Services Project

The Integration Services Project creates a new SSIS project — but without stepping you through the wizard to build the required connections and destinations. An SSIS project contains logical folders to organize elements of the project such as Data Sources, Data Source Views, SSIS Packages, and Miscellaneous items, as shown in Figure 11-9.

Report Server Project Wizard

The Report Server Project Wizard walks you through creating an SSRS report using the Report Wizard (for more about SSRS, see Chapters 6 and 8). Using the wizard, you can select a data source, design a query to obtain data, choose the type of report you want to create, set the layout of the report, and format the report.

You can access the same New Report Wizard by right-clicking the Reports folder in an open SSRS project and choosing Add New Report.

Report Model Project

The Report Model Project is used to create a Report Model — a database object that shows end users how to develop their own ad-hoc reports, using a data source that's easier to use than a working database.

Here's why a model is needed: An operational database is usually optimized for inserting, storing, editing, and deleting data — but not necessarily for ease of use. Usually the database administrators have broken tables apart in an effort to normalize the data and store it *only once* in the database system.

In addition, database objects such as tables and columns often have names that don't make a lot of sense to end users. A column may be named (for example) RX34TYZZ1 — which may mean something to the database designer but absolutely nothing to an end user. To help the rank-and-file users make practical use of the database, you could develop a Report Model that provides a logical view of the data, puts descriptive names on the columns, and acts as a view into the data. The end user would then connect to the Report Model using an ad-hoc report tool such as Report Builder (about which you can find more in Chapters 6 and 8).

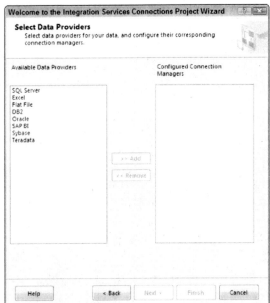

Figure 11-8:
The SSIS Connections Project Wizard.

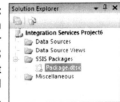

Figure 11-9:
The Solution Explorer of an SSIS project in Visual Studio.

Report Server Project

The Report Server Project creates a project that can be used to develop SSRS reports (described in Chapters 6 and 8). After the project is created, you can add data connections, create queries, and build and format reports.

You can also launch the New Report Wizard from your project by right-clicking the Reports folder and choosing Add New Report. If you right-click the Reports folder and choose Add➪New Item, you can add a blank Report or Data Source without walking through the wizard, as shown in Figure 11-10.

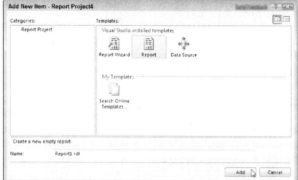

Figure 11-10: Adding a new item to an SSRS project.

Examining the .NET Framework

The .NET Framework is at the root of nearly all Microsoft application development, integrated into everything from SQL Server to SharePoint, and it helps to have a basic understanding of what it is and how it works.

The .NET Framework is essentially a storehouse of code — a resource that Microsoft makes available to help programmers write code more efficiently — and all the code it contains will run on (of course) the Windows operating system. To help you get a handle on what the .NET Framework is and how it works, here's a quick overview of how programming languages work — and why they're necessary tools for building software.

A language only a computer chip can love

If time and money were no object (instead of the same thing, which is usually an obstacle), then every software program could be developed by writing code in a language that the CPU chip could understand. But the language that the CPU *does* understand is made up of 0s and 1s; to do even the simplest interaction means feeding tens of thousands of strings of 0 and 1 codes into the CPU. Since this is theoretically possible — but not realistic for people to do — programming languages were developed. A *programming language* uses English syntax that's easier for humans to understand and write. The English-style programming code is then fed into a software application called a *compiler* that converts it into the 0s and 1s that the CPU understands.

Intermediate Language (IL)

Programming languages and compilers have made writing computer code very efficient; unfortunately, not all CPUs understand the *same* 0 and 1 codes. For example, if you write a program and compile it for a CPU made by one company and then move the program to a computer with a CPU made by another company, the program will break. The reason: The second CPU won't understand what to do with the 0s and 1s of the program. To get around this problem, computer scientists came up with a very smart idea: Instead of having the compiler translate a computer program from the English syntax to 0s and 1s, they have the compiler translate the English syntax to a language that various CPUs can translate into the languages *they* understand. This intermediate language is called, aptly enough, *Intermediate Language (IL)*. (It's sort of like naming your dog "Dog.") How it's translated into 0s and 1s for the CPU is the topic of the next section.

The Common Language Runtime (CLR)

Another computer program called the *Common Language Runtime (CLR)* actually translates the Intermediate Language into the 0s and 1s that the CPU can understand. Thus a developer can write a piece of software code, compile it once into Intermediate Language, and then run it on any computer that has the CLR software already installed. This entire process — including the English-syntax computer languages, Intermediate Language (IL), and the Common Language Runtime (CLR) — is called *.NET* (pronounced "DOT-net"); nobody's quite sure why — maybe it just sounded cool.

A number of English-syntax computer languages are available in the .NET environment — in particular, Visual Basic, C# (pronounced "C-sharp"), F#, and C++, among many others. All these languages compile the English-syntax code into Intermediate Language (IL) that can be understood by the Common Language Runtime (CLR). As with spoken languages, however, each language has its own subtleties and nuances. Some people prefer the C# language over Visual Basic as a programming tool. Others have been writing code in languages such as C++ for many years, and changing to a completely new language can be a painful experience. Whatever their quirks, however, all these languages can be used to write software code that can be compiled into IL code and understood by the CLR.

Reusing code is another standard part of the programming scene. After all, people have been writing code for decades, and a lot of it is very well written — so why make every developer write all the code needed for a software program from scratch? Life is short. So Microsoft developed a vast library of pre-built code that developers can use to write software programs. Put together enough of this ready-made code, and you have a solid frame for the rest of your program — which may be why this library of code is called the .NET Framework.

Exploring Report Builder

The Report Builder application is a separate download from SQL Server and Visual Studio. Report Builder is designed to provide an easy-to-use report development application for non-developers so they can build SQL Server Reporting Services (SSRS) reports (see Chapters 6 and 8) — an essential capability if you want to gather BI information from folks in all the departments of your company. The good news: Report Builder has the same usability features as the Office productivity suite:

- ✔ The Ribbon at the top of the application contains functional tabs similar to Word or Excel but geared towards report development.
- ✔ The tabs contain visual components that are grouped together by purpose.

    For example, the Insert tab contains groupings for Data Regions, Report Items, Sub-Reports, and Header and Footer, as shown in Figure 11-11.

One of the biggest challenges around BI information involves providing the users who understand the information with the ability to share it. I've found that critical information often comes from non-assuming sources. For example, on numerous occasions I've worked with executive-level resources who are trying to answer particular questions about their business. They're looking for a BI solution that will give them the answers but are struggling with the exact questions to ask. As I go through the process of interviewing people up and down the organization structure, I always find nuggets of knowledge that nobody knew existed.

It's a mistake to think that only the people whose job it is to analyze data have the answers. People throughout the organization often have areas of interest and specialties, and empowering them with the tools necessary opens up a whole new world of actionable BI information. For example, say the CFO is having trouble understanding the intricacies of expense reports throughout hundreds of offices around the globe. The CFO could spin up a SharePoint site designed to host SSRS reports and then communicate a request to office managers throughout the organization. The office managers could all go to the site and create their own reports from scratch (using Report Builder). The reports could be viewed and collaborated on in the SharePoint environment and since the office managers are developing the reports in Report Builder they do not have to spend time spinning back and forth with a report developer in order to create the content. Since the reports are hosted and stored in SharePoint every manager can communicate and collaborate. The result is that the absolute best reporting solution bubbles up from the overall crowd. Everyone in the crowd has a say and everyone also has the power to solve the problem by posing and answering questions.

Empowering the crowd by creating a level playing field for BI content development in a collaborative environment increases the efficiency and competitiveness of the overall organization. The organizations that continue to do things the old way will soon be left in the dust as the adaptive companies pull further and further away into the future. Report Builder provides a simple to use and ubiquitous (through a SharePoint intranet) tool that leverages the power of reporting using SQL Server Reporting Services (SSRS).

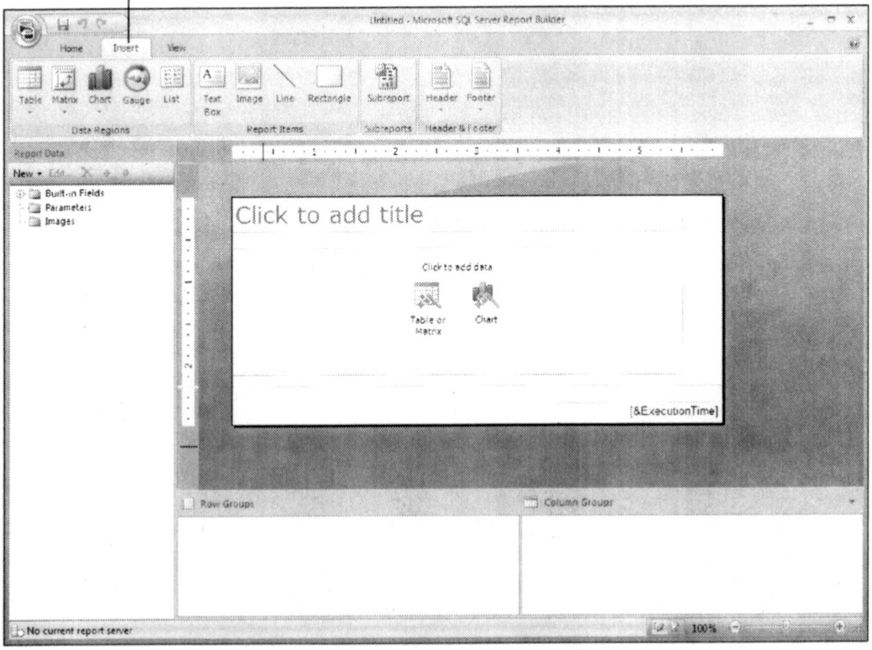

Report Builder's Insert tab

Figure 11-11:
The Report
Builder
application.

Diving In to SQL Server Management Studio

The primary tool used to build and manage SQL Server databases, including developing stored procedures, is SQL Server Management Studio. (For a look at how managing a database fits into the larger BI picture, see Chapter 6.) You can install this tool with the SQL Server media by choosing the Management Tools check box on the Feature Selection window when you're installing SQL Server, as shown in Figure 11-12.

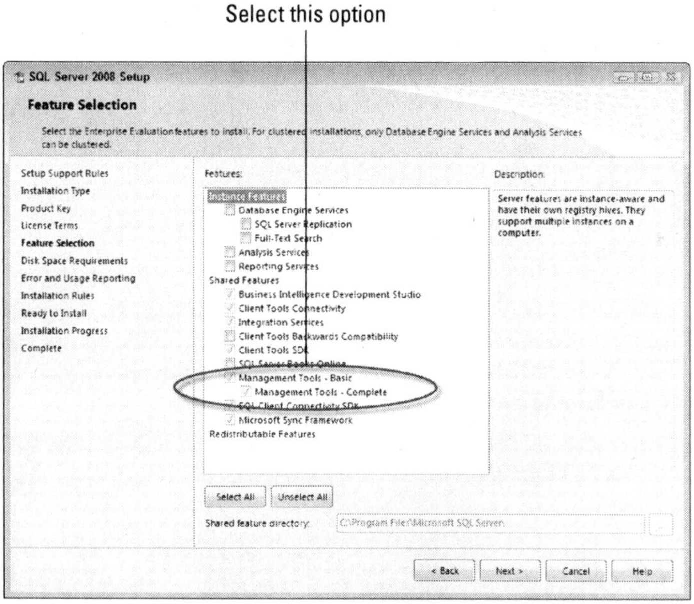

Select this option

Figure 11-12:
Installing Manage-
ment Studio from the SQL Server installation media.

With Management Studio in place, you may as well use it. Follow these steps:

1. **Launch Management Studio by clicking Start, choosing All Programs, navigating to the SQL Server 2008 folder, and then clicking SQL Server Management Studio.**

2. **With Management Studio up and running, enter the server instance type, server name, and authentication mechanism into the initial connection dialog box.**

   After making these specifications, you can use Management Studio to connect to and administer all the BI capabilities of SQL Server — including the Database Engine, Analysis Services, Reporting Services, Integration Services, and SQL Server Compact Edition.

3. **Use the Object Explorer window to browse and explore your databases.**

   Management Studio provides a view into all of the objects contained in the database instance from the Object Explorer window. For example, when Management Studio is connected to a database engine, the Object Explorer shows the databases contained within the instance, along with the current situation regarding security and server objects, replication, and management (as shown in Figure 11-13).

4. **A new query can be created by clicking the New Query button.**

5. **Develop your query in the top-center pane of the application using the Query Editor.**

Figure 11-13:
The Object
Explorer
window in
Manage-
ment Studio.

6. **Run your query by clicking the Execute button. You can also verify that you have entered the correct syntax by clicking the Parse button. The Parse button is the button with a blue checkbox just to the right of the Execute button.**

   The results of the query appear below the query design window as shown in Figure 11-14.

Getting to Know SharePoint Designer

When you point your Web browser at a SharePoint site, you're not headed for a normal browser experience — it only looks that way: The content appears in your Web browser, but nearly all of it actually lives on your SQL Server database. SharePoint works this sleight-of-hand by pulling the content (including any Web-site pictures, colors, and configuration) from the database, assembling it, and displaying it in the browser.

Of course, when you're customizing and developing SharePoint pages, you need a window that shows you the actual content that's stored in the SQL Server database. Technically you *could* manipulate the actual data in the SharePoint database, but the design of that database is extremely complex — and it's way too easy to mess something up. So Microsoft recommends strongly against interacting with the actual SharePoint content database. It's pretty insistent about that; if you *do* decide to work with the SharePoint content database without using the

SharePoint user interface, Microsoft won't provide support for you — or for your implementation of SharePoint. You'd be going it alone without a net, so to speak. Very risky.

To avoid the madness and mangled data that can crop up in such a scenario, Microsoft provides SharePoint Designer — a development tool that connects to the SharePoint database and allows you to create and edit pages, lists, libraries, and workflows, among many other developmental tasks. In essence, SharePoint designer is a window into the SharePoint databases. This window let's you interact with the databases on an intimate level without having to risk throwing something off kilter by tweaking the databases themselves.

SharePoint Designer is designed to provide a window into the databases that power your SharePoint site. These databases are very complex, and thus SharePoint Designer acts as an intermediary, or maybe dignitary, to these complicated databases.

The New Query button

The Execute button

The Query Editor

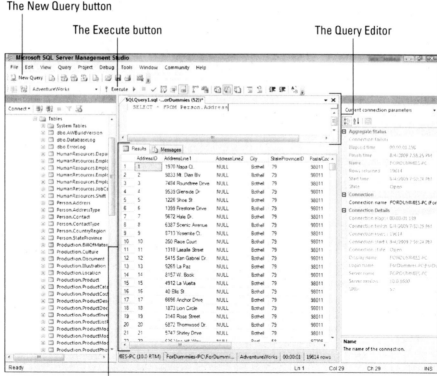

Results of the query

Figure 11-14: Designing and running a query in Management Studio.

SharePoint Designer is a free download from the Web. It can be downloaded from the following location:

```
http://office.microsoft.com/en-us/sharepointdesigner/
```

After SharePoint Designer is downloaded and installed, it shows up in the Microsoft Office folder on the Start menu. You fire up SharePoint designer just like you would fire up Microsoft Office Word or Excel. Click on Microsoft SharePoint Designer from within the Microsoft Office folder. To get started, you first need to connect SharePoint Designer to your SharePoint site. From the File menu, select Sites, as shown in Figure 11-15.

Figure 11-15:
Connecting
SharePoint
Designer
to a
SharePoint
site.

 You can get the URL of your SharePoint site by opening up your site in your Web browser and then copying and pasting the URL. Make sure, however, that you only including your site and not the actual Web page at the tail end of the URL. For example, if your URL is

```
www.mydomain.com/sites/mysite/Pages/default.aspx
```

then you would need to chop off the Pages/default.aspx and simply include the URL to the site, which would be as follows

```
www.mydomain.com/sites/mysite/
```

After your site is open in SharePoint Designer, you can click the Site tab and work with SharePoint in all sorts of 'under the covers' ways. All of the SharePoint 'objects' such as Lists and Libraries, Workflows, and Pages show up in the Navigation window on the left-hand side as shown in Figure 11-16.

A new SharePoint object can be created by clicking back over on the File tab at the top of the screen and then selecting Add Item. After the new item is created, it will show up on the Site tab, and you can click on it to configure and customize it. Figure 11-17 shows a Document Library that was created called Created from Designer.

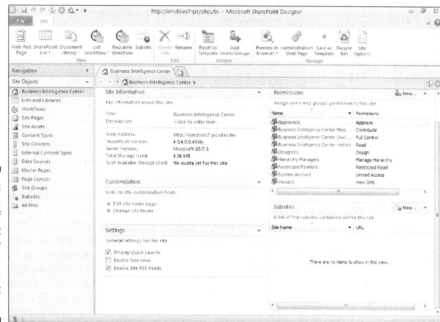

Figure 11-16: The Site tab of SharePoint Designer after connecting to a SharePoint site.

Whenever you interact with SharePoint, you are editing the content databases since all of the content is stored in a SQL Server database. Most users interact with SharePoint using their Web browsers. Whenever they make a change in their Web browsers, they're really making a change in the database. Whenever they add content to their SharePoint site, they're really adding content to the database. While many things can be done to SharePoint sites through the Web browser, not all development tasks can happen through the Web browser. SharePoint designer provides a connection to the SharePoint databases with more power and customization functionality than the browser alone.

Figure 11-17:
Configuring
a Document
Library
using
SharePoint
Designer.

Seeing the (Silver)light and Tasting Expression Blend

Delivering software applications over the Internet and through a Web browser is an increasingly popular method among software makers — no boxes, no shipping, no postage, what's not to like? Well, there is one problem: The World Wide Web was designed to make information accessible — not to make it especially user-friendly. These days, however, users expect the kind of convenience online that normally comes with a well-designed software product. To fulfill those expectations in the Web environment, Microsoft developed Silverlight — a specialized subset of .NET that runs in the browser on your desktop instead of on the server, providing a smoother, more seamless user experience.

The Silverlight user interface is made up of a special subset of .NET commands called Windows Presentation Foundation (WPF) — essentially code that creates a presentation-like user experience. To build a Silverlight user interface, a designer would use Expression Blend, one of the features of Expression Studio (a design tool intended for the artistic designer — as compared to Visual Studio, which is strictly a programming tool). The idea is that the designer can build a user interface in Expression Blend and then hand the design over to a programmer — who can open up the same project in Visual Studio and build the underlying program. It's sort of like delivering a sleek car body to a shop that installs the engine and running gear.

Understanding PerformancePoint

PerformancePoint is in a transition period. It used to be part of a Microsoft product called PerformancePoint Server, which is now discontinued. The analytical and reporting components of the old PerformancePoint Server are now reborn as part of SharePoint Server 2010, where they go by the name PerformancePoint Services for SharePoint. These capabilities include Key Performance Indicators (KPIs), scorecards, dashboards, reports, Strategy Maps, and Trend Analysis reports. Here's a closer look:

- **Key Performance Indicator (KPI):** KPI normally refers to a vital piece of information that provides performance information about your organization. Examples of KPIs include sales figures, manufacturing data, and financial information. (For more about the SharePoint KPI feature, see Chapter 10.)

- **Scorecard:** A scorecard is a collection of information about your organization that's organized in a single view, usually tracking progress toward a specific goal. For example, a CEO may outline a goal for sales-per-store figures throughout the country. A scorecard can be developed that tracks sales for each store and provides a visual indicator (such as a red, yellow, or green light) to indicate relative progress. (For more about scorecards, see Chapter 6.)

- **Dashboard:** A dashboard is similar to a scorecard, except a dashboard usually takes a snapshot of how an ongoing operational task is performing and displays it in real time. A scorecard tracks progress; a dashboard shows you current status. For example, you may have a dashboard for manufacturing that outlines the current status of all machines — showing (say) a red flashing icon when a machine is down or a solid green icon when a machine is up. Anyone in the organization can view the dashboard and quickly understand the current health of the manufacturing process. (For more about dashboards as BI tools, see Chapter 6.)

- **Reports:** A report is an organized package of information describing the status of some topic that matters to your business. In PerformancePoint, you can create reports that match the features you're using. You can use the Dashboard Designer (for example) to build Strategy Map reports and Trend Analysis reports. Dashboard Designer also excels at creating analytical charts and grids with drill-down, drill-up, and cross-drill capabilities. Drill-down means that you can click on an aggregated value and drill down to see the values that make up the aggregate. Drill-up means that you can take values and drill up to a higher level. For example, you may be looking at individual products and decide that you want to drill-up to see the same information aggregated by product group. Drill-through means that you can click on a value and drill to see the data in a different way. For example, say you're looking at bike products and you want to see all products that are red. If you clicked on the color red, you could cross-drill to see all of the products (not just bikes) that have a color of red.

Dashboard Designer is an application that installs on your desktop and allows you to develop PerformancePoint content. After you've developed the content, you can upload it to a SharePoint site for others to view, or you can embed the content directly in an Excel spreadsheet or PowerPoint presentation and take it offline.

KPIs, scorecards, dashboards, and reports are handy concepts — but by themselves, they're just concepts. Implementing these concepts is what often gets confusing. You can scrawl these concepts on graph paper or a cocktail napkin, but that approach takes a long time to refine — and each time you want to update the concept, you have to erase, redraw, or start over. (How twentieth-century.) Fortunately, you can use Excel as a powerful tool to build these visualizations. Note, however, that you still have to update the data that drives the chart, graph, or other visualization. And in BI, the update has to happen continually because the latest data is the most useful. That's where PerformancePoint Dashboard Designer comes in; it's a tool intended for the design of those very pesky KPIs, scorecards, dashboards, Strategy Map (Visio documents) reports, and Trend Analysis (which use SSAS data mining, see Chapter 7) reports. Sure, you can still use Excel, SQL Server Reporting Services (SSRS), or even pencil and paper, but why not use a tool created specifically to produce the BI-friendly components you need?

The SharePoint Dashboard Designer application can be started by clicking the Add New Item link from within a Document Library that contains the PerformancePoint content types. SharePoint Dashboard Designer will download and launch. This instant download and launch capability is called ClickOnce technology because you don't need to download and install an application manually on your local computer. You simply click the link in your SharePoint site to add a new PerformancePoint item, and the Dashboard Designer application launches automatically. Figure 11-18 shows SharePoint Dashboard Designer being used to create a new dashboard.

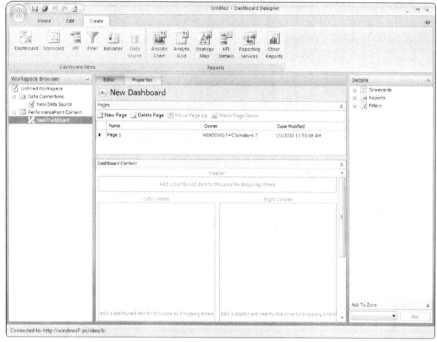

Figure 11-18:
Using
SharePoint
Dashboard
Designer to
create
a new
dashboard.

Part IV

Incorporating Microsoft Business Intelligence into Your Business Environment

The 5th Wave — By Rich Tennant

"Don't laugh. It's faster than our current system."

In this part . . .

This part walks you through the process of incorporating Microsoft Business Intelligence into your organization. Every organization is different; some are more techno-crazed than others. Some already have mature Microsoft IT departments; others tiptoe into the Microsoft waters.

The size of your organization also comes into play when incorporating Microsoft Business Intelligence. A small- or medium-sized organization has more flexibility in its internal bureaucracies; large organizations often rumble with internal politics when a new solution looms, generating pushback that hasn't much practical or technical merit but must still be dealt with. But identifying the best hardware and software is only the beginning. Getting everyone on board can be a big challenge; the success of your BI project may hinge on managing the impact of change.

In this part, you find out how to set your BI goals and implementation plan. You explore the process of evaluating and choosing the best parts of Microsoft BI to fit your existing infrastructure and knowledge base. You get a look at testing and rolling out a BI system, one iteration at a time. Finally, you get pointers on involving users from the get-go as sources of priceless feedback for your BI implementation.

Chapter 12

Setting Your BI Goals and Implementation Plan

In This Chapter

▶ Creating the goals for your BI implementation

▶ Picking the best method to get BI up and running

▶ Defining your implementation plan

It is a mistake to look too far ahead. Only one link in the chain can be handled at a time.

— Winston Churchill

In my experience as a consultant, I've found that technology is a double-edged sword: It can make great business processes extraordinary — or turn poor business processes into impassable hurdles. Doing BI right is more than just buying computers and software. If technological solutions aren't *implemented* in the correct way — turned from concepts into real tools that provide real benefits for your specific situation — they can make your business perform worse than it would if you went back to pen and paper.

In one vital respect, implementing a BI system is just like getting any high-tech solution up and running: The more knowledge you have about the topic when you start, the more likely you are to succeed. Of course, that sword also has two edges: Software vendors and consultants can tell you a lot, but as they get wind of a new opportunity to sell their wares and services (that's *you,* starting your journey toward business intelligence), they'll tend to overwhelm you with whiz-bang slideshow presentations and promises of amazing success. Pretty soon your head is buzzing like a bug around a dazzling light — but watch out: Ineffective implementation can turn into that light into a zapper that makes your investment dollars disappear in a puff of scorched-smelling smoke.

Don't get me wrong — bringing in consultants and vendors to help you understand your options (and help make the solution work) definitely has its place. However, don't let those folks drive the show until you're intimately familiar with where you're headed and why. Like real estate agents, consultants and vendors get paid when you buy something or do something (anything) they recommend. Of course there are honest and trustworthy consultants, vendors, and (for that matter) real estate agents. But the more knowledge you can obtain before you call them in, the better. Your knowledge not only gives you better questions to ask, but also provides a counterbalance to the financial incentive that drives consultants and vendors.

Setting Your Business Intelligence Goals

The goals of a business intelligence (BI) project are vastly different depending on the size and industry of an organization. Asking what your BI goals should be is like asking what road you should take: Before you can answer that question, you have to know where you're going — and where you're starting from. Then you can figure out the terrain and what roads are available — and have a solid basis for your answer.

Here's an example using real roads: We travel to Montana every year to my grandparents' homestead. The cabin is in the northwest corner of the state, and if you look at a map, you'll see that a major freeway (I-90) runs a relatively short distance away. The problem: There's a mountain range between I-90 and the cabin — and the only roads that connect the two are winding dirt logging trails. The hundred-or-so miles look tantalizingly close on a map, but it can sometimes take more than a day to drive through the mountains. If, on the other hand, we turn off at US 95 and head north and then east on Highway 2, I can arrive at the cabin in only four hours. A look at the map makes the four-hour route seem well out of the way; in reality, it's by far the best route.

Depending on where your organization currently stands and where it wants to go will have a huge impact on your business and BI technology goals.

Understanding the components of business goals

Modern business has gone through many different evolutionary changes. In some parts of the world, companies are just now computerizing their businesses and starting to work with Enterprise Resource Planning (ERP) systems. Other companies have had ERP capabilities for years and are now moving toward integrating collaboration, communication, and content management — using systems such as SharePoint. Regardless of where your organization is in this evolutionary cycle, you can achieve real value with Microsoft BI; the trick is to determine which of its tools are right for the job you want done.

Finding your way to an effective BI system starts with taking a look at the size of your business, its processes, and how well (or badly) those processes serve its goals. The approach for a company with predominantly manual processes is much different from what works for a company with a great deal of automation. The goals of a small or medium-size company are much different from those of a Fortune 500 multinational. The next subsections explain how these differences affect the way you put BI to work for you.

Politics, politics, politics!

I've spent a lot of time working with large, billion-dollar companies, and one of the first things I try to ascertain is the level of *sponsorship* for a new project — who's behind it, who's on board with it, who's not too keen on it, and who has the power to make it or break it. Here are just two typical features of the corporate terrain:

- ✔ Large companies often work piecemeal — a vice president (for example) will commission a BI project without the knowledge or support of other vice presidents. (That's often an early whiff of trouble.)

- ✔ In large organizations, the projects often involve interactions across divisions and with people who have no vested interest — or worse, with people who secretly hope the BI project will fail because it seems to threaten their own interests within the organization. (In smaller organizations, on the other hand, a BI project is often known and understood by leadership throughout the organization.)

The organization's internal political environment is often one of the most difficult parts of any BI implementation. That's because the data and information that are the lifeblood of BI are intricately dispersed throughout the organization — and you have to get a lot of different agendas, job titles, and personalities to work together at turning it into a BI resource.

I've found that one of the most critical parts of any BI project is getting key stakeholders and decision-makers on board early. Stakeholders are like stockholders — they all have something to gain and something to lose when the environment changes — so you have to show them how the BI project will add value that directly benefits their roles in the organization. For example, if a vice president in charge of manufacturing is known to be a "naysayer," then an early stage of the project should display real-time information to this VP — a chance to sample the better insight that BI offers into the manufacturing process. Working through the political environment can be tedious, but diplomacy in a BI project is always a requirement.

Keep your own particular organizational structure and political environment in mind as you proceed through the process of creating your BI goals.

Asking a genie

To determine your primary BI goals, start with this simple exercise: Pretend you've just rubbed a magic lamp: A genie pops out, willing to answer any question you have about your organization. Try not to think about the limitations of the data or the processes you already know about ("Oh, I could never find *that* out!"); instead, you want a pure list of the questions you most want to answer. The genie exercise is an attempt to set aside your pre-existing, insider knowledge.

Don't worry at this point if the questions seem out of scope or unreasonable. Your goal is to capture the *most important questions* involving your organization. Here are some sample questions you may want to ask:

- ✔ What are our current daily sales by product, by product category, by store, by region?
- ✔ What do my customers often purchase in the same basket?
- ✔ How much do sales increase in response to my different marketing campaigns?
- ✔ What are our biggest cost/profit drivers?
- ✔ How much overtime are our people working?
- ✔ Which shifts are the most productive?

In the realm of imagination, a genie (Microsoft BI solution) can answer *any* question for you about your organization. A genie is not restricted by the data contained in the current systems and processes. A genie does not rely on existing data-capture points. What you want is a snapshot of the most important aspects of your organization — and of the kind of information that will allow you to run your business more intelligently.

Given an unlimited budget and time, absolutely anything is possible since a Microsoft BI solution can be infinitely extended and customized. It's important to start your genie goal exercise without restricting yourself based on your knowledge. Some of your difficult questions may be easily solved with out-of-the-box Microsoft BI technology, and others may require extensive customization and process changes. Don't worry about *how* to do something at this point, just worry about *what* you need to better run your business. Later in the process you'll rank your needs based on factors such as budget, time, and resources required for implementation.

Prioritizing

When you have your list of the questions you'd most like to have answered, arrange them in order of importance. For example, if you're in the business of manufacturing toothpaste, then the question "How many tubes, boxes, and cases do we sell on a daily, weekly, monthly, and yearly basis?" would most likely have the highest priority (as compared to, "What is the tire pressure in

all of the delivery trucks?"). The tire pressure question may be very beneficial and important, but it's strongly argued that it is much more important to
first focus in on slicing, dicing, and analyzing the sales figures.

Assigning complexities

Once you've created your list of important questions and prioritized each of
them, rank their *complexity* (meaning how easy or difficult it is to answer each
question). A question that is important *and* has low complexity is an ideal
candidate for use in developing a quick down-and-dirty prototype of your BI
system. For example, if you choose a high-priority sales question ("How many
tubes, boxes, and cases do we sell on a daily, weekly, monthly, and yearly
basis?"), you know that the data for sales figures is stored in existing operational systems. Each sales transaction also has a date stamp — so all the data
you need to answer this particular question is already being captured. As "low-
hanging fruit" goes, this is a nice shiny apple without a worm — an ideal candidate question for a prototype.

You may find you also have very high-priority questions that bristle with
complexity. In such cases, you may need to tinker with some of your business processes, perhaps installing data-capture points where there were
none before. As a general rule, make sure your BI system works *before* you
tackle the high-complexity monsters. When your prototype BI system is functioning and adding value, you can try new iterations of the prototype — say,
after you install those new data-capture points — that get you closer to the
more complex goals.

By beginning with a goal that answers a high-value, low-complexity question,
you give your project its best shot at early success — and better momentum
from the start.

I've seen BI projects that attempt to answer all questions in one fell swoop —
and set up that Sword of Damocles to fall when the system goes live at the end
of the project. This sounds dramatic in PowerPoint presentations — pointing
to all those important questions and claiming the solution will solve them.
The problem, however, is that the project gets bogged down by its complex,
ambitious goals — and never provides any value. Then, after months (or even
years) and millions of dollars, the only result is a pile of documentation and
PowerPoint presentations. At this stage, the project's sponsors are in a pickle:
Do they put even more time and money into implementation or do they cut
their losses and pull the plug? I'd never wish anyone to end up in that situation. Too many do.

Examining technology goals

Business goals should drive technology goals, however I often find it's just
the opposite in many organizations: The Information Technology (IT) department has a de facto monopoly on those goals, thus the business has no

choice but to accept the services they're providing. But what if those services aren't meeting some specific needs within the organization? Well, that's when "shadow" IT groups start to appear in the various business groups — people outside IT who create their own tools to help them do their jobs. Such a group may start as just some technically-inclined person building an Excel spreadsheet or Access database, but it quickly builds to the point where specialized IT people are hired into the group *with the business budget* just to accommodate the needs of the business. I've even been involved in projects where business groups have hired me as a consultant to build a solution without the knowledge or support of IT. (Not an ideal approach — by a long shot. Trust me.)

In the end, businesspeople need to be able to do their jobs. If IT can't fulfill the technology requirements of the organization, then (the business groups figure) who can really blame them if they go outside their local IT departments? Unfortunately, the business still has a major problem here, and not just from the extra expense: Such a workaround is a bad precedent and makes it harder for everyone to work together toward a common goal.

For the sake of efficiency, morale, and a healthier business, technology goals should align with systems already in use throughout the organization. And if those systems aren't getting the job done, maybe it's time to use BI capabilities to integrate and co-ordinate them so they work better.

If the organization uses Microsoft Office for productivity, then it makes little sense to move from a mail system using Exchange to one using Lotus Notes. Exchange is already tightly integrated with Office, so moving to Lotus Notes would only exacerbate the problems people will experience when interacting between their mail system and their productivity tools.

The following are some sample goals to consider when thinking about implementing a Microsoft Business Intelligence solution:

- ✔ Making the best possible use of your employees' current Microsoft knowledge. (See Chapters 3 and 13 for some pointers.)

- ✔ Getting the most value from your current Microsoft licensing. (You may already have some hidden BI gems in the Microsoft products you have; see Chapters 3 and 13 for the word on what to look for.)

- ✔ Increasing worker productivity through Microsoft Office integration with a BI solution — especially SharePoint. (For more about integrating Office applications into SharePoint for collaboration, communication, and content management, see Chapters 9 and 10.)

- ✔ Using SQL Server and SharePoint to co-ordinate your core BI capabilities — especially reporting and dashboards — with ongoing collaboration, communication, and content management. (See Chapters 8 and 10.)

- ✔ Using SQL Server and SharePoint to encourage and optimize "human business intelligence" (for details, see Chapter 10.)

Determining Your Implementation Plan

The goal of a BI *implementation plan is* to lay out a roadmap that you can follow to a successful BI system. It's similar to starting a new enterprise with a business plan. Entrepreneurs often say that building a business plan is as useful for the person starting the business as it is for potential investors or debtors. The business plan forces the entrepreneur to think through all the key components of the business — and to make sure nothing is left out, overlooked, or forgotten. Developing an implementation plan — as an actual document — fulfills the same purpose for a BI project: You can just start building stuff, but what you build will work better if everybody who's doing the building has the same clear idea of what they're doing.

BI implementation plans come in all shapes and sizes — and consultants are always happy to lay out detailed graphs, charts, and documentation to sell their particular methodologies. In the end, however, BI implementation plans come down to two basic approaches: waterfall or iterative.

Comparing waterfall and iterative methodologies

In technology circles people talk about waterfall methodologies and iterative methodologies. *Waterfall* is a metaphor that pictures the stages of the project as cascading headlong from one to the next: You collect all your requirements, and then waterfall over to the next step of designing the system — and then waterfall over to the next step of developing, and so on. At each stage, you move on and don't go back. This approach, of course, assumes that everything goes right the first time, at every stage — how likely is that, *really?* — which is the worst mistake a technology project can make, though it doesn't stop many project teams from implementing a plan using this model.

I suspect that the waterfall model is popular for one simple reason: It looks nice on paper and the PowerPoint jockeys and project managers can fit the portions of a project into nice, neat buckets. The problem, however, is that the waterfall model is as rigid as the rock ledge under Niagara; it doesn't work so well for creating a working BI system. For that you need the flexibility to test, revisit, and improve the stages of implementation — for example, being able to develop something quickly and then let the users see and get a feel for it. An iterative approach is common sense really. How is a user expected to know what they like, what they dislike, what works, and what doesn't if they haven't even seen the system.

The *iterative* method — also called the *agile development* in custom development circles — starts with small baby steps, revisits each stage to try out improved versions (*iterations*) before moving on, and proceeds with these gradual steps throughout the entire project. With each new iteration, the scope and complexity of the project increases — but a working solution begins to emerge from the outset. Iterative steps should incorporate power-user feedback throughout the project. Often, power users don't fully understand what feedback they'd like to provide *until* they've seen and played with the product. By exposing power users to a rough-cut solution early on, you get them thinking about the feedback that is truly important to them.

Some benefits of getting power users' input include these:

- ✔ Finding out early what's the most important in adding value to users.

- ✔ Gaining user acceptance, user buy-in, and generally getting people on board with the solution.

- ✔ Doing user training as the solution evolves. User knowledge of the system grows as the solution is developed.

- ✔ Getting continual validation of the project throughout the implementation. When problems show up, they're dealt with immediately.

- ✔ Molding the user experience to exactly what user's need, in response to feedback provided throughout the process.

- ✔ Keeping communication lines open so users don't feel like something was dumped on them. Asking them to provide important feedback throughout the process encourages them to feel they're part of the solution.

One of the most important things to communicate to the power users in the beginning is that the early iterations of the system are rough drafts — not a final solution. They shouldn't think about details such as whether the data is exactly formatted correctly or if the design is cool enough — these touches can be finished in later iterations (you put the hood on after you get the engine running, right?). The key to early iterations is functionality, validity, and a user experience that solves the problem and adds value.

You want to make your users feel comfortable providing constructive and critical feedback early on. You're not looking for a mere shrug of acceptance. You *want* to hear the gripes and complaints — if the old way of doing something was better, then *why* it was better? All these points can then be incorporated into the solution as it evolves.

Identifying the phases of the waterfall approach

The typical phases of a waterfall approach to implementing BI (as outlined in Figure 12-1) display a full-speed-ahead optimism:

- ✔ **A requirements-gathering phase:** During this phase you try to figure out who may need to use the system. You then interview the people and attempt to ascertain what they want and need from the system in order to better perform their jobs. The biggest problem is that people generally don't know what they want until they have seen the system.

✔ **A design phase:** This is where the requirements guide the shaping of the solution. The design phase attempts to take the requirements gathered in the first phase and design a BI system. One of the biggest problems that I often see encountered here is that the consultants doing the design work are not the same ones doing the development work. It is one thing for a design to look good on paper but something entirely different when it comes time to develop it.

✔ **A development phase:** This is where the solution is built. Often one consulting company will be hired for the design phase, and then another consulting company will be hired for the development. The development team curses and blames the design teams, and the design teams shrug it off and assume the development team doesn't know what it's doing.

✔ **A deployment/going-live stage:** This is where the solution meets the real world: The hardware is connected and running, the software is installed and configured, and the users are aware that the new system is ready for a test drive. With the waterfall approach you hope and cross your fingers that everything works because your budget, time, and resources have already been used in the previous phases. If at deployment the system makes users pull out their hair and curse and scream then you have to either scrap the system and start over or pour additional budget, time, and resources in what amounts to another trip through the waterfall cycles.

✔ **A training and transition phase:** This is where users are trained on the solution and a full-time staff takes over maintenance of the system.

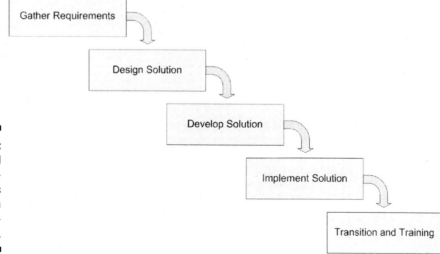

Figure 12-1:
A waterfall methodology looks like a smooth progression.

Gather Requirements

Design Solution

Develop Solution

Implement Solution

Transition and Training

The problem with the waterfall approach is that things never work exactly as planned. Users don't really know what they need until they see something and try it. Designers aren't really sure how long something will take to develop until they've actually developed it. Another pitfall is the rapid and massive change that's forced on the users at the conclusion of the project.

Using an iterative approach to implement a BI system

An iterative approach to adopting a Microsoft BI system builds an end-to-end solution extremely rapidly and with a relatively small team. You identify power users whom your team will consult throughout the process so they can influence the solution and identify what works (and what doesn't work) before it's financed and made available to the entire user base.

The phases of an iterative approach are similar to that of the approach except they become extremely short, and a lot more familiar — because you continue to circle through those phases with new improvements as the project progresses. Figure 12-2 illustrates the iterative approach.

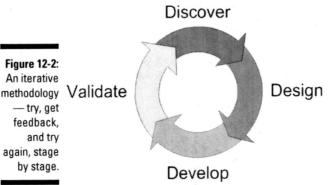

Figure 12-2:
An iterative methodology — try, get feedback, and try again, stage by stage.

The iterative approach consists of the following phases:

- ✔ **Discover:** The Discover phase involves identifying the problems and requirements that should be added to the solution in order to add value. Every iteration includes a discover phase; users often don't have a detailed idea of what they need until they see a working solution — after which they can provide additional information (from "this feature rocks" to "back to the drawing board") to incorporate into the system.

- ✔ **Design:** After the problems and requirements have been discovered, this phase incorporates them into the solution. For example, a user's initial request may be for sales-per-product-per-store information. Seeing that information on-screen may prompt a realization — "Say, it'd be nice to see the profit margin on each product per store as well." The design team gets wind of the new request during the Discovery phase and builds it into the solution during the Design phase; at the next iteration of the system, the newly requested information shows up on-screen.

✔ **Develop:** At this point, the components are designed — so now they're worked up as real capabilities and added to the overall solution — for each iteration. With each round of development, the next iteration shows users their feedback in a working environment.

✔ **Validate:** In this phase, after you've incorporated the feedback provided by users into the project, you show them the results in a new iteration. You want make sure that the problems and requirements identified in the Discover phase were correctly understood and addressed. The current working version of the solution gives users a look at how their feedback helps shape the solution — which will, in turn, probably lead to more feedback.

Each iteration — even the first — produces a working solution that can be shown to the power users. The idea is to show them something that works and get them to help you figure out how to make it work *better*.

One major benefit of an iterative approach is that it tends to use its support money efficiently. The waterfall approach often entails a risk of blowing through the budget and finding yourself with not much to show for it but a dilemma: Either you have to pull the plug or watch *another* barrel of money go over the falls to get a working system that delivers some of the promised value.

An iterative approach lets you refine the project at every stage, as long as you have the budget for resources. Even if the budget runs out before you've completed the project, you still have a solution that adds value and provides a return on your investment.

Discovering how things really work

A successful business is not a set-it-and-forget-it proposition; if you're going to improve how it runs, you have to know how it *actually* runs. A BI solution relies heavily on business processes to generate the data that it turns into strategic information. So if you're going to implement a BI system that does its job properly, you have to know the truth about what's really going on in your business processes. (The accompanying sidebar provides a look at why.)

The ugly truth . . . ?

I often interview work groups to nail down the details of business processes and map exactly what's happening. Sometimes the first thing I see happening is a mismatch between what management assumes and the employees know. For example, one group I was interviewing included the manager — who was explaining the flow of a business process, not noticing that the employees were growing more and more fidgety and aggravated. It was a symptom: What the manager thought was happening definitely wasn't what was really happening. I fully expected one of the employees to jump up and yell that classic Jack Nicholson line from *A Few Good Men:* "The truth? You want the truth? You can't handle the truth!"

In the end, the manager was completely baffled by the truth: The people involved in the process had to jump through tremendous hoops just to achieve the correct outcome. The computer system could be relied on — to freeze. The functionality that was supposed to make their jobs easier didn't work. In the end, the employees had to work around these obstacles, building extensive Excel and Access databases to produce information that the manager saw on a routine basis — and thought *was* the routine result of an efficient process.(Oops.) The truth: The process was about as workable as a nightmare — in desperate need of a redesign — ever gets.

To get a realistic view of your business processes, you'll need to build *process maps* — diagrams that are also called "flow charts" — to describe them. You get the best ones by enlisting the help of the people who are actually doing the work.

Make sure the folks who are doing the work understand that you're after the truth of the process — and that their jobs aren't on the line if they describe a sequence of events that doesn't match management's idealized picture. This is assuming, of course, that you're in a position to ensure their jobs aren't on the line. If you're not in this position, then make sure to bring management on board and explain that it's completely acceptable and expected that the way a process actual works is probably not how they think it works. Emphasizing a culture that covets the truth beyond politics is difficult, but it's as important as any other part of a BI implementation. Get leadership buy-in first, and the rest of the players will fall into place — even if they're just doing it to look good for the boss.

Building process maps and process flows

With an accurate process map, you can quickly visualize what's happening in a process. A process map (also called a *process flow*) shows the major components of a process as well as the interactions between the components. Documenting a process might be producing a bird's-eye view, with pretty pictures showing a general flow (as shown in Figure 12-3) or very detail-oriented diagram with *swim lanes* (functional areas of ownership that run parallel) and narrated interactions (as shown in Figure 12-4).

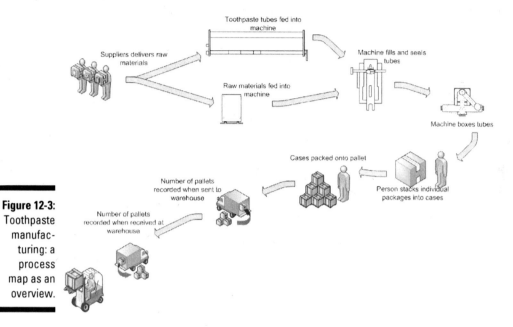

Figure 12-3:
Toothpaste
manufac-
turing: a
process
map as an
overview.

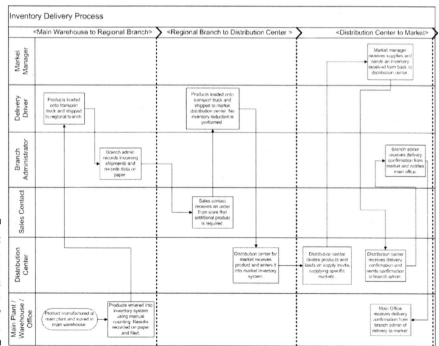

Figure 12-4:
Detail-
oriented
process
map: the
flow, blow
by blow.

It's one thing to have an idealized big picture of how a process *should* be performing — and quite another to see how it *actually* performs. Sometimes process maps can offer insight into that difference — especially if you base one of them on management feedback and one of them on what you hear from the people actually doing the tasks (take another look at the sidebar called "The ugly truth . . . ?" and imagine what those maps would have shown). When you create a process map, be sure to include feedback from both management and the individuals who carry out the tasks — and (here's a word to the wise) you may want to get them talking honestly to each other about the process first.

Process maps and process flows exist to make processes visible. They can also stimulate a three-stage process of their own:

1. Optimizing the processes.

2. Tapping in to the improved processes to gather critical — and accurate — data.

3. Combining the data from various processes into a component of the information that drives sound business decision-making.

Sending in the BI version of a SWAT team

No, I don't mean anybody has to get shot — but I do love watching action movies with specialized police forces known as SWAT (Special Weapons And Tactics) teams. The heart of this metaphor is expertise: SWAT teams are made up of the best-trained, most highly skilled people — they have to be, if they're going to perform superhuman feats of crime-fighting. When undertaking a BI project, you need a highly trained and highly skilled team of BI and organizational specialists who can help you build an understanding of the truth quickly and efficiently. Organize this "BI SWAT team" to provide a quick assessment of your organization. Their mission: Make those elusive processes *visible* so you can develop an initial implementation plan. Your BI SWAT team should include the following roles:

✔ **Business process expert:** This person interviews people, quickly ascertains what's really happening, and creates process maps and narratives that give you a clear picture of what's really working and what isn't. For example, if it takes people 20 minutes to open a Web application and then 5 more minutes every time they click to do something in the application, then they're not likely to use that application — even if it's being forced on them from upper management. People are smart and adaptable; they'll figure out what they need in order to do their jobs most effectively. What the business expert needs to figure out is what the employees are doing — and what information and tools they *really* need to make their jobs more efficient and valuable.

✔ **Fixer:** This person understands the political landscape of the organization and can get things done. No, I don't have in mind some shady character who bribes people in back alleys. What a fixer really does is understand how people work and whom to talk to, department by department, to get the work of the organization done. A fixer should be at ease in each department, and treat none of them as outsiders, or worse, adversaries. Fill that fixer role very carefully; this person should be a diplomat with a knack for getting people to open up without causing a defensive reaction. The fixer should understand the political landscape of your organization and be able to maneuver past hazards (personality conflicts, territorial clashes, you name it) that an outsider wouldn't be aware of. In general, the fixer shouldn't be a high-ranking person — high rank tends to attract idealized, what-they-want-to-hear answers from employees; what you want from the fixer is realistic employee feedback, provided in an atmosphere of support and trust.

✓ **Technology expert:** This person intimately understands Microsoft Business Intelligence and has experience at crafting Microsoft BI solutions. The person in this role has to soak up the organization's environment, develop a comprehensive vision of what's needed, and find the most economical way to make it happen. If something is possible but will cost a fortune for custom development, there may be other ways. After this initial analysis, the technology expert's task is to match appropriate system components with the company's real business processes — and then offer up a way to use technology efficiently to reach business goals while giving the employees a shot at greater, less stressful productivity. The goal is to make the best use of Microsoft BI capabilities — those you need to bring in and those you may already have.

✓ **Project manager:** This person keeps the project on track — making sure the meetings are set up, the notes are taken, and the information coming out of the team is cohesive and comprehensive. After all, a BI project should embody the improvements it's trying to bring about through implementing business intelligence.

Identifying the power users

One outcome of the BI SWAT team's assessment is an understanding of the *power users* — the people who explore the systems already in place and try to get a handle on the benefits and roadblocks. Power users are your ultimate weapon in a successful implementation — here's why:

✓ They can tell you which hardware and software components in your systems currently work well — and which ones don't.

✓ They can tell you where data lives, how to access it, and what data is missing.

✓ They are the go-to people for the overall user base because they know the current systems inside and out.

✓ They can provide useful insights for each iteration of your system and should be heavily involved in its planning and design.

When project teams build a solution using the waterfall model, it's too easy to try implementing a pretty BI strategy without asking the troops in the trenches first. Identifying power users and garnering their knowledge, expertise, and experience with the systems and business processes can bring the implementation down to earth and give it a solid footing. Granted, the project team *may* successfully identify the correct components and a workable strategy all by themselves — but that (to put it politely) is a roll of the dice. When the power users finally dive in to the new system at the end of the process, they have one of two reactions: Either they find it useful and promote it, or they discover it's a time-wasting monster, rail against it, and maybe start some trouble in Transylvania.

Getting the power users on board early takes the dice rolling out of the equation because the power users will give feedback at all stages of the implementation. If they don't like it after the first iteration, you'll be able to make adjustments and incorporate what they like and don't like into the plan.

Solidifying the goals of the BI project

With an understanding of how your organization really works, you're ready to revisit the genie goals you dreamed up (see the "Asking a genie" section earlier in this chapter) and determine which of those goals should be part of your system's earliest iterations.

The quick wins that bring a high return on investment (ROI) — that is, high-importance, low-complexity questions that can be of immediate benefit to your business — belong in the early iterations. Save the more advanced and difficult goals for later iterations.

Identifying the data needed to attain your goals

Process maps and process flows should include a data component. You need to know what data is being generated by what processes and where it's stored. If a data-generation point doesn't exist for a specific point in a process, then you know that you'll need to integrate that capture point into the process. A great example: a machine that manufactures toothpaste. If the machine has a data-generation point that isn't being captured digitally, then the company's approach to this business process may be too broad — say, counting the output as cases or pallets of toothpaste, sending people in to count them manually, and leaving it at that. Tapping in to the actual data coming from the machine, however, can give the company many more insights into the process — without additional manual effort. Some of those insights can answer questions like these:

- How many times has the machine jammed?

- How many individual tubes of toothpaste have been filled?

- How many times has the machine been filled with ingredients?

- How long does each batch take to complete?

- How many times was the machine stopped during a batch or shift?

- How often does a missing tube cause a gap in the filling line?

- Does the number of tubes filled match up with the number of cases being recorded?

All these questions can be answered by simply capturing and using the digital data that the machine may already be producing — and figuring out how to get it into the rest of the BI system. If you have an accurate sense of the data you already have available, you're already a step closer to answering those big business questions. If data isn't currently available, then you need to determine how much effort it'll take to capture the data that's required. It can be as simple as plugging in to an existing machine — or as complex as implementing a complete Enterprise Resource Planning (ERP) system before you move on to bigger BI goals (for more about ERP, see Chapters 3 and 5).

Setting a solid foundation for a BI implementation

As with most things in life, you'd better give your BI system a solid foundation, or it could fall right over. A BI solution can provide excellent visibility into your organization — but if its processes rest on a broken foundation, its potential benefits can end up buried under the rubble.

A BI system needs solid components to make up its foundation in order to be successful — in particular, these two:

- **Solid processes throughout your organization.**

  A solid process is the real deal — what's actually happening as your business pursues its goals — given enough careful attention and enhancement that everybody has the same (positive) picture of what it is and what it does.

✔ **Solid data flowing from those processes.**

> Solid — that is, reliable — data includes valid and relevant data-capture points and a mechanism for storing the data they generate. Usually these systems are made up of an ERP solution or specialized software, depending on the scenario. For example, if you're in the manufacturing business, your processes and software for capturing data will be much different than if you're in the retail business.

Two initial steps to success in any BI implementation are (a) intimately understanding your business processes and (b) constantly updating that understanding with fresh data. Result: Accurate, reliable, timely information about your organization — the essence of business intelligence.

Scope creep can be your friend

Having worked on hundreds of projects, I can attest that scope creep is a part of every project. No, *scope creep* isn't some unsavory character squinting at you through a telescope; it's a tendency — common to all projects — to take on larger, more complex goals than the project planners originally intended.

When a little of it, under conscious control, produces a better project — as it does when successive iterations of BI systems get better at their intended tasks — maybe it should be called something else — say, scope *refinement*.

If a person or team could, without a doubt, cover all of the requirements at the beginning of the project, then every project would be a success. Unfortunately this is never the case, and as anyone who has been involved in a technical project will tell you the requirements and needs of the project are never as straightforward as many a consultant would like you to believe. A set of defined requirements is a great starting point as long as you keep in mind that as they change the project will change. Using an iterative approach, you'll be able to adapt to the changes as the project progresses. You can try your best to manage scope creep, but some of it will always work its way into your project. In my experience, a project that perfectly defines all of the requirements upfront is sort of like Bigfoot — it may exist, but I've never seen it.

Another battle I often see rage on is when requirements are treated like a legal contract. Yes, a requirement gives the designer and developers a guide on what the system should do, but the process breaks down completely when a requirement is treated like a legal case. For example, a requirement may be to show sales by product for each specific store. The designer and developer may perform this task and spit out a PDF of the results with each row showing a purchase and its store. Technically, the requirement was met since the rows and columns contain all of the information, but the essence of the requirement was completely lost. The user is quickly overwhelmed by the massive amount of data and needs to further analyze it. If the data is in a

PDF, it's extremely difficult to export in a usable format. The result is a battle over who's right and who's wrong.

All too often technical people get caught up in the words of a requirement and lose sight of the meaning of the requirement. The requirement was really around providing the users with the ability to slice and dice data with a couple of the variables being product and stores. A good team that's constantly working together will infer this and provide a system that meets the original needs of the user — but a team of dispersed groups may call it quits with the requirement and push it down the waterfall to the next group. When this happens, it's a little like musical chairs . . . and you don't want to be the team standing around looking accountable when the music, or waterfall, stops.

The fundamental reason for BI scope creep is that users don't know what they need until they actually see a new tool, play with it, and get a feel for it; then they can then tell you what's wrong with it, what's right with it, and what other needs it brings to mind. This after-the-fact feedback is what drives scope, ah, *refinement*.

In a waterfall approach to a BI project, scope *creep* is your worst enemy — the true requirements may get buried somewhere in all the new tasks that glom on to the project, but those requirements don't poke their heads out of the mess until after the project is over. At its best, the iterative approach can scope creep into scope refinement: You receive valuable feedback that helps you fine-tune each iteration of your BI system-to-be.

When you're working through an iterative approach to implementing a BI system, you start with a very small initial scope, get that working, and then add scope *as needed* while you're incorporating user feedback into the *next* working solution. Figure 12-5 illustrates this happy prospect.

The BI project's initial scope starts off very small; it only expands to match real needs, stage by stage, as it's being implemented. For example, the initial scope may be to build a rudimentary data warehouse so you can pull sales data for a particular store into it. That's plenty to do for this iteration; pulling data into the data warehouse involves extracting it from the source systems, transforming it into a standard format, and then loading it into the data warehouse. With the transformed data ensconced in the warehouse, you can make it available to decision-makers — using a report created in SQL Server Reporting Services (SSRS) and displayed on a SharePoint site in the form of a dashboard. Getting all this stuff to work end-to-end is a monumental step. Once you have data on the products being sold in a single store, you can work up other data in the same way for future iterations. You can add ways to slice and dice the data — by product, product group, time of day, and customer Zip code, you name it. In even later iterations, you can branch out to include all stores — and then divide the purchases by store, county, state, country, or sales person.

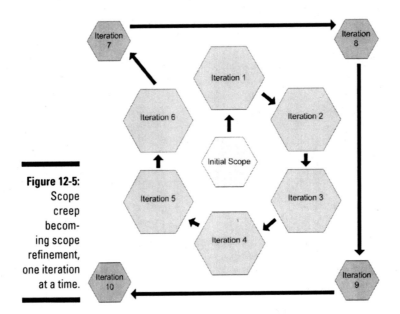

Figure 12-5:
Scope
creep
becom-
ing scope
refinement,
one iteration
at a time.

By this point, the scope has expanded, sure — but each expansion is controlled and gradual, and has a real, practical reason behind it.

An iterative approach gets you to a useful solution very quickly — and then continues to add value as the project progresses. At the conclusion of the project, the total scope may be the same as you'd get with the waterfall approach (see Figure 12-6) — minus the chaos. The primary difference is that in an iterative approach you manage the scope of the project, limit scope expansion, and use it to your advantage. The *estimated* scope for an iterative approach and a waterfall approach may be equal, but there's one more expansion of scope that happens at the end of the waterfall stages: When users finally interact with the solution, it's their first chance to provide their feedback — and here it comes, from everywhere, all at once, like a raging river that *somebody* has to manage (head for the hills!) — or else you get a deep, resentful silence settling over the cube farm.

If you manage the scope of your BI project throughout its stages, the users feel much more engaged and satisfied at its conclusion — and you're another step closer to having everyone buy in to a system that offers real worklife improvements and business advantages.

Total Scope

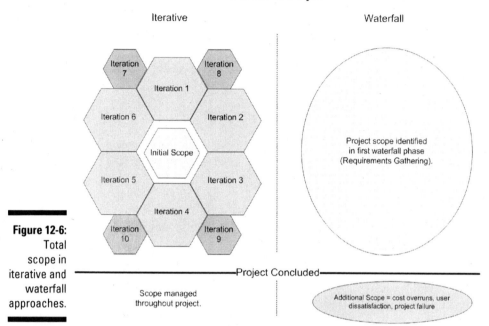

Iterative

Waterfall

Iteration 7

Iteration 8

Iteration 1

Iteration 6

Iteration 2

Initial Scope

Iteration 5

Iteration 3

Iteration 4

Iteration 10

Iteration 9

Project scope identified
in first waterfall phase
(Requirements Gathering).

Figure 12-6:
Total
scope in
iterative and
waterfall
approaches.

Project Concluded

Scope managed
throughout project.

Additional Scope = cost overruns, user
dissatisfaction, project failure

Chapter 13

Evaluating and Choosing Technologies

In This Chapter

▶ Identifying your current business intelligence capabilities

▶ Picking hardware and software to incorporate

▶ Discovering the value of "free" (as in "open source") BI software

▶ Increasing your success factor by reducing risk

Any sufficiently advanced technology is indistinguishable from magic.

— Arthur C. Clarke

*B*efore you start evaluating and choosing components to include in your BI system, you need a complete understanding of your organizational environment — as it is now, and as may come to look if you choose to move forward with Microsoft Business Intelligence. Knowing where you are and where you're going help you get a good working sense of how much effort will be required to implement a BI system. To get to that understanding, you need two kinds of savvy:

- ✔ A deep knowledge of your current business processes — what they are, what they do for your business, and how they fit into its long-term goals.

- ✔ Familiarly with the technology presently used in each process — where hardware, software, and human work habits combine to do the job.

In this chapter, you will explore ways that you can identify the Microsoft products you may already be using such as SQL Server. You will also assess your current environment including the licensing you are using and the skill-sets of your people.

Assessing Your BI Capabilities

To build a successful implementation plan (see Chapter 12 for more about implementation plans), you need an accurate assessment of your current BI capabilities — those you have, those you need, and those you may not know you have. These components form the foundation of business intelligence for your company. You can begin by taking a careful look at the hardware and software you currently have in place, including the licensing that governs their use and the employee skill-sets that already exist. Read on.

Identifying your current BI-friendly tools

As you plan your BI implementation, it's well worth finding out whether your organization is already using some Microsoft products that can put you a step ahead. For example, if your IT department is already heavily Microsoft-focused, you already have some Microsoft BI components in place. (Of course, if the folks in your organization have never heard of Microsoft; you may want to ask what they *do* use on the planet they come from.) I'm going to hazard a (pretty safe) guess that your organization has at least some Microsoft products up and running, and has had them for a while. But no matter who made your hardware and software, you need to know how much of it — and which parts — will fit smoothly into a Microsoft BI system.

Some Microsoft BI components to look for that you may already be using include these:

- ✔ Servers running the server version of Windows, as well as SQL Server for database needs, SharePoint for communication and collaboration, Communicator and Communications Server for internal instant communication, Exchange for e-mail.

- ✔ Desktop and laptop computers running the client version of Windows, as well as Microsoft Office (which includes Outlook, Excel, Word, PowerPoint, Project, Visio, Access, InfoPath, Communicator, Live Meeting, OneNote, Publisher, SharePoint Designer, and Groove).

In addition to the products I've just mentioned, Microsoft has an enormous range of other software products, and one of the *really* nice things about them is that when you've developed some skill using one product, you're well on your way to developing a skill-set for using the rest. You couldn't ask for a handier bit of ready-made Microsoft BI training.

In addition, you may have another potential BI advantage already in place: some existing, installed hardware and software that are already generating raw data about your business processes — but may as well be hiding under the covers for all the higher-ups know. Yes, some system (maybe even a custom system) is in place, and the data are being captured and stored, but it is never being accessed. Microsoft BI tools such as SQL Server Integration Services (SSIS) can tap in to these hidden data stores and pull them into a SQL Server data warehouse where the data can provide real value — quickly and cheaply. As a consultant, I often walk into an organization and find it's already using some would-be (*should*-be) great data sources that are off the radar of leadership (see Chapter 3 for a tantalizing hint). Sometimes, however, those legacy systems are lurking horrors . . . .

As you plan your BI system, looking under the hood of each business process to identify its components can reveal not only potential BI data sources, but also potential roadblocks to implementation. If (for example) one of your business processes depends on legacy software created by a small vendor who has long since gone out of business, then you may have to slog through a large custom-development project before you can gather inventory data for BI purposes. Figure you'd need to know something like that early on? Get it into the first iteration.

For example, you may find an ancient custom software application (created by a developer hired long ago in the pre-BI dark ages) that tracks truck deliveries. As your business evolves, you find you have a need for the delivery data buried in this custom software — but the old system did nothing more with the data than generate it and store it. Digging out the data for BI purposes will require additional custom work — the old system's creator is long gone — complete with additional custom fees. You may also be on much more intimate terms with the Enterprise Resource Planning (ERP) system your company has installed — and decide it's time to replace the old custom component with something ERP-friendly while you're at it. Good plan.

So where do you begin this seemingly arduous task of finding out what technologies (BI-friendly or BI-ignorant) you're currently using? Simple: You start with the Microsoft Assessment and Planning (MAP) toolkit, which is designed to assess your current IT environment. It's a software tool that reports on your hardware inventory, compatibility, and readiness. You can use the MAP toolkit to get a handle on what it'll take to upgrade your operating system for clients and servers — *and* a detailed look into the Microsoft Business Intelligence capabilities you may already have (high on that list is SQL Server).

Happily, the Microsoft MAP toolkit offers some built-in BI-friendly conveniences:

- ✔ You don't have to install extra software on existing client machines — or servers, for that matter — to obtain a MAP assessment.
- ✔ The MAP toolkit can also do other IT assessments, including a look at how feasible it may be to consolidate your servers into an integrated virtual environment.

✔ You can download the MAP toolkit for free from the following location:

`http://technet.microsoft.com/en-us/solutionaccelerators/dd537566.aspx`

When you've downloaded the MAP toolkit, you can run your assessment right away. The MAP results are presented in the form of Excel reports and Word documents that outline the findings in an easy-to-read format. The SQL Server report includes tables and graphs that outline any existing instances of this vital Microsoft BI component that you have running in your organization. Figure 13-1 shows versions of SQL Server found running in a sample organization and outlined in the MAP report's graph; Table 13-1 shows what that report's table looks like.

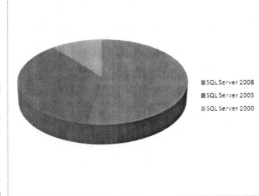

Figure 13-1:
Versions of
SQL Server
graph from
sample
MAP report.

Table 13-1	SQL Server Versions Table (from Sample MAP Report)		
SQL Server Version	**Computer Count**	**Instance Count**	**Percentage of Instances**
SQL Server 2008	39	51	57%
SQL Server 2005	27	31	34%
SQL Server 2000	8	8	9%
Insufficient Data	0	0	0%
Total	**74**	**90**	**100%**

The editions of SQL Server running in the sample organization are outlined in the MAP report's graph in Figure 13-2; Table 13-2 shows the report's table.

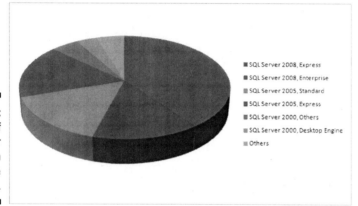

Figure 13-2:
Editions of
SQL Server
graph from
sample
MAP report.

Table 13-2	SQL Server Editions Table (from Sample MAP Report)		
SQL Server Version	*SQL Server Edition*	*Computer Count*	*Instance Count*
SQL Server 2000	Desktop Engine	3	3
SQL Server 2000	Others	4	4
SQL Server 2000	Standard	1	1
SQL Server 2005	Developer	1	1
SQL Server 2005	Enterprise	2	2
SQL Server 2005	Express	14	14
SQL Server 2005	Standard	13	14
SQL Server 2008	Enterprise	12	12
SQL Server 2008	Express	33	39
Total		**83**	**90**

If MAP turns up instances of SQL Server running in your organization, it shows you a table such as Table 13-3. Note that the sample report provided by Microsoft does not contain a graph of this table, but it's easy enough to import this data into Excel and insert your own graph in order to provide a visualization of the data. See Chapter 9 for more information on working with Excel to create graphs.

MAP also shows you a graph that depicts the operating systems running SQL (shown in Figure 13-3) and the report's table (shown in Table 13-4).

Table 13-3   **Instance Count of SQL Server Components (from Sample MAP Report)**

SQL Server Component Name	Number of Instances
SQL Server Database Services	90
SQL Server Integration Services	26
SQL Server Analysis Services	35
SQL Server Reporting Services	14
Insufficient Data (Not Inventoried)	0
Total	**165**

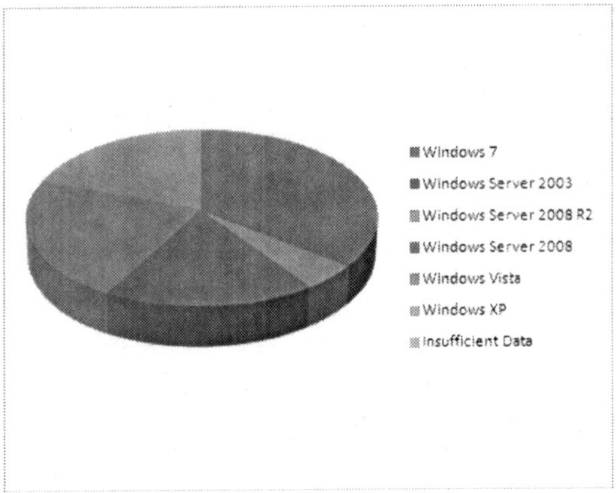

Figure 13-3: Graph of operating systems running SQL Server, from sample MAP report.

Table 13-4   **Operating Systems Running SQL Server (from Sample MAP Report)**

Operating System	Computer Count	Instance Count
Windows 7	4	6
Windows Server 2003	18	27
Windows Server 2008	11	16
Windows Server 2008 R2	3	5
Windows Vista	14	19
Windows XP	12	17
Total	**62**	**90**

Knowing your current licensing

A large cost with any software implementation involves licensing. Licensing involves paying Microsoft in order to use the software it develops. Large-scale licensing can put a hurt on your company's IT budget — but here's where Microsoft licensing brings a potential windfall: For some Microsoft products with BI capabilities, you may already have an enterprise-scale license in place that you're not using — because you didn't even know you had it. (See Chapter 8 for more about BI tools that already come with Windows Server and SQL Server.) It's important to fully understand your current licensing contract before deciding to move forward with a Microsoft BI solution. To find out more about your current Microsoft licensing contract, determine who in your organization is responsible for software licensing (usually the head of your IT department).

If you're *really* lucky, you may not have to pay any additional licensing fees — but if you have no Microsoft licensing in place, you'll have to pay up before you can take that final step in implementing Microsoft BI. Note that I said "final" step since Microsoft products are available for free trials so that you can determine exactly what functionality you want to use *before* you go ahead with paying for licensing. I've found that most organizations already have *some* licensing agreement with Microsoft but may need to revise it to include Microsoft Business Intelligence features.

Determining your current skill sets

If you happen to be Microsoft and want to offer BI capabilities to the world, you have a fairly obvious advantage: Your products are already widely distributed and used throughout the world. Your legion of users is vast; the depth of available knowledge is very deep. You *are* the 900-pound gorilla of software. Life is good; have a banana.

If (like most of us) you're not Microsoft, you're still probably running some of its products. As you think about creating a Microsoft BI system, keep in mind the Microsoft skills your people may already have. For example, if you already use Microsoft Exchange Server and Active Directory for e-mail and login information, and they're running on the Microsoft Windows operating system — whether the server or client version (the most recent of which is Windows 7), then your organization already has a wealth of Microsoft experience — belonging not only to the rank-and-file users but also to the administrators.

There's a range of Microsoft skill sets to look for. The more of them your organization has, the lower the potential cost of contracting or hiring specific Microsoft skills. The next several sections outline what they are.

Windows client OS

The *Windows client operating system* (OS) is the software that runs a standard desktop computer. The three most recent versions of the Microsoft client OS are Windows 7, Windows Vista, and Windows XP; don't be surprised if you run across all three of these on various machines in your organization. Managing these computers is usually the bailiwick of an Information Technology (IT) department that connects the computers to a company network and/or an online domain. The computers are then updated (and software patches installed) by the IT staff. The *domain controller* is a server computer that manages the tracking of the computers and users in the organization's domain; it runs on a Windows server operating system. The IT skills involved in managing all those Windows clients come in handy when you're setting up a Microsoft BI system.

Microsoft Office productivity suite

Microsoft Office is one of the most widely-used software products in the world. Available in several versions, the suite consists of productivity tools such as Outlook, Excel, Word, PowerPoint, Project, Visio, Access, InfoPath, Publisher, and Groove. The skills that users develop while working with Office don't need to be re-learned; the Office applications are tightly integrated with SharePoint and SQL Server, the heart of Microsoft BI.

Windows Server

The *Windows Server operating system* hosts and runs Microsoft server applications. Some versions of the Windows Server OS that you're likely to run across include Windows Server 2008, Windows Server 2003, and even Windows Server 2000 — and they're compatible with a wide range of software products from non-Microsoft vendors. You may be surprised to find how much of the non-Microsoft software you currently run is running on the Windows Server OS platform — and probably won't have to be replaced when you implement Microsoft BI. Administering a client/server system that runs the Windows Server OS, regardless of which compatible applications are running on the system, is a strong step in the direction of administering Microsoft BI.

Server products and features

Some standard Microsoft software products designed to run on Windows Server are common in many IT environments. Exchange Server, for example, handles e-mail traffic, and is the program that the Outlook e-mail client software often connects to. Outlook users are, in fact, using a more powerful and complex system to send and receive their e-mails (as well as to manage their tasks, calendars, contacts, and notes) than they may know; that system becomes an ally to Microsoft BI capabilities when reports live in SharePoint and the user connects his Outlook client to the SharePoint report libraries.

Active Directory (AD) is a feature of the Microsoft Windows Server operating system product, used to manage an organization's *domain* — the total of all online accounts, policies, and connected devices that reside on its intranet (including user accounts, computers, and printers). Presided over by AD administrators, this tidy electronic kingdom stores and manages information about users such as usernames, passwords, and named groups.

The Internet Information Services (IIS) is the part of the Microsoft Windows Server operating system product used to serve up Web pages, basic e-mail, news feeds, and FTP sites. It's the Microsoft version of providing software as a service — as such it's the foundation of SharePoint and many other Web applications that run on Windows Server.

Developers familiar with Visual Studio and .NET

Just as wooden sailing ships used to carry carpenters to make repairs, so many organizations have developers on staff who customize (or create) software capabilities as needed. Typically the developers who do so for the Microsoft platform use Visual Studio and .NET — the same application (see Chapter 11) used to fit the capabilities of Microsoft Business Intelligence to particular organizational needs. Microsoft BI development involves creating Visual Studio projects for SQL Server Analysis Services (SSAS), SQL Server Reporting Services (SSRS), and SQL Server Integration Services (SSIS).

SQL Server Database administrators

Many software applications use the SQL Server Database Engine as their data-storage mechanism when they work with databases. Many IT professionals think of SQL Server as only the database engine and forget that powerful BI components come with SQL Server. SharePoint uses a database running SQL Server to store all its content; often the knowledge that a database administrator has amassed working with the SQL Server Database Engine is applicable to other components of the SQL Server as well.

Microsoft products all over the place

As a software giant, Microsoft offers a plethora of software products to do all kinds of BI-friendly jobs — such as security, server management, communications, and networking. When you assess the Microsoft-savvy skills available in your organization, you may be surprised (though probably not astonished) at the sheer number of Microsoft products already deployed in your organization. There's a built-in benefit: If your people already have the skills required to manage Microsoft products, they're in a good position to use those same skills in the context of a Microsoft BI, when those familiar products take on the enhanced powers of server applications.

Choosing Technologies to Incorporate

Choosing which Microsoft BI capabilities to incorporate into your overall BI system can be a tricky endeavor. Here's where knowledge — in particular, familiarity with the business processes of your organization — is your most important weapon. For example, if Excel is your standard software tool for tracking sales figures, how do you get that data to flow smoothly to the decision-makers when they need it? Should you use a dashboard or score-card (see Chapter 6)? How about generating automatic reports (see Chapter 8) — and if that looks good, how often do you generate them? The quick answer is that there is no quick answer; every business is different, and you'll have to choose BI tools that fit your business processes.

A solid knowledge of your business processes includes not only what they do but how long they take, who does them, and how they fit into the bigger picture with all the other processes. (Those sales figures, for example, can have an impact on such processes as manufacturing, inventory, and marketing — for openers.) When you have a good handle on your business processes, you can then focus on their problems — and on which Microsoft BI tools can help you solve those problems. (For example, if the West Coast sales region has been going great guns for two quarters in a row, how come nobody has asked what they're doing right — and helped the other regions do the same things right? Would a timely automatic report help alert the brass to a potential advantage?) Combining these two steps is the strategic component that must precede any implementation of business intelligence — and Microsoft BI is no exception.

Understanding your business foundation

The first step in choosing the components of your BI system involves understanding the business processes that act as the foundation of your business. Here the quest is to identify the processes that

- ✔ **Produce what your business is known for:** If it's a service (such as data retrieval), how is it delivered to your customers? If it's a tangible product (such as a hybrid car), how is it made?

- ✔ **Directly relate to how your business makes money:** After all, the point of most businesses (unless you are a non-profit) is to make money. You have a good or service that you sell to consumers, other businesses, or other organizations and you need to understand what is going on with these sales. How many hours are we billing? How much honey did we sell?

- ✔ **Encompass how your business is being operated:** Business moguls often say that there are two ways to increase profitability. You can either increase revenue or decrease costs — or both. Incorporating operational processes into your BI system is an important step in increasing productivity and reducing eliminating inefficiencies. How much overtime are we paying? How many breakdowns are we having in our machines? How much turnover do we have with our employees?

In short, what *really* makes your business run? To find out, start with these three steps (and a quick review of Chapter 12):

1. **Create process maps and process flows.**

   These charts document and solidify your understanding of what's really taking place.

2. **Optimize your processes and identify data-capture points.**

   When you have an accurate read on your present situation, you have a strong basis for planning.

3. **Before you choose components for your BI system, get a good working answer to each of these practical questions:**

   - How do your business processes *currently* operate?

   - How *should* your business processes operate when optimized?

     No, "better" or "like gangbusters" are not useful answers, even if they express what you'd like to see. You need numbers here — such as, "By how much should sales increase in the Northeast sector to match what the West Coast sector is doing?"

   - How should data flow from these processes to where it's needed?

     Here the idea is to identify which data should go to whom to meet your BI goals. What's the most vital data? Who most needs to know it? How do you get it there?

Putting together the BI technology puzzle

In addition to understanding the processes that make up your business foundation, you also need a good working knowledge of the tools and capabilities that Microsoft Business Intelligence offers — what each can do, what problem each tries to solve, and how they all work together in a fully functional BI system. Take, for example, the SQL Server Integration Services (SSIS) that comes with the Microsoft SQL Server product:

✔ **What it does:** The SSIS component of SQL Server is used to perform the ETL duties of a BI implementation. Remember that ETL stands for Extract, Transform, and Load. The ETL portions of a BI system are used to connect to the disparate data that are being stored in various other products and databases throughout your organization.

✔ **What problem it tries to solve:** The problem that SSIS is trying to solve is that you have a ton of software and systems that capture and store data all over your organization. SSIS connects to these systems, pulls the data out, transforms it into a standard company-wide format, and then loads it into your data warehouse. Some of the data may be in custom software and some may be in your company-wide ERP system database. Some of the data are in text files and some are in Excel spreadsheets. The data flowing through an organization take many different shapes. The result of using SSIS is that you have standard data that are usable for analysis in your data warehouse.

✔ **How it works with other BI components:** The SSIS technology works with the rest of your Microsoft BI system by providing a useful and potentially automated stream of data that can then be reported on, analyzed, and mined using the other Microsoft BI stack. For example, after you have useful data in the data warehouse, you can have analysts build reports using Report Builder or Excel.

Keep in mind that just because a Microsoft BI product exists it doesn't necessarily mean you have to adopt it. If you're a small business and can accomplish your reporting with Excel, then you don't necessarily need a full-blown implementation of SQL Server Reporting Services.

In all due modesty, I'd say taking an extra spin through this book is another step toward identifying the right tools for the BI job specific to your organization. Parts I and II guide you through the functions that Microsoft BI tools can serve. Part III shows where to find the BI capabilities that are included in various Microsoft products — and how they fit together from a technical perspective. Both views of Microsoft BI — the functional and the technical — are needed. (Ask yourself: "Which of these is the most appropriate tool for the job I have in mind?")

Plugging in the pieces

When you've built a stronger understanding of both your business foundation and Microsoft BI, you're ready to decide which BI components to implement. Figure 13-4 shows how these two bodies of knowledge fit together.

By using an iterative approach (see Chapter 12 for more about what that is and why it works) you can try various BI tools, find what works best (one iteration at a time), and put some tested parts of your BI system into action — even before you finish the full implementation project. Here are a couple of sample scenarios:

✔ If you want to make more efficient use of human business intelligence (see Chapter 10) throughout your company's workforce and get people communicating and collaborating across the globe, you may want to get SharePoint up and running *before* you create a data warehouse for the entire enterprise.

✔ If you want to bring your sales figures into sharper focus, you may want to implement a sales-specific data mart early in the implementation so you can provide sales data that's already gathered, cleaned, sliced, diced, and served up fresh to the powers that be.

Every organization is different; what's important to one may not be as important to the next. Combining your understanding of the business foundation and the Microsoft BI with an iterative approach to implementation (more about that in Chapter 12) provides usable results from real data early on — with minimal upfront investment — what's not to like?

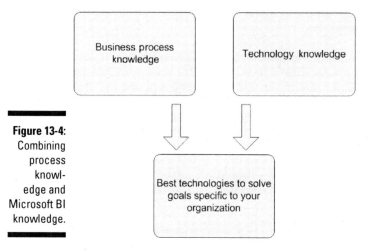

Figure 13-4:
Combining process knowledge and Microsoft BI knowledge.

Utilizing Free BI Tools: Try Before You Buy

Even proposing — let alone implementing — technology projects can generate a huge debate over the total cost of ownership. Business intelligence is no exception. Some of that cost is usually in the form of license fees (even if your company's Microsoft licensing already covers the excellent BI tools built in to some of its products — as described in Chapters 8, 9, and 10). Some organizations have chosen to take the open-source approach to BI. *Open source* means software created by a community of developers who make it available free of charge and provide tech support online forums; the Linux OS is a famous example. Such software is free of licensing fees (as long as it isn't then sold for a profit). For-profit software companies, on the other hand, pay developers to develop software and then sell the licensing to use the software.

There's a perpetual argument over at least two bones of contention:

- ✔ Whether open-source software is robust enough for professional use.
- ✔ Whether tech support is best entrusted to the professional (paid) staff of a large corporation.

I've seen both sides of that debate firsthand. In graduate school, I used open-source software extensively; in my consulting career, I've worked with software from many different companies — including Oracle, SAP, and of course Microsoft. What I've found is that for most business situations, it's much easier to work with a large, professionally-managed corporation that has an extensive customer base and a vast army of people who understand and use the company's products.

In addition, a for-profit organization such as Microsoft has an excellent support system. It's a huge benefit to know that the resources and expertise of the company that developed the software is only a phone call away. I've even been on projects where the issue was escalated to the product team members responsible for a particular piece of software. Even if it takes creating a unique software patch for an unexpected bug, you can be assured that it will happen since you're paying for the software and the support.

Granted, licensing is expensive — but here's a trade secret: The tools that make up Microsoft Business Intelligence are available for trial before being purchased. In particular . . .

- ✔ You can get SQL Server in a trial version with a 180-day free trial period.
- ✔ The Report Builder BI tool is a free download that is used to build reports for SQL Server Reporting Services (SSRS).
- ✔ You can download SharePoint from the Microsoft Web site to try the Business Intelligence Center site capability.
- ✔ For more about trial versions of Microsoft BI tools, check out these Web sites and look for the Try It tab at the top of the page:

    www.microsoft.com/sqlserver

    www.microsoft.com/sharepoint

All too often, decision-makers buy lots of software licensing after a slick presentation promises to solve a raft of business problems. What the demo doesn't show is that the capabilities it displays often depend on having a lot of *other* software from the same vendor installed — which can get really expensive in a hurry. In addition, these demos also assume that your business processes are already optimized and ready to roll down a BI path. Be careful if someone tries to sell you software that will solve all of your BI needs and forgets to mention your business processes. Building your BI foundation, as described in Chapter 12, is just as important as picking the right BI tools and should not be neglected in your BI implementation.

If you've got the money, purchasing licensing is easy — the difficult part is creating an implementation plan that fits your organization. A BI system that really delivers the desired results must take into account the processes and procedures of the organization; without that knowledge, half of Figure 13-4 is missing, and the BI implementation bogs down. Without a successful implementation, the software sits on a shelf and gathers dust as *shelf-ware.*

The best advice I can give is to follow a sequence like this:

1. Know your business processes well — *first.*

2. Download a trial version of the Microsoft BI tool(s) that best fit a low-risk, high-value business process (see Chapter 12).

   For example, you may try SharePoint to address the problem of isolated business knowledge.

3. Make full use of trial software throughout early iterations of your BI implementation.

4. When you start seeing the real results that the trial software generates — and are confident, you can then commit fully to purchasing the software license — go for it.

Trying SQL Server

You may as well try one of the heavy hitters of Microsoft BI: You can download a free trial version of SQL Server (yes, you read that right) at the following location:

```
www.microsoft.com/sqlserver
```

Click the Try It tab to navigate to the trial download page. The download page is very straightforward and easy to navigate, as shown in Figure 13-5.

There are two methods for obtaining the installation media for the trial version of SQL Server. The first is a simple download (which can then be burned to a DVD); the second involves ordering a physical DVD (which will be mailed to you), as shown in Figure 13-6.

Figure 13-5:
Download
page for
the trial
version of
SQL Server.

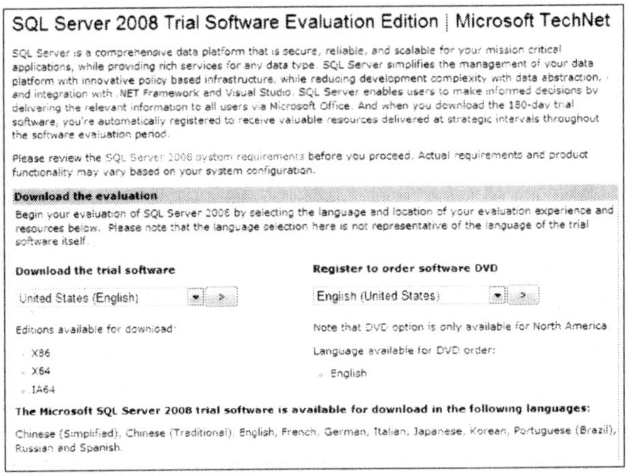

Figure 13-6:
The
Microsoft
page for
obtaining
a trial ver-
sion of SQL
Server as a
download or
a DVD.

Checking out SharePoint

How about trying another major Microsoft BI tool? A free trial version of
SharePoint can be downloaded by navigating to the following location and
then clicking the Try It tab:

```
www.microsoft.com/sharepoint
```

On the SharePoint trial page, you can find a simple mechanism to download the trial version of SharePoint — as well as case studies, whitepapers, and other resources to help you get to know both SharePoint and its user community. You can even chat with a SharePoint Specialist in a pop-in window.

Reducing Risk

No less than financial or construction projects, BI projects automatically entail risk. Taking as many risks out of the project as possible — before you shell out big bucks for software licensing — is critical to overall success. So take a look at the upcoming checklist (and maybe flip back through Chapter 12 and 13 for a refresher) as you get ready to select the components for your BI system.

You can greatly reduce risk in your implementation of Microsoft BI by

- ✓ **Intimately understanding your business processes.**
- ✓ **Building a solid foundation of business processes and data.**
- ✓ **Using an iterative approach to the implementation.**
- ✓ **Understanding the technologies and skill sets that you already have available.**
- ✓ **Using trial software to understand the value before paying large licensing costs.**

Chapter 14

Testing and Rolling Out

In This Chapter

▶ Getting real results early to add value persistently

▶ Exploring the different types of testing involved in a BI project

▶ Rolling out specific functionality to users

▶ Finding out how change affects a BI implementation

▶ Winning the hearts and minds of users

The test is to recognize the mistake, admit it, and correct it.

— Dale E. Turner (Oingo Boingo)

Chapter 12 discussed two different approaches to implementing a business intelligence (BI) plan: the waterfall approach and the iterative approach. The waterfall approach completes all design and development of a BI project before presenting the result to the users; it's up to the testers to find and fix any problems before releasing the new system — for better or worse — to the users. The result is tremendous pressure to *get every detail exactly right the very first time* — which rarely happens in the real world. An *iterative* approach, however, follows a cycle of "try it out, check your results, make changes, try it out again, repeat until you're satisfied with the way it works, and then move on." The iterative cycle turns the testing and rolling-out of components into gradual phases that get better and better results as they go along. With each new iteration, you can quickly verify whether a component is working as it should, roll out the shiny new iteration so users can see it and try it out, and then capture their responses for incorporation into future iterations — both the likes and the dislikes. Iteration by iteration, you find out what works and what doesn't work *before* the project ends . . . and before your entire BI budget is vaporized.

In this chapter, you explore testing and rolling out Microsoft BI functionality to users. You also examine the different types of testing involved in a Microsoft BI solution and discover some of the keys to rolling out a solution that users will love.

Continuously Adding Value

In an iterative approach to BI implementation, each iteration goes through four phases: Discover, Design, Develop, and Validate. Over the course of the project, this process loops back through these phases continuously; each cycle adds BI functionality, tests it, gets user feedback, and provides real results — all of which adds value to the overall BI system. Testing and rollout of each BI component will occur in the Validate phase, as shown in Figure 14-1.

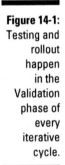

Figure 14-1:
Testing and rollout happen in the Validation phase of every iterative cycle.

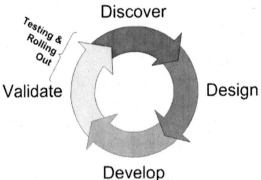

Discover

Design

Develop

Validate

Testing & Rolling Out

You don't have to complete every detail of each BI component before you present it to the users for their feedback. You can test, try out, and present each component as it becomes available — using the sequence of phases mentioned earlier for each iterative cycle. For example, the first iterative cycles may introduce a collaborative component such as a SharePoint discussion board. Presenting this component to the entire user base early in the implementation makes sense — the collaborative environment gives users a way to provide direct feedback and discuss not only this new component but also other components as they become available — while getting the users started using a part of the new BI system. Here you're already generating real value: (a) improvement in each BI component as you fit it into the system and (b) getting your users accustomed to using the new capabilities.

Testing Your BI Implementation

Testing a BI implementation is, of course, more complex than simply testing software code. The components of a BI implementation must be tightly integrated with the processes driving the business and the data flowing from those processes; you have to test the integration as well as the component itself. BI testing consists of a number of different techniques including testing for diversity, process testing, data extraction, transformation, and storage testing (also known as ETL testing), and unit testing.

BI testing diversity

To serve its function (which is analogous to that of military intelligence in wartime), BI information has to go through specific changes on its way from the front lines up to the top brass. It starts at the level of your business processes — not only an accurate picture of how they work, but also the data they generate. That data is captured by an ETL mechanism (see Chapter 5), given a usable format, and loaded into a data warehouse; finally it surfaces as usable business information — accurate, timely, and readily available to the decision-makers. End-to-end testing of the information at various stages of this journey is a vital part of BI implementation (as shown in Figure 14-2).

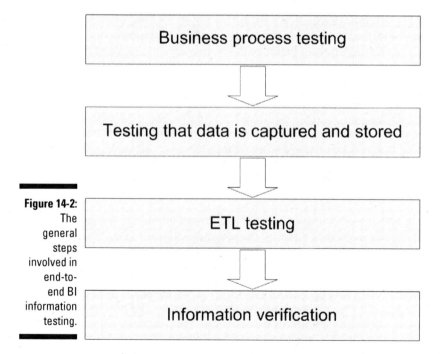

Figure 14-2: The general steps involved in end-to-end BI information testing.

This entire end-to-end testing process must be performed at each iterative cycle during the Validate phase.

The way you test a business process is very different from the way you test a database design. Because business processes are as diverse as businesses themselves, the testing process for a BI implementation is uniquely diverse. The following sections examine the general steps involved in end-to-end BI information testing.

Business process testing

The processes that drive your business form the foundation (the "it's-what-I-do") of the business — the creation of books, for example, is one such process that serves this function for a publisher. The entire BI system must reflect those processes — and be tested to ensure that it's serving them.

These days business processes commonly require interaction between humans and computers. Therefore testing a business process requires the human intuition and guidance of the people who perform the tasks that make up each business process — for example, the people who actually build the vehicles if your company makes hybrid cars. As you may imagine, the best people to recruit to test a business process are the very people who will be affected when it's optimized. They'll be able to guide you to the best places in the process to put data-capture points for your BI system (for example, should you monitor production rates for batteries, engines, chassis, completed vehicles, or all four?). The goal is to end up with a business process that's not only optimized but includes the necessary data-capture points — all of which adds more value to your BI system as you go along.

Testing to ensure data are captured and stored

En route to becoming usable business information, the data generated by a business process have to be captured and stored in an operational system. Capturing the wild business-process data mechanism involves not only the technical components (the hardware and software that do the capturing can vary widely), but also a deep understanding of the data itself: You have to ensure that it's correct and relevant to the process that generates it.

To confirm that the data are captured and stored correctly, the people performing the tasks that make up the process will need to form a working alliance with the data managers who run the data warehouse. These two groups should work closely together to verify that the data flowing into the operational system is not only technically correct but functionally correct. For example, data flowing into an inventory database needs to be tested on the technical level by database administrators and on the functional level by the people working in the distribution center. The database administrators can confirm that the data is in the correct format; the people in the distribution center can confirm that the numbers are in fact correct.

ETL testing

Once the data is captured and stored in the operational system, the computers take over. Extracting the data from the source operational systems, transforming it into a standard format, and loading it into the data warehouse — Extract,

Transform, and Load (ETL) — is detailed in Chapter 5. Here you're in luck: The SQL Server Integration Services (SSIS) packages that perform this transfer (see Chapters 5 and 8) are software-based — which means you can automate the testing. For example, you can create an SSIS package that includes tasks specifically designed to send testing information to files or to any other destination on the company network. In addition, SSIS includes tools for error handling which can also automate the process of detecting and responding to problems throughout the ETL process.

When you test your SSIS packages, be sure to verify that

- ✔ The amount of data showing up in the destination matches the source.
- ✔ The number of tables transferred is correct.
- ✔ The number of columns transferred is correct.
- ✔ The number of rows transferred is correct.
- ✔ The data in the destination system are functionally correct. For example, the database is looking for a piece of datum that is a number. If it's tracking the price for a stick of gum and receives $1,932,123,432.00, then it will not show an error because this information is a valid value from the database point of view. Functionally, however, it's a little bit steep for a pack of gum. You need to make sure data are correct both technically and functionally.
- ✔ The length of each data element is correct (for example, a first name may be 50 characters in the source system but stored as 20 characters in the destination system).

Keeping the project honest — did you answer the question?

By the time your business-process data are stored in the data warehouse, they're ready to be used as full-fledged business information; your BI system can surface (display) it in various forms to the users who need it — as reports, KPIs, scorecards, dashboards, graphs, and charts (see Chapter 6 for more about these). Before you go parading the information in front of the brass, however, be sure you've determined how important and valuable the information is by checking with the people who'll be using it.

Verifying that the surfaced information is both correct *and* useful involves another rollout: presenting the information to the users who expect to base business decisions on it — and requesting feedback. If you've run the iterative cycle often enough while developing your BI system, you already know that the feedback you receive is best used by incorporating it into later iterative cycles. And yes, those go on throughout the life of the BI implementation. Business realities change; your BI system has to gather, prepare, and present *current* information — that is, keep it real. As an ongoing aspect of business intelligence, the iterative approach is as essential and practical as regular car maintenance.

Unit testing

So what's going on under the hood of an iterative cycle? Well, the first thing you'll find is that it's made up of units of work. A *unit* is a finite piece of work that makes sense and has an easily identifiable starting and stopping point. For example, you can subdivide the process of getting a particular piece of information ready to surface to the decision-makers as a sequence of tasks, each one a unit of work:

- ✔ Documenting the goal
- ✔ Mapping the current the way the processes currently work
- ✔ Using SQL Server to create a data-storage mechanism in the data warehouse
- ✔ Mapping the way the processes will work once they are modified and optimized
- ✔ Modifying the current processes so that they contain the needed data capture points and are optimized
- ✔ Creating the ETL package using SQL Server Integration Services (SSIS)
- ✔ Creating information in ready-to-use forms such as SQL Server Reporting Services (SSRS) reports, PerformancePoint dashboards, SQL Server Analysis Services (SSAS) cubes, Excel Services reports, and KPIs and then making them available to other users in SharePoint

Documenting the goal

Business intelligence must provide information that helps you run your business more effectively, efficiently, and (yes) intelligently. So the first intelligent thing to do is set goals — to determine the specific information you want your system to provide. For example, you may decide that you need a detailed view of your sales data for a particular store — slicing and dicing the data by products, time of day, and customer basket.

Mapping the current state of your business process

In order to fully understand your current business processes, remember to get the rank-and-file perspective; the people involved in your processes can help you map out exactly what tasks they're performing. Process maps and process flows give you a bird's-eye view of how your business processes currently operate. What you get from diagramming the state of a business process can include

- ✔ A visual representation of what tasks are being performed
- ✔ What data is being captured
- ✔ Where the data is being stored
- ✔ What inefficiencies can use some tuning up

Creating a data-storage mechanism

Before you begin pulling data out of your source systems and transforming it, you need a storage mechanism in place that can provide the information that your higher-ups need. You can use SQL Server to create that storage mechanism — a data warehouse (see Chapter 6).

Early in your BI implementation — in the early iterations of the storage mechanism — you can fill it with dummy data and test the surfacing process to see how the information will play in the board room.

Be sure you create your storage structure *before* beginning the ETL process so you don't limit yourself to only the data that are currently being captured. If the word comes down from on high that critical data are missing about a particular business process, you can introduce additional data-capture points into that process to snag what's needed. After all, the whole point of a BI system is to answer critical questions and provide valuable information. That point is mounted on a moving target. (But you knew that.)

Mapping the future process state

When you have an appropriate data-storage mechanism in place — and have a good handle on what data are needed to answer your critical business questions — you're ready to map out how your business processes will look when the proper data capture points are in place and the processes are optimized. You don't need a time machine; all you need do is

1. Take a close look at the current process maps.

2. Figure out what the tasks would look like when optimized.

3. Include any data-capture points needed for the data warehouse.

For example, maybe a current process doesn't have a data-capture point for products by group. Here you'd have to identify the product groups and then modify the process so the required information is captured.

Modifying the current processes

When you have *two* business-process maps — one showing the current state and one showing that gosh-wow future state — you have the "before" and "after" views that should guide you in modifying the process appropriately. The BI aspect of this step is to introduce the data-capture points required for the data warehouse. For example, if you your goal is to provide information on a manufacturing machine, then you need to make sure the proper data are being captured. You may need to purchase a scanner and software that scans each new product as it rolls off the line and records the data in an operational database.

Creating the ETL package using SSIS

Up to this point, you've done a fair amount of magic but have barely touched any BI technology. You've created the storage mechanism for the data warehouse in SQL Server, but the bulk of the work has been in transforming your business processes. With that foundation in place, you're ready to create the SQL Server Integration Services (SSIS) package (see Chapters 5 and 8) — the tool that does the Extract, Transform, and Load process — ETL (see Chapter 5): It extracts the data out of the source systems, transforms it into a standard format, and loads it into the data warehouse.

Visual Studio is the tool you use to develop SSIS packages. In essence, you create a package by selecting tasks to add to the design surface in the SSIS development environment (for details, see Chapter 5). For example, if you want to make a copy of an Excel file on a network drive and store it in a backup folder on a different drive, you'd add a File System Task to the SSIS package, as shown in Figure 14-3.

Figure 14-3:
Adding a
File System
Task to
an SSIS
package.

Creating information and surfacing data

At this point, all the hard BI work is done. It's time to dress up the info in the digital equivalent of a pinstripe suit, — brush off its lapels, and surface it: Send it up to meet the end users and tell them what they need to know. The Microsoft BI tools you use to accomplish this feat include

✔ SQL Server Reporting Services (SSRS) reports (see Chapter 6)

✔ Key Performance Indicators (KPIs — see Chapters 6 and 11)

✔ PerformancePoint dashboards (see Chapter 11)

✔ SQL Server Analysis Services (SSAS) cubes (see Chapters 4 and 8)

✔ Excel Services reports (see Chapter 10)

So, to reiterate . . .

When all these units — each one a discrete task — are combined, they make up a full *iterative cycle.* Note that an iterative cycle presents just the latest version of a unit of work, a capability, or piece of the BI system you're putting in place. It's not a mighty megawatt heat-ray designed to boil the ocean; its goals are human-scale. Be sure to focus each iterative cycle on a small goal that results in real value. You can add functionality (and, if necessary, scope) in later iterations. As the project progresses and feels the beneficial shaping effect of user feedback, one iterative cycle at a time, you get usable business information *and* a demonstration of what BI can do for you — all with minimal budget and risk. Each progressive cycle adds incremental value — not only while you're developing the BI system, but also as you make business intelligence a valuable, ongoing part of your organization's future.

A common misconception is that you're somehow "done" with BI. That's like saying you're done with selling your products or services. You may have goals in place for selling a certain number of products within a given timeframe, but you're never done. The same mindset should be used for BI as well. You continually improve. When you have a bigger budget and bring in consultants, you'll improve faster. When you have a smaller budget and internal resources, you'll improve slower. In the end, however, you'll always be iterating your BI solution and always improving your BI solution.

Rolling It Out — Again and Again

In the aerospace industry, often the most exciting time is when a new jet rolls out of the hangar, into the sunlight, and flies for the first time. But business intelligence is more like a series of rollouts: As soon as each BI component is ready, be sure you roll it out to end users so they can ooh, ahh, kick the tires, complain, and generally improve it. When users can begin exploring BI functionality and discovering its strengths and weaknesses, what you get is a system that will (to continue the metaphor) fly better before it even gets off the ground, and continue to fly better as you use it. Hindsight may be 20/20, but that's often the attitude of folks who never expected to go back to the drawing board. By involving your end users in a series of BI rollouts and incorporating their feedback into future iterative cycles, you gain the benefit of 20/20 hindsight even before the overall project is complete. (Who *needs* a time machine?)

Your power users should be involved throughout the entire testing process. When your completed BI plan is in place, then you can have a *big* rollout to the rest of the user base. By the time the rest of the users are ready to use the BI system, they'll surely have heard about what's brewing from the power users. That's one critical reason to have the power users on your side (as they're likelier to be if they've been involved from the start): winning the hearts and minds of the rest of the users. In addition, the rank-and-file users can go to the power users for help and assistance. The power users are much likelier to champion a new system they helped create.

Training is a topic for Chapter 15; for the moment, however, I can mention that I've found the best training happens when users explore a system on their own — while trying to accomplish part of their job duties. A system that provides useful information will have a viral affect. Word of the system spreads; users get wind of, investigate, and start to use the system. They talk to each other and discover how to do things; their social networks actually boost the informal training process. To make this whole thing work right, however, the most important thing is to collect feedback from users *as they move through the acceptance process.* That means taking the gradual route — capturing their feedback and incorporating it, not only early on, but iteration by iteration. The parts that the users like and find useful should be expanded, and critical feedback should be embraced. The idea is to arrive at a BI system that everyone finds valuable in all the corners of the organization.

Surfacing information

Surfacing information to users — making it available in a ready-to-use format — can take many forms. The upcoming sections offer a closer look at some of the primary ways Microsoft Business Intelligence delivers the goods: Excel, SQL Server Reporting Services (SSRS), SharePoint Key Performance Indicators (KPIs), PerformancePoint Services, and Report Builder.

Excel

Microsoft Office Excel is so commonly used for data analysis and report building that you'll probably find it all over the place in your organization. An Excel report is very versatile; you can print it, e-mail it, place it on a shared drive, put it in a document library in SharePoint, embed it into a SharePoint site using Excel Services, or make a paper airplane out of an old Excel spreadsheet at the next big meeting. (Just kidding about that last one. But you knew that.)

Although Excel reports are fairly easy to connect to a BI system so you can import data for analysis, I prefer to use other methods to surface business info from the data warehouse. The problem with Excel is that it can produce independent documents that become competing (and confusing) sources of business information. To keep your BI story straight, what you need is software that can connect to the data warehouse and display its data but can't pull the data out of there. The idea is to ensure that there's only one authoritative source of the information you're using — and that the authoritative source isn't choked with obsolete data. For example, an SSRS report is usually connected to live data that's *updated every time the report is run*. When the data in the warehouse is updated, the report reflects the changes. On the other hand, if you just yank the data and drop it into Excel, you've introduced the possibility of acting on stale data. Bad idea. There are ways to keep Excel data fresh, of course, but they're more complex and hassle-prone than simply viewing an SSRS report that surfaces fresh data on a Web site.

One of the best ways to use Excel in a BI solution is to pair it with SharePoint. Using Excel Services, you can control the Excel sheet using SharePoint features and allow only a select group of people to own the spreadsheet, yet you can surface the sheet to the entire user base in a read-only format by embedding it in a SharePoint site. Excel Services provides content producers with the ability to continue to use the Excel program they're comfortable with and it also provides your IT department a control and governance mechanism that maintains one source of the truth. With the introduction of PowerPivot in Excel 2010 and SharePoint 2010, Excel can now handle millions upon millions of rows of data in an analysis. These powerful Excel documents can then be uploaded and embedded in the SharePoint 2010 environment and made available to the rest of the user base. The end users can then perform an analysis based on the Excel spreadsheet without spawning new versions of the document like water on a gremlin.

SQL Server Reporting Services (SSRS)

The reporting component of the SQL Server — SQL Server Reporting Services (SSRS) — is a reporting engine that can render reports and use them to surface fresh business information. SSRS can be used in two ways:

- ✔ **Stand-Alone mode:** The reports are stored, managed, and surfaced in a Web application called Report Manager.

- ✔ **Integrated mode:** Here SharePoint takes over completely, and Report Manager steps out of the picture. In Integrated mode, you can hot-rod your SSRS reports with the advanced content-management features of SharePoint — check-in/check-out, versioning, alerts, security, and workflow (see Chapter 10 for the juicy details). That'll stamp out mutant documents before they start.

SharePoint Key Performance Indicators (KPIs)

A Key Performance Indicator (KPI) is a *really* vital piece of information about how well your organization is doing its job — so vital that it may give the brass apoplexy if it starts looking anemic. SharePoint also contains a specialized list called a *KPI list* that's designed to surface the KPI information on a SharePoint Web site. (See Chapter 10.)

PerformancePoint Services for SharePoint

PerformancePoint is designed especially for creating information visualizations such as dashboards and scorecards (for more about those, see Chapter 6). Although you can create a dashboard and scorecard in other Microsoft programs (such as SSRS or Excel), using PerformancePoint is often the most efficient method. In particular PerformancePoint Services for SharePoint provides business users with the ability to create their own dashboards, scorecards, and analytical reports using PerformancePoint Services Dashboard Designer without having to rely on BI developers. For more about developing for PerformancePoint Services using Dashboard Designer, check out Chapter 11.

PerformancePoint Server was recently discontinued as a separate product. Its mightiest powers — the dashboard, scorecard, and analytical capabilities — became new SharePoint features that go by the name PerformancePoint Services for SharePoint 2010.

Report Builder reports

In days of old, at the very dawn of BI, traditional SSRS reports were crafted using the Visual Studio development tool. A report developer would take a list of requirements and then labor faithfully with a database administrator to retrieve the correct data, format the report, and display it in an informative fashion. Unfortunately, the information in the finished report ran the risk of being obsolete when presented. (See the accompanying sidebar.)

The Report Builder application was designed with the business user in mind. Report Builder has the familiar ribbon navigation of Office applications such as Word and Excel. Report Builder allows for the development of SSRS reports without having to use a development environment such as Visual Studio. Using Report Builder, an end user can build reports and surface fresh information without the need to enlist a technical developer.

The reports they are a-changin' . . . slowly

With traditional reporting, a database administrator would generally work with an SSRS developer to build a report and then surface it to the end users. An end user who wanted to revise or update the report would have to submit a requirement change request — which would funnel back through the development process. Now, if a report is especially complex (or rarely changes except in the event of an asteroid strike), a full development process may make sense. But these days businesses need *much* faster reflexes. Report Builder speeds up the reporting process by empowering end users to provide ad-hoc reports without the need for a full development cycle.

Having a BI Management Plan

As you've probably guessed, business intelligence is itself an ongoing business process that generates content (ready-to use business information). As such it needs its own management plan — for both the process and the content — to keep it on track. That means providing a management scenario for every BI component you roll out during every iterative cycle. That may sound complex, but if sound, authoritative business information is what your system produces, then (no less than any product) it needs some quality-control measures in place. For example, if you introduce an end-to-end data flow that handles sales data — taking it from the business-process level up through its emergence as surfaced information in SharePoint — then you'll need a management plan for each stage of that process.

If a business process might require maintenance, then you need a policy that manages the changes, the downtime, and the effects that the downtime has on the rest of the business. If you've set up some new data-capture points in the process, those will need their own management plan — as will the operational data-storage mechanism. For example, if your company makes toothpaste and you're tapping in to a toothpaste machine in the manufacturing department, here's what you'll need to manage — at minimum:

- ✓ A technician will have to monitor the machine to confirm that it's operating correctly.

- ✓ The data flowing out of the machine must be captured in an operational database.

- ✓ The database requires the attention of a database administrator.

- ✓ The SQL Server Integration Services (SSIS) package that performs Extract, Transform, and Load (ETL) as it grabs the data from the operational system and prepares it for the data warehouse will have to be monitored.

- ✓ The data warehouse itself requires a management plan that performs backups, restores data as needed, and monitors physical servers and networks.

- ✓ Turning the data into information and surfacing that information requires the skills of business analysts, report developers, and database administrators.

- ✓ The SharePoint environment requires a *farm administrator* (a farm is the term for an overall SharePoint implementation, which includes many different departmental and intranet sites).

- ✓ The overall network architecture requires Microsoft-savvy infrastructure and network teams.

Looks like the dawning of a golden age for managers, doesn't it?

Your organization may already have many of the necessary skill-sets. But don't assume that's true. Check. If you discover holes in your team that must be filled, you want that revelation to happen in *early* iterations. You don't want to find out at the end of the project that you need to hire 20 additional people just to manage the BI system. But don't panic: Using an iterative approach to BI implementation will give you a realistic picture of the people and skills needed to make your BI system work. In addition, by using a Microsoft BI solution you can leverage the wisdom and resources of the overall business user base. Business users will become content creators using tools such as Report Builder, Dashboard Designer, and Excel.

Managing Change

Some of the best consultants I've ever worked with were completely focused on the change process that every major project entails — they understood that even an improvement is a change, and change can be disruptive. Unfortunately, many organizations see the role of managing change as secondary to the technical challenges of implementing a new system.

Be sure to include a person who understands the impact of change — on your processes and on your people — in your team from the get-go — and that means from the first iterative cycle onward. Each iterative cycle will produce some amount of change; the role of the change guru is to make sure that the changes are as transparent (easy to understand and minimally disruptive) as possible, user-driven, communicated effectively, and incorporated into every iterative cycle of your BI implementation.

In many years of experience, I've found that change is one of those basic, built-in components of any BI implementation. The other basic component is just as built in: the business processes that drive the business and produce data. Software demonstrations and implementation plans often overlook those basics. But when the rubber hits the road and the BI implementation moves forward, those basics can either make or break the entire project. Granted, getting a handle on the business processes and preparing for change *during the first iteration* may be painful — but it pays dividends throughout the process of implementation, in the form of practical lessons about how the company works and the kind of immediate 20/20 hindsight that makes each iteration an incremental improvement.

An undisputed fact is that humans are creatures of habit, and disrupting that habit can create chaos. It doesn't matter if the old business process is very inefficient and unproductive and the new process is extremely efficient and productive. The process of changing behavior is painful and must be addressed *throughout the BI implementation.*

Change is painful

As humans we are creatures of habit — how many people do you know who park in the exact same parking spot every working day? When something causes a change in our habits, we often react with anxiety and discomfort. As a consultant, I'm forced to change constantly; every new client has a different culture, climate, and environment. You'd think that a life filled with constant change would get me used to it.

Nope.

Like most people, however, I avoid change whenever possible. When we go shopping at the mall I always park in the exact same place at the bottom of the parking garage next to the elevator. It drives my wife crazy that I pass up tons of open spots just so I can get to the spot I always park in. When I work out of our Seattle office, I park in the exact same spot every day. I stand in the same security line every week at the Seattle-Tacoma airport, even though there are probably shorter lines around the corner.

In a nutshell, I'm living proof that even when change occurs, human nature wants to avoid it.

A good friend of mine was teaching a course on change in the corporate world to a bunch of executives. He seated the executives and had them take out their pens and sign their names. Next, he told them that the change being thrust into their lives was minor: They would all have to sign their names with the opposite hand from this point onward. No big deal, right? (Good luck trying to get a legible signature — on everything you sign.)

The habits involved in everyday business are no different than the habits in our everyday lives. Business analysts come in every day and over time become so comfortable with the tools that they use they're often immune to think that there may be something better. Executives become so used to the basic text reports that they receive on a weekly or monthly basis that they forget to think that there may be a better, more efficient, and more informative report.

Gaining early adoption

Every organization has its power users who understand the systems intimately. These are the go-to people in every office or group who can answer questions and guide others through the systems . . . and these folks are your best friends when you're doing any kind of technical implementation. The power users already understand the current systems; bring 'em on board at the start of the project. Here are some starting points in that process:

- ✔ **Take the time to explain the reasons behind your BI implementation to the power users.** They already understand the current state of the business processes, but once they understand the reasons for the implementation, they can help optimize your business processes and help bring the rest of the user base up to speed.

- ✔ **Be completely transparent about the big picture and vision.** Don't minimize the work involved, but be clear about the expected advantages. Changing any business process often involves additional work —

at the very least, you have to create the correct data-capture points —
and your users will want (naturally enough) to know why this additional
work is critical. If you can clue them in to how your BI project fits into
the big picture, your users are less likely to resist the change. Involving
the power users early on sets up a flow of trustworthy information —
which boosts the project's credibility and merit.

✔ **Turn to your power users for solid information on how the current
systems work, for practical input on the design of the new system, and
to help get communication and feedback underway at each rollout of
BI functionality.** That involvement is another advantage of the iterative
approach. Figure 14-4 illustrates the central role that power users play
in a BI implementation.

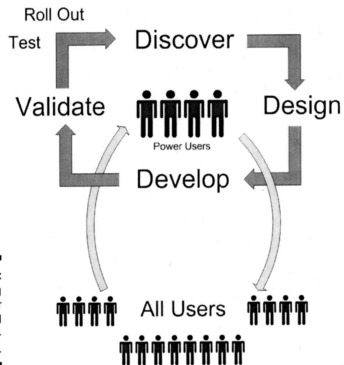

Figure 14-4:
Involving
power
users in a BI
implementa-
tion.

Transparency is crucial

One of the biggest mistakes I often see in large organizations when they try
to change a business process is an automatic do-as-I-say assumption: The
leadership believes they know best and that they'll simply make decisions
and then dictate what the worker bees should do. This command and control
structure is outdated and inefficient, especially in an age that gives information

workers increasing responsibility in their roles. What I've found is that most workers will understand and accept that management doesn't have all the answers all the time — and will provide valuable insights along the path to an answer.

Taking advantage of the knowledge your people already have gives you two major advantages right off the bat:

✔ You add their experience to the equation and thus come up with a more realistic, more workable solution.

✔ You help manage the change process by being inclusive.

By including people, you create a feeling of involvement and contribution. ("You mean my opinion matters? Cool. Let's get it done.") A leader without all the answers is not a bad thing as long as there's a clear vision. As a leader, you can provide the goal and then let the people figure out how to get there; the leader's role is to watch to make sure the path is being forged in the correct direction. This leadership-from-behind is, in my opinion, one of the keys to success in the modern business environment.

The explosion of popularity that Microsoft SharePoint enjoys has happened because it makes this inclusive style of leadership easier and more effective. SharePoint provides the mechanism for communication and collaboration — leaders can communicate a vision on an executive blog and then people can work together to discuss the vision and provide a clear path to success. Communication is iterative by nature; as people from throughout the organization participate, the organization as a whole gets a clearer picture of the best solution possible — a "what's best for *us*" perspective. This massive collaboration is often called *crowd sourcing* — the solution emerges from a wide range of diverse individual thinking that goes on in the crowd.

SharePoint allows everyone to log in, see what's going on, and participate. Using a communication-and-collaboration mechanism that's available to everyone reinforces a feeling of inclusion and contribution. By communicating early and often, the entire organization has a sense of the change and a stake in it; having a seat at the table allows people to understand and accept change instead of moving against it.

Delegating ownership

Ownership of an idea is a powerful force. People who are identified as responsible for a particular issue are often more engaged and dedicated. Such ownership triggers the best in people; they have a stake in the outcome. I've often worked with people who seem completely unengaged, but once they're given ownership of a particular task, they light up and come alive. The task becomes an extension of the person; the result directly reflects the owner's personal decisions and work ethic.

One of the biggest factors in the success of a BI project is how much ownership you can delegate to your most adept power users. As a consultant, when I walk into a new organization I usually already have a pretty good idea of how the official organizational structure is put together. One of my first objectives is to find out how the hierarchy really works; I've often seen organizations in which "officially" lower-ranking people have tremendous influence on the outcome of a decision. Why waste good brains?

Understanding how groups function is a whole book unto itself, but keep in mind that identifying the power users and influencers quickly — and giving them ownership — can be the key to a successful BI implementation.

Changing business processes

Don't be surprised if you run into a very traditional attitude when you start talking about improving business processes: "If it ain't broke, don't fix it." Sure, those processes may be clumsy, inefficient, and outdated, but hey, they're *familiar* — people have been doing the same thing for years. And now you're telling them the old familiar way isn't good enough?

Yep. Welcome to the twenty-first century.

A BI implementation needs a solid foundation. That means making sure the processes that drive the business are as effective and well-understood as they can be. So the question isn't whether to change, but how; that's what this section is about.

Deciding on the best change mechanism

There are three schools of thought when it comes to the most effective way to change a business process:

- ✔ You can create a new process, bring it up to run parallel to the old one, and then move from the old to the new.

- ✔ You can make a clean break from the old process and charge ahead into a full adoption of the new process.

- ✔ You can change the most important components of a process gradually, in iterative cycles, until you've transformed the entire process.

An element common to all three approaches is the need for a route to get from the old process to the new process. Whichever approach you choose, you start by mapping your current process and then mapping your future process — preferably in the form of process maps and process flows (see Chapter 12). Then you figure out what has to happen, in what order to get from the old way to the new way. The route you come up with should include as much detail as possible. Finally, decide which mechanism you'll use in order to actuate the change. Of course, if you think I'm in favor of the iterative approach . . .

Iterative and inclusive change

. . . you're absolutely right. I've been involved in all three types of change mechanisms and have found that, as with most things, an iterative approach works best. Making change happen *one careful iteration at a time* helps you to identify mistakes or misconceptions in the map that future business process — and take corrective action before the new process is fully in place.

To get the iterations to do their job — getting you closer and closer to what works best — it bears repeating — be sure you get the people performing the tasks on board. When they've participated in creating the future state of their process, they feel ownership, are likelier to become your allies in getting the new process off the ground, and can help everybody glide into the new way with scarcely a squawk.

Be inclusive in the entire change process; starting out with involvement and ending up with the same old do-as-I-say won't create the ownership and interested input that are the heart of an iterative approach to BI implementation. Sure, adding a data-capture point to a business process usually entails adding a step to the process — one more darn thing to do — but the data generated will benefit the whole organization: Accurate data on what's really going on means more realistic and effective business decisions. That's hard to attain if you just post a bare-bones directive that boils down to "This is what you're going to do, so do it." Staying inclusive by keeping your people clued in to the "why" of BI — every step of the way — conveys respect and encourages the best input.

Introducing new technology without mutiny

Introducing new technology into an IT department can often be a delicate matter — and business intelligence is a case in point. If it's "not developed here" — or seems (at first glance) to add needless complexity — even the idea of a new system can meet with fierce resistance. Being a technical person myself, I can understand the IT perspective. What IT despises is when a consultant gives a slick demo to upper management, without the involvement of IT, and then management goes to their IT team and orders them to make it happen. Maybe the IT team is a Microsoft shop through and through and the product that was just purchased is Oracle. Try to avoid purchasing technology just for technologies sake (or the demo looked so cool and easy).

Getting familiar with any new technology is a lot like learning a new language — or even a new culture. It takes years to fully understand the nuances engrained in the view of the world that always seems to be built in to products of a particular vendor — especially if your IT department has been using those products for years and has grown adept at tweaking them. Someone who has spent a career teaching (say) Microsoft or Sun applications to jump through hoops won't want to change and work with something else.

Of course, if your IT shop is already running Microsoft products and you approach it with a proposal for implementing Microsoft BI, your task may be a little less thorny. But if IT is running Macs, Unix, or other non-Microsoft systems, well . . . *diplomacy* is the byword.

Imagine growing up in the United States having never heard a language other than English. Then, all of a sudden, the mayor of your town declares that from now on, everyone is going to be speaking Chinese — say, because the town wants to build a tight relationship with a manufacturer in China and the best way to do that is to completely adopt the language. The town would probably not react well to this decree that makes a forced change. The kids may not resist (they may even quickly pick up the language), but older people who are set in their ways would rebel and refuse. Well, implementing Microsoft BI system for your whole organization could encounter similar troubles: The rank and file may shrug and force themselves to learn enough of the new procedures to get by — but IT may want to man the barricades. The challenge here is to get everybody to see

- ✔ How a Microsoft BI system can work with existing systems: Better do your homework on this one — IT can help. (See Chapter 13 for some starting points.)

- ✔ How an iterative and inclusive approach can make the changeover less traumatic: In addition to this chapter, see Chapter 12 for pointers.

- ✔ How a full implementation of Microsoft BI can benefit the whole organization: Yep, we're talking the vision thing here. See Chapter 12 for some talking points.

Chapter 15

Training, Using, and Evaluating Results

In This Chapter

▶ Discovering how training and feedback should be incorporated throughout implementation

▶ Exploring the results you get from each BI iteration

▶ Incorporating feedback into future iterative cycles

▶ Growing a corporate culture that embraces business intelligence

Culture is the name for what people are interested in, their thoughts, their models, the books they read and the speeches they hear, their table-talk, gossip, controversies, historical sense and scientific training, the values they appreciate, the quality of life they admire. All communities have a culture. It is the climate of their civilization.

— Walter Lippmann

*B*ack in graduate school, I had a professor give me some advice about software development. He told me I could build the most elegant and beautiful software solution ever seen, but if nobody knew about it, nobody would use it and nobody would care. Moral: Getting the word out about a solution is just as important as actually building it. Business intelligence is a case in point.

In this chapter, you discover how training and feedback should be incorporated throughout the entire implementation process. You also find out how important it is to incorporate feedback into every iterative cycle in order to capture what's really important to the people who will be using the BI system. Finally, you get some insights into how important a company culture is to business intelligence. A company culture can make or break a business, and it's an important aspect to consider when undertaking a BI implementation.

Tackling Training Efforts

Training your people to use your Microsoft Business Intelligence system, component by component, should begin with the first iterative cycle. Truly effective BI training is a grassroots effort — it works best if you include your organization's power users from the beginning (see Chapter 14) and provide a mechanism for communication and collaboration (of which SharePoint just happens to be a stellar example; see Chapter 10).

Continuous education

A number of years ago my wife and I were in Vancouver, British Columbia, as tourists. We decided to go up into a lookout tower and had to purchase tickets. At the time we were both just finishing our graduate degrees, so I flashed my student ID to get the student rate. I didn't really think a student "should" look like a twentysomething undergraduate — even if I was going to graduate school later in life than most (and my hairline was already retreating), I was still a student! The attendant looked at me strangely and said, "Well, I guess we're all students of life."

True enough. But the student discount isn't always available.

This episode stuck with me because it reminds me that people are always learning and building their knowledge; BI is no exception. Training should not be thought of as a onetime event that's scheduled, attended, and then checked off. Training is a continuous process that begins with the first iterative cycle and doesn't end — because the business world keeps changing.

Enabling self-service training

To create a continuous training environment that gets the job done (and keeps on getting it done), you have to ensure that people can take in new knowledge at their own pace. That's why it's important to provide self-service training that employees can use to find their own way through the new BI system and its future iterations. There should be extensive documentation that provides a self-service help section on the company intranet.

When people find things for themselves, they're much more likely to retain the knowledge; when they just sit in front of a lecturer, they only retain a small percentage — and not just because doodling takes up paper.

In the waterfall model of BI implementation (see Chapter 12), training is just another do-it-once-and-move-on stage. It isn't even addressed until the end of the project — offered once and that's it. When users finally get through the training (with a little knowledge, a few notes, and lots of doodles), often they catch a glimpse of the new system in all its complexity — and are overwhelmed. If they have any doubt that the solution solves their problems, suddenly that doubt looms large too. Then they'll likely reject the new system and resist any change that it tries to impose.

SharePoint training resources

Microsoft — probably aware that SharePoint can look scary and complex at first — has some free SharePoint self-service training materials that you can either download to your local computer or install on a SharePoint site where the entire organization can use them.

SharePoint training roadmap

The SharePoint training roadmap is a broad overview of the SharePoint product that lays out how its pieces fit together. Call it a bird's-eye view of SharePoint capabilities. After going through the roadmap, users have a better handle on what SharePoint can do — and on where they can benefit from diving deeper into SharePoint functionality.

The SharePoint roadmap can be found at

```
http://office.microsoft.com/en-us/sharepointserver/HA102486841033.aspx
```

The SharePoint roadmap site includes Collaboration, Portals and Personalization, Search, Enterprise Content Management, Business Process and Forms, and Business Intelligence.

SharePoint training

Microsoft has created a packaged training system for the SharePoint product. The training system includes documents, articles, interactive demos, and videos. The great thing about the SharePoint training system is that it can be installed right into the SharePoint product itself. The system can be installed as a SharePoint site, which can then be accessed by users throughout the organization. If you prefer to install only the training on your local machine you can do that as well.

The SharePoint training system can be downloaded from

```
http://office.microsoft.com/en-us/sharepointserver/HA102488011033.aspx
```

After the application is installed, double-click the icon that appears on your desktop (it's labeled *Microsoft Office SharePoint Server 2007 Training*). Your default Web browser will launch, and the initial training page will appear on-screen, as shown in Figure 15-1.

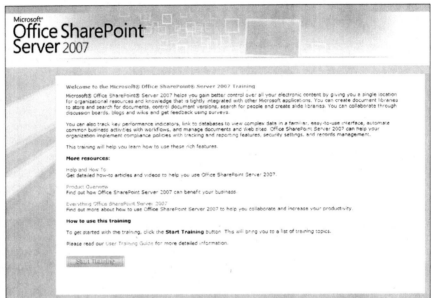

Microsoft®
Office SharePoint
Server 2007

Welcome to the Microsoft® Office SharePoint® Server 2007 Training

Microsoft® Office SharePoint® Server 2007 helps you gain better control over all your electronic content by giving you a single location for organizational resources and knowledge that is tightly integrated with other Microsoft applications. You can create document libraries to store and search for documents, control document versions, search for people and create slide libraries. You can collaborate through discussion boards, blogs and wikis and get feedback using surveys.

You can also track key performance indicators, link to databases to view complex data in a familiar, easy-to-use interface, automate common business activities with workflows, and manage documents and Web sites. Office SharePoint Server 2007 can help your organization implement compliance policies with tracking and reporting features, security settings, and records management.

This training will help you learn how to use these rich features.

More resources:

Help and How To
Get detailed how-to articles and videos to help you use Office SharePoint Server 2007.

Product Overview
Find out how Office SharePoint Server 2007 can benefit your business.

Everything Office SharePoint Server 2007
Find out more about how to use Office SharePoint Server 2007 to help you collaborate and increase your productivity.

How to use this training

To get started with the training, click the **Start Training** button. This will bring you to a list of training topics.

Please read our User Training Guide for more detailed information.

Start Training

Figure 15-1:
SharePoint
training
start page.

Clicking the Start Training button takes you to the *functionality tree* — a diagram that resembles a file hierarchy and lists each SharePoint capability as an individual *node*. You expand a node by clicking the plus sign to the left of it, which displays all the training methods available for that particular SharePoint feature. Figure 15-2 shows the training available under the Collaboration node.

SharePoint Designer training

SharePoint Designer is a development tool designed to enable users to customize the SharePoint product. Now, you *may* think that you can just waltz into the SQL Server database that SharePoint uses to store all its content and configuration information and tweak away. But beware: Here be dragons . . .

Figure 15-2:
The
expanded
Collabor-
ation node
within the
SharePoint
training
system.

It's incredibly difficult to get into the actual database directly and make changes to the SharePoint environment. That's intentional. In fact, Microsoft issues dire warnings against users blundering into the content-and-configuration database because it's way too easy to mess things up. So adamant is this prohibition that if you succumb to the lure of tinkering directly with SharePoint content and configuration, Microsoft probably won't support your implementation. You may think that you need to get into the SQL Server content database for SharePoint in order to do the serious development. This is not true. You can do everything you need to do with SharePoint Designer or Visual Studio. You should never need to go into the actual content and configuration databases.

Fortunately, SharePoint Designer is a straightforward tool that's not hard to use. It connects you to a special SharePoint site that gives you a window into that notorious content and configuration database — and a safe way to view, edit, and develop the content and design of your SharePoint site.

The SharePoint Designer training system is very similar to the standard SharePoint training system. (That's intentional too; consistency helps restore sanity.) The system can be installed on your local desktop machine or placed on a SharePoint site where the whole organization can access it — all without messing up that finicky database. You can download the SharePoint Designer training system (and its built-in peace of mind) at

```
http://office.microsoft.com/en-us/sharepointdesigner/HA102632321033.
                    aspx?pid=CL100796271033
```

SQL Server training resources

A quick trip to your local bookstore should reaffirm just how much material has been published about Microsoft's SQL Server product. Scads. Vast hordes. Big honkin' heaps. There are books and magazines dedicated to everything from database administration to data mining to querying SQL Server Analysis Services (SSAS) cubes and building SQL Server Reporting Services (SSRS) reports. For openers.

One of the greatest treasure troves of information about the product, however, comes directly from Microsoft. The Microsoft SQL Server Books Online is a training package that details nearly every aspect of the product. SQL Server Books Online is freely available online and also downloadable. Books Online is frequently updated as new functionality is incorporated into the SQL Server product. To get the latest version of Books Online, use your favorite search engine and search for SQL Server Books Online. The most recent release of Books Online is for SQL Server 2008 R2 but Books Online contains documentation for prior versions as well. If you would like to download the Books Online documentation to your local computer for offline browsing, then simply search for SQL Server Books Online Download.

Be sure to check this Web site now and then for updates.

Once downloaded, Books Online is easy to install: Simply double-click the downloaded MSI file. A wizard appears on-screen and walks you through the whole installation process. Once installed, Books Online is also easy to access: Click the Start button and choose Microsoft SQL Server 2008⇨Documentation and Tutorials⇨SQL Server Books Online, as shown in Figure 15-3.

Figure 15-3:
Accessing
SQL Server
Books
Online.

Books Online is organized in a tree format that lays out the features and capabilities of SQL Server. For example, The Report Builder 2.0 section is shown in Figure 15-4.

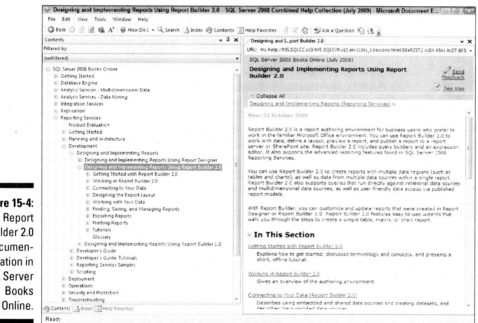

Figure 15-4:
Report
Builder 2.0
documen-
tation in
SQL Server
Books
Online.

SQL Server Books Online has a wealth . . . a plethora . . . a great huge (okay, okay, you get the idea) of information on nearly every aspect of the SQL Server. Invest a little time in getting to know how the documentation and tutorials are organized and where to find what you want to know about SQL Server. It'll come in handy later because SQL Server lives right at the core of Microsoft BI.

Training users at the grassroots level

One of the most successful methods in getting your organization trained is to involve your users at the grassroots. First off, you should be keeping in touch with the power users throughout your BI implementation process. They not only help define the new system in a practical and usable way when their colleagues come to them with questions, but they can also help champion adoption of the new system. And then there's the benefit they can bring to the nifty Microsoft self-service training tools: Don't be surprised if your power users are the first people to figure out where those tools are and how to access them.

Power users can point the rest of the users in the right direction and evangelize the solution, sure, but rank-and-file users should come up to speed pretty quickly when they've had a crack at self-service training.

A grassroots training effort, seeded by the power users early on in the BI implementation, can help encourage participation and ownership. That is not to say however that there is no room for official training provided by Microsoft Certified Training (MCT) professionals. Let the grassroots effort take hold and then bring in the MCT's. The people taking the training will already have an excellent understanding of the products and will not be overwhelmed by the training. Instead they will be engaged and will be able to question and speak intelligently to the trainers about the issues they have already been trying to figure out on their own.

Evaluating Results

Maintaining a close connection with users is critical in order to understand the pulse of the organization around BI functionality. You need to know what users like and what they dislike — you need to get feedback from them so you can incorporate it into future iterative cycles. You also need to update the feedback with each iterative cycle; the components that people dislike should be updated in order to address the complaints of the users, and the components that people do like should be embraced and expanded in order to provide as much value as possible to the organization.

The biggest problem with technology projects is also a hidden strength — namely, that you never really understand something until you've done it. Using the traditional waterfall approach (outlined in Chapter 12), the understanding of having-done-it only comes at the completion of the project — and at that point, all you've done is to put the system in place. The advantage of the iterative approach, however, is that your understanding grows with each iterative cycle; people get to do some learning-by-doing — and then can improve quality of the doing by learning what works and what doesn't.

Each cycle in the iterative approach to Microsoft Business Intelligence is made up of four phases: Discover, Define, Design, and Validate (as outlined in Chapter 12). Each phase entails its own tasks. The Validate phase, for example, includes the testing and rolling out of each BI component. The Discover phase scrutinizes the feedback received from users during previous cycles and looks to incorporate it into the next cycle.

Okay, it's true: Change can be a pain (but you knew that). The first iterative cycle can be difficult and fraught with mistakes and frustration. After all, it's "first" because nobody's done it that way before — but when it's over, somebody *has*. It's like a locale that's "a great place to be *from*" — you appreciate it best in the rearview mirror. After that first cycle, you have the advantage of looking back and viewing what went right and what went wrong. You get 20/20 hindsight early on — on a manageable scale — instead of all at once at the end of the project.

Getting feedback with SharePoint

There are a number of ways to gather feedback from users, but one of the most effective is Microsoft SharePoint itself. SharePoint provides a number of collaboration and communication mechanisms, including some tools that are familiar to users of social networking Web sites — surveys, discussion boards, blogs, and wikis.

If your organization already uses SharePoint — and you use these features to collect feedback in the course of your BI implementation — you can embed the SharePoint tools directly into a site on the company intranet. Doing so reduces complexity and provides a simple, easy-to-find location where users can provide feedback without disrupting the rest of their work duties.

In addition to SharePoint, good old-fashioned face-to-face interviews can provide feedback — sometimes more detailed — and the personal contact helps foster a sense of participation and involvement.

SharePoint surveys

A SharePoint survey works just like any other online survey tool: You create a set of questions and then send it to users. Users respond, and then you can collect and analyze their feedback. Since SharePoint often sits at the center of an organization and *is* the company intranet, people are familiar with the location and navigation of the site; they can complete the survey with minimum hassle.

Happily, creating a Survey in SharePoint is straightforward: You click the Survey link on the Create page under the Lists category and then fill in the questions you want to ask, as shown in Figure 15-5. The Create page can be accessed by administrators of the site by clicking on View All Site Content and then clicking the Create link at the top of the screen.

Depending on the SharePoint template that your site is based on you may not have all of the collaboration features discussed in this section. You can turn on the collaboration features by clicking on Site Actions in the upper-left corner of the screen and then choosing Site Settings. Under the Site Actions grouping click the Manage Site Features link. Look for the Team Collaboration Lists feature and then click Activate. You should now have all of the collaboration features. Note that in order to make this change you must be an administrator of the site.

Discussion boards

A *discussion board* is an online location that posts and gathers messages. There users can post feedback, respond to feedback from other users, and so provide you with a realistic impression of how your latest BI iteration is doing. A discussion board is great for viewing feedback because it also captures responses and discussions from multiple users. For example, one user may be very outspoken and provide a lot of feedback — whether positive or negative — but that also gives the rest of the crowd a chance to post different opinions and balance the total response.

Discussion boards already come with SharePoint. You can create one simply by clicking the Discussion Board link on the Create page under the Lists category and then giving it a name (as shown in Figure 15-6). The Create page can be accessed by administrators of the site by clicking on View All Site Content and then clicking the Create link at the top of the screen.

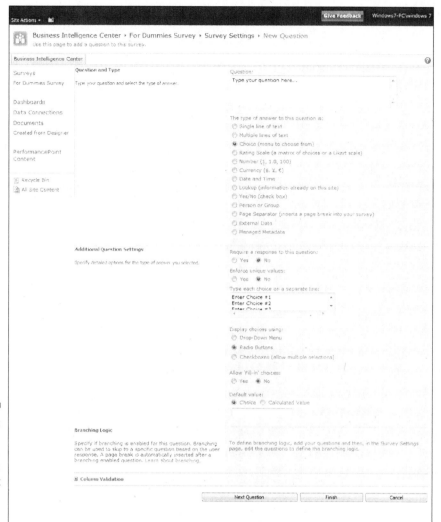

Figure 15-5:
Creating a
survey is
as easy as
filling out
a form in
SharePoint.

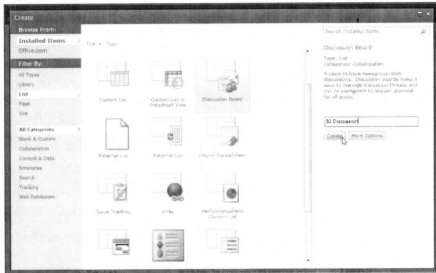

Figure 15-6:
Creating a
discussion
board in
SharePoint.

Blogs

If you've just arrived by time machine from the late 20th century, a *blog* is not some iffy fruit punch fixed up in a wastebasket. The term comes from *Web log*. Blogs started as online journals and evolved into online forums for publishing articles and thoughts — these days many of them have official business uses and corporate sponsors. I've seen those blogs used in a number of ways, but some of the most effective are produced by company leadership and experts on various topics.

Leadership can use a blog to broadcast the organization's message to the world, but in-house people are also free to comment and discuss the content of the blog. Result: two-way communication that starts out with a formal declaration of the company's direction (or other leadership decisions) and offers an opportunity for the exchange of useful ideas.

Another popular way I've seen organizations use blogs is to have experts post about topics of common interest that have a direct bearing on the organization. Representatives of the organization can then ask questions and discuss the content of the entry. For example, a marketing executive may post an article on the effectiveness of a recent promotional effort to a marketing blog. Other folks throughout the organization can view the expert knowledge of the marketing executive, respond, comment, and ask questions about the promotion.

You can use SharePoint to add a blog to your intranet. It's as easy as (pardon the expression) falling off a log. Microsoft even gives you the log — a template that forms the basis of your new blog. Simply click the Blog link from the Create page under the Site category and then fill in the name of the blog and the URL. A sample SharePoint blog is shown in Figure 15-7. The Create page can be accessed by administrators of the site by clicking on View All Site Content and then clicking the Create link at the top of the screen.

Figure 15-7: A basic SharePoint blog.

Wikis

A *wiki* is a dynamic Web page that multiple people can edit and modify. For example, an expert on Reporting Services can create a wiki page on how to build a report using Report Builder. As users gain skill with Report Builder, they can expand on the wiki page and add tips and tricks that fit with the organization's data systems — a very handy resource, regardless of whether those systems are all-Microsoft or a mixed bag of software products.

A SharePoint wiki page is easy to create: Click the Enterprise Wiki link on the Create page under the Site category and then give it a name and URL, as shown in Figure 15-8. The Create page can be accessed by administrators of the site by clicking on View All Site Content and then clicking the Create link at the top of the screen.

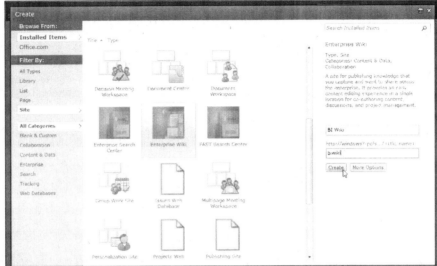

Figure 15-8:
Creating an
Enterprise
Wiki page in
SharePoint.

Interviews

Remember smileys — those funny faces made of punctuation that people started putting in e-mail messages because typed words on-screen just don't convey tone of voice or other subtle cues? Well, you can restore some of those cues to your feedback by conducting interviews — face to face — with power users throughout the implementation process. Be sure to interview the power users most affected by each new BI component you roll out — preferably just after each iterative cycle is complete. The goal of the interview is to get a good working sense of the power users' honest reactions to the BI functionality you've introduced.

Many times I've seen BI features presented as beneficial to users — only to be met with yawns and neglect. If a BI component doesn't offer a clear or immediate benefit to the users — or they don't yet see how it can help them — you need to find out why. Gathering this information as the project progresses allows you to adjust your implementation plan: You can expand the functionality that users find valuable, jettison the stuff they don't need and won't use, and maybe fine-tune your effort to communicate how your latest offering helps the big picture.

A particularly effective way to conduct interviews is to take a preliminary look at (and analyze) the information collected using SharePoint surveys, discussion boards, blogs, and wikis, and *then* seek to clarify those results during the interview process.

Incorporating Feedback

Feedback won't do you any good if you don't incorporate it into the next iteration of your BI system. The whole idea of an iterative approach to implementation is to keep using feedback to stay connected to the people who expect to use the new system. That means making sure you incorporate what they tell you into future iterative cycles. Otherwise you may as well be using the waterfall approach described in Chapter 12 — waiting until the end of the project to get a big, indigestible lump of feedback all at once — at which point it's too late to go back to the initial phases since they've already been checked off and completed. Suppose (just hypothetically) just one component of your new BI system turns out to be user-unfriendly or just a really bad idea. Oops. With the waterfall approach all you can do is extend the timeline — and thus the budget (good luck with that) — or muddle on with a system that has already stirred up frustration for users (good luck with that too — you'll need it). With the iterative approach you can incorporate that feedback into the next iteration.

Creating a BI Culture

Being a consultant has often been a painful experience; I'm ripped from one corporate culture to another and never get to really integrate with any particular group. The upside to this painful existence is that I've been given a look into the best and worst of company cultures.

For better or worse — but universally — every organization has a company culture — a mix of customary attitudes, habits, practices that express the organization's collective self-image and expectations. Those cultures can range from knuckle-dragging low morale to cheerful exuberance and a feeling of invincibility. A company's culture can take a great team and destroy it, or take an average team and make it great.

There's no shortage of books and articles on building a great company culture — everybody wants one and wants to know how to get one. In my experience, a great company culture consists of five primary components: Inclusion, communication and collaboration, ownership, merit-based recognition, and trust. (If you've read Chapter 14, you already know that many of these qualities would be highly compatible with a well-made BI system.)

Building a complete company culture based on those five pillars is, of course, beyond the scope of this book. But if you have strong company culture that clearly rests on at least three of them, I'll venture a prediction: A BI implementation will be fully adopted and embraced, and will result in adding tremendous value to the organization. The following sections explain why.

Inclusion

Inclusion is deeply engrained; everyone wants it because we're social creatures. Remember how it felt not to be included in some collective activity (whether important or just for fun) back in school? It's completely awful. As adults, we like to think that we've matured, that being included doesn't matter to us, and that we aren't kidding ourselves about that. If only it were that simple.

Being excluded often causes pain and uncertainty; people close down and start to build their own fiefdoms of relative safety and perceived trust — within which an "us versus them" mentality crops up within the organization. Result: rampant political motivations, hidden conflicts, knee-jerk defense of personal fiefdoms. By encouraging a culture of inclusion, you tend to remove the "us versus them" from within your organization and transform it into a competitive attitude by turning it outward: The "us" becomes the organization, and the "them" becomes its competitors. Business intelligence — both the process of implementing it (iteratively!) and the ongoing process of using the system that results — can help bring about this transformation.

Communication and collaboration

In many organizations, a light is dawning: They're discovering that communication and collaboration are vital to success in the current business world. This understanding has fueled the rapid growth of software products such as Microsoft SharePoint — which is designed to enable communication and collaboration. Those products were answering a need that already existed. Extending their strengths into business intelligence is a natural next step.

As SharePoint continues its march into many organizations, it's a natural fit for a new concept: *human business intelligence* (see Chapter 10). When ready-to-use BI information is made available to a collaborative environment, users throughout the organization have a new potential advantage: to progress at the same speed in understanding and learning — about their organization, its goals, its competition, and how well it does its work.

Ownership

Whenever people become directly responsible for solving a specific problem — essentially, when they *own* a particular issue and have a stake in resolving it — they're much more likely to be actively engaged in working it out. It's easy to "zone out" when you're not the one on the hook. If everyone in the organization is truly working toward the same goal, such ownership is a powerful advantage; holding people accountable for carrying their portion of the load can help create a feeling of unity.

Microsoft BI can help bring ownership to the user base by providing self-service BI capabilities to everyone. For example, using Excel (see Chapter 9), Dashboard Designer, and Report Builder (see Chapter 11), users can create content that can then be shared to their direct colleagues as well as the rest of the organization. Giving people the correct tools to do their job and then allowing them the opportunity to take ownership of their tasks are critical components of business and business intelligence.

Merit-based recognition

Recognition — in the sense of acknowledging and rewarding accomplish-ment — can be one of the best or one of the worst components of a corporate culture. Much depends on how it's done. Many organizations have a relatively feudal style of providing recognition: It's often based on nominations from leadership or managers. The idea is to highlight star performers so leadership can bestow recognition as if it were a sword-whack on a knightly shoulder. This approach is familiar — which may be one reason it looks like it should work — but what usually results is a storm of resentment, bickering, political maneuvering, and gossip. Or (worse) a kind of stressed indifference: "No time for kudos — I've got to get the next thing done."

Using an open communication platform that provides collaboration (SharePoint, see Chapter 10) removes the politics and brown-nosing from the recognition equation. When discussions, blog entries, wiki pages, and surveys are all out in the open for anyone in the organization to log in to and check out, then nobody will feel they are not being recognized for their contributions. Everyone has the opportunity to contribute, and contribution is what drives the human factor of business intelligence.

Recognition is an aspect of every company culture — but here's a notion to ponder: Would it work better to have the recognition come from the base of the organization up — essentially the same way BI information moves — and not the other way around? For example, instead of having managers nominate people, survey people and ask them to anonymously nominate peers and exclude themselves. Have them provide real examples of people going above and beyond. When you compile the results, you'll probably have a clear picture of how the crowd feels about the people they work with, day in and day out. The idea is to recognize the people who help their peers the most as star performers — instead of the people who have perfected the art of telling their leaders what they want to hear.

Trust

In the corporate world, there's a saying going around that seems obvious at first glance: "Nobody likes to be thrown under the bus." (Gee. No kidding?) Call it a metaphor for being sacrificed to expediency. It's happened to me, and I'm sure it's happened to many of the folks reading this book. One day you read down through an e-mail thread and find that someone you trusted has blamed some major problem on you, while claiming to be on your side. Your natural reaction (if you're like the rest of us): instant recoil and distrust. The corporate culture itself is damaged because there's now one less trusting person.

When this behavior is witnessed or brought to the attention of leadership, it should be strongly discouraged. Reward people who accept blame where blame is due instead of throwing their direct reports and peers under the bus to save face to their leaders.

Again, open and collaborative communication platforms such as SharePoint provide the opportunity for a company culture that is more transparent. Transparency builds a feeling of trust. As is often the case, when people don't know what is going on, they always assume the worst. It always boggles me to watch leadership let people assume the worst instead of getting the truth (which is usually not as bad as what people are assuming) out into the open.

A successful BI strategy requires a strong company culture. Carefully used and thoughtfully implemented, Microsoft Business Intelligence can encourage the growth of a strong, collaborative, more unified company culture. Call it, human business intelligence, which is one more major advantage that can come from a well-done BI implementation.

Part V
The Part of Tens

The 5th Wave   By Rich Tennant

In this part . . .

This part walks you through some of the most important aspects of Microsoft Business Intelligence, laid out in sets of ten. You start with ten pitfalls to avoid when you're implementing a Microsoft BI system. You behold the ten keys to a successful implementation. Finally, you discover the ten ways that a Microsoft Business Intelligence solution can boost your bottom line and provide a juicy return on your software and implementation investment.

Chapter 16

Ten Microsoft BI Implementation Pitfalls

In This Chapter

▶ Getting drenched with the waterfall methodology

▶ Buying shelf-ware that just sits there

▶ Letting politics destroy your BI project

▶ Disregarding IT

▶ Snubbing power users

▶ Ignoring business processes

▶ Promising extravagant results

▶ Failing to include everyone in the BI solution

▶ Skimping on the BI basics

▶ Misusing consultants

> *You only have to do a very few things right in your life so long as you don't do too many things wrong.*
>
> — Warren Buffett

There are potential hazards in any environment — and the business world has plenty of its own. Some of these are especially likely to lurk when your organization implements a new technology — and Microsoft Business Intelligence is no exception. To reduce risk and increase the odds of a successful and valuable BI solution, keep an eye out for the following ten pitfalls.

Drowning Under the Waterfall

The waterfall methodology (see Chapter 12) is still a popular approach to implementation — following a clear-cut series of one-time-only steps in a cascading sequence because it makes a project easier to understand on paper. In theory, this methodology looks straightforward and easy to plan: Start off with an initial phase and when that phase is complete, move on to the next phase, as shown in Figure 16-1.

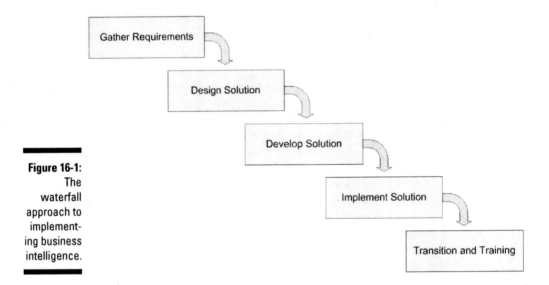

Figure 16-1:
The waterfall approach to implementing business intelligence.

Simple, right? Well, not necessarily. The problem is that the project isn't fully summed up, evaluated, and understood until all phases are complete . . . at which point, any significant changes cost extra time and money to make. Postponing complexity doesn't make it go away.

Hindsight may provide 20/20 vision, but if what it shows you is a glaring flaw (or an overwhelming pile of them) at the "end" of the project, then you still have a lot of work to do — or redo. The alternative is an iterative approach to implementing Microsoft BI: introducing, testing, and tweaking one component of the system at a time, incorporating feedback to improve each iteration. It's covered throughout Part IV (specifically Chapter 12) and is also discussed in Chapter 17.

Getting Stuck on the Shelf (-ware)

Watching a recorded software demo can be a powerful and seductive experience if you're looking for a fast route to a business advantage (who isn't?). It's easy to be dazzled by the spectacle of software features in action. Such a canned demo (a demo that is scripted and uses a basic set of predetermined data) illustrates the *potential* of software — but it can also be misleading because

- ✔ What you're seeing is a generic use of the functionality; the demo doesn't (and can't) confront the specific problems facing your organization.

- ✔ A demo completely ignores the business processes specific to your company because (obviously) it wasn't designed around them.

- ✔ A demo assumes the data is already perfectly arranged for optimal performance. (Yeah, right.) It's like the old joke about the shipwrecked economist who sees a crate of canned food wash up and says to his companions, "Our problem is solved! Now, if we assume a can opener . . . ."

Beware the "wow" factor. Often decision-makers are so impressed by demos that they're instantly off and running — purchasing licensing, rushing to start a project, spending like mad. This can be a huge mistake; in practice, of the route to a successful BI project involves very little technology — you just have to be sure it's the right stuff for your needs. Get the tool that fits the job; don't try to fit the job to the tool.

If new BI software is going to do you any good, it has to be a good fit with your existing business processes (you know — the ones you're expecting to generate data and feed a data warehouse when BI is up and running). As mentioned in Chapter 12, here's where the people performing the tasks that make up your business processes can provide vital information. Be sure you get them on board with your BI implementation. You can use what they tell you about how the work really gets done to get a handle on whether the foundations of your business processes need shoring up — preferably *before* you start putting BI in place. You don't want that gosh-wow new software to sit on the shelf unused — slowly morphing into shelf-ware.

The capabilities of Microsoft Business Intelligence are available in free trial versions, in downloadable packages (see Chapter 13). May as well make vigorous use of all those free megabytes of BI power — specifically to make sure your organization is a good fit with Microsoft BI *before* you commit a lot of time and money to implementation.

The best place to start this tryout process is with the primary Microsoft BI components: SQL Server and SharePoint. Trial versions of these products can be downloaded from the following locations (look for the Try It tab):

- ✔ **SQL Server** (www.microsoft.com/sqlserver)
- ✔ **SharePoint** (www.microsoft.com/sharepoint)

Letting Politics Kill the BI Project

Business intelligence, by its very nature, spans many different divisions and groups within an organization — used wisely and well, it can be a unifying influence. Getting there, however, can be a challenge; after all, it's no secret that in many organizations, not everyone is on the same page — to put it politely. At worst, that situation results in an environment of political infighting — not just in multibillion-dollar corporate giants, but even in small organizations that you'd think would know better (until you've worked with enough of them).

The lords of the corporate fiefdoms tend to cling to "the way it's always been done around here," which can plant some political landmines in the path of your BI project. Having a *fixer* — someone who understands the politics involved in the organization — is a must (for more about fixers, see Chapter 12).

Ignoring IT

The IT (Information Technology) department is a vital organ in the body of any modern business. Modern organizations rely on IT for everything from phones to e-mail to building access. The IT department often has a complete monopoly over the vital services it provides. Thus it's a critical make-or-break component of any BI project.

The IT team already has a stake in the very processes that BI would modify. These folks understand how your systems currently work — and they'll be responsible for all the building, installing, configuring, and maintaining that goes along with a new BI system. When you propose implementing BI, the first thing they're likely to see is . . . a whole lot of work. That's why it's wise *and* diplomatic to bring IT to the table when you're first fleshing out the stages of your BI implementation (preferably iterative, of course, as outlined in Chapter 12).

Disregarding Power Users

Ah, nostalgia — remember when terms like "workgroup" were new? Even back then, some users went above and beyond the help files and the manuals (remember *those?*) to grapple firsthand with the intricacies of the systems and processes their companies were putting in place. These were the *power users,* and guess what? They haven't gone away. You'll still find them in any organization that uses computers (know of any that don't?). Ignoring them can result in a BI system that nobody uses. Making allies of them can give you a big-time boost toward BI success.

Power users have no identifying marks, distinctive fur patterns, or secret jungle habitats. They don't fit any particular profile or gather at any particular level in an organization. To identify power users, you need to interview the various workgroups in your organization (see Chapter 12). Use survey questions not only on the users own knowledge but also the knowledge of the other members of the group. Here are some examples of useful survey questions:

- ✔ What systems do you use in your everyday job duties?
- ✔ Who do you go to with questions about Systems A, B, and C?
- ✔ List in order the three most knowledgeable people in your group for Systems A, B, and C.
- ✔ Who is the most technically-savvy and adept person in your group — especially the one who comes up with good workarounds?
- ✔ Who in your group is responsible for adding functionality to processes and systems within your group?

Try to go after the same type of information from several different angles; phrase several questions a little differently, emphasizing slightly different aspects of what makes a power user. For example, asking "who knows the most about the systems," "who do you ask when you need to tweak the software," and "who is the most technically adept" will start to give you a picture of the group dynamics and help identify the power users.

Power users should be identified in the beginning of your BI project and have a seat at your decision-making table throughout the project.

Snubbing Business Processes

Sorry, but business intelligence isn't a magic gadget you can bolt onto a business any old way for instant results. In fact, if you charge into implementing a BI capabilities before you've had a chance to analyze and optimize your business processes, it's a classic case of "cart before the horse." The data flowing out of your business processes has to be accurate; the data-capture points have to be placed right, and the processes themselves have to be working well (the closer to optimal, the better). If all that vital tinkering hasn't been done when you try to implement BI, you're building a beautiful house of cards on a wobbly table — at the first little bump, look out below.

For a BI system to do its job — turning raw, real data into ready-to use, valuable information — your business processes have to give it a sound foundation. The old computer adage is especially true for BI systems: Garbage in, garbage out.

Overpromising Results

Here's one area of BI implementation where human issues are at least as important as technical issues: Although BI can legitimately offer your organization some powerful advantages, you have to manage people's expectations. You're likelier to win the hearts and minds of the overall user base if what you promise matches what you can actually deliver. If an overzealous decision-maker — fresh from the screening of a demo of what Microsoft BI *can* do — starts spreading the word to the user base about the world of wonders just around the corner, well . . . what you've got there is like a picture of a rocketship: Thrilling to look at, but it won't take you anywhere.

Any BI solution takes time to evolve and grow — hence the iterative approach outlined in Chapter 12. If you can show very small (but real) improvements in the system during each iterative cycle — and deliver small-but-real benefits cycle by cycle, you're already getting somewhere. Allow users to find the value in what you're providing; let their feedback help drive changes to the system. The idea is to get users to grow *with* the BI system as it becomes a more familiar part of their everyday environment.

Getting Squashed by Top-Down Decree

I've found that business intelligence is nearly impossible to impose from above. (Ever try to build a house from the roof down?) A BI solution that really works throughout the organization — as it should — tends to happen best from the bottom up. The people performing the tasks that make up the processes that generate the data that becomes the information that makes for effective business decisions — that's the house that BI builds. From the ground up.

One of the biggest pitfalls I see in any business is a leftover from the last century: a top-down command-and-control structure. Word comes down the hierarchy from on high: "Lo, the powers have decided what ye will do, and if ye like it not, tough." Treating people like pawns in a game of business chess is a surefire way to lower morale and deteriorate the corporate culture. Communication and involvement are critical to the team environment in which a BI system thrives. If leadership sets goals that take into account a range of useful input (whether data or ideas) from the entire organization, the result is more than viable business intelligence — it's an increasingly intelligent business.

Skimping on the Foundation

If budget, time, and resources were unlimited, all technology projects would be successful — and we'd be living in a wildly unlikely science fiction story. Back here on Earth, when real-world budgets are created and a BI project is looking to cut costs, it's tempting to cut back on some BI essentials — in particular, changing the business processes, identifying and including power users, or (here's a big one) changing the management process.

Letting the budget ax fall on any of these components may seem to cut costs, but what it's actually cutting away is the foundation of BI success. For example, deciding that a business process "has enough data capture points" already and then pushing forward with building a data mart or data warehouse around the data being captured can be shortsighted. It may cost more to introduce data capture points into a business process, but the data those updated processes capture are critical for the overall usefulness of the information being produced. Using the iterative approach (see Chapter 12) helps ensure that value results from the available budget.

Misjudging How to Use Consultants

Speaking as one of the breed, I can tell you that consultants are a factor that can either lead to the destruction of a project or be the saving grace of a project. There's definitely a place for consultants, and nearly every successful Microsoft BI implementation I've seen has used them.

Think of a consultant as a tool in your BI arsenal — with both appropriate and inappropriate uses. If you're trying to attach two pieces of wood and you have a box of screws, then you don't need a hammer — you need a screwdriver. A look at the accompanying sidebar would also help.

Moral: Doing your homework on (a) what Microsoft BI can do, (b) how those capabilities can fit into your organization, and (c) what an iterative BI implementation would look like for your shop puts you in a better position to work with consultants. Then you can make knowledgeable use of the insights they offer — and ensure that they're doing what's best for you and your organization.

Take me to your (BI project) leader

Using the wrong tool for the task at hand can make the job incredibly difficult; using the correct tool can make even a seemingly impossible job seem blissfully easy. Here are a couple of quick examples of how consultants can affect BI implementation (the names have been changed for the sake of professional courtesy):

✔ The Acme Retro company tried a BI implementation that went awry when upper management decided to listen to consultants who assured them the waterfall approach was easier to manage and fit in nicely with the consulting company being paid at each successful phase. The project went smoothly, and the consultants were paid — until the end of the project when the system didn't work, and management had to decide if they wanted to scrap the BI system or fund another round of fixes.

✔ The Acme Vision company's approach to BI took a different tack: The company began the BI endeavor by first examining its business processes and document what was really going on in its business. Next, they had their IT team download the trial versions of SQL Server and SharePoint and begin to understand the features and functionality of the products. Finally, consultants were hired to fill expertise gaps such as change management, Microsoft SharePoint and BI expertise, and project management. The consultants used an iterative approach that seemed to get off to a rocky start. The first iteration was a nightmare that had everyone on edge, questioning whether BI could work in the organization. As the second iteration rolled around, the kinks were worked out, and the progress of the working BI system began marching forward — providing consistent and valuable results after each iteration.

Chapter 17

Ten Keys to Successful Microsoft Business Intelligence

In This Chapter

▶ Getting comfortable with an iterative approach

▶ Securing executive-level sponsorship

▶ Analyzing your current environment

▶ Creating an implementation plan

▶ Picking the right people for the implementation team

▶ Fostering an inclusive environment

▶ Establishing a culture of communication and collaboration

▶ Beginning with the right goals

▶ Minimizing risk

▶ Keeping the big picture in mind

There are many paths to the top of the mountain, but the view is always the same.

— Chinese Proverb

Some strategies for implementing Microsoft Business Intelligence are already coming to the fore, even though the field is relatively new. Try the following ten keys to success and see which ones unlock the potential of your BI implementation. (My bet is that they'll all help. I'll also bet you saw that one coming.)

Reiterating an Iterative Approach

Yep, this is a theme I harp on elsewhere in the book, but only because (a) it can bring heavenly business results but (b) it may take some getting used to at first. The iterative approach to BI implementation (see Chapter 12 for details) breaks up the project into specific BI components and introduces them in small, iterative cycles, each one following a complete set of stages before circling back to the beginning, incorporating what's been learned, and sallying forth again (as shown in Figure 17-1).

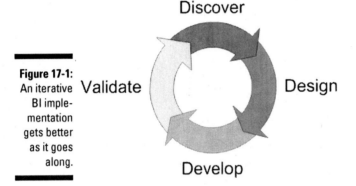

Figure 17-1:
An iterative BI implementation gets better as it goes along.

Discover

Validate

Design

Develop

Note that each cycle goes full circle before moving on to additional cycles. That's a departure from the more traditional waterfall approach (also described in Chapter 12) that slams the books shut on one stage of a project before moving on to the next stage. The first iteration is always the hardest. The first iteration is a complete end-to-end cycle, just like every other iteration. The first iteration is a time to work out all the kinks and find any major problems up-front so adjustments can be made. The first iterative cycle forges the initial trail through the organizational landscape; by the time your BI implementation starts to involve a vast swath of your organization, it's had lots of opportunities to get better and better at doing its job.

Because each iterative cycle incorporates feedback from users into future cycles, you're far likelier to end up with a solution that your people find usable and valuable — because they've grown familiar with how its parts work and they've seen it produce usable information.

Now, any business veteran steeped in the lore of the marketplace will tell you time is money. And it's uncanny how quickly both can end up in short supply — especially when you're trying to get a new technology up and running. No wonder overruns are such a common headache. If you are using the waterfall approach and have been cruising along from one phase of a project to the next, checking them off with a decisive flourish moving on — nary an iteration in sight — you may get to the end of your allocated budget and time blissfully unaware of lurking flaws. Then . . . surprise! A review at the end of the project turns up something you have to fix. Do you extend the budget and stretch the timeline or abandon the project in an incomplete (unusable) state. Devil or deep blue sea? (No, thanks.)

Of course, if you've been faithfully working through iterations of your BI components, you've been generating some useful information and gaining insights into your implementation all along, from the get-go. The budget has barely been scratched; but the implementation is improving, the information is starting to accumulate, and folks are starting to get the hang of this newfangled BI stuff. And behold: Increasing value reverberates through the project and out into the organization. As each iterative cycle progresses, the team gets better and better at the development process. Practice makes perfect, and with each iteration, the team is practicing. Just remember: You don't have to go overboard and try to conquer the world (where would you put it, anyway?). Although your BI system will always need to run iterative cycles to stay at peak performance (just as a sports car needs tuning up from time to time), they'll become a natural part of doing business.

Obtaining Executive-Level Sponsorship

Many BI projects begin life at the middle management level. Makes sense. Middle managers have familiarity with two distinct levels of the organization: the employees on the front lines and the executive decision-makers. And though I've found that a grassroots-up approach is a natural for implementing Microsoft BI, gaining executive-level sponsorship for such a project is crucial.

A BI project by its very nature touches many parts of the organization. That means both the rank-and-file and executive levels have indispensable roles to play: The rank and file keep the system supplied with practical feedback and solid data captured from the business processes; the execs make strategic use of the information flowing out of the data warehouse. Working in tandem, they're formidable. But folks at both levels have to have a stake in the system's success.

I've seen a number of BI projects begin life with a single executive sponsor and then slowly die off because the rest of the executives weren't brought on board. Gaining cohesive executive-level sponsorship is critical; two ways I've seen middle managers handle that mission are as follows:

✔ A formal steering committee that is made up of executives and stakeholders (including power users) from across the organization.

✔ An open forum where middle managers meet, discuss, and stay connected to the business users in order to relay to executives exactly what is happening in the organization. This concept all hinges on the company culture however. If the culture of the organization follows the lines of the workers telling the managers what they want to hear instead of what is really happening and then the managers telling the executives what they want to hear instead of what is really happening, then the executives have a false sense of stability. The culture of finding out what is really happening needs to come down from the top. Managers should not be afraid to tell their executives exactly what is happening, and the workers should not be afraid to tell their managers exactly what is happening. A culture that embraces truth, accepts critical feedback, and searches out faults in its systems and processes in order to fix them is well on the way to a successful BI implementation.

Assessing Your Current Environment

To get your BI implementation off the ground, you have to do first things first: Take a look at where you're taking off from. That means getting an accurate picture of how your current business environment really works.

If you're going to give your BI project a solid foundation for its characteristic activities — capturing data from business processes, addressing (and accurately conveying) the change that your BI implementation will bring, embracing power users, and providing an inclusive and interactive business environment through communication and collaboration (whew!) — pay attention to these elements of your current business environment:

✔ Business processes themselves (see Chapters 2 and 12).

✔ Data that your business processes generate (see Chapter 3).

✔ Your operational systems (see Chapter 3).

✔ Your software licenses (see Chapter 13).

✔ The technical skills that your people already have (see Chapter 13).

The best tools for understanding your current environment include building process flows and process maps (see Chapter 12) that paint a big picture about what is really happening. When building these process flows and maps, make sure you're only after the real stuff — not the idealized picture that folks paint when they're trying to tell management what it wants to hear. Interview frontline employees and include them in the assessment process at the end of each iterative cycle. The results may surprise (or disillusion) the supervisors and managers, but be discreet and stay focused: If you provide the straight goods on what's really happening, it helps your implementation — and eventually the whole organization when your system comes online.

Developing an Implementation Plan

The Western world loves plans for the future. The business world loves plans for becoming more efficient, profitable, timely, whatever. And whether or not you love plans, you need them for doing just about anything. A BI implementation is one of those undertakings that really needs a good plan — after all, it requires a vast array of resources and affects a wide swath of the organization — including (yep) the organization's *plans*. You don't want it to just go blundering around aimlessly, even if it could.

A Microsoft BI implementation plan should include

- ✔ Business and technology goals (see Chapter 12).

- ✔ Project milestones (see Chapter 14).

- ✔ Internal and external resources (see Chapter 12).

- ✔ Communication and collaboration (see Chapter 15).

- ✔ Training (see Chapter 15).

To keep your BI implementation on track and human-scale, break up the overall plan into *units* (see Chapter 14) — discrete tasks that can be accomplished during each iterative cycle of the implementation. Begin the iterative cycles with low-risk, high-value tasks (see Chapter 12) — the low-hanging fruit so well loved by people who want to do things fast. For example, if one of your business goals is to gain a window into your sales figures, then begin with a single store or product. At the conclusion of the first iterative cycle, you'll have

- ✔ Some accurate, timely, usable BI information about a real part of the business (while demonstrating that it can be done).

- ✔ A model for later iterative cycles.

- ✔ An end-to-end path through the implementation process.

Not bad for a first time out. As the iterative cycles continue, the breadth of the window into your business expands, and user feedback helps improve the process. Future iterations are able to build on the previous iterations in a solution that continues to gain functionality and usefulness.

Choosing the Right People for the Implementation Team

Having the right people on the implementation team (see Chapter 12 for more details) is very important in achieving a successful BI implementation. It's a big, complex job, and a range of roles comes with it; your team needs people with BI-friendly skills.

Your in-house team members

The general roles that your BI project team has to fill include these:

- ✔ Experts in your business processes (see Chapters 2 and 12).
- ✔ Experts in the hardware and software essential to BI (see Chapter 10).
- ✔ Project managers (see Chapter 12).
- ✔ Fixers who know your organizational politics (see Chapter 12).

Calling in consultants

Given that business intelligence is still a relatively new set of tools, it's no accident that consultants often play a big part in a BI implementation. Before you start combing the Web for Microsoft BI hired guns, however, here are some principles to keep in mind:

- ✔ **Hire the right consulting firm.** What "right" means will vary from one organization to the next, but in general, look for a partner for the long haul. You want to build a relationship with your consulting firm and know that you can trust it to do the right thing. I recommend looking for a firm with a strong local presence with a proven track record. It also doesn't hurt to ask them about their BI experience and methodology.

- ✔ **Decide consciously how to integrate consultants into your project.** In what areas of BI implementation are you likeliest to need help?

- ✔ **Do your homework.** If you take some time to study up on what Microsoft Business Intelligence does, enough to get a good working sense of what it's for, how it works, and what you can realistically expect from it, then you'll be less easily dazzled by demos — and in a better position to make the most of what consultants have to offer.

Just like attorneys, real estate brokers, and stock brokers, consultants get paid when they're doing something for you. If you've got a handle on BI capabilities, your implementation plan, and the role you expect consultants to play, you're ahead of the game.

Creating an Inclusive Environment

Even in the busy midst of a BI implementation, I often see organizational leadership make the mistake of silence. When the people who are out there building, testing, and evaluating the new system's components send an e-mail (or some other clear communication) to a leader, they should receive some response right away — even if it says, in effect, "I don't know yet — give me some time." At least then the sender knows the message got through — and that helps head off feelings of isolation or abandonment. The worst possible thing is not responding — it gives the impression that the leader's head is firmly planted in the sand.

Some of the best leaders that I work with are very inclusive. They communicate constantly and aren't afraid of showing the mistakes they make while learning what works. Communication builds an inclusive environment where everyone feels they have some control of (or at least influence on) the outcome of any decision.

Delegating the ownership of problems or issues is a surefire way to create an inclusive environment. Delegation is not about passing the buck to the next person but engaging other people and using their input to move the project forward. Let employees come to the table with their proposed solutions before assuming they don't know what they're doing.

Beware, however, of leadership that only responds to good news. As soon as something comes up that either requires a tough decision or the delivery of difficult news, our Pollyanna higher-up simply stops responding and communicating. This behavior is not only bad for business but also damaging to the company culture.

When a leader fails to communicate, the culture breaks down; people automatically assume the worst and lose all respect for leadership. That's especially dire if the leaders in question are making a classic big mistake — assuming that they always know best and that the natural order of things is for them to make the big decisions unilaterally, pass those decisions down to their employees, and just watch the results roll in. (**Hint:** The results may bear no resemblance to what those folks had in mind.)

Bring employees into decisions early and often. Maintaining a constant flow of communication and collaboration helps address problems from various angles in a timely way, while ensuring that employees have a forum for discussion. (Hint: SharePoint happens to be designed for this sort of thing. For more about that, read on.)

Fostering a Culture of Communication and Collaboration

As potent as Microsoft Business Intelligence is in transforming how a company does business, company culture always plays as big a role in BI as any technology. Business intelligence is, in essence, making intelligent decisions based on valuable and relevant information. Microsoft BI facilitates the collection and delivery of information, but without a receptive company culture, a BI system will struggle (and may fail) to survive.

If the products and capabilities that make up Microsoft BI are any indication, Microsoft has already recognized the importance of communication and collaboration in organizational culture and is encouraging such cultures to grow and prosper. The main components of Microsoft BI reflect this approach:

✔ Designed to sit at the center of the organization — essentially to be the heart of its intranet — SharePoint provides tools for communication, collaboration, and content management that make the intranet an active tool for encouraging company unity.

✔ Integrating the power of SQL Server product with the features of SharePoint and user knowledge of Office applications (such as Word and Excel) strikes a balance between providing enhanced capabilities and keeping a familiar way of getting the work done.

✔ Presenting ready-to-use BI information in the SharePoint environment provides not only a resource for decision-making, but also a way to integrate two bodies of knowledge: the information produced by the BI system and the employees' existing knowledge. Combining these two fronts is a huge step toward a more intelligent and efficient organization.

Being a consultant is a relatively unsettled way to make a living. I tend to bounce from one culture to another and never settle in with any particular group. The upside is that I get to see what works and doesn't work in a lot of different settings. I've seen how a culture can build a team up to do extraordinary things with seemingly average people — or tear down a team of superstars into a pile of mush that's barely able to accomplish even the most basic tasks. So it seems to me that one of the best uses of SharePoint —

especially in the context of implementing a BI system — is to connect the people within the organization. A SharePoint site dedicated to the BI project provides a window into what's happening and why. Leadership can use the SharePoint blogs, discussion boards, wikis, and surveys to create and encourage a transparent and inclusive environment — of which BI then forms a natural part.

Starting with the Right Goals

The information that flows from your finished BI solution should be valuable and relevant to you and your organization. The best way to ensure that you get those goods is to start with the right goals — to ask the genie at the beginning of the BI project (a handy little brain-stretcher from Chapter 12).

Relax. You don't have to break out the magic Eight Ball. Just imagine that a genie has appeared, and you can ask it anything at all about your organization. Instead of worrying about what's possible and what isn't possible, focus on what information you need to make better decisions and run your organization in a more intelligent manner. For example, if it would be a tremendous help to understand your sales cycles and customer buying habits, then start with those broad goals — and then narrow down to very specific questions.

The genie exercise can also give you some good hints about appropriate human-scale BI information to start with as you begin the initial iterative cycles of your BI implementation.

Reducing Risk

As bold as boardroom rhetoric can be in a flush year, nearly everybody in business gets a bit more timid in the face of risk. And risk is everywhere — especially where technology is concerned (and *that's* everywhere too). It's common, even customary, to be mystified by technology — to not-quite-understand all the components (and potential snags) in a new system until they've already been encountered and overcome.

I often see project managers ask developers how long it's going to take to complete some aspect of a technical project. The reply can go one of two ways:

  ✔ If the developer has already completed the tasks and knows that a new component works, then the estimate can be pretty accurate because the remaining tasks (say, packaging up the code, documenting, and testing) are known.

✔ If the developer has not yet figured out how to perform some key piece of functionality, then the estimate is at best a guess — and at worst a nearly-random number tossed out to appease the project manager.

Using an iterative approach to implementing Microsoft Business Intelligence reduces risk by reducing the unknown that all team members will face during each phase of the project. Since each iterative cycle spans the entire Discover, Design, Develop, and Validate lifecycle for each component, the biggest hurdles and risks are determined early in the project. And because practice makes perfect, the team gets more and more familiar with what works as they go along.

Another way to reduce risk is to make full use of your existing equipment. In this case, review the software your company already owns, and see whether it's packing already-licensed BI capabilities (or whether they're readily available). You may be pleasantly surprised:

✔ If you already own the Enterprise edition of Microsoft SharePoint, then you already have a wealth of BI features at your fingertips — including the Business Data Catalog (BDC), the Report Center template, Key Performance Indicators (KPIs), Excel Services, and InfoPath Form Services (see Chapter 10 for details).

✔ If you already own SQL Server, then you also own the Database Engine, Reporting Services, Integration Services, and Analysis Services (which includes OnLine Analytical Processing and Data Mining functionality — (see Chapter 8).

✔ If you don't already own the licensing for SharePoint or SQL Server, you can download trial versions of both these products and use the free trial period to test-drive them. It's a risk-free way to see how they may benefit your organization (see Chapter 13).

Maintaining Perspective

For a relatively new field, business intelligence has already sprouted a large and complex array of tools, techniques, products, experts, and expectations. Even so, its basic goal remains pretty simple: Transform raw data about how a business works into readily usable information that can help it make solid plans, use what it has to best advantage, become more collaborative, and get closer to its stated goals.

On a smaller scale, a look under the hood of Microsoft Business Intelligence shows two major components — SharePoint and SQL Server — that bristle with enough powerful features to seem intimidating at first. Even so, all these capabilities came together under the label of Microsoft BI for a straightforward reason: The new century has brought not only some stiff economic challenges, but also a newly collaborative way of doing business — which needed new tools. Microsoft saw the need; the current form of Microsoft BI is a powerful — but still early — response to that need.

On a smaller scale yet, Microsoft Office applications are expanding their powers way beyond the individual desktop machine, becoming familiar packages for powerful new functionality. Microsoft BI allows them to issue commands to servers and send sophisticated queries to databases. Excel (for example) already has so many features that surely only a small number of people fully understand the product — and now it's hobnobbing with databases? But it retains a familiar look and feel — and a savvy user base, because Microsoft figured out that familiar productivity software can help make new capabilities more understandable and usable. (Pretty smart.)

As a consultant, I've seen yet another intimidating complexity: the sheer number of different ways organizations use Microsoft products. The mind boggles. Of course, some of those uses work better than others. But feature-rich products can go in one of two directions: (a) they get used as a basic tool that just happens to have a trunkful of unused bells and whistles or (b) organizations will make sophisticated use of different components. Either way, the need is simple: Find the tool that works and get on with the job.

Whatever the broad similarities between organizations, every one has ways in which it's unique — especially in how it sets up its internal culture, its business processes, and even its computer systems. In-house folks who work in the corporate environment every day have experience in navigating that invisible maze. It's another complex form of valuable knowledge (vital, by the way, to setting up a BI system that both fits the company and invites frequent use). But the corporate goal is simple: Be your corporate self and keep going, taking on new capabilities as they prove useful. From the perspective of the individual employee, that's the big picture.

Arming yourself with knowledge about one such new capability — Microsoft Business Intelligence — gives you a perspective that nobody else in your organization possesses (at first, anyway — but just wait till they get a load of the new system you have in mind). It's often a struggle to avoid getting distracted by details such as how an SSIS package runs or what fields should be included in an SSRS report. But persevere. It's important to maintain a larger perspective and keep the overall goal of the BI-project-to-be in mind: Contribute to the longevity and effectiveness of your organization by introducing and implementing a new, more effective way for it to work.

Chapter 18

Ten Ways to Boost Your Bottom Line with Microsoft Business Intelligence

In This Chapter

▷ Using Microsoft BI to increase efficiency, agility, and visibility

▷ Making deep use of SQL Server and SharePoint

▷ Finding out how data mining can increase ROI

▷ Boosting your bottom line through human business intelligence

A penny saved is a penny earned.

— Benjamin Franklin

Walk in the door of any organization, and sooner or later you hear some buzz about *operating in a more optimal and efficient manner* — the mantra and primary driving force for just about every technology project for the last thirty-or-so years. No surprise that the expected return on the dollars invested in all that high-tech stuff is the deciding factor that gives the green light to a technology implementation. Unfortunately, sometimes realism can go out the window at that point. Used (ahem) *intelligently,* Microsoft Business Intelligence can help your organization add to its bottom line in a number of realistic ways. *Return on investment* (ROI) can be difficult to determine, but you can zero in on where a Microsoft BI solution can increase your ROI — the secret, O seeker of optimal efficiency, is to identify and closely track the appropriate metrics.

That's exactly what this chapter helps you do. In ten different ways. Read on. In this chapter you will explore how Microsoft BI can be used to increase efficiency, agility, and visibility using products such as SQL Server and SharePoint. You will look into the power of data mining and understand how human business intelligence can be quantified into real value.

Increasing Efficiency

Increasing efficiency in an organization is a selling point for a lot of hardware and software, but if you're serious about actually getting there, you need something a lot more basic: the proper knowledge of your business processes, systems, and procedures. After all, how are you supposed to make something *more* efficient if you don't know how efficient it already is?

A Microsoft BI solution increases efficiency in a number of different ways — largely because it starts with a realistic examination of your actual business processes (see Chapter 12). A few of the efficiencies realized with Microsoft BI in place include these:

- ✔ Tight integration among technology products — including productivity applications such as those in Office, operating systems, and SharePoint — provides seamless interaction for users.

- ✔ Powerful data-mining algorithms help improve the accuracy of forecasting and analysis.

- ✔ The growth of versatile skill sets. For example, software development using Visual Studio is similar development for other Microsoft products such as Reporting Services, Integration Services, Analysis Services, and custom .NET solutions.

- ✔ Surfacing BI data in SharePoint — making it visible in Web browsers across the organization — communicates business realities to everyone, encourages collaboration, and manages content by restricting edits to the data. In effect, everybody's on the same (Web) page where business information is concerned.

- ✔ Providing employee self-service tools for creating reports using Report Builder, Excel (which includes PowerPivot in 2010), and SharePoint sites entails a consistent form for reports and timely delivery of fresh data.

In addition to its BI capabilities, SharePoint helps boost efficiency for sales pursuits (by performing content management duties around documents containing sales materials — why re-write a new document or PowerPoint presentation when the sales people in a different region have already created one and marketing has approved it, for example) and for other tasks that use packaged material — for example, creating Word or Excel documents that follow a standard company template. You can also make reports available using the advanced content management features of SharePoint, which enhances efficiency of reporting and analysis by leveraging features such as versioning, check-in and check-out, workflow, and security.

Improving Agility

Okay, how *do* you get a big hulking company to turn on a dime and respond right away to market conditions and customer questions? Well, one way is to give users a handy, familiar way to use sophisticated databases. Microsoft BI can give employees such tools so they can answer incoming questions quickly, using minimal company resources: Excel, for example, can connect directly to OLAP cubes built using SQL Server Analysis Services (SSAS). Excel acts as a client to the cube; from the user's perspective, what shows up on-screen resembles a familiar Pivot Table (see Figure 18-1).

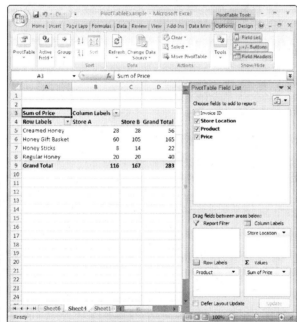

Figure 18-1: An SSAS cube can be navigated in the same fashion as a Pivot Table in Excel.

Users can drag and drop different fields into columns, rows, and summations. Hot-rodding Excel with SSAS capabilities gives users the tools to slice and dice data at will — and they can analyze data without having to bug the IT department or hunt up a report developer. Report Builder is designed for business users as opposed to Visual Studio which is designed for developers; they can create their own reports without having to struggle with undue complexity or go pound on IT's door. Report Builder reports can then be stored and managed in SharePoint — just as any other content within the organization — and displayed on a SharePoint site as appropriate. The resulting time savings, along with the ready availability of focused reporting, add up to an agility advantage.

SharePoint is also designed to help create and encourage an environment of communication and collaboration — which brings greater agility to decision-making. For example, an engineer in San Francisco that has a question about a company product built in China can post it to the internal discussion board — and a company engineer in China can respond right away.

Increasing the Visibility of Business Processes

Microsoft BI offers better visibility into many of your organization's activities, branches, and processes. Here are some examples of questions you can answer fast with BI tools:

✔ Which stores are outperforming or underperforming?

✔ What are sales and revenue figures by store, by year, by quarter, by month, by week, by sales person, by product, by product group, by state?

✔ How effective are marketing campaigns?

✔ Which people are outperforming or underperforming?

✔ Are newer, more expensive manufacturing machines more efficient than older manufacturing machines that may require more maintenance?

✔ How many products are being produced in a given shift, week, or month?

✔ What's actually causing the problem on the factory floor?

✔ How is current performance stacking up against previous years?

Forecasting

An area of business intelligence that's gaining popularity is *data mining* (also known as *computer learning* or *predictive analytics*): Complex mathematics create ready-to-use formulas that take in numbers *and predict results* — essential if you're peering into the business future or analyzing a complex set of data looking for groupings that would not otherwise be obvious. The SQL Server Analysis Services (SSAS) component of SQL Server provides a number of data-mining algorithms for use in forecasting numeric data or doing market-basket analysis (see Chapter 7).

And then there's that handy Microsoft BI way of giving Office desktop applications extra database muscle. Excel, for example has a Data Mining plug-in that calls up the power of the SSAS Data Mining Engine, using algorithms that reside in Excel itself — or on the SQL Server host machine — to find ad-hoc answers to business questions that suddenly crop up and demand answers. Figure 18-2 illustrates this use of Excel as a client to make powerful use of data-mining functionality.

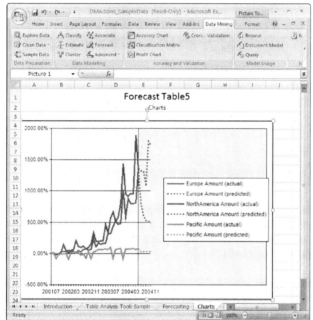

Figure 18-2:
Using SSAS data-mining functionality with Excel.

Taking Advantage of Existing Skill Sets

It'll come as no surprise that every company I've ever talked with uses Microsoft products in some capacity. Chances are really good that you've used Microsoft products or know someone who does, or has, or will. They're all over the place — and they've been a familiar part of the business landscape for decades. As potential advantages go, that one's a sleeping giant.

May as well wake the giant up. When you assess the skills that your employees bring to your organization, be sure to catalog the existing Microsoft skill sets. If you have people who can make Word turn out stellar documents or Excel crunch numbers with extra gusto, you have a resource with some serious BI potential. That's because the skills needed for using one Microsoft product are often transferable from one product to another — and that's especially true of the skills people gain from an everyday use of Office applications, Microsoft operating systems (especially the current Windows client and server OSs), Access databases, and .NET development tools. Microsoft Business Intelligence can use and extend them all.

Taking advantage of the existing Microsoft skills in your organization can directly improve your bottom line by reducing the number of people you have to hire — whether full-time employees, consultants, or contractors — when it comes time to implement Microsoft BI. A major advantage of implementing Microsoft BI is that it puts the power of BI right in front of the people who are best suited to analyze and respond to that information. You may hear this idea of self-serve BI and that is what Microsoft BI is all about.

If Microsoft products were Martians, most of us Earthlings would be speaking Martian by now — and (metaphorically speaking) some of those who do are already fluent. For true Microsoft adepts, certification is available — for the truly elite players there are the Microsoft Most Valuable Professional (MVP) programs for every component of Microsoft Business Intelligence.

Collaborating and Communicating

If you're intent on running a more intelligent business, you may as well harness the considerable knowledge and information that your company's workforce carries around in all those human heads. I like to call this resource *human business intelligence.*

How to access it? Just give it the right tools. SharePoint provides an excellent environment for collaboration and communication — universally important components of any business, just made more accessible, easier to use, and designed to be compatible with BI goals and processes. Surfacing BI information to a SharePoint site, for example, brings fresh business information together with the information flowing from your people (in forms that include feedback, comments, discussions, and company blogs). Combining these two types of information creates a synergy of content, interaction, and value to the company.

Reusing Code in Various Functional Areas

To a developer, efficiency often means reusing the code created for a particular solution; if a piece of code can be used over and over again in various projects, there's an obvious time saving. The BI world is no different.

Functionality developed for one aspect of a BI implementation can be used again throughout different stages of the project. For example, you can create a program for use with SQL Server Integration Services (SSIS) that pulls data from an inventory-management system; the same code can be extended to pull data from a manufacturing system.

I've been involved on a number of SQL Server Reporting Services (SSRS) projects, and one common theme is the reuse of reports. Often a number of the reports that a company needs to see regularly are very similar in nature; slight modifications can custom-tailor the report to a new purpose. When designed properly, a *base report* can be built once to handle a number of different scenarios. When an entirely new report is built from the report, the amount of work — and the time spent — is greatly reduced.

Consolidating Content

From the viewpoint of the content-management system in SharePoint (see Chapter 10), BI information is just more content to be *managed.* One efficient way to manage content is to consolidate it. Then you don't have to have a zillion different systems for collecting and storing information, workflows, documents, reports, KPIs, scorecards, and dashboards.

The SharePoint system provides an easy, one-stop shop for users throughout the organization: All the information and content generated by the business lives there. Add to that centralized convenience the security features, group management, and access control built into SharePoint, and consolidated content becomes a serious timesaver. The result is a single content store and thus a single version of the truth. No longer do employees have to go hunting through their local and shared drives. All of the content they own or relate to is summarized right on their SharePoint site.

Increasing Productivity

Increasing productivity has been a goal (and a promise, sometimes imperfectly kept) ever since personal computers started showing up in offices a couple of decades ago. These days a change is afoot in the pursuit of greater productivity: empowering users with BI capabilities. When multiple people from different teams need to interact to achieve a goal — and have powerful, easy-to-use tools at hand to make it happen — well, fasten your seat belt and prepare for takeoff.

Users can be empowered with tools such as Report Builder, SharePoint sites, discussion boards, wikis, KPIs, blogs, and data-warehouse components such as OLAP cubes and models (see Chapter 6). When a user can answer a business question by analyzing an OLAP cube or reading a discussion board about similar issues, you get a time saving, a reinforcement of a collaborative business culture, and . . . yes . . . a boost to the bottom line.

In addition, non-technical users can provide assistance to superiors (what a concept). For example, an administrative assistant supporting an executive can build reports and dashboards using Report Builder — and deliver a tool much like what a business analyst would usually produce. Administrative assistants are always in close contact with the people they're supporting, so the flow of communication is quick and to the point; it's a lot faster than the extended, formal requirements-gathering sessions common to traditional projects and business relationships.

Making Deep Use of SQL Server and SharePoint

The products that make up Microsoft Business Intelligence — in particular, SQL Server and SharePoint — include a wealth of capabilities. These two products are by no means a pair of one-trick ponies.

- ✔ SQL Server includes the Database Engine, Reporting Services, Integration Services, and Analysis Services (which includes OLAP and data-mining functionality — for openers).

- ✔ SharePoint is available in a base edition that is included with Windows Server called SharePoint Foundation. In addition, there is a Standard and Enterprise edition for Internet sites as well as Intranet sites. For more about the editions of SharePoint see Chapter 10.

Before you implement Microsoft BI products and features, be sure to study up on what they can do, evaluate how they fit into a realistic assessment of your business processes, and wring as much use out of each capability as you can. Given the effectiveness of the iterative approach to BI implementation detailed throughout this book, your company will get better and better at using BI tools and techniques as it goes along — and because Microsoft has a history of keeping its tools consistently usable, you'll probably be ahead of the game when new Microsoft BI features hit the market.

Glossary

balanced scorecard: A type of scorecard application that tracks an organization's progress from various perspectives simultaneously. The Microsoft version of the balanced scorecard tracks Financial, Operational, Sales, and Human Resources objectives. Various Microsoft tools are available for building balanced-scorecard visualizations; they include PerformancePoint, SQL Server Reporting Services (SSRS), and Excel.

business intelligence: As described in this book, using computer software systematically, throughout an organization, to get a handle on the mountains of data that flow from modern business. BI turns the raw data into ready-to-use business information that becomes an ongoing part of strategic decision-making.

Business Intelligence Development Studio (BIDS): When SQL Server is installed there is an option to install Business Intelligence Development Studio (BIDS). When this option is chosen the installation looks to see if Visual Studio is already installed. If Visual Studio is already installed, then the Microsoft BI development features are added to the already installed version of Visual Studio. If Visual Studio is not installed, then a version of Visual Studio is installed that only contains the Microsoft BI features. This Microsoft BI–only version of Visual Studio is called BIDS.

cube: A database object that organizes data for accessibility in an OLAP database.

dashboard: An on-screen array of indicators that show what a business process is doing in real time — presenting an up-to-date snapshot of how an operational task is performing. Distinct from a scorecard (which shows progress toward meeting a specified list of goals), a dashboard shows the current status of ongoing operations. For example, you may have a dashboard for manufacturing that outlines the current status of all machines. If the dashboard is designed to show a red flashing icon when a machine is down or a solid green icon when a machine is up, then anyone in the organization can view the dashboard and quickly understand the current health of the manufacturing process.

data mart: A smaller, more specialized version of a data warehouse that includes data from a specific functional area or department.

data mining: The process of using mathematical algorithms (usually implemented in computer software) to attempt to transform raw data into information that is not otherwise visible (for example, creating a query to forecast sales for the future based on sales from the past). Data mining is a component of Analysis Services, which is part of SQL Server.

data warehouse: A data warehouse is a large, enterprise-wide database that acts as a central storage location for data that has been through the Extract, Transform, and Load (ETL) process. A data warehouse often includes historical data as well.

dimension: An aspect of data that provides a way to divide it in an OLAP database (for example, a carmaker's OLAP database may organize product data by the dimensions of model, body style, engine type, and price point).

Excel Services: Excel Services is a feature of SharePoint that makes Excel documents available to the organization on a SharePoint site through a Web browser.

Expression Blend: A Microsoft software application designed for building Silverlight applications.

Extract, Transform, and Load (ETL): The process of connecting to a source database, pulling data out of the source database, transforming the data into a standard format, and then loading the data into a destination system. Microsoft provides ETL functionality in SQL Server Integration Services (SSIS), which is a part of SQL Server.

fact/measure: Often used interchangeably, these terms refer to numeric (or aggregated non-numeric) data contained in an OLAP database.

key performance indicator (KPI): A piece of information that an organization considers a crucial reflection of how well it's doing. Examples of KPIs include sales figures, manufacturing data, and financial information.

Microsoft Business Intelligence: The Microsoft products, tools, and capabilities that operate together to convert raw business data into strategically usable information (the "intelligence" component of BI).

Microsoft .NET: A set of programming languages and libraries designed to help developers produce compatible programs for Microsoft client and server computers.

multi-dimensional: The way an OLAP database is structured: The database organizes the various distinct aspects of the data in the OLAP database so a query can find them, whether individually or in combination; each aspect is called a *dimension*.

Multi-Dimensional eXpressions (MDX): A computer language designed to query OLAP databases in much the same way that SQL queries OLTP databases.

OnLine Analytical Processing (OLAP): An approach to database design that focuses on analytical activities such as viewing data in various aggregations, slicing and dicing data to meet different criteria, and grouping data.

OnLine Transactional Processing (OLTP): An approach to database design that focuses on data transactions — in particular inserting, updating, and deleting data.

PerformancePoint: A set of software tools from Microsoft designed for building analytical visualizations such as scorecards, dashboards, KPIs, and reports. (*Note:* The former stand-alone product known as Microsoft Office PerformancePoint Server is now a feature included in the current version of SharePoint, where it's called PerformancePoint Services for SharePoint.)

report: Organized information describing the status of some topic. BI often involves creating reports that focus on specific aspects of business operations; Dashboard Designer, for example, is a tool for building Strategy Map and Trend Analysis reports.

Report Builder: An application that gives information workers (especially end users who don't develop software) tools for building SQL Server Reporting Services (SSRS) reports without having to use Visual Studio. Report Builder offers familiar usability features such as the Office Ribbon.

scorecard: A collection of information — organized in a single view — that tracks an organization's progress toward a specific goal. For example, the CEO may set a goal for sales-per-store figures throughout the country, and set up a scorecard to track the progress of each store toward the sales goal with at-a-glance indicators such as a red, yellow, or green lights.

SharePoint: Networked communication-and-collaboration software from Microsoft that's available in two versions: a basic, free version known as SharePoint Foundation that comes with the Windows Server operating system, and a full-featured commercial software product known as SharePoint Server. SharePoint has become the leader in communication, collaboration, and content management; as such it forms a major component of Microsoft Business Intelligence. SharePoint continues to evolve, taking on new functionality and features; SharePoint Server 2010 is the latest version.

SharePoint Designer: A software application used to develop SharePoint applications that keep their content in SQL Server databases. SharePoint Designer provides a window into the SharePoint database that allows a developer to customize database content without accessing the database directly (which can be disruptive).

Silverlight: A Microsoft plug-in that enables a Web browser to mimic the fast, responsive performance of an application running on a local computer. Most Web applications (and the World Wide Web in general) are not designed to provide such a user experience. When a server sends a page to a client machine for viewing, the client uses a Web browser; each time the user interacts with the application, the Web browser sends a message back to the server — which causes the Web page to refresh and flicker. Silverlight runs on the Web browser of the client computer, where it eliminates the need for the entire page to update whenever a user interacts with the page, making the overall user experience smoother and more consistent.

SQL Server: A product from Microsoft that contains four primary components (Database Engine, Reporting Services, Integration Services, and Analysis Services).

SQL Server Analysis Services (SSAS): A component of SQL Server that contains functionality for OnLine Analytical Processing (OLAP) and data mining.

SQL Server Database Engine: Many people think of SQL Server as only the database engine. The database engine is the component that is responsible for storing data in databases. When you think of a software program that is used to store data, that is the database engine in SQL Server.

SQL Server Integration Services (SSIS): A component of SQL Server that connects to source databases and performs the Extract, Transform, and Load (ETL) procedure.

SQL Server Management Studio: A software application that provides development tools for managing the components SQL Server.

SQL Server Reporting Services (SSRS): A component of the SQL Server product and designed to provide reporting functionality across source data platforms.

Structured Query Language (SQL): A standard computer language designed to query any OLTP database, regardless of operating system.

Transact-SQL (T-SQL): A superset of the SQL query language that adds support for the Microsoft-specific database product known as SQL Server.

Visual Studio: A software application designed as a development tool for Microsoft-compatible programs. Visual Studio is called an *Integrated Development Environment (IDE)* because it provides many built-in development features that work together — including features that run and test code, color-coded key words, and IntelliSense (a feature that helps the developer find the correct key word without having to type the entire word).

Index

• A •

Accenture consulting company, 52
Access, SSIS support for, 85
ad-hoc data analysis
  described, 32–33
  SSAS support for, 33, 35–36
ad-hoc reports
  BI capabilities for, 32
  defined, 160
  report models for, 160–161
  SSAS support for, 35–36
  tools for creating and editing, 161
adopting BI. *See* implementing Business
    Intelligence
Adventure Works database, 201
aggregating values
  defined, 81
  overview, 81
  PivotTables for, 191
  pre-aggregated data with OLAP, 68–69
agile development. *See* iterative approach
    to implementation
agility, improving, 377–378
Alaska-Canadian (ALCAN) Highway, 41
algorithms
  data mining, 126, 140–143
  defined, 124
  peanut-butter-and-jelly example, 124, 126
  SSAS data-mining algorithms, 126,
    140–143
analysis. *See* data analysis; SQL Server
    Analysis Services (SSAS)
Application Programming Interface
    (API), 182
Architecture Journal site, 55
artificial intelligence. *See* data mining
"Ask the BI genie" exercise, 42–43, 278
ASP.NET language, 215

assessing BI capabilities
  current BI tools, 298–302
  current environment, 366–367
  current licensing, 43–44, 303
  current skill sets, 40–41, 47–48, 303–305,
    379–380
  MAP toolkit, 299–302
association data-mining algorithms, 140
Avanade consulting company, 52
averages, in data mining, 128
Azure Services Platform, 154–155

• B •

Balanced Scorecard, The (Kaplan and
    Norton), 120
balanced scorecards, 120–122, 383.
    See also scorecards
barcode scanners, 98
base-ten numbering system, 125
base-two numbering system, 125
BCS (Business Connectivity Services),
    228–229, 243
BDC (Business Data Catalog), 243
benchmarks, 60–61
BI. *See* Business Intelligence
BI culture
  communication and collaboration in, 350,
    370–371
  inclusion principle for, 350
  merit-based recognition in, 351
  need for, 349
  ownership in, 350–351
  trust in, 351–352
BIDS. *See* Business Intelligence
    Developer Studio
binary numbering system, 125

blogs
  by BI experts, 53–54
  getting feedback using, 346–347
  SharePoint, 235, 346–347
  uses for, 235
bottom line, methods for boosting
  communication and collaboration, 380
  consolidating content, 381
  deep use of SQL Server and
    SharePoint, 382
  forecasting, 378–379
  importance of, 375
  improving agility, 377–378
  increasing efficiency, 376
  increasing productivity, 381–382
  increasing visibility of business
    processes, 378
  reusing code, 380–381
  using existing skill sets, 379–380
boutique consultancies, 52
Buffett, Warren (investment expert), 147,
    175, 355
Business Connectivity Services (BCS),
    228–229, 243
Business Data Catalog (BDC), 243
business goals of BI project
  "Ask the BI genie" exercise, 278
  assigning complexities, 279
  factors affecting, 276–277
  prioritizing, 278–279
  sponsorship issues, 277, 365–366
  technology goals driven by, 279–280
Business Intelligence (BI). *See also specific*
    components
  agility improved by, 377–378
  core components, 10, 12–15, 47, 118
  culture, 349–352, 370–371
  in data lifecycle, 34–36
  defined, 27, 383
  development tools, 10, 18–21, 247–271
  ease of use, 46
  efficiency increased by, 376
  identifying current BI tools, 298–302
  presentation components, 10, 15–18
  project team, 368
  self-powered information flow with, 46
  terminology, 11
  tunnel vision with, avoiding, 65–66

Business Intelligence Developer Studio
    (BIDS). *See also* Visual Studio
  Analysis Services Project, 256
  Data Mining Designer, 137
  Data Mining Wizard, 129, 135–137
  defined, 383
  described, 20, 83, 129–130
  features, 254
  as IDE, 113
  Import Analysis Services Database,
    256–257
  Integration Services Connection Project
    Wizard, 257
  Integration Services Project, 257
  New Report Wizard, 259
  overview, 112–113
  Report Model Project, 257–258
  Report Server Project, 259
  Report Server Project Wizard, 257
  report-building tools, 159, 160
business processes
  canary processes, 50
  changing, 332–333
  collaborative, SharePoint for, 212
  data generation by, 25–27
  in data lifecycle, 26–27
  data points in, 25, 38
  data-generation points in, 62, 63
  documenting, 50
  efficiency critical for, 26–27
  expert on BI SWAT team, 288
  foundation for BI implementation,
    291–292
  identifying current BI tools, 298–299
  increasing visibility of, 378
  Key Performance Indicators (KPIs), 50
  management/employee mismatch
    regarding, 286
  mapping during testing, 320, 321
  mapping future process state, 321
  mapping IT processes, 44–46
  metrics needed for, 59–60
  modifying during testing, 321
  process maps and process flows for,
    286–288
  scorecard perspective, 120
  software products for, 25–26

SSRS as dashboard for, 112
understanding before implementing BI,
    285–289, 306–307, 360
buzzwords, 1, 11, 148

• *C* •

Campaign Analysis algorithm, 143
canary processes, 50
Cartesian/Gantry robots, 97
charts and graphs (Excel)
    creating, 189–190
    inserting in other Office programs, 189
    PivotCharts, 191, 195–196
    Scorecards using, 205–206
    uses for, 182–183
check-in and check-out
    described, 112
    SharePoint Ribbon functionality, 240
    with Word/SharePoint integration, 237
Churchill, Winston (British statesman), 275
Churn Analysis algorithm, 141
Clarke, Arthur C. (science writer), 297
classification data-mining algorithms, 140
cleansing. *See* data cleansing
Codd, E. F. (father of the database), 66
collaboration
    in BI culture, 350, 370–371
    bottom line increased by, 380
    Report Builder for, 261–262
    SharePoint for, 212
collection. *See* data collection
Color Scales feature (Excel), 184, 185–186
Comma Separated Value (CSV) files, SSIS
    support for, 85
command-line utilities
    PowerShell, 153
    for SQL Server installation, 168
    SQLCMD, 152
Common Language Runtime (CLR), 260–261
communicating
    in BI culture, 350, 370–371
    bottom line increased by, 380
    with power users, 282
computers
    data generation speeds due to, 95–96
    numbering system of, 125
    SharePoint hardware, 213–214

conditional formatting (Excel)
    Color Scales feature, 184, 185–186
    Data Bars feature, 184–185
    described, 184
    Icon Sets feature, 186–188
    setting rules for, 188–189
consolidating content, 381
consultants. *See* experts or consultants
Control Flow Toolbox (SSIS), 86, 88
core components. *See also specific*
        components
    common use of, 48
    overview, 10, 12–15, 47
    SQL Server components, 12, 47
core editions of SQL Server, 163–164
count, defined, 61
CSV (Comma Separated Value) files, SSIS
        support for, 85
cubes
    databases versus, 70
    defined, 64, 70, 383
    Excel use of, 64, 180, 197, 200–205
    geometrical analogies for, 72–74
    PerformancePoint Services analysis of, 118
    with PivotTables and PivotCharts, 200–205
    PowerPivot for building, 14
    sample for Excel, 201
    SSAS for building, 64
culture. *See* BI culture
customer perspective of scorecards, 121
customer relationship management
        (CRM), 228

• *D* •

dashboards
    automatic updating of, 119
    Dashboard Designer for, 118, 119, 270–271
    defined, 17, 119, 383
    PerformancePoint Services feature, 269
    scorecards versus, 120
    SSRS as, for business processes, 112
data analysis. *See also* SQL Server Analysis
        Services (SSAS)
    ad-hoc, 32–33, 35–36
    in data lifecycle, 32–33
    defined, 32
    Excel for, 16, 177, 191–197
    granularity of, 75, 76

data analysis *(continued)*
  high-level, 75
  low-level, 75
  PerformancePoint Services analysis of
    cubes, 118
  SSAS data-mining algorithms, 126, 140–143
  statistical, in data mining, 128
Data Bars feature (Excel), 184–185
data cleansing
  for date formats, 79
  defined, 29, 79
  for naming conventions, 79–80, 82
data collection
  data silos for, 28–29
  described, 28
  digital format for, 63
  Excel for, 177, 179–181
  extracting data, 78–79
  from legacy systems, 29
  methods for, 27
  understanding the source data, 88, 89
Data Definition Language (DDL), 151–153
Data Exploration algorithm, 142
Data Flow Toolbox (SSIS), 88
data generation
  by business processes, 25–27, 62
  computers increasing speed of, 95–96
  described, 27
  by ERP systems, 96
  Excel for, 177, 178–179
  at point of sale, 98
  retail store example, 37–38
  by robots, 97
  by scanners, 98
data lifecycle
  analysis, 32–33
  business processes in, 26–27
  data mining, 33
  Excel use throughout, 176, 177
  generation and collection, 25–29
  Microsoft BI in, 34–36
  overview, 24–25
  transformation and organization, 29–30
  visualization and reporting, 31–32
data marts
  data flow to, 107–108
  defined, 13, 29, 106, 383
  purpose of, 106
  storage across many servers, 13

data mining
  averages and extremes, 128
  building your models, 129
  connecting Excel to SSAS server, 199,
    201–204
  continuous iteration in, 130–131
  in data lifecycle, 33
  Data Mining Designer, 137
  defined, 15, 33, 124, 384
  defining the problem, 127
  deploying and updating your models,
    130–131
  ETL needed for, 126, 127
  Excel add-in for, 16, 132, 133–134, 138,
    177, 198–200
  Excel use for, 177, 197–205
  exploring and validating your models,
    129–130
  exploring the data, 128–129
  forecasting using, 378–379
  integrating with Microsoft Office, 133–134
  iteration 1, 128–129
  iteration 2, 129–130
  Microsoft process for, 127–131
  Microsoft resource page, 200
  models, 129–131, 132
  need for, 123, 124
  phases of, 127
  preparing the data, 127–128
  role in BI process, 126
  sample Excel document, 199
  SQL Server Management Studio for, 139
  SSAS algorithms for, 126, 140–143
  SSAS engine for, 33, 36
  SSIS tools for, 138–139
  statistical analysis of data, 128
  structures, 131, 132
  videos on, 200
  Visio add-in for, 16, 134, 198
  Visual Studio wizard for, 129, 135–137
Data Mining Client for Excel, 134, 198
Data Mining Designer (Visual Studio), 137
Data Mining Extensions (DMX), 129, 132,
  138–139
Data Mining Templates for Visio, 134, 198
Data Mining Wizard (Visual Studio), 129,
  135–137

data models
  dimensional, 108–109
  hybrid, 109–110
  model, defined, 110
  relational, 109
  as schemas or patterns, 110
data organization
  in data lifecycle, 29–30
  defined, 29
  Excel for, 177, 181–183
  SSIS capabilities for, 30, 34, 64
data points
  defined, 25, 179
  retail store example, 37–38
data silos
  defined, 28
  overview, 28–29
  SSIS with, 30
data sources supported
  by Excel, 180
  by Report Builder, 159
  by SSIS, 85–86, 128
  by SSRS, 11, 35
data storage. *See also* data marts; data
    warehouses
  centralized, need for, 100
  creating a mechanism, 321
  data silos, 28–30
  dimensional models of, 108–109
  hybrid models of, 109–110
  models, 108–110
  patterns, 108–110
  relational models of, 109
  schemas, 110
  varieties and need for data
    transformation, 79, 82
data transformation
  aggregating values, 81
  calculating new values, 80
  checklist for building ETL processes, 88–89
  cleansing, 29, 79–80
  in data lifecycle, 29
  mapping for, 80, 89
  SSIS capabilities for, 30, 34, 64
  SSIS data-flow transformations, 139
  storage varieties and need for, 79, 82
  time saved by, 81

Data Transformation Services (DTS),
    83. *See also* SQL Server Integration
    Services (SSIS)
data versus information, 105–106
data visualization
  charts and graphs for, 182–183, 189–190
  conditional formatting for, 184–189
  in data lifecycle, 31–32
  Excel capabilities for, 177, 183–184
  Excel charts and graphs for, 189–190
  Excel conditional formatting for, 184–189
  Excel PivotCharts for, 191, 195–196,
    200–205
  Excel Scorecards for, 205–206
  for KPIs in SharePoint, 227–228
  PerformancePoint Services capabilities
    for, 36
  PowerPoint themes with SharePoint for,
    241–242
  as small project, 31
  starting point for, 31
  Visio Services for, 242
data warehouses
  as central storage mechanism, 100–102,
    107–108
  data flow to data marts from, 107–108
  data formatting consistent in, 102
  defined, 13, 29, 100, 384
  ETL used for, 104
  getting data from, 104, 106
  need for, examples demonstrating, 101,
    102–103
  overview, 100–103
  reasons for, 104
  SQL Server database engine running, 103
  storage across many servers, 13
database engine, defined, 150
database mirroring, 153–154
databases. *See also* data marts; data
    warehouses
  creating using the DDL, 151–153
  creating using the GUI, 151, 152
  cubes versus, 70
  data-mining models as, 132
  de-normalization with OLAP, 71
  Excel support for, 180
  federated, 103
  multidimensional, with OLAP, 71
  multiple, in organization systems, 13

databases *(continued)*
  normalization with OLTP, 70–71
  relational, with OLTP, 70–71
  retail store example, 37–38
  snowflake design, 108–109
  star design, 108–109
data-flow destinations (SSIS), 139
data-flow transformations (SSIS), 139
    data-generation points
  defined, 62
  determining, 63
date formats
  data cleansing for, 79
  SSIS walk-through for transforming, 89–95
DB2. *See* IBM DB2
DDL (Data Definition Language), 151–153
deadlines for BI adoption, 42
decimal numbering system, 125
decision making
  getting decision-makers on board
    early, 277
  hierarchies of detail for, 76
  identifying relevant data for, 63
  providing relevant data for, 63–64
delegating ownership, 331–332
Design phase of iterative methodology,
    284–285
Develop phase of iterative methodology, 285
Developer edition of SQL Server, 166
development tools. *See also specific tools*
  .NET Framework, 259–261
  overview, 10, 18–21, 247
  PerformancePoint Services for
    SharePoint, 269–271
  Report Builder, 261–262
  SharePoint Designer, 264–268
  Silverlight, 268–269
  SQL Server Management Studio, 263–264
  Visual Studio, 248–259
digital format for data, 63
dimensional data-storage models, 108–109
dimensions of a database
  data-storage patterns, 108–110
  defined, 71, 384
  hierarchies of, 75–76
  values at intersections of, 72

Discover phase of iterative methodology,
    284
discussion boards (SharePoint)
  attaching to Outlook, 238–239
  creating, 344–346
  getting feedback using, 344–346
  overview, 235–236
DMX (Data Mining Extensions), 129, 132,
    138–139
document libraries (SharePoint)
  adding an Excel document, 220–223
  content management functionality,
    231–232
  creating, 232
  defined, 209
  embedding an Excel document in a
    SharePoint page, 223–226
  overview, 231–232
  Ribbon functionality, 240
documentation
  of goals, 320
  of key business processes, 50
  SharePoint wikis for, 234
drilling in analytical technique, 68
drilling out analytical technique, 68
drilling through analytical technique, 68
Drucker, Peter F. (management expert), 23
DTS (Data Transformation Services),
    83. *See also* SQL Server Integration
    Services (SSIS)
.dtsx filename extension, 85
Dynamics (Microsoft)
  described, 25
  SSIS support for, 85

• *E* •

early adoption, gaining, 329–330
efficiency
  critical for business processes, 26–27
  increasing, 376
Einstein, Albert (scientist), 9
Electronic Data Interchange (EDI), SSIS
    support for, 85
embedding an Excel document in a
    SharePoint page, 223–226
engine, defined, 103, 150

Enterprise Content Management (ECM)
systems, 18, 36. *See also* SharePoint
Enterprise edition of SQL Server, 163–164
Enterprise Resource Planning (ERP)
   companies providing products, 85, 96
   data generation by, 96
   Excel used with, 116
   as shelf-ware, 43
   SSIS connections for systems, 85–86
Epicor ERP systems, SSIS support for, 85
ETL. *See* Extract, Transform, and Load
evaluating results
   need for, 342–343
   SharePoint feedback tools for, 343–348
Event Handlers Toolbox (SSIS), 86
Excel. *See also* Excel Services
   adding a document to a SharePoint
      library, 220–223
   as analysis tool, 16
   as BI front end, 176–178
   bus factor for spreadsheets, 208
   charts and graphs, 182–183, 189–190,
      195–196, 205–206
   Color Scales feature, 184, 185–186
   common use of, 116, 175–176
   conditional formatting, 184–189
   configuring for data mining, 199
   connecting to SSAS server, 199, 201–204
   cube data with, 64, 180, 197, 200–205
   data analysis using, 16, 177, 191–197
   Data Bars feature, 184–185
   data collection using, 177, 179–181
   data generation using, 177, 178–179
   data lifecycle spanned by uses of,
      176, 177
   Data Mining Add-in, 16, 132, 133–134, 138,
      177, 198–200
   Data Mining Client, 134, 198
   data mining using, 177, 197–205
   data organization using, 177, 181–183
   data sources supported by, 180
   data visualization using, 177, 183–190
   described, 15, 47, 175
   embedding a document in a SharePoint
      page, 223–226
   future of, 209
   Get External Data feature, 180–181
   Icon Sets feature, 186–188
   installing the Data Mining Add-in, 198
   limits of, 207–209
   maximum rows of data, 208
   as OLAP analysis tool, 200
   PivotCharts, 191, 195–196, 200–205
   PivotTables, 14, 68, 191–194, 200–205
   PowerPivot feature, 14, 68
   purchase-order form, 179, 180
   reasons for dominance of, 176
   Ribbon, 176–178, 198–199
   Rights Management feature, 208
   sample document for data mining, 199
   sample OLAP cube for, 201
   scalability issues for, 207–209
   Scorecards, 205–206
   SharePoint integration with, 220–226
   SSAS integration with, 35
   SSIS connections for spreadsheets, 91–93
   SSIS integration with, 85
   surfacing information during rollout,
      324–325
   Table Analysis Tools, 134, 198
Excel Services
   adding an Excel document to a
      SharePoint library, 220–223
   dashboarding using, 17
   defined, 384
   embedding an Excel document in a
      SharePoint page, 223–226
   needs addressed by, 17
   overview, 116–117, 209
   security features, 17, 117
   Web service, 209
experts or consultants
   on BI SWAT team, 288, 289
   finding, 53–54
   in-house expertise, 51
   principles for hiring, 368–369
   pros and cons of, 52, 275–276, 362
   prototype phase agreement for, 51
Express editions
   SQL Server, 164–165
   Visual Studio, 251, 255
Expression Blend (Silverlight),
   268–269, 384
Extract, Transform, and Load (ETL). *See
   also* SQL Server Integration Services
   (SSIS)
   checklist for building processes, 88–89
   data mining and need for, 126, 127

Extract, Transform, and Load
        (ETL) *(continued)*
    defined, 14, 78, 384
    drag-and-drop development using Visual
        Studio, 83, 84
    extracting data, 78–79
    focusing on "what" not "how," 83, 127
    loading data, 81–83
    need for, 82, 104
    package creation using SSIS, 322
    SSIS as ETL tool, 14, 77, 82
    SSIS walk-through, 89–95
    testing, 318–319
    transforming data, 79–81, 88–89
extremes, in data mining, 128

• *F* •

Fact Tables, 74
facts, defined, 61, 74, 384
failover clustering, 153
feedback after implementation
    blogs for, 346–347
    discussion boards for, 344–346
    incorporating, 349
    interviews for, 348
    need for, 342–343
    SharePoint tools for, 343–348
    surveys for, 344
    wikis for, 347–348
filename extension for SSIS packages, 85
financial perspective of scorecards, 121
fixer, on BI SWAT team, 288–289
Flat Text files, SSIS support for, 85
Ford, Henry (auto inventor), 123
forecasting, 378–379
Forecasting algorithm, 141–142
Franklin, Benjamin, 375
FTP, SSIS support for, 85
fully articulated robots, 97

• *G* •

Gates, Bill (Microsoft founder), 39, 211
generation. *See* data generation
global consultancies, 52
goals of BI project
    "Ask the BI genie" exercise, 278
    assigning complexities, 279

business goals, 276–279
    documenting, 320
    factors affecting, 276–277
    as key to success, 371
    prioritizing, 278–279
    sponsorship issues, 277, 365–366
    technology goals, 279–280
granular, defined, 75
granularity of data, 75
graphs. *See* charts and graphs (Excel)
Groove Networks, Microsoft acquisition
        of, 244
Groove Workspace, 244
grouping analytical technique, 68
Grove, Andy (business leader), 77, 99

• *H* •

hierarchies of detail
    defined, 75
    high-level versus low-level, 75
    uses for, 75–76
high-level analysis, 75
high-tech tunnel vision, avoiding, 65–66
HTTP and HTTPs, SSIS support for, 85
hybrid data-storage models, 109–110
Hyperion
    SSIS support for ERP systems, 85
    SSRS support for Essbase, 35

• *I* •

IBM DB2
    SSIS support for, 85
    SSRS support for, 11
Icon Sets feature (Excel), 186–188
icons in margins of this book, 5
IDE (Integrated Development
        Environment), 113
IIS (Internet Information Services), 214–215
IL (Intermediate Language), 260
implementation plan, 367
implementing Business Intelligence.
        See also assessing BI capabilities;
        prototype for BI project
    ALCAN Highway example, 41
    "Ask the BI genie" exercise, 42–43, 278
    BI SWAT team for, 288–289

business goals for, 276–279, 371
choosing BI components, 308–309
determining which software to purchase, 46–47
documenting business processes, 50
effective versus ineffective, 275–276
employee ownership and engagement in, 41
evaluating results, 342–348
foundation for, 291–292, 361
free BI tools, 309–313
identifying data needed to attain goals, 290–291
inclusive environment for, 369–370
incorporating feedback, 349
involving power users, 282, 289–290, 324, 329–330, 359
IT department involvement, 43–44, 280
iterative approach, 281–282, 284–285, 293–295, 315–316, 364–365
keys to success, 363–373
maintaining perspective, 372–373
management plan for, 327–328
managing change, 328–334
MAP toolkit for assessment, 299–302
mapping business processes, 46, 286–288
mapping IT processes, 44–46
overpromising results, avoiding, 360
phases of iterative approach, 284–285
phases of waterfall approach, 282–284, 356
pitfalls to avoid, 355–362
plan for, 367
reducing risk, 313, 371–372
resources for guidance, 51–56
rolling out, 323–326
scope creep, 292–295
shelf-ware, avoiding, 357–358
solidifying the project goals, 290
step 1: determining knowledge needed, 40, 42–43
step 2: investigating current licensing and capabilities, 40, 43–47, 303
step 3 and 4: determining knowledge and skills available, 40–41, 47–48, 303–305
step 5: prototype development and iteration, 41, 48–50
team for, 368–369
technology goals for, 279–280
testing, 316–323
timelines and deadlines for, 42
top-down control issues, 361
understanding BI tools, 307–308
understanding business processes, 285–289, 306–307, 360
unknowns involved, 42
waterfall approach, 281, 282–284, 290, 293, 315, 356
inclusion principle for BI culture, 350
inclusive environment, creating, 369–370
inclusive leadership style, 331
indicators, defined, 61
InfoPath Form Services, 226–227
InfoPath (Microsoft Office), 226
Information Quality algorithm, 143
information versus data, 105–106
Infosys consulting company, 52
installing
Excel Data Mining Add-in, 198
SQL Server, 166–169
SQL Server Management Studio, 263
Visual Studio BI components, 135, 159
Integrated Development Environment (IDE), 113
Integration Services. See SQL Server Integration Services (SSIS)
IntelliSense feature, 171–172
Intermediate Language (IL), 260
Internet Information Services (IIS), 214–215
Internet resources
Azure Services Platform, 154
blogs, 53–54
data mining resource page, 200
data mining videos, 200
Excel Data Mining Add-in, 198
for experts or consultants, 53–54
magazines, journals, and newsletters, 55
MAP toolkit, 300
Microsoft Developer Network, 55
Microsoft Support, 54–55
MVP directory, 53, 54
sample Excel document for data mining, 199
sample OLAP cube, 201
SharePoint Designer download, 266
SharePoint Designer training, 340
SharePoint training roadmap, 337
SharePoint training system, 337
SharePoint trial version, 310, 312
SharePoint versions, 217

Internet resources *(continued)*
  SQL Data Services (SDS), 155
  SQL Server Books Online documentation, 340–342
  SQL Server software download, 166
  SQL Server trial version, 166, 310, 311
  TechNet site, 55, 56
  Theme Builder, 242
  user groups, 53
  Visual Studio trial version, 248
  whitepapers, 55
  Wikipedia, 234
interviews (SharePoint), 348
intranets
  defined, 48
  SharePoint as portal, 122
  SharePoint blogs for, 235
introducing new technology, 333–334
ISO image for SQL Server installation, 167
IT department, involving in BI decisions, 39, 43–44, 280, 358
IT processes, mapping, 44–46
iterative approach to implementation
  changing business processes, 333
  continuously adding value, 316
  iterative cycle for testing, 317–318, 323
  as key to success, 364–365
  managing change, 328–334
  overview, 281–282
  phases, 284–285
  prototype iteration, 41, 48–50
  scope refinement in, 293–295
  testing and rollout in, 315
  using, 284–285

• J •

JD Edwards ERP systems, SSIS support for, 85
journals online, 55
juggling data, 36–37

• K •

Kaplan, Robert (*The Balanced Scorecard*), 120
Key Performance Indicators (KPIs)
  canary processes, 50
  defined, 50, 61, 227, 384

Excel Scorecards for, 205–206
PerformancePoint Services feature, 269
SharePoint KPI lists, 119, 227–228
surfacing information during rollout, 325

• L •

Lawson ERP systems, SSIS support for, 85
learning and growth perspective of scorecards, 121
legacy systems, data collection from, 29
licensing
  adoption rate for Microsoft, 43
  checking before adopting BI, 43–44, 303
  determining which software to purchase, 46–47
  IT department knowledge of, 39, 43–44
  Microsoft Support options with, 55
  needless, for shelf-ware, 43
  Site Licensing (Microsoft), 43–44, 55
  Volume Licensing (Microsoft), 43–44, 55
  Web site for information, 44
Line of Business (LOB) systems
  SharePoint BCS with, 228–229, 243
  Word/SharePoint integration for, 243
Lippman, Walter (journalist), 335
Lists (SharePoint)
  built-in lists, 232
  custom, creating, 232–234
  defined, 232
  sorting and filtering dynamically, 243
loading data
  defined, 81
  mapping numeric values before, 80
  practical decisions for, 81–83
log shipping, 154
low-level analysis
  defined, 75
  granularity of, 75, 76

• M •

machine learning. *See* data mining
magazines online, 55
maintenance, 327–328
management plan
  managing change, 328–334
  minimum, 327
  need for, 327, 328

Management Studio. *See* SQL Server Management Studio

managing change
  benefits of, 328
  changing business processes, 332–333
  delegating ownership, 331–332
  gaining early adoption, 329–330
  inclusive leadership style for, 331
  introducing new technology, 333–334
  resistance to change, 329
  transparency for, 329–331

MAP (Microsoft Assessment and Planning) toolkit, 299–302

mapping
  business processes, 46, 286–288
  business processes during testing, 320
  for data transformation, 80, 89
  IT processes, 44–46

Market Analysis algorithm, 141
Market Basket Analysis algorithm, 141
Master Data Management (MDM), 105
MDX (Multi-Dimensional Expressions), 173, 385
Measure Groups, 75
measurements. *See* metrics

measures
  defined, 61, 74, 384
  varieties of, 74–75

merit-based recognition, in BI culture, 351

metrics
  data-generation points for, 62
  defined, 27, 61
  determining relevant data, 62–63
  gut feelings versus, 61
  measuring changes, 60
  need for, 59–60, 61
  for prototype development, 42–43
  terminology, 60–61

Microsoft Access, SSIS support for, 85
Microsoft Assessment and Planning (MAP) toolkit, 299–302
Microsoft Business Intelligence, 384. *See also* Business Intelligence (BI)
Microsoft Developer Network (MSDN), 55

Microsoft (Dynamics)
  described, 25
  SSIS support for, 85

Microsoft Message Queuing (MSMQ), SSIS support for, 85

Microsoft .NET. *See* .NET Framework

Microsoft Office. *See also specific programs*
  current skill sets for, 304
  data-mining tools, 133–134
  SharePoint integration with, 236–239, 243–244

Microsoft Office SharePoint Server (MOSS), 216, 217. *See also* SharePoint

Microsoft Support, 54–55
mission-critical applications, 153
Model Designer (Visual Studio), 161

models
  data mining, 129–131, 132
  data-storage patterns, 108–110
  defined, 110, 132
  for reports, 159–161

Most Valuable Professionals (MVPs), 53, 54
multi-dimensional databases, 71
multi-dimensional, defined, 384
Multi-Dimensional Expressions (MDX), 173, 385

MySQL
  SSIS support for, 85
  SSRS support for, 11

• N •

naming conventions, data cleansing for, 79–80, 82

.NET Framework
  ASP.NET language, 215
  Common Language Runtime (CLR), 260–261
  current skill sets for, 305
  custom code for SSIS using, 79, 89
  defined, 384
  described, 18, 19, 21, 259
  as development tool, 259–261
  English-syntax languages supported by, 260
  Intermediate Language (IL), 260
  as SharePoint framework, 214

newsletters online, 55

normalization
  defined, 70, 109
  de-normalization of OLAP databases, 71
  normalized data models, 109
  in OLTP databases, 70–71

Norton, David (*The Balanced Scorecard*), 120
numbering systems, 125

• *O* •

Object Linking and Embedding, DataBase (OLEDB), 35, 182
ODBC (Open DataBase Connectivity), 35, 182
OLAP cubes. *See* cubes
OLTP. *See* Online Transactional Processing
Online Analytical Processing (OLAP). *See also* SQL Server Analysis Services (SSAS)
  ad-hoc data analysis provided by, 33
  defined, 24, 385
  de-normalization for, 71
  described, 14
  drilling in technique, 68
  drilling out technique, 68
  drilling through technique, 68
  Excel as analysis tool, 200
  grouping technique, 68
  multidimensional databases for, 71
  OLTP compared to, 66–67, 69
  power of, 69
  PowerPivot cubes as, 14
  pre-aggregation by, 68–69
  speed of, 67–69
  as SQL Server component, 70
  SSAS as, 14
Online Transactional Processing (OLTP)
  defined, 385
  OLAP compared to, 66–67, 69
  relational databases for, 70–71
Open DataBase Connectivity (ODBC), 35, 182
open-source software, 309–310
operating system (OS). *See* Windows Operating Systems
Oracle
  Report Builder support for, 159
  SSIS support for, 85
  SSRS support for, 11, 35
organizing data. *See* data organization
Outlook, SharePoint integration with, 237–239

ownership
  in BI culture, 350–351
  delegating, 331–332
  employee, in BI project, 41
Ozzie, Ray (Microsoft executive), 244

• *P* •

Package Explorer Toolbox (SSIS), 86
packages (SSIS)
  building by dragging tasks, 86
  configuring task properties, 86–87
  defined, 84, 86
  ETL package creation, 322
  filename extension for, 85
  Package Explorer Toolbox, 86
  procedures for building, 162
  testing, 319
  Visual Studio projects versus, 84
PASS (Professional Association for SQL Server), 53
PerformancePoint Server, 117–118, 119
PerformancePoint Services for SharePoint
  advantages of, 270
  cube analysis feature, 118
  Dashboard Designer, 118, 119, 270–271
  dashboard feature, 269
  defined, 385
  described, 17
  as development tool, 269–271
  KPI feature, 269
  as MOSS feature, 36
  overview, 117–119
  reports using, 269–270
  scorecarding feature, 117, 269
  surfacing information during rollout, 326
perspective, maintaining, 372–373
PivotCharts (Excel)
  changing the chart type, 196
  creating, 195–196
  cube data with, 200–205
  described, 191
  updating, 195
  uses for, 195
PivotTables (Excel). *See also* PowerPivot feature (Excel)
  adding pivot points, 194
  calculations available, 194

creating, 191–193
cube data with, 200–205
data grouping by, 68
described, 14, 191
dragging fields into boxes, 193–194
slicing and dicing a dataset, 194
updating PivotCharts using, 195
uses for, 191
PL/SQL (Procedural Language/SQL), 172
point of sale, data generation at, 98
political environment of organization, 277, 358
post-backs, 240–241
PostgreSQL
 SSIS support for, 85
 SSRS support for, 11
power users
 benefits of input from, 282, 289
 communicating with, 282
 gaining early adoption by, 329–330
 getting on board early, 290
 involving in implementation, 329–330, 359
 involving in testing, 324
 as keys to successful implementation, 289–290
 training by, 342
PowerPivot feature (Excel), 14, 68
PowerPoint themes with SharePoint, 241–242
PowerShell, 153
pre-aggregated data with OLAP, 68–69
predictive analytics. *See* data mining
Premium Edition of Visual Studio, 251–254, 255
presentation components, 10, 15–18. *See also specific components*
private contractors, 52
Procedural Language/SQL (PL/SQL), 172
process maps and process flows
 for BI project prototype, 46
 for business processes, 46, 286–288
 for IT processes, 44–45
productivity, increasing, 381–382
Professional Association for SQL Server (PASS), 53
Professional Edition of Visual Studio, 251–254, 255

programming languages
 ASP.NET, 215
 IL (Intermediate Language), 260
 .NET environment support for, 260
 overview, 259–260
 PL/SQL (Procedural Language/SQL), 172
 T-SQL (Transact-SQL), 151, 152, 172, 386
project manager, on BI SWAT team, 289
project team, 368
projects (Visual Studio), SSIS packages versus, 84
prototype for BI project
 ALCAN Highway example, 41
 benefits of, 40, 48–49
 business process map for, 46
 consultant agreement for, 51
 employee ownership and engagement in, 41
 iterating and expanding upon, 41, 49–50
 key questions and metrics for, 42–43
 before large-scale implementation, 42
 value generated by, 39, 40, 46, 49–50
publishers, defined, 154

• R •

Radio Frequency Identification (RFID) scanners, 98
RDL (Report Definition Language), 156–157
regression data-mining algorithms, 140
relational databases, 70–71
relational data-storage models, 109
relevant data, determining, 62–63
Remember icon, 5
render, defined, 150
replication, 154
Report Builder
 ClickOnce downloads for, 158
 collaborative use of, 261–262
 data sources supported by, 159
 defined, 385
 described, 18, 19, 20, 45, 114
 as development tool, 261–262
 integration with SharePoint and SSRS, 45–46
 overview, 114–115, 158–159, 261–262
 Ribbon, 115, 261

Report Builder *(continued)*
  SSRS capabilities supported by, 114
  surfacing information during rollout, 326
  user-friendly features, 115
Report Definition Language (RDL), 156–157
Report Explorer (SSRS), 219
Report Manager (SSRS), 161, 219
Report Viewer (SSRS), 219
Reporting Services. *See* SQL Server
    Reporting Services (SSRS)
reports. *See also* SQL Server Reporting
    Services (SSRS)
  ad-hoc, 32, 160–161
  in data lifecycle, 31–32
  defined, 385
  importance of, 32
  models, 159–161
  need for, 13
  PerformancePoint Services feature,
    269–270
  as small projects, 31
  starting point for, 31
  surfacing information during rollout,
    325, 326
  tools for building, 157–159
resources for BI adoption. *See also* Internet
    resources
  experts, 51–54
  in-house expertise, 51
  Microsoft Support, 54–55
  online, 55–56
reusing code, 380–381
RFID (Radio Frequency Identification)
    scanners, 98
Ribbon
  Excel, 176–178, 198–199
  Report Builder, 115, 261
  SharePoint, 240
Rights Management feature (Excel), 208
risk, reducing, 313, 371–372
robots, data generation by, 97
rolling out
  changing business processes, 332–333
  delegating ownership, 331–332
  gaining early adoption, 329–330
  introducing new technology, 333–334
  managing change, 328–334
  overview, 323–324

  phase of iterative methodology for, 316
  surfacing information, 324–326
  transparency during, 329–331
RS. *See* SQL Server Reporting Services

• S •

Sage ERP systems, SSIS support for, 85
SAP
  described, 25
  Report Builder support for, 159
  SSIS support for, 85
  SSRS support for, 11, 35
scaleout approach, 34
scaleup approach, 34
scaling
  Excel limits for, 207–209
  prototype iteration, 41, 49–50
  scope creep, 292–294
  SQL Server database engine, 34
scanners, data generation by, 98
SCARA (Selectively Compliant Articulated
    Robot Arm) robots, 97
scope creep, 292–294
scorecards
  balanced, 120–122, 383
  BI products useful for, 121–122
  business process perspective, 120
  customer perspective, 121
  dashboards versus, 120
  defined, 120, 385
  Excel, 205–206
  financial perspective, 121
  learning and growth perspective, 121
  Microsoft approach to, 121–122
  PerformancePoint Services feature,
    117, 269
SDS (SQL Data Services), 155
security
  Excel Rights Management feature, 208
  Excel Services features, 17, 117
  SharePoint features, 17, 112, 117
segmentation data-mining algorithms, 140
Selectively Compliant Articulated Robot
    Arm (SCARA) robots, 97
self-service training, enabling, 336–337
semiconductors, 125

sequence analysis data-mining algorithms, 140
servers. *See also* SQL Server
  current skill sets for, 304–305
  defined, 214
  for SharePoint, 214–215
  SSAS, Excel connection to, 199, 201–204
servers-in-the-clouds, 154–155
service, defined, 150
Services Oriented Architecture (SOA), 226
SharePoint
  adding an Excel document to a library, 220–223
  BI features, 115–116, 118
  blogs, 235, 346–347
  Business Connectivity Services (BCS), 228–229, 243
  check-in and check-out functionality, 112, 237, 240
  components of environment, 213–216
  computer hardware for, 213–214
  content management functionality, 222–223
  as core of Microsoft BI, 118
  dashboards, 119
  data visualization using, 241–242
  deep use of, 382
  defined, 385
  described, 15, 16, 47, 212–213
  development ladder, 218
  discussion boards, 235–236, 238–239, 344–346
  document libraries, 209, 231–232
  document versioning with, 111, 222–223
  as ECM solution, 18, 36, 111
  embedding an Excel document in a page, 223–226
  Excel integration with, 220–226
  Excel Services, 17, 116–117
  feedback tools, 343–348
  fluid user experience with, 240–241
  IIS servers for, 214–215
  inclusive leadership style aided by, 331
  InfoPath Form Services, 226–227
  interviews, 348
  as intranet portal, 122
  KPI lists, 119, 227–228
  Lists, 232–234, 243
  My Site pages, 46

  Navigation Ribbon, 240
  .NET framework for, 214
  new features for SharePoint Server 2010, 239–245
  Office integration with, 236–239, 243–244
  operating systems for, 214
  Outlook integration with, 237–239
  overview, 115–116
  PerformancePoint Services, 17, 117–119, 269–271
  PowerPoint themes with, 241–242
  Report Builder integration with, 45–46
  scorecards, 120–122
  security features, 17, 112, 117
  SharePoint Designer, 264–268
  SharePoint Foundation, 215, 216, 217, 218
  SharePoint Server, 215–216, 217, 218
  SSRS integration with, 17–18, 36, 112, 115, 161, 218–219
  SSRS SharePoint Integrated mode, 219, 325
  surfacing of information by, 64, 229
  surveys, 344
  Theme Builder, 242
  training resources, 337–340
  trial version, 310, 312–313
  uses for, 211–213
  versioning features, 111, 222–223, 237, 240
  versions and editions, 216–217
  Visio Services, 242
  Web site, 17
  Web sites, 230–231
  wikis, 234, 347–348
  Word integration with, 237, 244
  workflow monitoring with, 112
  Workspace, 244–245
SharePoint Designer
  connecting to SharePoint site, 266–267
  creating a new SharePoint object, 267
  defined, 385
  downloading, 266
  overview, 264–265
  training, 338–340
  uses for, 267–268
SharePoint Foundation. *See also* SharePoint
  described, 215, 216, 217
  in SharePoint development ladder, 218

SharePoint Server. *See also* SharePoint
  described, 215–216, 217
  in SharePoint development ladder, 218
shelf-ware, 43, 357–358
Siebel ERP systems, SSIS support for, 85
Silverlight
  defined, 386
  described, 18, 19, 20
  as development tool, 241, 268–269
  Expression Blend, 268–269, 384
Site Licensing (Microsoft), 43–44, 55
Slalom Consulting, 52
SMTP, SSIS support for, 85
snowflake database design, 108–109
SOA (Services Oriented Architecture), 226
software licensing. *See* licensing
sponsorship issues for BI goals, 277,
  365–366
SQL Data Services (SDS), 155
SQL Server. *See also* SQL Server database
  engine; *specific components*
  Books Online documentation, 340–342
  core BI components, 12, 47, 149–150
  core editions, 163–164
  as core of Microsoft BI, 118
  Data Mining Engine, 140–141
  deep use of, 382
  defined, 386
  described, 148
  Developer edition, 166
  Enterprise edition, 163–164
  Express editions, 164–165
  installing, 166–169
  PASS user group for, 53
  Standard edition, 163
  training resources, 340–342
  trial version, 166, 310, 311–312
  Web edition, 165
  Workgroup edition, 165
SQL Server Analysis Services (SSAS)
  ad-hoc data analysis provided by, 33,
    35–36
  as back end for Excel, 178
  BIDS features for, 254
  connecting Excel to server, 199, 201–204
  Data Mining Engine, 33, 36, 163
  Data Mining Extensions with, 129, 132
  defined, 386
  described, 12, 150

  Excel integration with, 35
  Measure Groups in, 75
  OLAP cubes built by, 64
  as OLAP implementation, 14, 163, 201
  overview, 162–163
  sample OLAP cube for, 201
SQL Server database engine
  on cluster of computers, 30, 103
  creating a database using the DDL,
    151–153
  creating a database using the GUI, 151–152
  current skill sets for, 305
  data warehouses run by, 103
  database mirroring, 153–154
  defined, 386
  described, 12, 149
  engine, defined, 103, 150
  failover clustering, 153
  federated database using, 103
  log shipping, 154
  replication, 154
  scaling, 34
  servers-in-the-clouds, 154–155
SQL Server Express (Runtime Only), 164
SQL Server Express with Advanced
  Services, 164
SQL Server Express with Tools, 164
SQL Server Integration Services (SSIS).
  See also Extract, Transform, and Load
  (ETL)
  BIDS features for, 254
  checklist for building ETL processes,
    88–89
  Control Flow design surface, 86–88
  custom code for, 79, 89
  data extraction by, 78–79
  Data Flow design surface, 88
  in data lifecycle, 30
  data sources supported by, 85–86, 128
  data transformation and organization by,
    30, 34, 64
  data-flow destinations, 139
  data-flow transformations, 139
  data-mining tools, 138–139
  defined, 386
  described, 12, 14, 150
  drag-and-drop development using Visual
    Studio, 83, 84
  ETL package creation, 322

as ETL tool, 14, 77, 82, 162
filename extension for packages, 85
overview, 307–308
packages, 84–87, 162, 319, 322
testing packages, 319
Toolbox, 86–88
walk-through, 89–95
SQL Server Management Studio
for data mining, 139
for database creation, 152
defined, 386
development in, 171–172
as development tool, 263–264
installing, 263
IntelliSense feature, 171–172
overview, 170–171
queries using, 263–264
terminology confusion with, 170
SQL Server Reporting Services (SSRS). *See also* reports
BIDS features for, 254
capabilities of, 31–32
as dashboard for business processes, 112
data sources supported by, 11, 35
defined, 386
described, 12, 13–14, 111, 149
history of, 155
Report Builder integration with, 45–46
Report Definition Language (RDL), 156–157
Report Explorer, 219
Report Manager, 161, 219
report models, 159–161
Report Viewer, 219
report-building tools, 157–159
in SharePoint Integrated mode, 219, 325
SharePoint integration with, 17–18, 36, 112, 115, 161, 218–219
stand-alone mode, 325
surfacing information during rollout, 325
Web Parts, 219
SQL (Structured Query Language), 386
SQLCMD utility, 152
SSAS. *See* SQL Server Analysis Services
SSIS. *See* SQL Server Integration Services
SSRS or SRS. *See* SQL Server Reporting Services
stakeholders, getting on board early, 277
Standard edition of SQL Server, 163
star database design, 108–109

statistical analysis in data mining, 128
storage. *See* data storage
Structured Query Language (SQL), 386
subscribers, defined, 154
surfacing information
by Excel, 324–325
KPIs, 325–326
by PerformancePoint Services, 326
by Report Builder, 326
during rollout, 324–326
by SharePoint, 64, 229
by SSRS, 325
during testing, 319, 323
verifying its value, 319
surveys, SharePoint, 344
SWAT team for BI, 288–289
swim lanes
in business process maps, 286–287
defined, 44, 286
in IT process maps, 44–45

• T •

Table Analysis Tools for Excel, 134, 198
task sequence for unit testing, 320
tasks (SSIS)
building packages from, 86
configuring properties of, 86–87
Data Flow Task, 88
for data mining, 138–139
SSIS Analysis Services Execute DDL, 138
SSIS Analysis Services Processing, 138
SSIS Data Mining Query, 138–139
TechNet site, 55, 56
Technical Stuff icon, 5
technology choices
business foundation for, 306–307
choosing BI components, 308–309
free BI tools, 309–313
introducing new technology, 333–334
open-source software, 309–310
reducing risk, 313
understanding BI tools, 307–308
technology expert, on BI SWAT team, 289
technology goals of BI project, 279–280
TERADATA
Report Builder support for, 159
SSIS support for, 85
SSRS support for, 11, 35

testing. *See also* unit testing
  BI testing diversity, 317–319
  business process testing, 318
  complexity of, 316–317
  ensuring data are captured and stored, 318
  ETL testing, 318–319
  involving power users, 324
  iterative cycle for, 317–318, 323
  phase of iterative methodology for, 316
  unit testing, 319–323
  verifying the value of information, 319
Text Analysis algorithm, 143
Theme Builder (SharePoint), 242
timelines for BI adoption, 42
Tip icon, 5
Toolbox (SSIS)
  Control Flow tab, 86, 88
  Data Flow tab, 88
  Event Handlers tab, 86
  overview, 86
  Package Explorer tab, 86
trainers, finding, 53
training
  continuous education, 336
  grassroots level, 342
  self-service, enabling, 336–337
  SharePoint training resources, 337–340
  SQL Server training resources, 340–342
Transact-SQL (T-SQL) language, 151, 152,
    172, 386. *See also* Data Definition
    Language (DDL)
transforming data. *See* data transformation
transparency, 329–331
trial versions
  SharePoint, 310, 312–313
  SQL Server, 166, 310, 311–312
  Visual Studio, 248
trust, in BI culture, 351–352
tunnel vision, avoiding, 65–66
Turner, Dale E. (Oingo Boingo), 315

• *U* •

Ultimate Edition of Visual Studio,
    251–254, 255
unit testing
  creating information and surfacing data,
    322–323
  creating the ETL package using SSIS, 322

data-storage mechanism creation, 321
documenting goals, 320
iterative cycle for, 323
mapping current business processes, 320
mapping future process state, 321
modifying current processes, 321
task sequence for, 320
Unsupervised Learning algorithm, 142
user groups, 53

• *V* •

Validate phase of iterative methodology,
    285, 316
versioning
  SharePoint features, 111, 222–223, 240
  Word/SharePoint integration for, 237
Virtual Private Network (VPN), 48
visibility of business processes,
    increasing, 378
Visio
  Data Mining Templates, 16, 134, 198
  described, 15, 16
  SharePoint integration with, 242
Visio Services (SharePoint), 242
Visual Studio. *See also* Business
    Intelligence Developer Studio (BIDS)
  Analysis Services Project, 256
  architecture and modeling features, 253
  avoiding for data mining, 138
  BI capabilities of, 137, 254, 255–259
  as container, 250–251, 254
  creating a new project, 249
  creating an Integration Services
    project, 90
  current skill sets for, 305
  Data Mining Designer, 137
  Data Mining Wizard, 129, 135–137
  database development features, 252
  data-mining model validation using,
    129–130
  debugging and diagnostics features,
    252–253
  defined, 386
  described, 18, 19, 129–130, 135
  development platform support, 252
  as development tool, 248–259
  drag-and-drop ETL development using,
    83, 84

editions compared, 251–254, 255
Express editions, 251, 255
Import Analysis Services Database,
    256–257
installing BI components, 135, 159
Integration Services Connection Project
    Wizard, 257
Integration Services Project, 257
interface, 248–250
lab management features, 254
Model Designer, 161
New Report Wizard, 259
Premium Edition, 251–254, 255
Professional Edition, 251–254, 255
projects, defined, 84
Report Model Project, 257–258
Report Server Project, 259
Report Server Project Wizard, 257
report-building tools, 159, 160
Solution Explorer, 250
start page, 248–249
Team Foundation Server features, 251
testing features, 252
Toolbox pane, 250
trial version, 248
Ultimate Edition, 251–254, 255
visualization. *See* data visualization
Volume Licensing (Microsoft), 43–44, 55
VPN (Virtual Private Network), 48

• *W* •

Warning! icon, 5
waterfall approach to implementation
    iterative approach compared to, 281,
        282–284
    as pitfall, 356
    power users ignored in, 290
    scope creep in, 293
    testing and rollout in, 315
Web edition of SQL Server, 165
Web Parts
    defined, 36
    embedding an Excel document in a
        SharePoint page, 223–226
    for SSRS, 219

Web resources. *See* Internet resources
Web services, 209
Web Site Analysis algorithm, 142
Web sites. *See also* Web Parts
    discussion boards (SharePoint), 235–236
    embedding an Excel document in a
        SharePoint page, 223–226
    fluid user experience with SharePoint,
        240–241
    post-backs, 240–241
    SharePoint sites, 230–231
    Silverlight for, 18, 19, 20, 241
    wikis (SharePoint), 234
Welch, Jack (GE chairman), 61
whitepapers, 55
Wikipedia, 234
wikis (SharePoint), 234, 347–348
Windows Operating Systems
    current skill sets for, 304
    described, 47
    for SharePoint, 214
Windows Presentation Foundation (WPF),
    268
Windows Server, current skill sets for, 304
Windows SharePoint Services (WSS), 215,
    216, 217. *See also* SharePoint
Word, SharePoint integration with, 237, 244
workflow monitoring features of
    SharePoint, 111
Workgroup edition of SQL Server, 165
Workspace
    Groove, 244
    SharePoint, 244–245

• *X* •

XML
    for BCS configuration, 228
    defined, 157
    Excel support for, 180
    opening documents, 157
    RDL formatted as, 156–157
    SSIS support for, 85
    SSRS support for, 35

Business/Accounting & Bookkeeping

Bookkeeping For Dummies
978-0-7645-9848-7

eBay Business
All-in-One For Dummies,
2nd Edition
978-0-470-38536-4

Job Interviews
For Dummies,
3rd Edition
978-0-470-17748-8

Resumes For Dummies,
5th Edition
978-0-470-08037-5

Stock Investing
For Dummies,
3rd Edition
978-0-470-40114-9

Successful Time
Management
For Dummies
978-0-470-29034-7

Computer Hardware

BlackBerry For Dummies,
3rd Edition
978-0-470-45762-7

Computers For Seniors
For Dummies
978-0-470-24055-7

iPhone For Dummies,
2nd Edition
978-0-470-42342-4

Laptops For Dummies,
3rd Edition
978-0-470-27759-1

Macs For Dummies,
10th Edition
978-0-470-27817-8

Cooking & Entertaining

Cooking Basics
For Dummies,
3rd Edition
978-0-7645-7206-7

Wine For Dummies,
4th Edition
978-0-470-04579-4

Diet & Nutrition

Dieting For Dummies,
2nd Edition
978-0-7645-4149-0

Nutrition For Dummies,
4th Edition
978-0-471-79868-2

Weight Training
For Dummies,
3rd Edition
978-0-471-76845-6

Digital Photography

Digital Photography
For Dummies,
6th Edition
978-0-470-25074-7

Photoshop Elements 7
For Dummies
978-0-470-39700-8

Gardening

Gardening Basics
For Dummies
978-0-470-03749-2

Organic Gardening
For Dummies,
2nd Edition
978-0-470-43067-5

Green/Sustainable

Green Building
& Remodeling
For Dummies
978-0-470-17559-0

Green Cleaning
For Dummies
978-0-470-39106-8

Green IT For Dummies
978-0-470-38688-0

Health

Diabetes For Dummies,
3rd Edition
978-0-470-27086-8

Food Allergies
For Dummies
978-0-470-09584-3

Living Gluten-Free
For Dummies
978-0-471-77383-2

Hobbies/General

Chess For Dummies,
2nd Edition
978-0-7645-8404-6

Drawing For Dummies
978-0-7645-5476-6

Knitting For Dummies,
2nd Edition
978-0-470-28747-7

Organizing For Dummies
978-0-7645-5300-4

SuDoku For Dummies
978-0-470-01892-7

Home Improvement

Energy Efficient Homes
For Dummies
978-0-470-37602-7

Home Theater
For Dummies,
3rd Edition
978-0-470-41189-6

Living the Country Lifestyle
All-in-One For Dummies
978-0-470-43061-3

Solar Power Your Home
For Dummies
978-0-470-17569-9

Internet
Blogging For Dummies,
2nd Edition
978-0-470-23017-6

eBay For Dummies,
6th Edition
978-0-470-49741-8

Facebook For Dummies
978-0-470-26273-3

Google Blogger
For Dummies
978-0-470-40742-4

Web Marketing
For Dummies,
2nd Edition
978-0-470-37181-7

WordPress For Dummies,
2nd Edition
978-0-470-40296-2

Language & Foreign Language
French For Dummies
978-0-7645-5193-2

Italian Phrases
For Dummies
978-0-7645-7203-6

Spanish For Dummies
978-0-7645-5194-9

Spanish For Dummies,
Audio Set
978-0-470-09585-0

Macintosh
Mac OS X Snow Leopard
For Dummies
978-0-470-43543-4

Math & Science
Algebra I For Dummies,
2nd Edition
978-0-470-55964-2

Biology For Dummies
978-0-7645-5326-4

Calculus For Dummies
978-0-7645-2498-1

Chemistry For Dummies
978-0-7645-5430-8

Microsoft Office
Excel 2007 For Dummies
978-0-470-03737-9

Office 2007 All-in-One
Desk Reference
For Dummies
978-0-471-78279-7

Music
Guitar For Dummies,
2nd Edition
978-0-7645-9904-0

iPod & iTunes
For Dummies,
6th Edition
978-0-470-39062-7

Piano Exercises
For Dummies
978-0-470-38765-8

Parenting & Education
Parenting For Dummies,
2nd Edition
978-0-7645-5418-6

Type 1 Diabetes
For Dummies
978-0-470-17811-9

Pets
Cats For Dummies,
2nd Edition
978-0-7645-5275-5

Dog Training For Dummies,
2nd Edition
978-0-7645-8418-3

Puppies For Dummies,
2nd Edition
978-0-470-03717-1

Religion & Inspiration
The Bible For Dummies
978-0-7645-5296-0

Catholicism For Dummies
978-0-7645-5391-2

Women in the Bible
For Dummies
978-0-7645-8475-6

Self-Help & Relationship
Anger Management
For Dummies
978-0-470-03715-7

Overcoming Anxiety
For Dummies
978-0-7645-5447-6

Sports
Baseball For Dummies,
3rd Edition
978-0-7645-7537-2

Basketball For Dummies,
2nd Edition
978-0-7645-5248-9

Golf For Dummies,
3rd Edition
978-0-471-76871-5

Web Development
Web Design All-in-One
For Dummies
978-0-470-41796-6

Windows Vista
Windows Vista
For Dummies
978-0-471-75421-3